UNIFICATION AND CONQUEST

A Political and Social History of England in the Tenth and Eleventh Centuries

PAULINE STAFFORD

Senior Lecturer, Department of Humanities
Huddersfield Polytechnic

Edward Arnold
A division of Hodder & Stoughton
LONDON NEW YORK MELBOURNE AUCKLAND

For my Mam

© 1989 Pauline Stafford

First published in Great Britain 1989

Distributed in the USA by Routledge, Chapman and Hall, Inc.
29 West 35th Street, New York, NY 10001

British Library Cataloguing in Publication Data
Stafford, Pauline
Unification and conquest: a political and social
history of England in the tenth and eleventh
centuries.
1. England. Social conditions, 924–1066
I. Title
942.01'7
ISBN 0–7131–6619–3
ISBN 0–7131–6532–4 pbk

Library of Congress Cataloging-in-Publication Data
Stafford, Pauline.
  Unification and conquest: a political and social history of
England in the tenth and eleventh centuries/Pauline Stafford.
  p. cm.
  ISBN 0–7131–6619–3. — ISBN 0–7131–6532–4 (pbk.)
  1. Great Britian—History—Anglo-Saxon period, ca. 449–1066.
  2. Great Britain—History—William I, 1066–1087.   3. Great Britain–
  –History—Canute, 1017–1035.   4.   England—Civilization—to 1066.
  5. Anglo-Saxons—History.   I. Title.
  DA152.S68 1939
  942.01—dc20   89–17858
                                                                CIP

Typeset in 10/11pt Ehrhardt by TecSet Ltd, Wallington, Surrey.
Printed and bound in Great Britain for
Edward Arnold, the educational, academic and medical publishing
division of Hodder and Stoughton Limited, 41 Bedford Square,
London WC1B 3DQ by Richard Clay, Bungay, Suffolk

Contents

Preface

This book is not an attempt to write a total history of tenth- and eleventh-century England. It is primarily a political and social history and its focus is the repercussions in both of these areas of the unification of the English kingdoms under one ruler in the tenth century and the two conquests of the unified kingdom in the eleventh. The first part of the book provides a political narrative whilst the second consists of thematic chapters centring on the king, nobility and churchmen who were most involved in these processes. Opportunity has been taken, however, to include discussion of family, marriage and women, beyond the obvious importance of these for understanding the noble group, and to provide a broader conspectus on the church than political history alone might require. In both these areas, as on the economy, new work and changing interests are transforming our view and much of this is not readily available to the general reader.

Modern history teaching pays particular attention to sources and their interpretation and this emphasis is reflected in the chapter on sources and elsewhere. An introductory chapter provides discussion of the framework within which the political sources were produced, the ideas which influenced them. Readers new to the period may find it useful to read the chapters on sources and the church together, and cross-referencing has been provided. At many points in the narrative problems of source-interpretation are made explicit. Throughout reference in notes has been made where possible to the most readily available modern translations, rather than always to standard editions, in the hope that students will follow up questions for themselves in the original material.

The book spans the tenth and eleventh centuries. Since the argument is that unification was equally if not more important than conquest all themes have been carried across 1066. A detailed political narrative beyond 1066 has not, however, been provided. This is partly because such narratives are readily available, in contrast to the period before 1066, partly also because the aim is not to offer a complete picture after 1066, which would involve broadening the scope to cover England and Normandy, but rather to approach the Norman Conquest and its aftermath from a new reading of tenth- and early eleventh-century English history. Special emphasis has been given to Cnut's conquest to bring out comparisons and contrasts with 1066. In the history of the eleventh century, as opposed to the longer-term history of England, both conquests were of significance, and William's invasion would never have happened without the political consequences of Cnut's conquest.

It is a central thesis of this book that tenth- and eleventh-century England share many of the characteristics of pre-industrial England and its politics. Early England should not be set apart by the tyranny of 1066. Its politics were those arising from personal monarchy in a framework of noble and ecclesiastical power in which court, war and family were central, where king, bishop, noble and local community were major actors. The unification effected by military conquest in the first half of the tenth century had important results for the growth of royal power and the initiation of that long dialogue between centre and locality which is a theme of English history. The development of an effective system of royal rule, often verging on tyranny, is a thread which links the late ninth century to the twelfth and much emphasis has been placed on how this was achieved. The nobility were a key group in the politics of the tenth as of later centuries. The effects on this group of unification and royal power, and their acceptance of both are questioned and discussed rather than assumed, and changes within this group are covered alongside their ideals and interests. The economy is discussed primarily in relation to noble and royal power.

The English kingdom in these centuries was a unity, in the sense of being ruled for much of the period by a single king acknowledged from Northumbria to Wessex. Its boundaries, however, were not inevitable, especially given the rise of a strong kingdom of the Scots to its north at this same date. The fact that England was unified under Wessex and in a context of threat from Scandinavian settlements in other parts of Britain played some role in determining its eventual shape, as did older ideas of English unity. The kingdom, however, exhibited many internal divisions and tensions. It is argued that these did not arise primarily from the Scandinavian settlements of the late ninth century nor simply from the survival of loyalty to older kingdoms conquered by the West Saxon kings. They are as much the product of unification as a survival into it, the result of the experience of southern royal rule and a development of relations between kings and nobles and the patterns of administration. As such they survived and complicated 1066.

Unification was effected by conquest, enhancing the prestige of the tenth-century monarchy and producing changes among the nobility, in royal power and in relations between English kings and their immediate neighbours. The two conquests of Cnut and William had significant results in all these areas. That of Cnut temporarily ended a serious recurrence of Scandinavian invasion which had laid bare the strengths and weaknesses of the tenth-century kingdom during the reign of Æthelred II. Tenth-century England was not isolated from its neighbours; eleventh-century England, as a result of invasions and Cnut's conquest, was drawn into an even more complicated set of links. The ousting of the native dynasty by Cnut ensured complications to the succession to the throne which were compounded by Edward the Confessor's failure to produce heirs. In some senses English political history from 1035 until the early twelfth century and beyond is the story of a protracted succession crisis resulting from two foreign conquests.

Political events across these centuries took place against a background of economic vitality and long-term ecclesiastical changes which may be described as 'reform'. Kings benefited from the coinage and towns though they were not entirely responsible for all changes here. Taxation and money demands were a growing feature of the time. Reform and change within the English church was afoot long before the arrival of William the Conqueror and Lanfranc, and the confrontations of the late eleventh and twelfth centuries between archbishops and kings have roots in the tenth and early eleventh. Insular patterns and peculiarities are clear, not least in the structure and relative wealth of the bishoprics. But in the church as in so many areas at this date, England cannot be seen in isolation either before or after 1066. England was a kingdom formed in the tenth and eleventh centuries on an island off the coast of Europe.

Constitutional struggles between king and parliament were long a theme of English medieval history. Since the seventeenth century Anglo-Saxon England and the Norman Conquest have been central to this debate, with Anglo-Saxon liberties frequently opposed to Norman tyranny. The debate arose in the political arguments between king and parliament in the seventeenth century, and as late as the nineteenth was producing a picture of an embryonic parliament in Saxon England and the rule of a strengthened king after 1066. Twentieth-century historians have often moved away from this picture of constitutional struggle to describe kings surrounded by nobles and churchmen in royal councils, to emphasize that such councils were as much the king's creatures as his opponents and to stress what drew this political elite together rather than what divided it.

I have been much influenced by this latter approach. But it is the argument of this book that royal power grew rapidly in these centuries. This occurred with the consent and support of many great nobles, for reasons which included both the self-interest and values of these men. However, royal power contravened some of those values and interests, in, for example, the area of family and its lands. I have highlighted the tensions in the system: the development of the coronation and its oath, the troubles at the end of Æthelred II's reign and around 1066, the coronation charters of Cnut and Henry I. In doing so I am not returning to a view of an embryonic parliament before 1066 nor of a proto-democratic system and I am certainly not arguing that 1066 was a significant turning point. Rather I am suggesting that with the growth of royal power these centuries saw conflict as well as cooperation between king and nobles, prefiguring later tensions. I am arguing that contemporaries recognized the difference between a good king and a tyrant, though, as in all periods, they may not all have agreed in consigning particular rulers to either category. It is, for instance, by these standards that I have judged William I.

Where relevant, brief biographical details on many persons mentioned in the text are provided in the appropriate index entry to aid the reader in coping with the complexities of the period. Readers are encouraged to consult this. Where 'man/men' is used in the text, members of the male sex are intended. Further guidance on reading has been supplied in footnotes, and many chapters and sections have an introductory note on further reading. A short bibliographical note supplements these. Place of publication is London unless otherwise stated.

My deepest gratitude is, as always, to my husband, Bill, who read the work in its entirety, improving its style. Without his constant help and support the book could never have been written. The dedication acknowledges the debts of a lifetime.

Abbreviations

The following abbreviations have been used

ANS   *Anglo-Norman Studies*, ed. R. Allen Brown (Woodbridge, 1978—), cited by volume number. The earliest volumes appeared as *Proceedings of the Battle Abbey Conference*

ASC   Anglo-Saxon Chronicle, together with manuscript and date. References are to the translation in *English Historical Documents*, vols. I and II

ASE   *Anglo-Saxon England*, ed. P. Clemoes (Cambridge, 1972—), cited by volume number

DB   Domesday Book, cited by volume number and folio in the edition by A. Farley (1783)

EHD I & II   *English Historical Documents* I, ed. D. Whitelock, 2nd ed (1979), and *English Historical Documents* II, eds. D. C. Douglas and G. W. Greenaway, 2nd edn (1981). References in each case are to the document number and page number in this edition.

Encomium   *Encomium Emmae reginae*, ed. and trans A. Campbell, Camden Series, 3, vol. 72 (1949).

Fl. Wig.   Florence of Worcester, *Florentii Wigorniensis Monachi Chronicon ex Chronicis*, ed B. Thorpe, 2 vols. (1848–9)

Harmer SEHD   *Select English Historical Documents of the Ninth and Tenth Centuries*, ed. F. Harmer (Cambridge, 1914)

               Laws are cited by number of code, name of king and chapter number, thus V Æthelred 20. The enumeration is that of F. Liebermann, *Die Gesetze der Angelsachsen* (Halle, 1903–16). Translations are available in *The Laws of the Earliest English Kings* ed F. Attenborough (Cambridge, 1922) and *Laws of the Kings of England, Edmund to Henry I*, ed. A. J. Robertson (Cambridge, 1925)

Leges Henrici *Leges Henrici Primi*, ed. L. J. Dornier (Oxford, 1972)
Primi

LE   *Liber Eliensis*, ed. E. O. Blake, Camden Series 3, vol. 92 (1962)

Orderic Vitalis *The Ecclesiastical History of Orderic Vitalis*, ed. and trans M. Chibnall, 6 vols. (Oxford, 1969–80)

R   *Anglo-Saxon Charters*, ed. A. J. Robertson (Cambridge, 1939), cited by number of document

S   *Anglo-Saxon Charters*, an annotated list and bibliography, P. H. Sawyer Royal Historical Society Guides and Handbooks, 8 (1968), cited by number

W   *Anglo-Saxon Wills*, ed D. Whitelock (Cambridge, 1930), cited by number

William of   *Willelmi Malmesbiriensis Monachi, De Gestis regum Anglorum libri quinque*, ed. W.
Malmesbury   Stubbs, 2 vols. (1887 and 1889), Rolls Series, vol. 90

Writs   *Anglo-Saxon Writs*, ed. F. E. Harmer (Manchester, 1952)

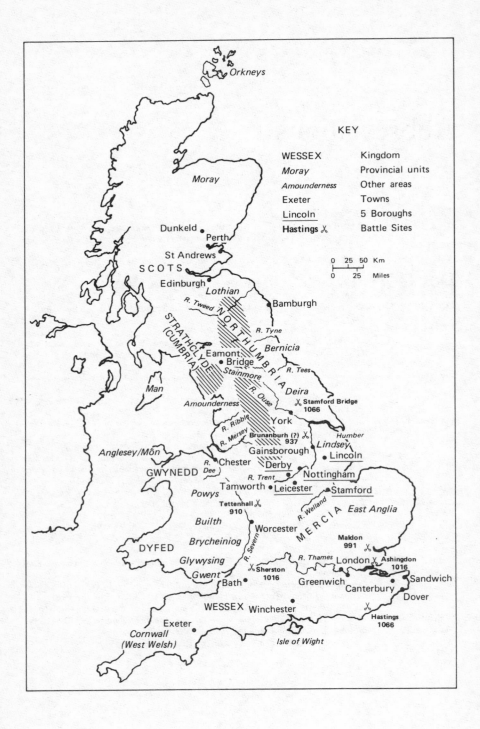

Orkneys

Moray

KEY

WESSEX	Kingdom
Moray	Provincial units
Amounderness	Other areas
Exeter	Towns
<u>Lincoln</u>	5 Boroughs
Hastings ✗	Battle Sites

0 25 50 Km
0   25   Miles

Dunkeld
Perth
St Andrews
SCOTS
Edinburgh
Lothian
R. Tweed
Bamburgh
NORTHUMBRIA
R. Tyne
Bernicia
STRATHCLYDE (CUMBRIA)
Eamont
Bridge
Stainmore
R. Tees
R. Ouse
Deira
Man
Amounderness
Stamford Bridge 1066 ✗
R. Ribble
York
R. Mersey
Brunanburh (?) 937 ✗
Humber
Lindsey
Anglesey/Môn
Gainsborough
<u>Lincoln</u>
R. Dee
Chester
<u>Derby</u>
GWYNEDD
R. Trent
<u>Nottingham</u>
Tamworth
<u>Leicester</u>
<u>Stamford</u>
Powys
Tettenhall 910 ✗
R. Welland
East Anglia
Builth
MERCIA
Brycheiniog
Worcester
Maldon 991 ✗
DYFED
Glywysing
R. Severn
R. Thames
London
Ashingdon 1016 ✗
Gwent
Sherston 1016 ✗
Greenwich
Canterbury
Sandwich
Bath
Dover
WESSEX
Winchester
Exeter
Cornwall (West Welsh)
Isle of Wight
Hastings 1066 ✗

PART I

Genealogical Table

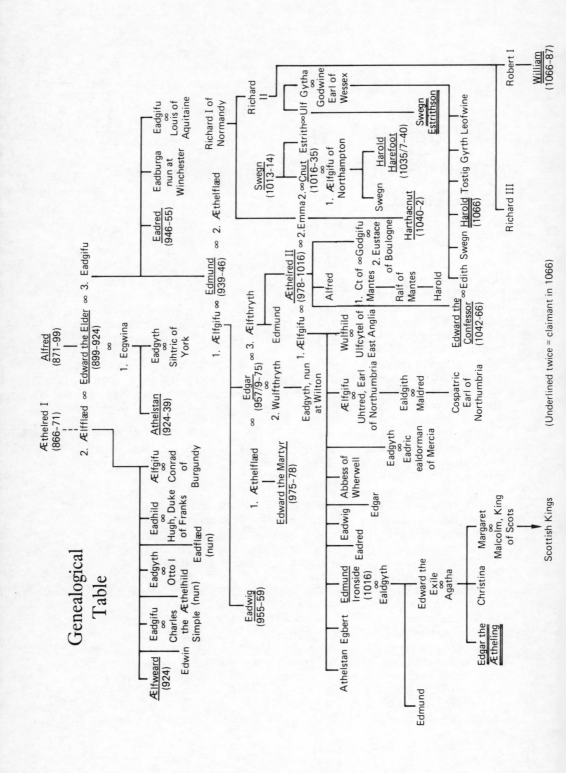

1

Historical Writing in England, Late Ninth to Mid Twelfth Centuries

The picture we can have of political development in tenth- and eleventh-century England is that which the sources will give us. That is not to say that only one picture is possible. Varied questions elicit different responses. But the range of answerable questions is limited by the sources. Tenth- and eleventh-century England is patchily covered, both by narrative sources with which this chapter is mainly concerned, and by law codes, charters and administrative or estate documents. For the period from 924 to 975, for example, narrative sources are so fragmentary and poor that a chronological picture is difficult to construct, conversely charters (records of land grants) are a rich source as are law codes, six or seven of which survive for the reign of Athelstan alone. Edward the Confessor (1042–66), by contrast, is relatively well-served in historical narratives, but no law code survives in his name. Æthelred II (978–1016) is known from a single but detailed chronicle, and is illuminated by a wealth of charters and sermons and apparently produced more law codes than any other early English king.

The thousand years which separate us from these centuries have meant much loss of documents. This applies especially to the ephemeral documents of administration, written in Old English, incomprehensible and irrelevant to the Latin world of the High Middle Ages. Loss alone does not explain the paucity. The entire period is transitional between an oral and a written culture. Much which we would expect to see documented they committed to memory and witness. If writing things down was not merely a compulsion of habit, we must ask not solely why have some documents survived but also what prompted people to record in the first place. Tenth-century literate men apparently gave the chronicling of events a low priority, but record of land grants a high one. The two conquests of the eleventh century sparked a more passionate interest in contemporary history. It was not merely the case that more general legal pronouncements were committed to writing before 1023 than after; more were made in the tenth century because current ecclesiastical views of the royal office considered law-making its appropriate instrument in tackling problems.

From the myriad factors which influenced documentation two were paramount: the concerns and preoccupations of churchmen and the changes which affected these, and the crises which sparked both a desire to explain and a need to record the immediate past, whether in narrative, law code or record of landholding. An influence on many sources, and the spur to some, was the unification of the kingdom, expressed in the growing power of kings and the sense of England as a unity. We need to be aware of the significance of growing royal power for all who held land or were involved in political life, that is, for all those who wrote our documents. We must recognize how many documents we owe to the reactions to the attacks on monastic land after 975, to the experience of Danish attack and conquest between 1006 and 1016, to the immediate and longer-term reactions to the Norman conquest of 1066. Such 'crisis-led' sources are not the easiest guides to history.

The documents and chronicles on which this book is based were written by churchmen; their study is inseparable from that of the intellectual milieu of the church. Some laypeople were certainly literate: legal and administrative documents were often in the vernacular so as to be accessible to them. *C.* AD 1000 literary works were dedicated to laymen and one man, ealdorman Æthelweard, even translated an English chronicle into Latin. In writing as opposed to reading Æthelweard appears exceptional. This was virtually an ecclesiastical monopoly. Throughout the period the outlook of churchmen on the political world was influenced by a long-standing tradition of the involvement of Christianity in the secular world, of alliance and cooperation with kings. Political sermons to be preached at court, law codes drafted and inspired by churchmen, records of land granted to and disputed with the church, the lives of saints who were also courtiers are among the products. Not only were churchmen accustomed to working with kings, they were themselves drawn from the nobility. Their view was not so separate from that of laypeople that to see this world through their eyes is wholly to distort it.

These centuries, however, saw major movements for church reform which are linked to a growing gulf between a secular and religious view of the world. In England an episcopal and monastic movement went hand in hand. The monastery not the cathedral was the intellectual centre, though the two were linked since most articulate bishops by the late tenth century had trained as monks. Monasticism waxed in importance with the foundation of many houses, accounting for the increasingly rich documentation as the tenth century progresses. Monks were the most separate group within the church. But to understand the outlook of writers at this date we need to remember that reform meant two things. It was return to first principles, the challenging of present compromises and the improvement of the clergy, a meaning it had had throughout Christian history, but also the completion of the process of conversion, the spread of the basic structures and beliefs of Christianity. In the first meaning reformed church and royal power tended to grow apart; their interests could conflict. The church as an arbiter of morality possessed a potential critique of power. The seeds of the conflict and separation often termed 'Gregorian', after Pope Gregory VII in the late eleventh century, were there in the ninth. In England they germinated before Gregory's influence, watered by the rising tide of reform and fertilized by the exactions of a growing royal power and by experience of two conquests. But the split cannot be maximized. In the second meaning of reform king and churchmen were essential partners. The tenth-century reform movements began in the court itself, and as late as the twelfth century churchmen could still see the need for royal protection. William of Malmesbury was still able to sympathize with the problems of kings as well as to criticize them. William is also one of the many English monastic writers whose focus lay beyond the monastic wall in England. English monks show little of the local particularism which characterizes many of their continental counterparts. They certainly produced documents, especially concerned with landholding, designed to protect their house. But their desire to write *English* history is one of the most remarkable things about the faltering growth of historical writing.

Alfred and after: the sources *c.* 900 to *c.* 980

The reign of Alfred

The blending of religious and secular concerns and their *English* focus is already clear in the reign of Alfred, as is the stimulus of external attack. The role of kings had been defined by Christianity. When Alfred issued his law code he aimed to produce and sustain an earthly order mirroring that of heaven; in the code itself he moves readily from sin to crime. Disturbance of the relationship between humans and God is akin to disturbance of the relationships among humans through murder or theft. Christianity has in turn been moulded by the secular world. In ninth-century England God exacts vengeance like any other aggrieved party. In his prose preface to the Pastoral Care, Alfred bemoaned the state of learning at his accession and linked that state with the condition of the Church and both with the plight of the English.[1] He set about collecting a group of scholars at his court and undertook the translation of a series of key texts into English to make them more readily accessible. It is scarcely surprising that Alfred saw it as his duty as a king to remedy the state of learning. Since Viking attacks were interpreted as a divine punishment for the state of the church and scholarship he took responsibility for both.

The Carolingians, especially the potent symbol of Charlemagne, are one possible source of Alfred's views. The influence of works produced in ninth-century Frankia remained strong throughout the tenth century. But Alfred and his Frankish counterparts shared the same world-view and it would not be surprising if they found similar answers to similar questions.[2] Alfred's desire to encourage learning and his revival of English law-making left a legacy to the tenth century, to its reform movements, its rulers and its intellectual development. His attitude towards the writing of history, whether past or contemporary, is more debatable. The Anglo-Saxon Chronicle cannot be attributed with certainty to him or to his court.[3] This is not to imply that he did not appreciate its value. The Chronicle may have been circulated at his command and

1. EHD 1 no. 226 pp. 888–90
2. J. Nelson, 'A king across the sea, Alfred in continental perspective', TRHS, ser. 5, 36 (1986), pp. 45–68
3. J. Bately, 'The compilation of the Anglo-Saxon Chronicle 60 BC to AD 890: vocabulary as evidence', *Proceedings of the British Academy*, 64 (1980 for 1978), pp. 93–129

additions made to it in the 890s probably originate from court. The chronicle tells the story of the struggle against the Danes. His children, Edward the Elder and Æthelflæd, were influenced by it. So too was an anonymous private writer of the early eleventh century who wrote the parallel but dramatically different account of Æthelred II's fight against the Danes. But the late ninth-century Chronicle did not found a continuous tradition of annal writing in England or in Wessex.The contrast with the tradition of law-making which Alfred reinvigorated is instructive. Law not history epitomized the intersection of religious and secular concerns in the tenth century.

The historical works produced in the reign of Alfred, the Chronicle, Asser's Life of the king, the translations of Bede's *Ecclesiastical History of the English People* and of Orosius, were stimulated by Viking attacks and the desire to explain or cope with them. Conquest and crisis remained the major stimuli to the writing of historical narratives in tenth- and eleventh-century England. The history of 'normal' conditions is correspondingly difficult for us to write. Many also shared a view of the English *as a people*; the Prose Preface casually refers to 'the English'. Alfred was king of Wessex, and questionably of Mercia; but in the late ninth century aspirations and ideals outran political reality. 'England' existed first in the realm of ideas.[4] In the twelfth century William of Malmesbury wrote a history of the kings of the English not merely of the church of Malmesbury. That he did so was due to a tradition dating back to the days of Bede, and powerfully reinforced from the late ninth century onwards.

After the comparative richness of the historical sources for Alfred's reign the tenth century appears a desert. Not until its end, during the reign of Æthelred, will sources again be produced in such quantity as to allow the construction of a historical narrative, or to study any area of life fully. The sparseness is a sign of how much was owed to Alfred personally in stimulating the writings of his own time, of how little his successors needed or inspired, comparable efforts, and of how long the church reform movement and its revival of learning took to come to fruition (see The Church, pp. 184–93). The writing of history was a low priority for that movement, though its interest in land and law ensure that royal patronage, land-holding and law-giving can be studied even before a political history can be written.

The Anglo-Saxon Chronicle

The Anglo-Saxon Chronicle, such an important source for Alfred's reign, dries up in the tenth century. There are long gaps and omissions in its coverage; the reign of Athelstan, 924–39, for example, has only eight entries in MS A and not all of them political. After the 890s 'Anglo-Saxon Chronicle' is a misleading term. By the end of the eleventh century, when the now surviving MSS were all in existence, there were effectively six chronicles, now generally known as MSS A, B, C, D, E (and the less useful F). These differ in so many respects that they can be seen almost as separate chronicles. Yet they are also interdependent, the products of borrowing, copying and collation of often identical sources; and

---

4. P. Wormald, 'Bede, the *Bretwaldas* and the origins of the *Gens Anglorum*', *Ideal and Reality in Frankish and Anglo-Saxon Society*, ed. P. Wormald *et al.* (Oxford, 1983), pp. 99–129

although produced in different places, in their final forms all have some aspiration to be chronicles in the vernacular of England. The study of these chronicles poses problems, some of them as yet unresolved. All are anonymous, most are the products of several hands few of which can be dated or placed precisely. But an understanding of their nature is essential and provides insight into the writing of contemporary history in tenth- and eleventh-century England.

The MSS can be divided into those which are contemporary, i.e. which exist in the form in which they were periodically added to during the tenth and eleventh centuries, and those which are synoptic, i.e. which were compiled from a collection of sources and earlier versions of the Chronicle, surviving only in a late form. The distinction is rather arbitrary, since all are contemporary for their final stages: E, for example, a classic synoptic chronicle, has contemporary entries for the twelfth century. Similarly even those which contain contemporary entries for the tenth and eleventh centuries are synoptic for earlier dates. The utility of the distinction lies in the awareness that few Manuscripts of the Chronicles survive in strictly contemporary form, and most are compilations whose sources themselves require identification and dating.

Only the so-called Parker or A MS of the chronicle is strictly contemporary for the tenth century. It was kept at Winchester and the different hands which added to it from time to time during the tenth century can still be identified.[5] It was moved to Canterbury *c.* 1006, and after this entries are sparse. Even for the tenth century when its authors were so well placed to record events in and around the court at Winchester, MS A is brief, with long gaps, and concerned after 924 with religious rather than secular events. It flowers in the reign of Edward the Elder (899–924) though it may not always be strictly contemporary: for example the section from 912 to 923 was entered in one go. The tradition of historical writing in Southern England in the tenth century was an impoverished one if A represents it.

MS B confirms the impression. This Chronicle was copied up in the late tenth century, its last entry being for the year 977. Its scribe used a Mercian chronicle, or sources including Mercian ones, and had access to an early tenth-century Mercian record of the doings of Æthelflæd, Edward the Elder's sister. This latter is the so-called Mercian register, which can be set alongside the fuller Winchester account of these years to provide a picture of the conquest of Danish England by these two children of Alfred. Its Mercian sources also included a brief but non-West-Saxon account of the division of the kingdom in the events of 955–59. B is *not* however a purely Mercian Chronicle. Its Mercian elements are stressed for the additional information they give, but after *c.*918 it is not an example of local particularism in historical writing. The similarities are more important than the differences between MSS A and B. The compiler of B or one of his predecessors used MS A or something like it. They share many entries. Borrowing and copying of MSS was already occurring in the tenth century itself and complicating the history of the Chronicle. By the end of the tenth century when this MS was written the desire was to give a history of

5. M. B. Parkes, 'The palaeography of the Parker manuscript of the *Chronicle*, Laws and Sedulius, and historiography at Winchester in the late ninth and tenth centuries', ASE, 5 (1976), pp. 149–71

England, or at least of Wessex and Mercia, not of Mercia alone. Such an enterprise was inhibited for the author, as for us, by the lack of earlier chronicles. But he shared the English perspective of his contemporaries. In the early tenth century Mercian pride focused on the court of Æthelflæd still played a part in the production of history, witness the Mercian Register. By the later tenth century that court had gone, and any such local feeling found little expression.

MSS C, D and E are all eleventh-century compilations (see also pp. 84–6). C was written during the reign of Edward the Confessor probably at Abingdon. Its sources, even for the mid eleventh century included non-Abingdon material. Until 977 C is merely a copy of B. From 985 until the end of Æthelred's reign it contains the best version of the detailed account of that reign which was used by almost all the eleventh- and twelfth-century chroniclers. That account was certainly not an Abingdon account, nor was it a chronicle produced year by year, but rather a single history written *c.*1016 (see below, p.000). Note the need to identify the sources behind the surviving chronicles. Purely Abingdon material in this chronicle may well be confined to odd entries like some of those from 977 to 985. Even these cannot be dated or placed with precision.

D and E pose in many ways the most complex problems for students of the Chronicle. In their final form they are part of that flowering of English historical writing which followed and was stimulated by the Conquest in 1066. D is a chronicle compiled in the North, probably at York, in the late eleventh century. E is a copy of a Chronicle which was at St Augustine's, Canterbury *c.*1066, later sent to Peterborough where it was continued as a contemporary work during the twelfth century. But in each case this is only the end product of a long evolution during which both these chronicles shared common ancestors and came in contact with each other at more than one point. The story of E gives an insight into the development and consequent problems of an Anglo-Saxon Chronicle.

E is the descendant of a long lineage which had undergone much inter-marriage and several changes of principal residence. Its remote ancestor was the Anglo-Saxon Chronicle of Alfred's reign which by accident or design found its way north. There a marriage occurred with a set of northern annals, some predating 890, others recording a skeleton of events in the northern kingdom of York until the end of that kingdom in 954. These annals for the tenth century can be presumed to be more or less contemporary. As in Mercia, the survival of the local court and kingdom is the necessary context for even the most fragmentary history. The traumatic events of the 940s and 950s as Viking and southern English rulers fought for dominance and ravaged the North may be the immediate stimulus for many entries. The descent of E's family during the tenth century cannot be traced in every generation. A northern Chronicle or chronicles may have gone through several stages during which some of the family links between D and E were formed. Some entries for the tenth century were certainly not contemporary. E and D's ancestors adopted the version of Æthelred's reign which they share with C and also during the early eleventh century received additions by way, for example, of the pen of Archbishop Wulfstan of York. It was he who wrote the long entries on Edgar recorded under 959 and 975, both of which thus belong not to Edgar's own reign and its immediate aftermath but the later stages of the reign of Æthelred after Wulfstan moved to York in 1002. If the family tree in the tenth century is obscure, what is clear is a major house move for E's ancestor between 1031 and 1045, most probably early in that period. The move was a southerly one to St Augustine's, Canterbury which was the home of E's mother until 1066 at least. The final move, the copying in the late eleventh century which produced E itself, took it finally to Peterborough.

Such a chronicle cannot be understood apart from its family history. Successive copyings may have produced errors, or even serious tampering with the account itself. Comparison of surviving chronicles is reassuring here as is the fact that the Peterborough additions to the pre-1066 chronicle in E stand out starkly from the rest. There was no premium on originality in the production of these earliest chronicles. More of a problem is the precise dating of the constituent parts. Their complex history is an offshoot of the growing desire by eleventh-century religious houses to have chronicles and histories, and English ones at that. It is a result of borrowing and copying to achieve that aim. The northern elements in D and E are important as were the Mercian ones in C. But after 954 those elements cease to be in any sense a localized history of the North. In the eyes of the educated monks who wrote its history England was a unity by the eleventh century.

Laws and charters

The tenth century lacks a continuous historical tradition. What historical writing there is before the eleventh century was stimulated by crisis, invasion and conquest and to a lesser extent by threat to churchmen. Even these troubles were not consistently recorded. A blank in the sources cannot be taken as indicating a lack of significant event. There was no historical vocabulary or tradition within which to discuss politics as we would understand it. Even kings whose relations with contemporary churchmen were manifestly good are often accorded the briefest of accounts. The lack of historical writing does not mean that nothing was being written in tenth-century England. A Golden Age of manuscript production was in full swing by the end of the century and can be traced back to the reign of Athelstan.[6] Athelstan gathered a court school or chapel comparable with that of Alfred and in direct contact with continental developments (see *The Church*, pp. 184–6). The manuscripts assembled and the scholars trained there were a foundation of later intellectual developments.

Historical writing was less important for this latter-day Charlemagne and his advisers than law, both secular and ecclesiastical law and the penitentials which helped regulate individual moral life. In the unified England which succeeded the conquests of Danish-controlled areas it was the pursuit of reform, seen as both a secular and religious enterprise, which engrossed scholars. Athelstan is the first English king in whose name a significant number of law codes survive. It was Archbishop Oda, trained in Athelstan's chapel, who produced the Constitutions

6.   ed. J. Backhouse *et al.*, *The Golden Age of Anglo-Saxon Art* (1984)

of Oda[7] the first surviving set of reforming decrees of a tenth-century English bishop. Edmund, Athelstan's brother and successor (939–46), issued laws which combined the religious injunctions of Oda's work and the pursuit of internal peace through royal power. For the ecclesiastical advisers of kings at least the tenth-century project was clear.

The history of the tenth century is largely devoid of personalities; even in stereotyped form they scarcely interested those who put pen to paper. This is a lamentable lack at a time when the court and its politics were of central importance, a lack stemming from the priorities of the period, albeit only of the ecclesiastical members of it. In those priorities land and law were central. The broad term 'charter' covers a varied assortment of documents. The bulk are records of royal grants of land, of patronage. Some are outright and straightforward gifts of land. Others confirm rights over land acquired in other ways, like the grant to the thegn (noble) Ealdred of land at Chalgrave and Tebworth in Bedfordshire which he himself had bought from the pagans.[8] In either case rights or immunities are being confirmed and recorded in solemn form in a document which also contains a record of the names of those present at the royal court when it was witnessed. In addition to charters, wills and vernacular accounts of court cases or legal disputes have also survived, like the account of the protracted case of the estate at Fonthill in Wiltshire[9] which stretched from the reign of Alfred into that of Edward the Elder. These are private accounts, often written by the victor, and give much insight into the tenth-century legal process in action and the frequent interference of the king in it. The development of both these and the wills during the tenth century especially is no casual accident. The increasing literacy of the revived monasteries plays some part, but more important are changes in royal power and its exercise.

It is because the patronage and legal activity of the king were of interest to churchmen that they have survived. Many laws were preserved by the interest of ecclesiastics like Archbishop Wulfstan (see below). Charters were often copied into later monastic and ecclesiastical cartularies (volumes in which the charters of a religious house were collected). Some were grants to churchmen, many more were grants to laymen of land subsequently given to or claimed by churches. Some were simply deposited in churches for safe keeping. There was no central register of royal grants, nor apparently of royal laws, a reminder that many of the habits of an oral society remained. It was pressure from the beneficiary not desire for record by the king which stimulated record, and which produced much of the change in the nature of the record of land transactions as the tenth century went on. It was the beneficiary's needs in a society in which land was changing hands fast amid constant dispute that prompted some of the records discussed above. The influence of the late tenth-century reformed religious houses on the production and preservation of these documents is one reason for the increase in their number as the century

7. The Constitutions of Oda, printed *Sacrorum Conciliorum nova et amplissima collectio*, ed. J. Mansi, vol. 18 (facs. ed. Paris, 1902), pp. 394–8
8. EHD 1 no. 103 pp. 546–7
9. EHD 1 no. 102 pp. 544–6

goes on. That influence on all areas of documentation is most marked in the reign of Æthelred II.

Post-revival illumination *c*.975–1016

The reign of Æthelred, or more correctly the half century after the death of Edgar, is the most well-documented period in early English history. A profusion of sermons, saints' lives and religious texts were produced alongside legal material, laws in the name of the king and private compilations largely associated with Archbishop Wulfstan II of York. Charters are not only plentiful but often blossom into detail of land disputes, vernacular accounts of which increase in number. One church at least, Worcester, produced a cartulary, others the first records of their endowments and losses. This plenty results from the fruition of the movement for ecclesiastical especially monastic reform and the sheer number of active scriptoria. As an expression of that reform and thus of the ideas current since the ninth century it is the ideal place to explore the assumptions of churchmen produced in this environment. Reform and revival, but also threat to monastic land were stimuli. The attacks on church property which followed the death of Edgar (see pp. 57–8) sharpened sensitivity to that threat. The need to record especially disputed claims became greater.

The traumatic events of these years after 975 had other repercussions. Trauma increased historical consciousness. Within a couple of years of his death the reign of Edgar was coming to be seen as a lost Golden Age; the reign of his son Æthelred has suffered by comparison. Æthelred's rule is peculiarly well illuminated in the resulting glare and some of its problems have been exaggerated as a result. The raised historical consciousness of this intellectual revival coincided with renewal of Viking attacks on England: the old stimulus to the writing of contemporary history had returned. The general result of this is a mass of documentation; the specific one the production of a chronicle of this reign more detailed and more passionate than any other.

Some of these sources stem from major political actors at the time. The views expressed in the many works of Archbishop Wulfstan, for example, are not merely academic. He reflects on events which he helped shape and his own reflections are public statements which went on to influence action. His laws or his Sermon of the Wolf to the English preached in the depths of defeat by the Danes[10] must be read in this light.

---

10. EHD 1 no. 240 pp. 928–34. Of the many works on Wulfstan the following are especially useful: D. Bethurum, 'Wulfstan', in *Continuations and Beginnings*, ed. E. G. Stanley (1966), pp. 210–46 and her *'Regnum* and *Sacerdotium* in the early eleventh century' in *England before the Conquest*, eds. P. Clemoes and K. Hughes (Cambridge, 1971), pp. 129–45; D. Whitelock's introduction to her edition of the Sermo Lupi ad Anglos, (3rd edn 1963); H. Loyn, 'Church and state in the tenth and eleventh centuries' in *Tenth-Century Studies*, ed. D. Parsons (Chichester, 1975), pp. 94–102; P. Wormald, 'Æthelred the lawmaker', in *Ethelred the Unready*, ed. D. Hill, British Archaeological Reports, British series 59 (1978), pp. 47–80, and P. A. Stafford, 'Church and society in the age of Ælfric' in *The Old English Homily and its Backgrounds*, eds. P. E. Szarmach and B. Huppe (New York, 1978), pp. 11–42.

Saints' Lives

The late tenth and early eleventh centuries saw a renewal of English hagio-graphical writing with a crop of saints' lives from the pen of Abbot Ælfric of Eynsham[11] and a series of lives of outstanding contemporary churchmen. Dunstan, Oswald and Æthelwold all attracted hagiographers.[12] The first and most influential life of Dunstan was written probably by a foreign clerk and dedicated to an archbishop of Canterbury.[13] Oswald's was produced in and for the monastic community at Ramsey which he had founded. The two early lives of Æthelwold were written by Winchester monks, the most famous by his distinguished pupil, Abbot Ælfric of Eynsham. Both were intended for the monastic audience of Æthelwold's own foundations. These lives have done much to shape our view of the later tenth century. The Life of Dunstan, for example, is the major source for the sharp contrast between Edgar and his older brother Eadwig, and especially for the charge that the older brother was a lascivious and easily led young man whose wanton cavortings at his coronation banquet denoted a character unfit to rule the kingdom. This Life and the Life of Oswald are the most detailed sources for the two succession disputes of the age, of 955–9 and 975–8. The three lives together defined the movement for reform which was seen to have taken place during the tenth century, and between them determine our differing pictures of these leaders of reform, especially the contrast between the politically involved Dunstan and the simple monastic reformer Æthelwold.

These lives are hagiography not history, lives of saints not descriptions of tenth-century politics. Dunstan's confrontation with Eadwig and the two women at the king's coronation, his upbraiding of a king whose crown is discarded as he wallows like a pig in a sty, is famous. Yet the black and white, hero and villain conventions of hagiographical writing have shaped it, and its details recall other famous encounters between loose women and fearless prophets from the time of Jezebel onwards. The audience of Dunstan's life were encouraged to expect bishops to act in this way. The association of the story with the coronation shows how important this event had become as an occasion for stressing the duties of kings. As an account of the events of 956 it is too simple. As an indication of the climate of moral judgement of kings in the late tenth century and a guide to political language of churchmen it is instructive.

The differing audiences and authorship of the Lives explain much of the contrasts among the three reformers, especially between Dunstan and Æthel-wold. Dunstan, counsellor and upbraider of kings, is an appropriate picture to present to his archiepiscopal successors. The reforming Æthelwold is a monk for monks. Saints' lives were didactic, images of idealized action for living

11.   e.g. Ælfric, *Lives of the Saints*, ed. W. W. Skeat, EETS 76 and 82 (1881). Of the many works on Ælfric the following are of special general interest: P. Clemoes, 'Ælfric', in *Continuations and Beginnings*, ed. Stanley, pp. 176–209 and the essays in *The Old English Homily and its Backgrounds*, eds. Szarmach and Huppe

12.   Lives of Dunstan, printed *Memorials of St Dunstan*, ed. W. Stubbs, Rolls Series (1874); of Oswald, *Historians of the Church of York and its Archbishops*, ed. J. Raine, Rolls Series (1879), vol 1; of Æthelwold by M. Winterbottom, *Three Lives of English Saints* (Toronto, 1972)

13.   Compare Stubbs, *Memorials of St Dunstan* with the views of M. Lapidge, 'The hermeneutic style in tenth-century Anglo-Latin Literature', ASE, 4 (1975), pp. 67–111 at pp. 81–3

audiences not biographies. Recent study of Æthelwold, for example, has shown how deeply he was involved in the politics of the tenth century.[14] We seek that involvement in vain from the pen of Abbot Ælfric, educator of monks. But all distinction should not be ironed out. The differences between the needs of a Canterbury and a Winchester audience are a reminder of the variety within the later tenth-century church.

These lives, like the later sources which use and reinforce them, have shaped the modern picture of tenth-century reform. The monastic viewpoint predominates in sources largely produced for and transmitted by monastic houses. Even more insidious is the idea that there had been a clearly identifiable movement of which all would have been aware since the beginning of the reign of Edgar, if not since that of Athelstan (see *The Church*, pp. 186–92).This message of the three lives must be seen as the retrospective on a movement defined not merely with hindsight but by the experience of vicissitude after 975. If tenth-century history often now appears as the story of reform and the relation of rulers and nobles to it that was the view from the late tenth century, not necessarily from the 940s, 950s or 960s.

Ælfric and Wulfstan

The view of the immediate past which had emerged by the end of the tenth century was one increasingly ready to judge kings and to label them as 'good' or 'bad'. A tale of harmonious alliance between the needs of kings and churchmen misses the double-edged nature of the reforming sword. The work of Abbot Ælfric of Eynsham and Archbishop Wulfstan of York encompassed the range of reforming interests and their expression. Ælfric was the most prolific and learned product of the tenth-century monasteries. A pupil of Æthelwold at Winchester and later an abbot, he was concerned for monastic education, though also for the general moral reform of society. Archbishop Wulfstan was a leading counsellor of Æthelred and Cnut, a committed reforming bishop who saw law as the instrument through which his ends could be achieved. He played a major role in the last four law codes of Æthelred and in the codifications of Cnut. Their sermons, translations, educational works, rules of life for the clergy, penitentials, laws are all linked by the underlying purposes of early church reform but concern with the politics and condition of the present is never absent. Whether in sermons on the last days, addresses aimed at a 'political' audience like the Wulfstan's Sermon of the Wolf or Ælfric's *Wyrdwriteras...*[15] scattered in the lives of saints or in translations of the bible, or clearly articulated in royal law codes and works of political theory like Wulfstan's Institutes of Polity,[16] the ideas and assumptions of the articulate churchmen of the day are clear. The overwhelming message is a positive endorsement of the rule of kings, though their audiences may have heard it differently.

14. B. Yorke, 'Æthelwold and the politics of the tenth century', *Bishop Æthelwold his Career and Influence* (Woodbridge, 1988), pp. 65–88
15. *Homilies of Ælfric. A Supplementary Collection*, ed. J. Pope, vol. 2, EETS (1968), pp. 725–33
16. ed. K. Jost, *Swiss Studies in English*, 47 (Bern, 1959), translated M. Swanton, *Anglo-Saxon Prose* (1975), pp. 125–38

Kings were essential and should work with churchmen, hence royal law codes written by an archbishop or the lives of saintly kings. Rebellion was unacceptable, a duly consecrated king must be obeyed – the people might not shake off his yoke. His ways, if evil, are a punishment for sin. Such general messages are reinforced by specific application to the current situation. In *Wyrdwriteras* Ælfric engages in special pleading for a king who does not lead out his armies in person but knows how to choose good deputies. A reply to criticism of Æthelred is implicit. In his final passionate analysis of the woes of the English in 1014, the Sermon of the Wolf, Wulfstan turns the blame not on the king but squarely on the English and their sins, which have included the betrayal of their own kings.

Yet Wulfstan also dwells on shameful tributes paid to the Danes, on public humiliation, devastation and famine. Like the moral commentators of any age his call for repentance required depiction of horrors as specific and full as possible. The articulation of present ills is as important as any analysis of their causes. Definition of 'good kings' may be as powerful as depiction of 'present ills' in fuelling criticism and dissatisfaction. Ælfric wrote in his translation of Judges:

> In England also kings were often victorious through God . . . just as King Alfred was, who often fought against the Danes, until he won the victory and protected his people, similarly Athelstan, who fought against Olaf and slew his army . . . and afterwards lived in peace with his people. Edgar, the noble and resolute king, exalted the praise of God everywhere among his people, the strongest of all kings over the English people; and God subdued for him his adversaries, kings and earls, so that they came to him without any fighting, desiring peace.[17]

Such a view of the tenth century strengthened the dynasty through its glorious predecessors. The mirror of the past held up now to the present included good kings defined in relation to their religious patronage and to their successes against the Danes. Contrast with contemporary defeats could be read even if it was not intended.

Wulfstan, like other tenth- and early eleventh-century reforming bishops, expresses traditional ideas invigorated by the ninth–century Carolingian revival. One concern of those ideas was the definition of the way of life of all ranks within society through law codes, penitentials, rules of life, treatises. The ordering of those ranks and their appropriate action is central. The separateness of cleric and lay, of sacred and secular grows easily out of this type of hierarchical definition, especially via stress on the ideal way of life of the clergy and a monastic environment with an emphasis on celibacy and separation. Such 'Gregorian' ideas are to be heard from the ninth century and with increasing insistence in the work of men like Wulfstan. His legal concerns dwelt especially on the ranks of society. He elevated the clergy, and bishops in particular, to a role above that of kings.[18]

Wulfstan expressed these ideas in early eleventh-century England under Viking attack. He enunciated them in the royal courts as well as in his bishopric

17. EHD 1 no. 239 p. 928
18. D. Bethurum, '*Regnum* and *Sacerdotium* in the early eleventh century', *England before the Conquest*, ed. Clemoes and Hughes, pp. 129–45

and they received wide implementation in the royal laws of Æthelred and Cnut in which he played a large part. He and the movement of which he forms a part had grown up during unification of the kingdom and the consequent strengthening of its monarchy. Working still with kings, it is scarcely surprising that he stops short of the full logic of his own statements, that he is a 'pre-Gregorian'. But already the tone and language of criticism is there and it derives not merely from his ideas but from their expression at a time of invasion, indeed in the last stages of successful Viking attack. Wulfstan's assessment of Edgar added to the northern versions of the Anglo-Saxon Chronicle is no simple panegyric. It praises, but also criticizes a king who brought heathen men and their ways to his court. It is the Vikings whom Wulfstan has in mind. It was they who made the terrors of the Millennium and the coming of Antichrist an urgent reality for him. It is they who prompt his picture of a society in disintegration which has brought its own ruin upon it which informs the Sermon of the Wolf. The tenth-century reform could but did not have to produce the critical tone of the Sermon of the Wolf or the comments on Edgar. That tone results from the current situation in England. The influence of current events on intellectual traditions, the beginnings of criticism of kings and society, the tone of the moralist in politics all anticipate the later eleventh-century.

The Chronicle of Æthelred's reign

The powerful evocation of these ideas in Wulfstan's Sermon is a product of the specific situation at the end of Æthelred's reign. So too is the account of that reign given in the Anglo-Saxon Chronicles. Apart from A, all versions have copied a common account. The anonymous author shares with Wulfstan the note of passion and nemesis, and like him looks inwards for the causes of defeat, not outwards to the nature of Viking attack. Unlike Wulfstan, he blames not moral collapse but treachery and poor leadership. It was not the English who were defeated, but their leaders, and especially some of their leaders, who let them down. The story he tells is compelling and has the deceptive appearance of a set of annals written up year by year from the 980s. In fact it is a tale told by a single man, at a single time, *his* story of a reign he now saw as dominated by Viking attack to the exclusion of all else. It is a coherent tale of the Viking invasions and the inadequacy of response to them. He may have been inspired by the story of Alfred and the Danes, inviting comparison between Alfred and Æthelred. The need to distinguish his purposes and perspective from that of Alfred's chronicler is all the more pressing. Alfred's tale was told from the perspective of victory, or wary peace; Æthelred's from the depths of defeat. It sought not so much reasons as scapegoats for that defeat. It was written in South East England by someone apparently remote from the court and its concerns, without the inside knowledge which could have revealed the complexity of political situations. Yet had he had such knowledge, the author would not have used it. It would not have served his purposes, and there was no precedent for the discussion of political troubles other than in black and white, loyalty and treachery. His account is a bleak picture of incompetence, arbitrariness and treachery, and such is the fullness and compulsion of his narrative that no subsequent chronicler or historian can free him or herself from it.

As a picture, one man's picture of England *c*.1016, it cannot be dismissed. As a story of the entire reign of Æthelred it is deeply flawed. The lack of alternative accounts for comparison is a major problem in using this source. No other individual or scriptorium is known to have produced an account of the late tenth and early eleventh century. Occasional entries were made at Winchester, Wulfstan at York added a few to the earlier tenth century but these merely highlight the lack of a strong tradition of historical or contemporary narrative writing. The role of passionate concern rather than habit in prompting our solitary chronicler makes his account even more problematic. This one chronicler did not produce a flowering of historical writing, the mid-eleventh-century spurt was still ahead. It was being fuelled by the chronicle copying which we do know was occurring in the late tenth and early decades of the eleventh century. When that flowering came it would however share some of the views which animated this chronicler of Æthelred, a desire to write contemporary narrative and an account of the immediate past as a prelude to and explanation of important events in the present. The stimulus of events like 1016 and 1066 in the creation of the English historical tradition is an important one.

Politics, Propaganda and History, 1016 onwards

After the detail of Æthelred's time the reign of Cnut returns to the sparse chronicling of the tenth century. The sources of Æthelred's reign had not been produced simply by the gathering momentum of the revival of intellectual activity. The desire to explain, present and defend the monastic movement after the reaction following 975 and the deaths of its first leaders had produced not only Saints' Lives but many of the judicial narratives, including such full ones as the Ely land pleas recounted in Æthelwold's *Libellus* and copied later in the *Liber Eliensis*. The severity of Danish attacks and their final outcome in defeat produced analyses and explanations of 'the condition of England' *c*.1016 from the Chronicler and Wulfstan. During the early years of Cnut the desire to chronicle a Danish takeover briefly sustained chronicle writing, whilst the survival of Archbishop Wulfstan until 1023 directly inspired the two law codes of Cnut. These are the closest to codification of all the old English laws and are intimately related to contemporary circumstances (see Ruling the Kingdom, pp. 138–45). They are the work of an English archbishop whose training and experience of Æthelred's reign had given him a passionate interest in law in the unique circumstances of conquest. They are the products of an opportunity to use law as a framework for the transition to rule by a conqueror, and of that conqueror's own desire to rule with the powers of an English king.

The consecutive narrative traditions of English historical writing date from the mid eleventh century. From the mid 1030s the Anglo-Saxon Chronicles provide detailed, but now often differing accounts. Perhaps earlier than these is the *Encomium Emmae Reginae* of 1041. This is the first of a relatively new b: ed of *pièces justificatives*, virtually propagandist works which increase in number in this century. It was written for a known patron, Queen Emma, by a foreign clerk. The lack of such writers in England itself prefigures the need for a Goscelin of St Bertin later in the century to produce lives of the English Saints.

The contrast between these faltering beginnings and the outstanding achievements of English historians less than a century later is stark. The fertilization of English writing by continental influences was important in producing this change. So too was the experience of 1066 and its aftermath. Both ensured that one of England's great contributions to the twelfth-century Renaissance would be the writing of History.[19] Crisis was the already established provocation for historical writing. From the late tenth century it was within a monastic framework that those crises had been recorded and interpreted. And already it was a national not a regional picture which writers aspired to paint. Faltering as the pre-conquest traditions were they are the foundations on which a Florence of Worcester or a William of Malmesbury worked. And the production of an orderly, balanced narrative from the raw materials of the often highly partisan accounts of the mid eleventh century was one of the latter's great achievements.

The Anglo-Saxon Chronicle

The development of the Anglo-Saxon Chronicles in the eleventh century is complicated by questions surrounding their relationship to the events of 1066 which altered all perspectives on earlier history. MS C is simplest. It had been completed by the end of 1066. The MS is written in several mid-eleventh century hands, and changes in the handwriting suggest, though cannot prove, that the period up to 1049 was written together and retrospectively, with near contemporary entries from 1049 to 1066. Those for 1065 and 1066 appear to have been written in awareness of the victory of William at Hastings.

E is post-conquest in its present form but there is every reason to believe that its account of the years before 1066 is a near-contemporary St Augustine's story. Its entry for the accession of Edward the Confessor was written during the king's lifetime.[20] Its account of key events in the Godwine story, like those of 1052, suggest a contemporary Kentish justification rather than one which is specifically pro-Godwine, or pro-Harold. Most of its amplifications and variations between 1035 and 1066 point to a Kentish observer and an important witness to the events he described. There is no indication of any rewriting or reorientation of material for the period before 1066 in the copy made after that date.

D is another story. It was compiled at the end of the eleventh century as a northern Chronicle with a definite interest in the family and career of Edgar the Ætheling, the surviving Old English claimant to the throne, and in connections between the Danes and England. D's scribe had access to pre-1066 sources, including some of those also found in C and E, and he made alterations to some of them in order to develop his own themes. D is closer to history than annal.

D had access to MS E or its sources for the period before 1066, but the relationship between these two after 1066 is unclear. Common material links them up to 1079, and it would be simplest to argue that the compilers of both

19. R. Thomson, *William of Malmesbury*, (Woodbridge, 1987) and 'England and the twelfth-century Renaissance', *Past and Present* no. 101 (1983) pp. 3–21
20. ASC E 1042

used a common set of annals for these years which they amplified. That common set has a Northern focus, which D occasionally extends. E received some Peterborough additions for this period, the most famous being the exploits of the English and Danes in and around the Fenlands. But Peterborough is not the source of all its account of the late century, nor is there any sign of a continued Canterbury or Kentish knowledge. The entries from 1085 change in nature, becoming specially concerned with the king and his doings and this chronicler's assessment of William and his reign in 1087 is famous. That assessment was made by someone who had lived at William's court and its mixture of praise and criticism articulates the contradictions inherent in the earlier attitudes to kings.

History and Propaganda

Already in these eleventh-century chronicles individual voices can be identified behind the anonymity: the South Eastern monk who wrote the story of Æthelred, the Kentish monk we can hear in the E chronicle for 1049–52, the Northern writer of MS D. The individual voice, often telling a highly partisan tale, becomes a feature of the eleventh-century sources whether English or Norman. Some are overt political statements designed to explain, exonerate, defend or promote their patrons. Many are related to the succession crises and conquests which dominated this century. In highlighting these crises they encourage a contrasting view of the tenth century as an age of peace, whose succession disputes easily appear less political and fraught. The contrast is partly illusion. Tenth-century succession produced its own character assassination and arguments about legitimacy. Some of them still echo in eleventh-century sources like the Life of Wulfhild, with its stories of Edgar's sexual exploits. The contrast is partly a reflection of the sparsity of tenth-century narrative compared with the fullness of the eleventh, a century which felt increasingly driven to document events. But it was the peculiarly complicated crises and the novel elements of conquest which prompted much of the eleventh-century revival of narrative. Some of the contrast is real, and the resulting works highly partisan political documents.

Such is the so-called *Encomium Emmae Reginae*. Emma was the widow of Æthelred and Cnut and the mother of Harthacnut and Edward the Confessor. Her situation between 1035 and 1042 posed political dilemmas and produced actions which she afterwards felt the need to explain. The Encomium was written for her in 1041, during the reign of Harthacnut, but after the return of her son, Edward, to England in that year. It covers the accession of Cnut, the coming of the Danish dynasty, but especially the events of 1035–40 after Cnut's death. It is an almost contemporary source written for a key actor in these years. As Emma's own version of the years 1016–40, albeit refracted through a cleric's eyes, it is crucial. Although written for a woman, and one who played a large part in politics, its treatment of Emma herself is cursory. The situation of a political woman who needed to stress the legitimacy and claims of the husband and sons through whom alone she could act speaks through it. In it Emma answers the criticisms of her, especially those which could be made by her sons. It can be read as a guide to the arguments and accusations current *c.*1040.

The *Life of Edward the Confessor* is also a historical piece produced for a royal patroness in the thick of political events. The author is again a Flemish monk, his patroness Queen Edith, daughter of Earl Godwine, sister of King Harold and widow of Edward the Confessor. The work can be dated between 1065 and 1067.[21] Its most recent editor divides it into two distinct parts: a eulogy of the house of Godwine and a more hagiographical account of Edward the Confessor, with the two parts separated by Hastings itself and demonstrating that its author and his purposes were overtaken by events. But there is no necessary incompatibility between the two halves. Edith as the patroness is its key. A work in praise both of her family and her husband, far from being disjointed, stresses her two claims to position in the political world. Such claims needed to be put forward after the conquest of 1066. The immediate aftermath of Hastings was uncertainty: would the battle be final and irreversible; would William be a conqueror or a legitimate king, would he be another Cnut; how were Harold and his family's claims to be treated? Norman apologists took some time to resolve this last question,[22] and in 1066–67 most of the others were still open. The *Life* is Edith's claim to continued importance in this context. The achievements of her family were still worth glorying in, her royal and saintly husband must be stressed. Edith's story thus becomes not just another important woman's voice from the eleventh century but a voice from the surviving great Old English nobility immediately after Hastings, uncertain that all was lost, still basing its claims and its pride in the recent English past. Such attitudes would have played a part in determining how William was received in these crucial early stages.

William of Poitiers's *History of William the Conqueror* does not speak with its patron's voice as clearly as do the Encomium or the Life of Edward. Edith and Emma supplied details themselves to their authors. Poitiers provides another historical form, the panegyric or adulatory life of the man in whose service Poitiers had been. If the *Life of Edward* speaks with a voice from the English nobility, Poitiers echoes the conversation of the Norman court by the mid 1070s. It was written no earlier than 1073–74. Its glorification of William presents a view of 1066 and its origins which is not as the Normans saw it on the eve of that year, nor in its immediate aftermath, but as they had come to see it. Still not entirely sure of their security in England, they had decided on both the need for and manner of legitimation of the Conquest. The line they developed was not one which sought to explain Hastings itself, that had been the concern of the Anglo-Saxon Chroniclers of 1066 for whom the defeat was central. Rather it gave a version of English and Norman history in the eleventh century which justified and legitimized the acquisition of England and the disappropriations which followed it. The battle itself played a central part in that argument: its outcome was a judgement of God, his military success vindicated William as well as making him king. But for Poitiers, as to a lesser extent for his source, William of Jumièges, all relations between England and Normandy since the 990s are woven into a story of promises and legitimate claims. The difficulty of

21. *The Life of King Edward*, ed. F. Barlow (Edinburgh, 1962) pp. xxv–xxx
22. G. Garnett, 'Coronation and propaganda: some implications of the Norman claim to the throne of England in 1066' TRHS, ser. 5, 36 (1986), pp. 91–116

writing English history in the eleventh century without seeing it as a prelude to
and result of 1066 begins with sources such as these.

The impact of 1066

The impact of 1066 on historical writing was felt immediately. That impact
grew rather than diminished in subsequent generations, and cast its shadow not
merely over the reign of Edward the Confessor but as far as that of Æthelred
and Edgar.

As the perception of 1066, its results and its finality, changed, so writers and
chroniclers variously tried to preserve and foster an English inheritance and
explain the drama of 1066. The losses of church land and the depredations of
Norman lords were one spur, but not the only one. Pride in the English past
played a part. The desire to record it brought the chroniclers of the later
eleventh and twelfth centuries up against the same source problems as we face,
viz. the lack of them. The best argument against substantial losses of chronicles,
annals and Saints Lives from before 1066 is the difficulty these chroniclers had
in compiling their works. The problems experienced and resolved by a
Florence of Worcester, William of Malmesbury or Henry of Huntingdon when
trying to write an English history from fragmentary sources is a measure of their
historical achievement. Their aim was the preservation, celebration and
explanation of an English past which was more than a prelude to 1066, but
which would help in the understanding of that event and its aftermath. One of
the certain effects of 1066 was its stimulus to the flowering of historical writing
in England.

The hundred years from the mid eleventh to mid twelfth century produced a
profusion of narrative and historical works: Saints' Lives from the pens of
Goscelin, Osbern, Eadmer, Heremann; local chronicles, or chronicles-cum-
cartularies like those of Hemming at Worcester, Hugh Candidus at Peterborough, Hugh the Chantor at York and of the anonymous authors of the
Ramsey and Abingdon Chronicles and the Book of Ely, and chroniclers who
painted on a broader canvas, the Anglo-Saxon Chroniclers, Florence of
Worcester, Eadmer, Orderic, Simeon of Durham, and pre-eminently William
of Malmesbury. The range of these authors, almost all working within the
English monastic tradition, is summed up by William of Malmesbury.

William was the greatest of the twelfth-century historians. The classical
studies and humanist traditions of his day affected him deeply, as did the
tradition of English historical writing epitomized for him by Bede. William was
a man of his day and its politics. His *Historia Novella*, an account of the civil war
which began in 1135 is a twelfth-century example of the partisan contemporary
history which succession problems had produced in the eleventh century. But his
De Gestis Regum Anglorum, Deeds of the kings of the English, is history. It was
dedicated to Mathilda, descendant of Æthelred II and wife of Henry I. It is a
deliberate attempt to tell English history to a generation which was the product
of the union of England and Normandy symbolized in the marriage of Mathilda
and Henry. William however was no crude political propagandist or political
apologist in the style of the *Encomium Emmae*. His writing deliberately sought to
draw on all sources, and he used the works of his immediate predecessors, men

like Florence and Eadmer, as well as earlier material. Like most of his predecessors he wrote history from within the English monastic tradition, which consciously dated itself from the Golden Age of Edgar and before. Early English historical writing was monastic not simply ecclesiastical though its focus was often England. As a historian William was aware of and presented the contradictions and inconsistencies in his sources. The closer he came to the Norman Conquest, the greater this problem became, and William was occasionally driven to stressing the difference between what the 'English' and 'Normans' said.

The Norman Conquest was a developing process and one which could not have appeared irreversible before the later 1080s at the earliest. English nobles and churchmen reacted to the circumstances of defeat, wished to see themselves giving the throne to William, later struggled to retain lands; Normans needed to prove their right to the throne against other claimants and to the lands they had taken. 1066 raised immediate questions of legitimacy and explanation.

The Norman arguments assembled by the early 1070s in Jumièges and Poitiers and graphically rehearsed in the Bayeux Tapestry are one side of the debate. They stressed Edward's promises of the throne to William, Harold's oath in 1064 confirming these promises, his subsequent perjury in 1066 making him an illegitimate ruler. The Tapestry, produced in England for a Norman lord, hints at an alternative English version.[23] There were, in effect several 'English' versions. Those writing closest to the event, MSS C and E, Edith, sought the immediate causes of their defeat and emphasized the tragedy of the 1065 revolt in dividing the English defence in 1066. As Norman actions and accounts took shape, English views reacted. Some sought to counter by emphasizing the legitimacy of Harold, or denying details of the Norman case against him. Thus the Bayeux tapestry depicts the designation of Harold by the dying Edward, Eadmer counters the Norman version of Harold's visit to the continent. William of Malmesbury referred to laudatory English views of the Godwine family still current in his day. Others, like the D MS of the Chronicle refrained from commenting on Harold, preferring to stress the continued importance of the Old English claimant, Edgar the Ætheling, the injustice of his treatment symbolic of the injustices of the Conquest and of the tyranny of a conqueror who had failed to stand by his coronation promises. Most of these reactions pre-date 1100. The first-generation response to the Conquest was highly charged if not united. Contemporary history was still being written as part of political debate.

By the 1090s if not before the immediate passion of the legitimacy debate was waning. The first Norman succession had been effected without successful challenge. William of Malmesbury's concern with the legitimacy and explanation of 1066 shows that this was far from a dead issue in the twelfth century, but as a spur to historical writing it was now joined by other questions. Domesday had set its own seal on the Conquest, convincing many perhaps of the need of written proof to land, but also of the strength of claims based in the Old English past. The respect which Domesday and the legal cases which preceded it gave

23. N. Brooks and H. E. Walker, 'The authority and interpretation of the Bayeux Tapestry', ANS, 1, pp. 1–34

to English law and proof spurred the recording of that past. So too did the growing realization of what Norman rule meant. Devastations, disappropriations, troubles over landholding, taxation, the high-handed attitude of some Norman bishops and abbots towards English monks. It was not solely an *English* response to *Normans*. Norman churchmen who had taken over English houses and sees threatened by Norman lords quickly developed an interest in recording the rights of the English past. The eleventh-century struggles between cleric and lay are as important as a nationalist response in producing late eleventh- and twelfth-century sources.

The experience of foreign rule under Cnut and his sons and a long history of growing royal exactions had been fostering the consciousness which now became articulate. Uneasiness with royal power was there in the sources for Æthelred's reign, in the laws of Cnut and in the readiness of Chroniclers to judge Harthacnut's harsh taxation and his unworthiness to be a king.[24] Events after 1066 and the urgent need of the late eleventh century for records brought unease to the point of criticism. When the literate churchmen came to see themselves at the receiving end of royal exactions, they were shocked into a critical view of royal and lay power itself.[25] Some saw it as a Norman innovation and combined it with disgruntled responses to 1066. At Worcester Hemming wrote a history which chronicled losses to royal officials which stretched back into Æthelred's time, but singled out the foreign conquests of Cnut and William for their oppressiveness. The angst of the E chronicler both praising and condemning William in 1087 speaks not only of the growing criticisms, but also of the difficulties they produced for writers trained to accept and laud royal power.

If 1066 did no more than articulate criticism growing for many years, the use of these sources to assess the severity of the effects of 1066 becomes difficult. We may not be seeing novel developments, but merely hearing about old ones in the improved records of the time. If English monks of the late eleventh century temporarily articulate the voice of the oppressed, if they criticize kings and nobles and put quill to parchment to do so, it was perhaps because Norman kings had hit them in their sensitive pockets. But the severity of the experience was one reason for the improved record. We should not view the responses of the clerical elite too cynically. Orderic Vitalis, safe in his Norman monastery was appalled by the devastation after the conquest and railed against the weight of the Norman Yoke.[26] The intellectual developments of the tenth and eleventh centuries had provided yardsticks of royal action by which to judge kings and the powerful. A history of growing royal power had encouraged their use. In England the more critical attitude to kings and secular rule pre-dates the arrival of specifically Gregorian ideas.

The chronicles after 1066 are more often informed by such ideas than by simple nationalism or xenophobia. Xenophobia certainly existed as did an awareness of nations. The Ramsey Chronicler relished stories of sharp local practice at the expense of the Danish followers of Cnut.[27] William of

24. ASC C 1040
25. M. Clanchy, *England and its Rulers, 1066–1272* (1983), pp. 52–5
26. Orderic Vitalis, vol. II, Bk IV p. 203 and compare vol. IV, Bk VII, p. 95
27. *Chronicon Abbatiae Ramesiensis* ed. W. D. Macray, Rolls Series (1886), pp. 129–43

Malmesbury used racial characteristics to explain the Norman Conquest, with frugal Normans pitted against dissipated English,[28] but he was too careful an historian not to hedge it round with qualifications.

By the mid twelfth century the tradition of historical writing was well established in England. It was the product of the classicizing, systematizing, humanist tendencies of twelfth-century thought, but grew on older foundations. To understand it we need to go back to the aspirations and ideals of Alfred's day, to the monastic changes of the tenth century and to the political crises of the eleventh. Developments which inspired changes in narrative writing, responses to unification and conquest, ecclesiastical reform, had an impact on all forms of documentation, laws and charters in particular. The documents which we use to construct the political, social and religious history of tenth- and eleventh-century England are not merely the sources for that history, they are part of it.

28. William of Malmesbury, Bk III, caps. 241, 242 and 245

2

Edward to Eadred, AD 899–955

When Alfred died in AD 899 he was succeeded by his eldest son, Edward the Elder. Edward's succession was challenged by his cousin, Æthelwold, son of Alfred's elder brother King Æthelred I. Æthelwold gained only limited support within Wessex, but the seriousness of his challenge grew as he attracted support north of the Thames. He fled north to be accepted as king by the Vikings settled in Northumbria. By the time of his death at the battle of the Holme in 902 he had been joined by the East Anglian Vikings and by a Mercian prince, Brihtsige son of the ætheling (throneworthy prince) Beornoth. The three-year crisis lays bare the situation which Edward the Elder faced. Within Wessex the immediate legacy of Alfred's reign was strong support for his son. But the challenge a cousin could offer indicates that succession from father to eldest son was no cut and dried rule. North of the Thames the settlements of the Viking armies in East Anglia, North-east Mercia and Northumbria were a permanent threat, ever ready to take advantage of troubles in Wessex or Mercia. Viking settlers were a novel element in relations among the kingdoms of the English, but not a totally transforming one. They acted as Northumbrian and East Anglian armies, identifiable at least to southern observers within older political divisions, and a West Saxon prince could happily ally with them. Mercia and Wessex themselves remained recognizably discrete kingdoms. Mercia was ruled in 899 by Edward's sister and brother-in-law, Æthelflæd and Æthelred. Under them it was allied with Wessex, but control and assimilation of one by the other was far from clear. And, as the aftermath of 899 showed, there were other claimants to the Mercian throne ready to take arms against a West Saxon king, if necessary with Viking aid.

Many of the issues of the early tenth century were clear. Could the rulers of Wessex and Mercia afford to ignore the Viking settlements on their doorstep? Had those settlements altered the relationships among the English kingdoms, and between them and their neighbours within the British Isles? Were those relationships amicable with or without Viking complications? Was there a common sense of Englishness, or strong local loyalties? And what was the situation within Wessex itself, the kingdom whose dynasty had survived the Viking invasions and which was to go on to conquer the remaining kingdoms of the English in the tenth century? Was the prestige of that survival, the legacy of Alfred, sufficient to carry it on to expansion and further victory? Did the aspirations of Alfred and his descendants lie in these directions? Was the dynasty itself internally united?

England c. AD 900

The kingdoms of the English

Although some notion of England was already in existence by AD 900 the political reality was of separate kingdoms, some of them by this date under Viking control. The kingdom of Wessex, consisting of the old kingdoms of Wessex and Kent, had survived the Viking attacks under its king, Alfred. Alfred was able to present himself as a member of a dynasty whose claims to rule in Wessex stretched back to the era of settlement. The historical truth of those claims is less important than the possibility of making them. Combined with the undoubted military reputation of the ninth-century representatives of the line they placed the kings of Wessex c. AD 900 in a uniquely strong position.

The situation in Mercia was less straightforward. Mercia was a kingdom equal to if not greater than Wessex. This is easily obscured by its immediate ninth-century history of dynastic change and rivalry which give a false impression of political weakness. Mercian rulers had threatened Welsh kings with domination in the mid ninth century, in alliance with Wessex had had their own successes against the Vikings, and independent Mercian rulers had survived the darkest days of the 870s when the Viking armies had seemed poised to reduce them to tributary status. Yet the Viking successes in Mercia had undoubtedly been facilitated by the rapid changes of dynasty. One of the rival kings, Ceolwulf, had been prepared to treat with the Viking army, if not to use it to gain control of Mercia. He, like Alfred, came close to paying regular tribute in the 870s. Unlike Alfred he was forced to divide his kingdom as the price of settlement with the Viking leaders. The division of Mercia and the takeover of its eastern half by Viking rulers and settlers was a result of Ceolwulf's disputed claim to the throne and his readiness to use Viking allies. Realization of the internal situation in Mercia may have played a more important part than geography in explaining why Mercia took the brunt of Viking attacks in the 870s, though its proximity to Northumbria, where the Viking armies had succeeded in establishing themselves at this date, its openness to new Viking armies coming from the North East and from Ireland, and the undoubted attraction of its wealth were all important factors. Mercia at the end of the ninth century should not be written off as a kingdom that had obviously had its day. It certainly lacked the advantages of a king or dynasty which could claim the antiquity or the history of family successes in war which Alfred could claim in Wessex. But by the 880s its western parts had a new ruler, Æthelred. We know nothing of his ancestry, but he chose to continue the alliance with Wessex already a feature of the mid ninth century.

The closer cooperation of Wessex and Mercia in the last half of the ninth century resulted from Viking attack and was marked by a series of marriage alliances. Burgred had married Alfred's sister, Æthelswith; Alfred himself had married Ealhswith, daughter of a Mercian ealdorman. The West Saxon ealdorman Æthelfrith married Alfred's Mercian niece by marriage. It is thus no surprise that when Æthelred became the effective lord of 'English' Mercia in the 880s, Alfred married his daughter to him. The marriage of the king's own daughter to Æthelred lord of the Mercians warns of the need to examine Æthelred's status carefully. The Anglo-Saxon, more correctly West Saxon Chronicle of the late ninth century calls him an ealdorman, i.e. a subordinate of Alfred. And no coins were struck in his name, not even after the taking of London in 886 and the delivery of the town and presumably its mint to him. Yet the chronicler Æthelweard, using a lost version of the Anglo-Saxon Chronicle, calls him *king* and Alfred's biographer Asser speaks of the rule of Æthelred in Mercia as if it were analogous to that of the Welsh kings who sought Alfred's alliance and made some form of submission to him.[1] During Alfred's own reign Æthelred recognized his authority, acknowledging the need for his permission to grant charters, for example. This situation did not survive Alfred's death. After 899 Æthelred and his wife Æthelflæd grant charters in Mercia without reference to West Saxon kings.[2] A chronicle of their military deeds, the so-called Mercian Register, was produced at or near their court to celebrate their actions. We must not assume that from the late ninth century onwards Mercia was politically subordinate to Wessex. The independence of that kingdom lasts in a real form until the death of Æthelflæd in 918.

In East Mercia, as in East Anglia and Northumbria, Viking rulers had taken over by AD 900. There is considerable debate about the nature of this takeover and especially about the density of the Viking settlement.[3] The evidence of linguistic changes in these areas suggests a Norse settlement which went beyond simple political takeover especially in parts of Lincolnshire and Yorkshire, but did not entail a swamping of the local communities. In assessing the impact of Viking settlement, however, its nature is as important as its scale. Widespread peasant settlement without the political coordination of Viking lords would have had little political importance. Viking *rulers* are more important than Viking *settlers* in the political history of these areas and their relations with southern kings. In AD 900 there were Viking kings at York and in East Anglia, and other Viking leaders, *jarls* or *holds*, in control of eastern England from Bedford northwards. The distinction between these two types of ruler may be less an indication of their status in the Scandinavian world from which they came than of the nature of the rule they took over in England. At York and in East Anglia the Vikings took over kingdoms and their rulers were known as kings. In the East Midlands they, like Æthelred in the West, took over not a kingdom but only a part of one. Southern chroniclers fitted them into the existing political geography of Northern and Eastern England and this says much about the way in which the Vikings had settled and adjusted to their new situation. But it should not lull us into assuming that the Vikings had made little difference to that geography.

1. *Chronicle of Æthelweard*, ed. A. Campbell (Edinburgh, 1962), pp. 49–50 and Asser, Life of Alfred in *Alfred the Great* ed. S. Keynes and M. Lapidge (1983), pp. 96 and 190
2. S. 221, 224, 225. Even before 899 only their grants to Worcester consistently call Æthelred *ealdorman*
3. P. Stafford, *The East Midlands in the Early Middle Ages* (Leicester, 1985), pp. 109–21

The old kingdoms of Northumbria, of Deira and Bernicia South and North of the Tees, and of East Anglia remained recognizable under Viking rule. Deiran political identity was given an extended vitality by the rule of Viking kings here until 927 and intermittently from 939 to 954. The independence of Northumbria, North or South of the Tees was no novelty; it had never been in subordination to either Wessex or Mercia. East Anglia had been controlled by Mercia for part of the ninth century, though its assimilation had been less successful than that of Kent by Wessex. Here too Viking rule can be seen as reasserting previous independence.

At York and in East Anglia the Viking rulers received local cooperation from an early date. In both places Christian Viking kings were ruling by the 890s. At York the archbishop and the community of St Cuthbert made their own successful adjustments to the reality of Viking rule. The art and archaeology of York suggest an assimilation of Viking and native Anglian traditions here,[4] and as late as the 940s and 950s Christian archbishops would find it possible to deal with pagan Viking lords. The Vikings were not the pariahs which some churchmen and beleaguered rulers tried to paint them. Once the transition from external looting as invaders to internal looting as kings had been made they could readily take their place within the political patterns of late ninth-century Europe. Rule by a Viking at York was arguably preferable to many in the North to rule by a remote southern king.

But relations between Northumbria and the South must be seen historically. It was a Dublin dynasty which constantly asserted its claims to York during the first half of the tenth century, and until the 920s it was aggressively pagan. Neither its paganism nor its external links need have endeared it to Northumbrian nobles and clergy. Athelstan found little difficulty in replacing it in 927. By the 930s these Dublin kings were Christian and the North had experienced remote southern rule. Irish Scandinavian rulers were more acceptable after 939. Attitudes towards southern and Viking kings oscillated. Thanks to the dearth of written sources the reasons for those oscillations can only be surmised. An influx of Viking lords and repeated periods of Viking control could have fostered existing independence, yet there need have been little constant common cause between Northumbrian and Scandinavian elites before both felt threatened by southern expansion. The tenacity of Scandinavian rule re-emphasized the Humber as a boundary.

Relations among neighbours

As far as their southern and western neighbours were concerned the Viking kingdoms had altered if not the geography then the political situation of the ninth century. The new Viking rulers of these areas were still heavily dependent on loot as a means of rewarding their followers; those followers still consisted of men drawn into Viking activity by the promise of such gains; rivalry for their support continued. All these factors, plus the momentum of their late ninth-century victories made their presence on the borders of Mercia and Wessex more aggressive and threatening than that of their English predecessors. The

4. J. T. Lang, 'Anglo-Scandinavian sculpture in Yorkshire', in *Viking Age York and the North*, ed. R. A. Hall, CBA Research Reports (1978), pp. 11–20

military campaigns of Æthelflæd and Edward were defensive as much as expansionary.

The overriding fact of the ninth century in the kingdoms bordering the North Sea had been the Viking invasions. Those invasions had not ceased by AD 900, but an important stage in their development had been reached. During the latter half of the ninth century Viking activity in Europe had been concentrated into the actions of one or two large and organized armies operating between Frankia and England. New armies and leaders were still gathering, but on the whole were joining those already established. The Channel and southern part of the North Sea were their highways. During the late ninth century these large armies had moved from looting, ransoming and pillaging to settlement, in England and Ireland especially but also in parts of northern France. Their military organization was not immediately lost. Edward and Æthelflæd would find that the settled Vikings of northern and eastern England easily turned to warfare again and readily regrouped, e.g. around fortified *burhs* in response to military pressure.

Settled Vikings who were still a military threat remained the backdrop to relations between rulers and kingdoms in the early tenth as in the late ninth century. This applied among the kingdoms of the English, between Wessex and Mercia, to links between Wessex and its neighbours across the English channel and to some extent to relations with the Welsh kingdoms. The rapprochement between some of the latter and Alfred had also been a response to the aggression of the sons of Rhodri the Great, king of Gwynedd.

The links among these kingdoms varied. Alfred and his father had joined themselves by marriage and alliance to several rulers whom the Viking menace drew together in a common enterprise. To the Mercian alliances, Alfred's father had added Frankish, marrying Judith, the daughter of Charles the Bald, ruler of West Frankia. Alfred continued to recognize the importance of the southern shores of the English channel. He married his daughter Ælfthryth to the count of Flanders. These marriages were attempts to foster and bind a sense of common purpose. The particular direction of Viking attack from the mid ninth century drew together Mercia and Wessex, rather than Mercia and Northumbria. The resulting alliance was confirmed when the Vikings took over York and eastern England.

The links between Alfred and the Welsh appear differently. The kings of South Wales are said to have submitted to Alfred's lordship (see above, n. 1). The writer, Asser, was a native of the southern Welsh kingdom of Dyfed. He explains the submission as a response both the the pressure of the sons of Rhodri the Great and also to that of Æthelred lord of the Mercians. Long-term pressure from rulers of Mercia and Gwynedd had led to a submission in search of a powerful lord and ally. Alfred is also said to have received the submission of Rhodri's son, Anarawd of Gwynedd. But Asser's description raises questions of interpretation which dog discussion of the relations of English kings with their mainland neighbours (see below, *England and its Neighbours*). Asser speaks of subjection to Alfred's lordship but also of alliance; Alfred showered Anarawd with gifts and became his godfather at confirmation. The subjection of Anarawd to Alfred is said to be on the same conditions as that of Æthelred with the Mercians. With the suspicion that West Saxon sources and the southern Welsh author deliberately talked up their significance, and lacking any other version, these events can only be interpreted within the history of relations between the actors and by comparison with similar contemporary action. Alfred's relations with Anarawd appear as alliance to end hostilities rather than as subjection. The gifts and the creation of a god-relationship recall the making of peace with Guthrum, the Danish leader. The seeking of Alfred's court is a hint of inequality in the relationship, but there is prior indication of the subjection of the sons of Rhodri. Asser's analogy between Anarawd and Æthelred corroborates Æthelred's independence and hints at Alfred's aspirations towards subjection of both.

During the first half of the tenth century relationships between West Saxon kings and Mercia and of English kings and their British and Frankish neighbours are important. Their background lies in the late ninth century, in Viking attacks and political pressures. The links varied from temporary subjection to simple alliance in a common cause. The potential was there for future expansion and development but there was nothing inevitable about it.

These relations among neighbours, English kings, Viking rulers, Welsh and Frankish princes are the legacy of the ninth century to the tenth. They form one element in a framework to which the nature of politics, the traditions of rule, noble and ecclesiastical power and ideals all contributed (see below, *Ruling the Kingdom*, *The Nobility*, *The Church*).

The nature of tenth-century politics

Tenth-century politics turned on relations between personal monarchy and powerful nobles and churchmen whose position was not solely a question of royal whim. Monarchy was well-established, underpinned by Christian thought and noble tradition; the West Saxon dynasty itself was relatively stable. The royal court was thus already a single political centre within which a politics of personality and faction grew. The bishops, abbots and nobles who attended court did so in the hope of patronage, in its widest sense. But the power and position they hoped to gain was to be exercised both inside and outside the court framework. Access to the king meant not only the hope of material rewards, land and increasingly office, but the less tangible influence which was equally important in maintaining status beyond the court. For few ninth- or tenth–century men was court office or standing an end in itself. Rather the patronage acquired there brought lands and powers in local tribunals, or influence over the king's own judicial decisions affecting local clients. The process was not however linear, attendance at court not a career stage en route to local power.What the king had to offer drew men back constantly to court, not least because the continued existence of the court as a source of patronage in one's absence allowed the growth in power of rivals, present or potential.

The royal court could only function in this way as long as the king had much to give, though when the desired gifts included such intangible and transient benefits as judicial favours its appeal was constant. The unification of England under Wessex during the first half of the tenth century increased royal assets both in land and office, magnifying both the problems of rule and the magnetic pull of the court. The pull of that magnet was not uniform. It was strongest where the possibility of gift was greatest, and thus the concentration of royal land determined the area of its greatest attraction – Wessex and to a lesser extent Mercia. The extension of the king's judicial activities during the tenth century widened the attraction by offering benefits of office, control of courts high among them, over a larger geographical area. Hope and expectation reinforced gift; giving need not be constant to be effective. Yet where the king had least to offer, nobles and churchmen were least attracted. The reality of royal control in northern England, if not in large parts of the East remains debatable throughout these centuries.

Because the court acted as a magnet for those whose power was already established in other areas, or who sought the court to achieve ends external to it, it attracted to itself wider issues. Thus for example, the concerns of reforming churchmen, which required royal backing, became a part of the politics of the court, as did concerns of nobles who were also ealdormen or local landholders. When factions formed, as they inevitably do in any system which revolves around patronage, the alignments might not reflect merely the personal issues which divide courtiers but also these wider religious or regional issues which had been drawn into court politics. Conversely the alignments of the court ramified into these other areas. It is regrettable that the tenth-century sources allow little detailed exploration of the fluctuation of factions which result.

In a personal monarchy the question of inheritance, of succession to the throne is central. The future heir and disappointed or aspiring princes are important political figures. Tenth-century succession norms did not clearly designate a single heir as the unquestioned successor. A range of possible heirs were thus legitimate foci for factional development and the succession became an issue around which the many questions drawn into court politics could crystallize. A system based to a large extent on patronage is bound to create a defensive in-group and a discontented out-group. For both, the choice of the next heir to the throne is crucial. Where succession is a central question of politics, politics itself becomes family politics involving potential future heirs and their mothers. The court as royal household, where the personal is emphatically political, is always an area of potential female activity; doubly so when succession is a burning question.

Both court and succession politics bring personality firmly into the political realm and at the same time encourage character assassination as a political tool. Court groupings thrive on gossip and accusations among tightly knit groups spread and fester even when rebutted. Where issues divide less than groupings of interest centred on individuals, character assassination rather than policy accusations become means of political advance. Too many other questions, most notably those of religious change, were drawn to the tenth-century court for it to have witnessed a pure form of such politics;[5] though this often served only to determine the type of accusation made. Succession intensified these features. The choice of successor turns on fitness to rule. This raises legitimacy, and invites speculation about the character of the mother and the nature of her union. It involves the personality of the claimant himself and invites comment on this, informed by what was expected of rulers and the moral codes of the day. Argument about succession generated some of the sources and many of the legends of the tenth and eleventh centuries.

5. On this see N. Elias, *The Court Society* (Oxford, 1983)

All this assumes a court centred around a personal monarch as the hub of politics. This is true of the tenth and eleventh centuries as of most of the Middle Ages. But the nature of medieval politics arises not merely from the power of the king and court, but from its coexistence with the semi-independent power, allegiances and interests of nobles and churchmen and from the importance of war. Warfare does not destroy the patterns suggested above but like principle, it adds its own complications. As a source of profit to be distributed through the mechanisms of the court it may merely reinforce the pattern. Yet the battlefield can function as an alternative focus to the court for the formation of political alliances and produce a different weighting of qualities. The threat of a common enemy can both exacerbate and override the factions of court; exacerbate them by sharpening the criticisms of incompetence, override them by suggesting that narrow factionalism is inappropriate. Warfare will only act in this way if the enemy is perceived as a common one – witness Alfred's problems in keeping the allegiance of his nobles even at the height of Viking attack. Yet the prestige of the successful warrior operates as a magnet to followers and a legacy to successors in the same way as gift giving. And it can operate over a wider geographical area, pulling in remote allegiances. At the same time it is more readily dissipated than the longer-term development of a balance of interests between centre and localities which was the centripetal strength of court politics.

Such was the political system and the specific situation inherited by Edward the Elder in 899. He, his sister Æthelflæd who ruled Mercia alongside him and his three sons who ruled after him were the military creators of the English kingdom. Their reigns are so lamentably ill-documented that in what follows they will be treated as a group. This is no indication of their relative importance in the history of these centuries. But necessity will be taken as an opportunity to set up the broad framework, whilst the period 955–1066 enables us to explore the politics of these centuries in more detail.

Edward the Elder to Eadred 899–955

Military problems and unification

The creation of the English kingdom through conquest is the primary theme of the first half of the tenth century. The story is well known and its outline can be briefly told. Edward the Elder and his sister Æthelflæd were its first actors. Æthelred lord of the Mercians lived until 911, but even before his death his wife Æthelflæd had for several years taken the active military role in the Mercian kingdom. She and her brother Edward followed broadly comparable tactics in the construction of large-scale fortifications, or *burhs*, at such places as Nottingham, Towcester or Derby as centres for their advance against the Danish rulers of northern and eastern England. The threat of these rulers was obvious from the time of Æthelwold's rising against his cousin Edward. It was writ on the landscape of southern England, where some estates were still impoverished as a result of earlier depredations.[6] Edward and Æthelflæd were aware of the threat and were already encouraging their nobles to acquire land in

6. EHD I, no. 103, pp. 546–7

areas controlled by the Vikings, perhaps hoping for peaceful extension of control.[7] The settled Vikings had been negotiated with, Edward's second law code refers to the *friðgewritu*, literally 'peace writings' which had been drawn up between them. These were at best settled enemies.[8]

In 909, whether in response to specific provocation or in recognition of the general threat, Edward led an army north from Wessex and Mercia and ravaged for five weeks. The retaliatory raid of the following year began a series of campaigns which resulted in the conquest of eastern England as far as the Humber or perhaps Lindsey by the time of the deaths of brother and sister. Æthelflæd until her death in 918 was especially concerned with defence against the Welsh, against what appears to have been a continuing Viking settlement from the Irish Sea in the Cheshire/Lancashire region and with the recovery of control of North East Mercia beyond Watling Street. Edward concentrated his efforts in Essex, East Anglia and in the East Midlands, moving up towards Stamford. By 920 when the rulers of North Britain met him at Bakewell in the Peak, Edward was king of all southern England to the Trent and Welland if not the Humber.

Were they uniting in an 'English' or a West Saxon family effort? Their spheres of action appear clearly demarcated and concerted, yet it might be argued that Æthelflæd was doing no more than defending traditional Mercian areas and that the appearance of cooperation is an illusion. The two courts remained separate. The Mercian Register concerns itself exclusively with Mercian events whilst the Winchester Chronicle is purely an account of Edward's successes. Yet Edward was moving into areas never considered West Saxon territory and the Mercian Register, at least once, uses the term 'English' to describe the joint West Saxon and Mercian forces.[9] It would be premature to speak of a fusion of Wessex and Mercia, but the drawing together of the later ninth century was continuing, against the background of the same threat.

Athelstan succeeded in 924. In 926 he met Sihtric, king of Northumbria at Tamworth and arranged a marriage between Sihtric and his sister: only a year later he drove out Sihtric's brother and successor Guthfrith and took over York. The rapidity of these events is difficult to understand when all immediate background to them has been lost. Sihtric, his predecessor, Ragnald and his immediate successor, Guthfrith were all Viking leaders active in Dublin and Ireland as well as at York. Ragnald's own takeover may have been resented by some in the North, including other Scandinavians. Neither Sihtric or Guthfrith may have enjoyed automatic united support there. Ragnald had been one of the northern rulers who met Edward the Elder in 920; Sihtric treated with Athelstan. Their actions may have been response to military threat, equally attempts to gain extra legitimacy in the North. Divisions in the North, not merely of Northumbrian v. Dane but of Viking v. Viking seem to lie behind the speed of Athelstan's takeover there.

Athelstan was now king of the English and continued to be so until his death in 939. The rapid rise of the West Saxon kings to be kings of all England reshaped the political geography of Britain and raised new fears and new

7. EHD I, no. 101, pp. 543–4
8. II Edward 5.2
9. ASC 910

enemies. On the death of Æthelflæd in 918 Edward had taken forcible control of Mercia. Some Mercian nobles were prepared to have Æthelflæd's only child, her daughter Ælfwyn, as their ruler, but Edward carried her off to a southern monastery and assumed rule himself. His accession to Mercia was also marked by what the Winchester Chronicler calls a submission of the Welsh kings to him,[10] an event which could be coupled with those of 920 to give a picture of Edward as an acknowledged ruler of Britain. In 920 the Chronicler tells how the rulers of North Britain, Ragnald of York, the kings of the Scots and Strathclyde Britons and the sons of Eadwulf of Bamburgh chose Edward as father and lord. The kings of the Scots might well have described this alliance sealed on the Pennine borders of York and Mercia in other ways. In both cases the language of submission and dominance we hear is West Saxon. Edward chose the moment of his seizure of power in Mercia to confirm friendship with Æthelflæd's allies, and with his own in South Wales. The meeting at Tamworth, not on the borders of any Welsh kingdom, implied more in the way of subordination than the 920 gathering at Bakewell. Both meetings demonstrated that a southern English king who had accumulated the several kingdoms of the English inevitably entered new relations with his British neighbours.

Athelstan's takeover of York rammed the point home. He went on in 927 to meet many of the rulers of Britain at Eamont Bridge on the borders of Strathclyde. There he was met by Hywel, the Welsh king of Dyfed, Constantine, king of the Scots, Owain, king of Gwent (and/or Owain, king of Strathclyde) and Ealdred, son of Eadwulf of Bamburgh. The northern annals preserved in MS D of the Anglo-Saxon Chronicle spoke of him bringing all the kings of this island under his rule and establishing peace with pledge and oath. The precise significance of the actions is debatable (see below, *England and its Neighbours*), but again the tenth-century message was of a king whose power was growing, at a date when the successes of a great warrior king could easily mushroom to engulf his neighbours.

Hence the alliance of the kings of the Scots, Strathclyde and Olaf Guthfrithson, king of Dublin which Athelstan defeated at *Brunanburh* in 937. In the early 930s Constantine had already confirmed friendship with Olaf by marriage. This had been one of the actions which prompted Athelstan's expedition into Scotland in 934. In 937 the alliance resulted in an attack on Athelstan's kingdom, a first attempt by Olaf to re-establish his family's control at York. *Brunanburh* was a great victory for Athelstan, but few tenth-century victories guaranteed the future. When Athelstan died in 939 the accession of his younger brother Edmund at the age of 18 was a signal for another attempt by Olaf to take York, on this occasion successful. Before his death in 941 Olaf had taken York and the North East Midlands. As with Athelstan's easy takeover in 927 internal support not military might alone was the key to Olaf's success. Rulers from Ireland and the Viking world continued to find support in the North throughout the reigns of Edmund and his brother Eadred. Olaf Guthfrithson, Olaf Sihtricson, Ragnald Guthfrithson and Eric Bloodaxe ruled at York, alternating with ravaging and rule from the South in a deadly political dance which only ended with the expulsion and murder of Eric in 954.

10. ASC 918

The confused history of Northern England between 927 and 954 and especially of the years after 939 is instructive. The takeover of the North was less straightforward than that of Mercia. Part of the reason for this was that it was more abrupt. The long history of rapprochement and sibling rule which had drawn Mercia and Wessex together for over half a century had no parallel in the takeover at York in 927. The common interests which had lain behind that rapprochement were lacking. Athelstan and his successors recognized both the need to buy loyalty here, and the difficulty of ensuring it. Amounderness and later Southwell were granted to the archbishop of York, a key northern leader. The monopoly of the York mint which Athelstan gave to a single moneyer is almost unprecedented. The North was distant, and the existence of a rival dynasty with military strength in Dublin and potential allies to hand was a complication. It was not only Danes who supported Olaf or Eric. The southern chronicler and the later Durham monk Simeon speak not of the faithlessness of the *Danes* of the North but of the *Northumbrians*. A term such as 'separatism' is insufficiently subtle to capture the transitory alliances, the fluctuations of regional feeling, the fears and the calculations of interest which the rapid changes of king in these years suggest. Yet 'separatism' pinpoints the part played by rule from the South in encouraging rather than assuaging such feelings.

In the North and elsewhere churchmen, churches and relics focused local feeling. Archbishop Wulfstan I of York was with Olaf in the campaign which captured the Five Boroughs. He was the leader of the Northumbrians who first pledged themselves to Eadred in 947 then broke their pledges by accepting Eric in the same year. Eadred ravaged and burned the minster at Ripon in his retaliatory raid in 948 and took the archbishop prisoner in 952. The more peaceful transfer or cult of relics often had a political dimension in the process of unification.[11] Athelstan, for example, who had a clear conception of himself as lord of the English, revered the relics of St Cuthbert in the far North, encouraged his cult in Wessex and began the deliberate accumulation of relics from Cornwall and the South West at Glastonbury.

In 954 Eric Bloodaxe, the last Viking ruler of York, was expelled. With hindsight the date has significance. No-one at the time could have appreciated it, and the Northumbrians were slow to declare an allegiance in the succession dispute of 956–59. It now appears as the end of the military unification of England, fitting our assumptions that that enterprise was a deliberate political undertaking with an inevitable *English* boundary. Unfortunately when we try to move from the all too fragmentary story of battles and harrying to the motives and intentions of the actors the problems of the sources are at their most intransigent. The consecutive political history of the early tenth century cannot be written, though tantalizing hints of what has been lost can be gained.

Lords of men, rulers of the English or kings of England?

The reign of Athelstan is now considered of great importance because of his political aspirations and achievements and wide European links. This revalua-

---

11. D. Rollason, 'The shrines of saints in later Anglo-Saxon England: distribution and significance', in *The Anglo-Saxon Church*, papers presented to H. M. Taylor, eds. L. A. S. Butler and R. K. Morris, CAB Research Report (1986), pp. 32–43 and his 'Relic cults as an instrument of royal policy *c.* 900–*c.* 1050', ASE, 15 (1986), pp. 91–103

tion has been based first on references in foreign sources to that king. No English king of whom the Annals of Ulster could write that he was 'the roof-tree of the dignity of the Western world' should be underrated. The study of his reign has relied heavily on his charters, and the records of meetings with other rulers of Britain and nobles from throughout England which they contain. It has given full value to the royal titles he used, including those of a quasi-imperial nature and to the organization of his coinage which the recent flourishing of numismatic studies has made clear. His aspirations and foreign contacts have been painstakingly reconstructed from study of manuscripts associated with his court, produced there or given away by him.[12]

With six law codes and an attempted reform of the coinage Athelstan and his advisers appear concerned with questions beyond the purely military. The titles used in his charters projected him as ruler of all England and in a quasi-imperial light. The 'Imperial' meetings of the royal courts especially in the 930s were attended not only by nobles from much of England but also by Welsh rulers, termed *subregulus* or *regulus*, underking, by the English scribes.[13] Did the unification which resulted from a series of military responses involve the pursuit of a political ideal, a deliberate pursuit of ideas formed at Alfred's court about the kingdom of the English?

The contrast between attitudes to Northumbria and Mercia on the one hand and the Welsh kings on the other is instructive. The determination with which rule of the *English* kingdom of York was pursued, in spite of the obvious difficulties, whilst the closer and more accessible kingdoms of South Wales were consistently treated as allies, albeit with overtones of subordination, indicates an apparent desire to unite the kingdoms of the English. From military campaigns to the fostering of the cult of St Cuthbert in Wessex the area north of the Humber was treated differently from the Welsh kingdoms. Mercia was deliberately and carefully taken over. Marriage alliances, joint military action, the raising of Edward's son Athelstan at the Mercian court appear as preliminaries to Edward's seizure of power there in 918.

But the picture is not so simple. Athelstan's moves into Cornwall (i.e. the West Welsh) are less the actions of a king whose major project was the unification of the English than those of a king of Wessex following traditional West Saxon lines of expansion. The greater effort put into acquiring and holding the kingdom of York may be less because of its Englishness than because the alternatives here were not Welsh rulers with traditions of alliance but Vikings from Dublin who posed a threat to the kingdoms of the South. The takeover of Mercia has parallels in earlier history, in Offa's relations with neighbours who began as kings and ended as Mercian lords. In the early tenth century the attendance of Welsh princes at court and their treatment as underkings looked like an ominous prelude to expansion.

12. On all this see M. Wood, 'The making of King Æthelstan's empire: an English Charlemagne?', *Ideal and Reality in Frankish and Anglo-Saxon Society*, ed. P. Wormald *et al.* (Oxford, 1983), pp. 250–72; S. Keynes, 'King Athelstan's books', in *Learning and Literature in Anglo-Saxon England*, eds. M. Lapidge and H. Gneuss (Cambridge, 1985), pp. 143–201; C. Blunt, 'The coinage of Athelstan, 924–939: a survey', BNJ, 42 (1974)
13. H. Loyn, 'England and Wales in the tenth century: the context of the Athelstan charters', *Welsh History Review*, 10 (1980–1), pp. 283–301

Edward and his sons, especially Athelstan, aspired to rule more widely than Wessex. A loose hegemony coupled with determined efforts to rule south of the Humber best describes the early tenth-century kingdom. The Imperial ideal of ruling over many peoples with subject kings was the self-image fostered at Athelstan's court; the suggestions of an English Charlemagne are not misplaced. At the same time some difference between those peoples seen as 'English' and others is evident.

From the 920s Wessex and Mercia were treated as a unit. Athelstan does not appear to have appointed any single ealdorman with control over the whole of Mercia. Mercia was treated like Wessex and was divided among several. East Anglia, more remote, was given a single ealdorman. How Athelstan ruled the North is unclear. He courted the archbishops with grants of land, gave the valuable York mint into the hands of a single man and may have allowed the lords of Bamburgh to extend some control here though our ignorance of events in the North at this date is profound. It is doubtful how far any of the developments in law and rule of the first half of the tenth century were extended into northern England. The reforms of the coinage which Athelstan undertook during the 930s only took real if brief effect in Wessex and East Anglia. Whatever their aspirations and ideals these kings remained bound by the realities of power and its limitations.

The capacity of loose hegemonies to expand rapidly aroused fear among neighbouring rulers; they certainly did not assume that the aim of West Saxon kings was merely to unite the kingdoms of the English. And within the kingdoms of the English themselves the notion of the loose rule of underkingdoms may have been the way West Saxon expansion was seen. When Edward sent his son Athelstan to be brought up in Mercia, its nobility would have envisaged a family underkingship with a degree of local autonomy. The presence of Welsh princes at court in the 930s and 940s reinforced this view. When in 957 the Mercians chose Edgar to be their king, a local ruler subordinate to Wessex could have been their aim. Difficulty in defining contemporary ideas of rule cannot be an excuse for our importing the concept of deliberate unification, nor of administrative or centralizing views of unity, and certainly not for imposing such views indiscriminately on all political actors of the day.

Athelstan especially is presented in a European context in contact with other rulers; again this is a continuation of older patterns. Alfred's stepmother was a Frankish princess, his daughters married a count of Flanders as well as a lord of Mercia and he attracted foreign scholars to his court. Edward the Elder had had links with the Breton church and had married his daughter Eadgifu to Charles the Simple. Edmund in 946 was still concerned with the claims to the throne of his Frankish nephew, Louis d'Outremer, was receiving Flemish monastic exiles and gifts and ambassadors from Germany. Athelstan's court was a refuge for Alan of Brittany, who became his godson; for his own nephew and sister, Louis d'Outremer and Queen Eadgifu, and Hakon, the son of Harold Fairhair of Norway may have been brought up there. Athelstan's embarrassment of sisters and half-sisters enabled him to be generous in marrying them to Hugh the Great, duke of the Franks, Otto, son of Henry the Fowler, Louis of Aquitaine, and Sihtric of York. Such marriages solved family problems as sisters were joined to men of appropriate rank at a comfortable distance. They continued the alliances formed against the Vikings in the ninth century and fulfilled the need for prestigious brides felt by newly rising stars like Hugh and Henry.

Marriages are only one facet of a range of contacts which encompassed exchanges of exiles, churchmen and gifts. Such contacts are a language whose meanings are ambiguous, often deliberately so. Alliance and prestige, opportunities for intervention, hostages for continuing friendly relations, tentative steps towards extension of power, traditional hospitality can all be read there. Some of the early tenth-century meanings look back into the world of loot and tribute where wide-ranging lordships were built up and held together by these means. The premises of that world were semi-nomadic, its views of the boundaries of power fluid since power was measured less by depth of control than by the accumulation of shifting personal loyalties.[14] Kings were lords of men not rulers of territory. Looking back to that world, Athelstan appeared to his contemporaries as a possible lord of Britain, certainly as ruler of the English. But he was also king of England, as Alfred had been king of Wessex. The move towards stable rule of territory was long since made, and politics had long been about the binding of enduring allegiance. Only at the margins could loyalty be transferred to another king. When the disappointed can no longer decamp, their disaffections turn inwards, into rivalry and faction.

Kings and nobles

Charters tell another story to set beside the familiar one of military unification. The reign of Edward the Elder is poorly served even by charter sources, and there are virtually none surviving from him after 909. Many charters of Athelstan remain, though a higher proportion than usual are dubious. Edmund and Eadred made a large number of land grants, abnormally large given their brief reigns. This set a pattern travestied by the huge number granted by Eadwig in the single year 956 (see below, pp. 148–50). The greater number of charters from mid century is obviously affected by the foundation or refoundation of so many monasteries from the 940s onwards. These preserved the records not simply of grants to them but of the original grants to laypeople who then endowed them. A concentration of charters beginning in the 940s and 950s is not surprising. But the rate is not maintained under Edgar, when the factors making for survival were if anything greater. Moreover a breakdown of the evidence reveals an underlying trend. Of Athelstan's surviving charters alleged ecclesiastical grants outnumber lay in a ratio of over 2:1. Under Edmund, Eadred and Eadwig, however, lay grants outnumber those to ecclesiastics in the proportions respectively of 2:1, 3:1 and 3:1. The sheer number of grants to laymen in these sixteen years is remarkable and never repeated in the reigns of later kings. The brute figures suggest a significant development of, if not a crisis in, the politics of patronage.

Whatever their intentions, early tenth-century kings extended their rule and in so doing created a group of great nobles whose descendants would be important until the 990s. Athelstan Half-King, appointed to East Anglia in the

14. cf. T. Reuter, 'Plunder and tribute in the Carolingian Empire', *TRHS*, ser. 5, 35 (1985), pp. 75–94

930s, and several of his brothers who gained ealdormanries in the 940s are one such family.[15] The family of ealdormen Ælfhere and Ælfheah, respectively ealdormen of Mercia and East Wessex under Edgar, first gained office in 940, when the father of these two brothers, Ealhhelm, was appointed in Mercia; its importance at court can be traced back into the charters of Athelstan.[16] Ealdorman Ælfgar, whose son-in-law succeeded him in Essex and whose daughters were important local landholders through into the 990s, was appointed in the 940s, and again is first identifiable at the court of Athelstan. Even a family like that of Wulfric Spott, whose rise to office belongs to the reign of Æthelred at the end of the century, was already receiving grants of land and being drawn into the orbit of royal patronage in the 930s.[17]

These families all profited from the process of unification. The lands and offices they received were a result of that process. Apart from the family of Wulfric Spott all originated from or had connections with Wessex. It was the West Saxon nobility who reaped benefit from these first stages of unification, causing problems in Mercia by mid century. These families formed a group connected together by marriage and blood. Brihtnoth, Ælfgar's son-in-law, was related to ealdorman Æthelweard of Wessex, himself a descendant of King Æthelred I; when Brihtnoth died in the battle of Maldon in 991 a grandson of Ealhhelm was with him. Their connections included close ties with the ruling dynasty. One daughter of Ealdorman Ælfgar married Brihtnoth, the other became the second wife of King Edmund. Ælfhere and Ælfheah claimed kinship with Kings Eadwig and Edgar. The idea of a group of great nobles bound together and to the royal dynasty, later espousing the royally backed movement for monastic reform, is a useful one. And a picture of tenth-century politics turning around this group and broken when Æthelred II ended their hereditary control in the 990s is tempting. But we should not overstress their coherence.

Their origins were more diverse than their West Saxon connections suggest. Some date back to the late ninth century. The family of Athelstan Half-King for example can be traced through his father to office-holders of Alfred's day. Their power and longevity coincided with the monastic revival, with which many of them were concerned; as a result we are peculiarly well informed about them. Other families, especially in the first half of the century appear to rise and fall more rapidly, but we may simply know less about their heyday of power. In the 930s, for instance, a man called Wulfgar was appointed to an ealdormanry. His family can be traced back to the 860s. His grandfather, Wulfhere, forfeited his lands to King Alfred; he was already an ealdorman, and possibly brother-in-law of Alfred's older brother, Æthelred I.[18] Lack of information prevents us following the family's fortunes beyond the 940s, but clearly we should beware of assuming that the unification created a group of new families, as opposed to

15. C. Hart, 'Athelstan Half-King and his family', ASE, 2 (1973), pp. 115–44
16. A. Williams, '*Princeps Merciorum Gentis*: the family, career and connections of Ælfhere, ealdorman of Mercia', ASE, 10 (1981), pp. 143–72
17. P. H. Sawyer, *The Charters of Burton Abbey* (Oxford, 1979), pp. xl–xli
18. EHD I, no. 100, pp. 541–2 for the forfeiture; R. 26 is Wulfgar's will and the notes on pp. 275 and 307–8 give details of his family. See also J. Nelson, 'A king across the sea: Alfred in continental perspective', TRHS, ser. 5, 36 (1986), p. 54–5

providing extra opportunities for some of those already established. Nor were tenth-century politics stable. This handful of families did not themselves maintain unbroken power. The family of Athelstan Half-King, for example, dates back to the late ninth century, and retained control of East Anglia until the 990s, yet its heyday was from the 930s to early 950s when Athelstan and his three brothers held offices.

The new kingdom magnified noble as much as royal power, provided new opportunities. Royal office as ealdorman was a key to success, but when ealdormanries passed from father to son, when families like those of Ealhhelm of Mercia or Athelstan Half-King in East Anglia became locally entrenched, there was danger they might 'go native' and ignore the king. The royal court remained sufficiently attractive to check such centrifugal tendencies. The king controlled new opportunities. Old families were not ignored, but families and individuals waxed and waned in power in ways which indicate royal whim and favour. This delicate balance turned not only on patronage but on forfeiture.

As the story of Wulfgar's family showed, forfeiture of land to the king was a reality by the late ninth and early tenth century in Wessex. Alfred had deprived Wulfhere of his land for breaking his oath, perhaps for desertion in the Viking wars, perhaps for supporting the claims to the throne of Alfred's and Wulfhere's nephews, more likely for some combination of both. Forfeiture, once developed as a royal power, had its obvious political uses against enemies: pretexts to move against such men are rarely lacking. Forfeiture became embroiled in patronage, with forfeit land recycled through royal hands. The rising proportion of lay grants in mid century is not merely a squandering of royal resources but partly a largesse utilizing forfeit land. Forfeiture, however, was not readily accepted; families tenaciously pursued their claims to lost land long after the original case. Such tenacity meant, for example, that a case involving Queen Eadgifu and land at Cooling was reopened on every change of power for a half century.[19] Gift or sale of any kind could create uncertainty in the tenth century. The desperation of Ealdorman Ordlaf addressing Edward the Elder about the problems of legal cases in general is eloquent of the difficulties of anyone who received land as a result of legal decisions.

'And lord, when will any suit be ended if one can end it neither with money nor with an oath? And if one wishes to change every judgement which King Alfred gave, when shall we have finished disputing'.[20]

Such problems applied *a fortiori* to land which changed hands through forfeiture. No case was ever so straightforward that there were no grounds for reopening it.

The king's largesse was fraught with insecurity, the need for his patronage extended beyond gift to the judicial cases in which gift and forfeiture were contested. Litigants appealed to the king. And as Queen Eadgifu found, the most dangerous moment of all was when power changed hands from one ruler to the next. A new reign meant new opportunities to regain losses. An heir to the

19. Harmer SEHD 23
20. EHD I, no. 102, p. 545

throne gathered discontents this type. The factional politics revealed in the struggles for the throne in the tenth century is rooted in the insecurity of patronage. For the winners and the losers in this game the control of the next heir to the throne was crucial. The 940s and 950s were a peak of patronage; that largesse and its nature was one cause of the bitter succession dispute of 955–57.

Succession to the throne and family politics

Succession disputes were the crucibles of tenth-century politics. In them met the centrifugal tendencies of fluctuating regional feeling and the centripetal strength of royal largesse. The ealdormen, facing janus-like between the pull of continued royal gift and the representation of local feeling, were symbols of the new kingdom. Religious questions were drawn in; the battleground was the court. Yet open conflict was virtually confined to the choice of successor. Opposition at other times appeared illegitimate. The pull towards the centre and the prestige of the monarchy was strong.

Struggles surrounding the succession to the throne punctuate the tenth and eleventh centuries. Æthelwold's challenge to his cousin Edward the Elder was the first. In 924–25 Athelstan's accession was complicated by the existence of a younger but more legitimate brother. In 933 Athelstan himself suffered problems with another younger brother, Edwin, who was drowned at sea. These are the open expression of the family politics which loom large over the early tenth century. The royal dynasty was large. Alfred's younger son, Æthelweard, survived his father, married and had sons of his own who were still alive in 937. Edward the Elder married three times, producing not only a large number of daughters but also at least five sons, all of whom survived him. Ninth-century precedents for fraternal succession in the West Saxon dynasty were strong; Alfred himself had been the last of four brothers to rule in succession; some of them too had left descendants. Two unmarried kings ruled during the first half of the tenth century and two royal women played an important role in politics. Neither Athelstan nor Eadred appear to have married; a notable fact given the importance of securing the family's future. Æthelflæd, Edward the Elder's sister, played a role written by family relationships, as did Eadgifu, third wife and widow of Edward the Elder, whose significance at court during the reigns of her two sons Edmund and Eadred is almost without parallel. To ignore the politics of the royal family would be to miss an important key to the unlocking of the early tenth century.

As long as succession is decided by a balance of claims and support rather than by binding rules the presence of such a large number of potential claims was dangerous. The idea that one needed to be the son of a king to be throneworthy was growing, as was a preference for older sons, but none of this was prescriptive. These very tendencies made *æthelings* (i.e. throneworthy men) more desperate to make their claims stick since claims might die with them. The nature of marriage and especially Christian influence on it left the issue of legitimacy debatable; echoes of the arguments about Athelstan's legitimacy could still be heard in the twelfth century.

Soon after his accession following the death of Alfred in 899 Edward the Elder married his second cousin Ælfflæd, and took the unusual step of having her consecrated as queen.[21] Edward had already contracted some sort of union with Ecgwyna the mother of Athelstan. But Ælfflæd was the niece of that Æthelwold who rebelled. The royal blood which ran in her family was to make it important throughout the tenth century. It later provided both a wife for King Eadwig and an ealdorman of South West England. On the death of Alfred his elder brother's family represented by Ælfflæd had to be placated. Marriage, and such a union as should admit of no question, was one answer. The legitimacy of this marriage underscored by the consecration of Ælfflæd meant that her sons' claims on the throne were strengthened: it was her son Ælfweard, not Athelstan who succeeded Edward the Elder in Wessex in 924, only to die fourteen days after his father. The marriage aimed to reunite a dynasty divided by Alfred's accession over the heads of his elder brother's children and by his handing on of the throne to his own son.

This second union was a threat to the claims of Edward's eldest and now questionably legitimate son Athelstan. At some stage Edward sent this eldest son to Mercia to be reared by his aunt Æthelflæd, lady of the Mercians. In the early ninth century West Saxon kings had sent their eldest sons to rule in Kent during their father's lifetime, providing a limited autonomy for Kent and satisfying the ambitions of a dangerous heir. Sending Athelstan to Mercia may have been a similar move with a longer-term aim of uniting Mercia and Wessex. His rearing at his aunt's court could equally have signalled that he was no longer to have claims to Wessex; that he was to rule in Mercia as an underking whether of his father or of his more legitimate brother. Athelstan may even have ruled as such an underking there between the death of Æthelflæd in 918 and the death of his father and brother in 924.

Mercian susceptibilities certainly played their part. Æthelflæd ruled in Mercia at a date when female rulers were a rarity; her daughter was accepted after her. Æthelflæd ruled as a daughter of Alfred and sister of Edward and enjoyed the legacy of the power of earlier Mercian queens. But she and her daughter are witnesses to a strong desire for an autonomous ruler in Mercia. Giving Mercia a king from the West Saxon ruling house was one motive in sending Athelstan there, whether or not he was ever intended to rule in Wessex. Mercian nobles chose Athelstan as their king on the death of his father in 924. He was fully accepted in Wessex only a year later. It was no foregone conclusion that he would become king of Wessex even after Ælfweard's death.

Athelstan's legitimacy and the arrangements for the sons of Edward's second marriage were problems. Athelstan's mother was rumoured by the twelfth century to have been a concubine.[22] The antithesis wife/concubine is too simple for the early tenth century (see *Family, Marriage and Women*). A union between man and woman was made in a series of ceremonies and arrangements. Ecclesiastical definitions and rulings combined with lay desires to manipulate

21. J. Nelson, 'The second English *ordo*', in her *Politics and Ritual in Early Medieval Europe* (1986), at p. 367
22. William of Malmesbury, Bk I, cap. 131

marriage and inheritance produced uncertainty about which act or action *made* a marriage. Given the unique position of the king, some royal unions were made without full dower of the bride, one of the easiest proofs of marriage. Other criteria for claiming legitimate marriage remained and differences of opinion were wide enough to both allow Edward to dispose of his first wife *c*.899, and for others to argue for Athelstan's legitimacy then and later.

Edward the Elder was able to bend the rules back and forth to suit his need. At some stage in his reign Edward married again, to Eadgifu daughter of an ealdorman of Kent. Ælfflæd was probably alive at the time of this marriage,[23] but Edward's political needs had changed. Eadgifu had landholdings in Kent, an area only recently absorbed into Wessex. No king concerned with Viking movements in the Channel and with the defence of both Mercia and the newly conquered Essex could ignore it. If Edward required separation, ecclesiastical rulings could have accommodated him. Edward and Ælfflæd were closely related, the original reason for their marriage. Yet incest, marriage within the kindred, was forbidden by long-standing Christian tradition. If Edward disposed of Ælfflæd in these circumstances, the situation faced by Athelstan was complex. He had a clutch of half-brothers some of whom looked more legitimate than himself yet whose mother had been set aside on the grounds of incest. He had other half-brothers who were no more than infants, fully legitimate if the arguments of incest were accepted, not so if the original marriage to Ælfflæd held. He had cousins, sons of his uncle Æthelweard, not technically *æthelings* since their father had never ruled but significant nonetheless. And he himself had the backing of the Mercian nobility.

Athelstan was chosen first in Mercia and with some delay in Wessex. His family are a submerged theme of his reign. His many sisters were found foreign husbands or entered nunneries. A king surrounded by men of royal blood had no wish to increase that number by allowing the marriages of his sisters within his kingdom. The battle of Brunanburh was a military triumph, and also a family affair. The poem which describes it commemorates the role of Edmund, Athelstan's brother and successor, in the fighting, and Athelstan's counsins, the sons of Æthelweard were present. Judging from the records of his court preserved in charter witness lists, Athelstan did not give his male relatives any formal political role. But he may have felt it expedient to keep them close to him, indeed may still have seen his kingdom as a family concern. His apparent failure to marry is difficult to understand. Alfred, a man who succeeded in spite of the claims of others, felt no reluctance to marry and to press the claims of his own son. Athelstan may have been another Confessor, married but childless. We cannot know, given the poverty of sources for his reign. Yet even in such a situation his failure to divorce and remarry argues a king who did not feel sufficiently secure to do so. Was an arrangement made for the succession of more legitimate brothers after his death, made even in the negotiations for his acceptance in Wessex in 925? What is certain is that the accession of his younger brother Edmund was one of the rare undisputed transfers of power in the tenth and eleventh centuries.

Athelstan's failure to produce heirs and the passage of time meant that Edmund faced a situation different from that of his older brother. The huge

23. P. Stafford, 'The king's wife in Wessex, 800–1066', *Past and Present*, 91 (1981), at p. 13 n. 29

royal clan of the early years of the tenth century was now reduced to himself and his brother Eadred, together with ever more remote descendants of Æthelred I. Edmund however was the third son of Edward the Elder to rule. Since the death of his great-grandfather Æthelwulf only three kings had directly succeeded their fathers. He was the fifth to follow a brother on the throne. The arguments for fraternal succession were growing stronger. The acquisition of Mercia raised the question of provision for brothers in an acute form. Old-established inheritance practices preferred older or legitimate sons for ancestral lands, but acquisitions could be more flexibly treated. With possible feeling in Mercia in favour of some autonomy the argument for endowing a brother with that kingdom, perhaps as a form of designation to rule later, was strong. Such arguments may lie behind the unprecedented importance of Edmund's brother Eadred during Edmund's reign. It was an importance matched only by the role of Edgar in 956, the first year of his brother Eadwig's reign, when it was a prelude to the division of the kingdom of Wessex and Mercia between the two brothers in 957. Were Edgar and Eadred given an underkingship in Mercia? Did the strong claims of both to such position force their brothers to give them power at court? Was the period 940 to 959 a protracted succession dispute involving the question of rule in Mercia, a dispute not resolved until in 959 when, as in 925 a king who had ruled first in Mercia came to be king of Wessex?

The doubt and argument around the succession brought the dowager Queen Eadgifu to the fore. She was the first tenth-century queen to achieve any prominence in Wessex. Fraternal successions had taken place at a time when the position of the queen was changing with the introduction of formal anointing (see above, n.21). In England as in tenth-century France anointing was developed as a strategy in succession politics[24] to benefit a woman's sons or husband rather than enhance her own power. But anointing gave a queen a unique position in the royal household with advantages which individual women like Eadgifu could exploit. But it was the fraught politics of the 940s and 950s which brought her to prominence. Her lands in Kent were important, and any arrangements which guaranteed the succession in turn of both her sons prolonged her role as dowager at court. During Eadred's reign she was second only to the king himself, acquiring both friends and enemies at court and becoming part of the factions which came into their own on Eadred's death.

By 955 a court group and great nobility had grown up which had profited from royal largesse, in which we might guess that the winners and losers were sharply delineated. The Life of Dunstan catalogues its hero's reversals of fortune from the 930s to the 950s, twice exiled from court, once saved from such a fate only by a miracle. Shorn of the hagiographical judgements the picture is of the instability and rivalries of court faction.[25] The build-up of tensions concerning the succession ramified to encompass questions of the rule of the unified kingdom. Edmund and Eadred had appointed new ealdormen in Mercia; where they can be identified they were outsiders. There was no sign that the Mercian

24. P. Stafford, *Queens, Concubines and Dowagers: The King's Wife in the Early Middle Ages* (1983), pp. 127–34
25. EHD I, no. 234, pp. 898–9

nobility were participating in the bonanza of royal patronage. Eric Bloodaxe had just been expelled from York and people north of the Humber had been given renewed proof of the warlike determination of southern kings to secure rule of Northumbria. Succession dispute between West Saxon noble factions at the West Saxon court was unlikely to be contained in these narrow West Saxon confines.

3

Eadwig to Æthelred II, 955–1016

Eadwig's brief reign was summed up by Bishop Æthelwold and by the author of the first Life of Dunstan.

> Through the ignorance of childhood, he (Eadwig) dispersed his kingdom and divided its unity, and also distributed the lands of the holy churches to rapacious strangers. After his death Edgar... obtained by God's grace the whole dominion of England, and brought back to unity the divisions of the kingdom, and ruled everything so prosperously that those who had lived in former times and remembered his ancestors and knew their deeds of old, wondered very greatly.[1]

> Eadwig... a youth indeed in age and endowed with little wisdom in government, though when elected he ruled in due succession and with royal title over both peoples... in the passage of years was wholly deserted by the Northern people, being despised because he acted foolishly in the government committed to him... they chose as king for themselves by God's guidance the brother of the same Eadwig Edgar... the state was divided between the kings as determined by wise men, so that the famous river Thames separated the realms of both.[2]

The narrative sources invite us to interpret the second half of the tenth century as a see-saw between good and bad kings. Eadwig (955–59), young, ignorant, immoral and easily led by poor counsel, ruining the wise and inviting disaster; Edgar (957/9–75) a glorious preserver of internal harmony and external peace, rewarded with such secular blessings because of his protection and advancement of ecclesiastical interests; Æthelred (978–1016) dogged by internal treachery and external attack, his own character flawed by a mixture of indolence and spasmodic violence. Given the nature and date of the sources from which they derive these contrasts must be toned down if not jettisoned in favour of a stress on the continuity of problems and attempted solutions across the period. At the same time the dynamic interactions of circumstances, events and people must be allowed their play in later tenth-century politics. Fundamental structures define the nature of problems and the range of answers without determining the unfolding of action.

The narrative sources on which the contrasting judgements of Eadwig and Edgar were based were written after the death of Edgar. By then Edgar's reign

---

1. An Old English account of King Edgar's foundation of monasteries, EHD I no. 238, p. 920
2. Life of Dunstan, Auctore B, EHD I no. 234, pp. 900–1

was already seen as a Golden Age which had just passed, especially by contrast with the attacks on churches and their property which were a feature of the 970s and the late 980s. Work produced in this climate insisted that a good king was one who protected the church; one attribute of a bad king was to attack it. Æthelwold explicitly contrasts the two brothers, Eadwig and Edgar, and Eadwig suffers by being cast as the dark which throws the light of Edgar into relief. The analysis of Eadwig's reign arose from the need to see Edgar's reign as glorious, a view which ran up against the problem that it began in the division of a unified kingdom, with a secession of the northern peoples which made Edgar king, a division with which reforming churchmen committed to the ideal of unity felt uncomfortable. Æthelwold and like-minded writers escaped the contradiction by blaming the division on Eadwig. His misrule had alienated the northern peoples. They had chosen Edgar. He could be presented as a restorer not divider of unity.

The picture of Edgar and the problems surrounding it are more complex. Edgar proved a name to conjure with until the twelfth century, and the account of him in the narrative sources continued to develop over a long period. Eadwig's chief importance was to writers of the later tenth century. His portrait was picked up by chroniclers in the twelfth century since it appealed to their love of a good story and proved a convenient peg on which to hang new definitions of 'a bad king', around which to develop anti-feminism and romance. But little of substance was added after AD 1000. The historical picture of Edgar's reign starts its life in the events after his death and especially during the reign of his son Æthelred. Already there were subtle variations in the picture depending on the precise date and authorship of the accounts. Æthelwold's account was spurred by appreciation of dangers to the reforming ecclesiastical movement of which he was a part; his portrait of Edgar is a mirror of princes, an instruction on the benefits to be reaped from support of the Christian church (for which read, reform). Accounts produced as Æthelred's reign progressed laid more emphasis on the peace of Edgar, in contrast with the Viking devastations of the day. Wulfstan added a concern with exalting God's law, a judgement appropriate to the legal expert of Æthelred's later years, but also a note of criticism: 'he loved evil foreign customs and brought too firmly heathen manners into this land, and attracted hither foreigners and enticed harmful people to this country'.[3] Praise was already balanced by criticism and this was developed in the stories about his marriages, emanating from succession propaganda and retold in hagiography, which circulated in the eleventh and twelfth centuries. Edgar's reign continued to be a part of a living historical development throughout those centuries. There was a cult at Glastonbury by the mid eleventh century;[4] contemporary political comment was couched in the guise of prophecy in his name, and by the mid twelfth century his life could be cast into the romantic moulds of lust, seduction and cruelty as well as idealized by monastic writers. At the same time Edgar became the reverse coin of his son Æthelred. Writers who sought the origins of the conquests of England in the weakness of Æthelred painted Edgar's reign as an apotheosis of the qualities they wished to associate

3. ASC MS D & E 959
4. William of Malmesbury, Bk II, cap. 160

with England pre-1066 but could not find in the fraught and well-chronicled history of the eleventh century. The surviving picture of Edgar's reign has much to tell of the use of history from the late tenth century to the mid twelfth, less of the years 959–75.

What happened in Eadwig's reign?[5]

The first Life of Dunstan had a simple answer to that question. The king proved himself from the outset unfit to rule. Young, foolish, dominated by bad counsel, easily led astray by the lusts of the flesh, he was an exiler of saints, morally deficient and politically incompetent. He was justly rejected by the northern peoples and the Mercians, and his early death then relieved Wessex of his presence, allowing God to instate the glorious rule of Edgar the Peaceable. The answer is a fleshed out reiteration of Æthelwold's judgement and its detailed picture has coloured all subsequent judgement of Eadwig. Had not Eadwig's brother-in-law, ealdorman Æthelweard left us the briefest of alternative assessments 'He, for his great beauty, got the nickname *All fair* from his people. He held the kingdom continuously for four years and deserved to be loved'[6]; there would be nothing in the narrative sources to contradict this image. Even Æthelweard was circumspect. He wrote in the reign of Æthelred II, Edgar's son. Eadwig left no family to cultivate his memory, was too easy a target for the moralists-in-politics of the late tenth century. The circumstances of his brief reign were complex and some arguments against him must have been strictly contemporary, part of the debate about succession which took place between 955 and 957. At best we have received only half of those arguments, those used to bury Eadwig not to praise him. The political situation and the evidence of the charters can legitimately be used to seek an alternative picture.

By 955 the royal court was riven by faction, in which Abbot Dunstan if not Archbishop Oda were already involved. Eadred's death had been preceded by long illness; whatever prior arrangements may have been, debate about the succession was inevitable. Trouble in the North had dogged the last reigns, and recent developments may have fanned rather than allayed local feeling in Mercia. In these circumstances the young Eadwig, no older than fifteen at his accession, came to the throne. Almost immediately a new ealdorman, Ælfhere, was appointed in Mercia and the young king's marriage arranged. His wife Ælfgifu linked him to the royally descended family into which his grandfather Edward had married c.900. It signalled or caused a breach with the dowager Queen Eadgifu; with its promise of children it had implications for the claims of Edgar, Eadwig's younger brother. At the coronation in January 956, or soon thereafter, Abbot Dunstan and Cynesige, bishop of Lichfield, disappeared from court. The Life of Dunstan explained this as punishment for their castigation of the immorality of the king and his young bride. Was this an

---

5. For recent insight see S. Keynes, *The Diplomas of King Æthelred the Unready* (Cambridge, 1980), pp. 48–70 and P. Stafford, *Queens, Concubines and Dowagers* (1983), pp. 16, 44, 75, 83, 85, 126, 148–9, 157–61 and N. Brooks, *The Early History of the Church of Canterbury* (Leicester, 1984), pp. 222–7 and 237–43

6. *Chronicle of Æthelweard*, ed. A. Campbell (Edinburgh, 1962), p. 55

impartial view of a marriage which was marking changes at court and the realignment of factions in which Eadgifu and Dunstan were losing ground?

Eadwig's younger brother Edgar was prominent at court from the beginning of the reign. The only parallel is the role of Eadred under his brother Edmund. The recent precedent of Eadred, and of the claims of brothers to the throne, combined with the strength of faction to push Edgar forward. The waning power of Dunstan and Eadgifu, if not of others at court, may have produced an alignment around Edgar and his claims. Arguments in his favour were strong, whether for a sub-kingdom in Mercia or for a recognition of his rights to succeed. The subtle shifts in favour at court in 955–56 cannot be recaptured, but the emergence of Edgar would have been enough to push some of them to the point of open breach.Dunstan was exiled, Eadgifu lost all her lands. But in 956 they took few with them. The pull of patronage and tradition was in favour of the crowned king. Unless the shift in patronage proved overwhelmingly partisan most preferred to test their chances in the new situation.

956 was a crucial year, its significance marked by an unparalleled number of royal charters. The scale of royal extravagance signals a king seeking support, bolstering his position; together with two new appointments to the office of ealdorman, Æthelwold to East Anglia and Brihtnoth to Essex, it caricatures the politics of the mid tenth century. But there was no immediate lurch to new or unknown favourites. The men advanced or wooed were members of established families, though often the sons of established men. Eadwig did not inaugurate a revolution at court but bound it closer to himself in a new generation. Some individuals do fall from power, like the thegn Wulfric who was deprived of his lands.[7] But the great men at court remained essentially the same, and Edgar if anything advanced in power. The charters of this year point to unease, but not as yet crisis.

That crisis came in the second half of 957. Edgar was chosen king by the Mercians, and before the end of 957 Wessex and Mercia were divided along the Thames. It was a territorial and not a factional split. The division was neat. All the bishops and ealdormen north of the Thames ceased to appear at Eadwig's court and attended that of Edgar in Mercia. There is no sign of the ragged geography which faction split would have produced. Yet the crisis arose out of the faction and family tension of 955–56 as much as out of separatist feeling. One bishop had already disappeared from court in 956, Cynesige bishop of Lichfield in the heart of Mercia. The strength of Edgar's situation in 956 could have led his supporters to advance the suggestion that he be given rule of Mercia. The question may at first have been of a sub-kingdom under his brother's control; the decision to break away more fully may only have been made in 957: we can only speculate whether the recreation of the Mercian kingdom came in stages or as a single blow in 957. Its results were dramatic. Edgar acted as full king in Mercia granting charters like his brother in Wessex, and in them was accorded the title of 'rex Merciorum'.

Dissatisfactions caused by the exercise of royal power found an outlet in 957. The deaths of most tenth-century kings were accompanied by a crop of attempts to reverse legal decisions taken in the previous reigns. Edgar's

7. S. 687

acceptance in Mercia was no exception. At least one man disappointed with a ruling given by Eadwig 'betook himself to King Edgar and asked for judgement'.[8] Such opportunism and contesting of royal rulings did not cause the succession disputes of the tenth century, though they did nothing to allay them. Edgar and his followers were not about to renounce the legal powers gathered by his predecessors, so useful as a source of land and patronage. In this case Edgar and his Mercian counsellors ruled against the appellant, confiscated the estate and used it to reward ealdorman Athelstan, one of those who had come over to Edgar in 957. Such need to woo support is a warning against interpreting 957 as a surge of Mercian nationalism anxious for its own king at any price. The loyalties of great men in Mercia were not be be won simply by appealing to 'Mercianness'.

Edgar's court was clearly seen as a rival to that of Eadwig, one where Eadwig's political exiles would be welcome. Dunstan returned there and was rewarded with a bishopric. Churchmen were party to the splits of these years. Late in 957 Oda, archbishop of Canterbury, ceased to attend Eadwig's court and in 958 he moved to divorce the king and his wife on the grounds of incest. Eadwig realized the importance of the archbishop's support. One of his last acts as king of all England was an attempt to hold Oda's loyalty with a grant of land at Ely. When the archbishop died in 958, Eadwig moved to appoint his own man at Canterbury, putting in one of his own kinsmen, and Edgar was not slow to appreciate the importance of the see when he became king of all England in 959. One of his earliest acts was to remove Eadwig's man and appoint Dunstan as archbishop. Oda's own motives in 958 are unclear. His family connections lay north of the Thames in the area now ruled by Edgar. He was also a religious reformer and may genuinely have objected to the incestuous nature of Eadwig's marriage, though the kinship of Eadwig and Ælfgifu was tenuous. It is always unwise to make a rigid separation of principle and preference in human motivation, to impute cynicism where interests and values chime in unison.

By late 958 the Northumbrians had accepted Edgar's rule. There is no indication that they formed part of the original division of 957, little sign that they remained faithful to Eadwig. Almost all the charters of Edgar in 957–58 call him king only of the Mercians, but a canvas of support north of the Humber is likely. By 959 one of his supporters, Bishop Oscytel of Dorchester, had been accepted as archbishop of York.[9] By the time of Eadwig's death in October 959 Edgar was in control of England north of the Thames. That death allowed him to become king of all England.

The reuniting of the kingdom again forbids a reading of these years as a straightforward expression of Mercian separatism. The events were cumulative. What started as court faction and family dispute pushing Edgar forward allowed separatism to crystallize around him. But the origins lay in the persons of men like Dunstan, who never lost their interest in the southern court and in unity. Had Mercian separatism played the major role, it was folly to have chosen a West Saxon prince whose claims and desire to rule the entire kingdom remained strong, though in 956/7 no-one could have anticipated the early death of Eadwig which would reunite the kingdom; and to have chosen any other candidate would

8. R. 44
9. No unambiguous evidence for this appointment dates before S. 681, AD 959

have invited retaliation. 956–59 indicates both the strength of local feeling and the limitations on that feeling which were already drawing southern England towards unity. Ealdormen in Mercia and East Anglia were ready to support the power of Edgar north of the Thames and to use it to advance their own and local interests. But the way the great nobility had developed meant that their own and local interests were not identical. Many retained strong commitments and links south of the Thames, just as Oda retained a southern archbishopric and Fenland ties. Ælfhere of Mercia had brothers and family land south of the Thames, his own hopes of patronage might be better realized on an English stage. The lack of any automatic allegiance to Eadwig or Edgar north of the Humber shows by contrast how little success southern kings had had in absorbing this area.

The role played by Eadwig and his character in all this is unfathomable. The later blackening of his character may have built on earlier judgements. His actions in 956–57 could have been interpreted as politically inept. Enemies who wished to justify their own actions or attract support could have pointed to his new, and often youthful appointments, to his technically incestuous marriage, to the changes he made at court. Moral defamation, always part of politics in Christian society, is the preferred line of church reformers. Yet the choice of counsellors in 956 appears neither rash nor poor. The men and families upon whom Eadwig relied were the mainstays of later tenth-century politics. Succession and court faction invite character assassination. Unfitness to rule defined as listening to the wrong people is a major line of attack in a hereditary monarchy where the choice and reward of advisers is the stuff of politics, especially when there is legitimate room for dispute over the succession.

The reign of Edgar 957/9–75[10]

Edgar is remembered as the king who backed the church reform movement and whose glorious reign of peace contrasted with the ignominious defeats of his son Æthelred. Sparse sources make the construction of any alternative to this plaster saint of monastic hagiography difficult. Edgar was a king faced by the problems and opportunities of tenth-century rule. He was concerned like his predecessors with his rights over the coinage and in the courts; the 940s and 950s ensured that he would be aware of the problems of ruling England north of the Thames. His relations with his nobles followed established patterns, and his attitudes to his own family continued to store up as much as to resolve tension. His support for the reform movements is undeniable, though its consistency throughout his reign and its motivation are both debatable. The troubles after Edgar's death are a commentary on a king whose strength had deferred them, but whose actions had precipitated them.

10. For recent work on the politics of this reign see N. Brooks, *The Early History of the Church of Canterbury* (pp. 243–9; P. Stafford, *Queens, Concubines and Dowagers* pp. 16, 21–2, 74, 125–6; A. Williams, 'Princeps Merciorum gentis: the family, career and connections of Ælfhere, ealdorman of Mercia', ASE 10 (1981), pp. 143–72; B. Yorke, 'Æthelwold and the politics of the tenth century', in *Bishop Æthelwold, his Career and Influence* (Woodbridge, 1988), pp. 65–88, and P. Stafford, 'The reign of Æthelred II, a study in the limitations on royal policy and action', *Ethelred the Unready*, papers from the millenary conference, ed. D. Hill (Oxford, 1978), pp. 21–3

Edgar's accession to Wessex in 959 was later presented as a restoration of unity, a prelude to a prosperous and tranquil reign.[11] The reality was more fraught. Dispute and division meant that nobles had openly taken sides, some opposing Edgar. Edgar added a legacy of debts owed to supporters north of the Thames to his new need to reconcile his brother's former allies in Wessex. Edgar's reign looks like that of Athelstan in its attempts to face the problems of unity, though in both cases what we see are kings with direct experience of ruling north of the Thames taking over the South where they needed to woo acceptance. Edgar, unlike Athelstan, faced no immediate rival. There was no alternative candidate to whom Eadwig's supporters could turn even had they wished. Nonetheless the inheritance of 956–59 was a need for care at the outset of the new reign.

The sixteen-year-old Edgar and his supporters seem to have understood the need both to take power and reward, yet not to overplay their hand. Eadwig's last-minute appointment to Canterbury was nullified in favour of Dunstan. Eadwig's appointee had not yet received his pallium from Rome, and such action was technically if not morally justifiable. Dunstan received his pallium, and with it the right to act as an archbishop, in September 960, and by 961 Oswald, the nephew of Archbishop Oda had been appointed bishop of Worcester. In that same year the thegn Wulfric, who had suffered forfeiture under Eadwig, was restored and at about the same time Edgar reinstated his grandmother Eadgifu in all her lands. A sharing out of rewards to those who had supported him in 956–59 was accompanied by more than a hint at the injustices of Eadwig's actions.

But this was more than denigration of a predecessor. Edgar was seeking active support in Wessex, including from his brother's followers. Between 959 and 961 he took a new wife, Wulfthryth. Later legend told how Edgar first pursued Wulfthryth's cousin, almost into the sewers of the nunnery, before he contracted this match. The king was determined not by passion but on a union with a powerful West Saxon family.[12] In 962 he granted land to Ælfheah, his brother's appointee as ealdorman in East Wessex, despite protests from Dunstan that the estate in question belonged by right to Canterbury.[13] Ælfheah was the brother of that Ælfhere of Mercia who had been an earlier follower of Edgar; such ties bound the kingdom together and made Edgar's task easier. But the sign that relations between Edgar and Dunstan were not the cosy partnership of later hagiography is clear. Dunstan is conspicuous by his absence in the land grants of Edgar's reign. Nor did Oswald and his religious houses fare especially well. The appointment of both men at the beginning of the reign was the repayment of debts not a deliberate espousal of reform; the alleged dominance of Dunstan must be suspect.

11. Old English account of Edgar's foundation of monasteries, EHD I no. 238, p. 920
12. Goscelin's life of Wulfthryth's daughter Edith states that she was 23 at the time of her death on 16 Sept. 984, giving a date for the marriage no later than 961, 'La legende de Ste Edith en prose et vers par le moine Goscelin', ed. A. Wilmart, *Analecta Bollandiana*, Vol. 56 (1938), cap. 24, p. 95. For Edgar's pursuit of Wulfthryth's cousin Wulfhild and the involvement of their aunt see 'La vie de S. Wulfhilde par Goscelin de Canterbory', ed. M. Esposito, *Analecta Bollandiana*, vol. 32 (1913), pp. 10–26
13. R. 44

Between 961 and 964 Edgar's actions show a king more secure in his position and anxious to remain so. The spurt of grants to lay nobles, normally a feature of the beginning of a tenth-century reign, came now, and Edgar showed that although he ruled from the South he had not lost sight of his Mercian supporters. For example, of the twelve grants to laymen in 963, five were to men in Northern and Midland England and East Anglia.[14] Reconciliation with the family of his brother's wife was effected.[15] Late in 963 Abbot Æthelwold of Abingdon was chosen and consecrated to the rich royal see of Winchester.

If a turning point were sought, the appointment of Æthelwold would be a better candidate than that of either Dunstan or Oswald. The political importance of this man has been obscured by his later, wholly monastic biographers. But his influence at court was immediately shown in religious changes. Oswald had already founded Westbury and may have begun the monasticization of Worcester, a slow and halting process.[16] Æthelwold's first recorded action as bishop was the dramatic expulsion of the married clerks from the New Minster Winchester, followed by changes at Chertsey and Milton. New monastic abbots were installed in all three houses. The king's role in all this was open. Winchester sources, like the A MS of the Anglo-Saxon Chronicle, heighten the profile but Æthelwold's appointment had brought monastic reform to the fore and the king into reform.

Æthelwold later claimed that Edgar's commitment to reform was conceived when that king was a child under the tutelage of Æthelwold as abbot of Abingdon.[17] Such an initial overriding commitment cannot be squared with the slow progress of the years 959 to 964. Even a long-standing alliance with Æthelwold sits oddly with the delay in appointing him to a bishopric. Æthelwold did not count among those who had to be rewarded in 959. Edgar may have deliberately waited to appoint him to Winchester. In any event the strength of their partnership belongs after 964.

In 964 Edgar put aside his wife Wulfthryth and married again, to Ælfthryth.[18] This match became a favourite story for twelfth-century chroniclers, who attached to it tales of seduction, of feminine wiles and of the murder of Ælfthryth's first husband, ealdorman Æthelwold of East Anglia. Such tales have origins in the tensions between Ælfthryth and the family of Edgar's wife Wulfthryth; they are heard in the Lives of Wulfthryth and Wulfhilde. They are rooted in Ælfthryth's implication in the death of her stepson (see below) and in the arguments between her son and stepson in 975. They must not obscure the politics of this marriage. Edgar already had a son by his first wife, Æthelflæd, whom he had married before his accession in Wessex; Wulfthryth had produced no male heir, a possible reason for her repudiation now. If his first wife belonged with his rule north of the Thames, and his second with his need for allies in Wessex, Ælfthryth signals Edgar's growing concern with South West England. A series of grants in Cornwall and Devon show Edgar as keenly aware

14. S. 712, 716, 717, 720, 723
15. Æthelweard, Eadwig's brother-in-law, becomes a regular attender at court from 963/4 and in 966 two grants of land were made to his sister, Eadwig's divorced wife, Ælfgifu, S. 737 and 738
16. P. H. Sawyer, 'Charters of the reform movement; the Worcester archive', *Tenth Century Studies*, ed. D. Parsons (Chichester, 1975), pp. 84–93
17. Old English account of Edgar's foundation of monasteries, EHD I no. 238, p. 921
18. On the basis of S. 724 this date is preferable to MS D's 965

of the need for supporters in this area as he was in Mercia.[19] Ælfthryth's father Ordgar had extensive lands here and was later buried at Exeter; her brother Ordulf was the founder of Tavistock abbey. Ordgar was appointed as ealdorman of South West England at roughly the same time as the marriage took place. Wulfthryth was disposed of on the grounds that she was a nun; she was raised at Wilton, easy ground on which to build claims that she had undertaken religious vows. Did Æthelwold play a part in the repudiation? He later appears as an ally of Ælfthryth, though this may have been a friendship arising from their almost simultaneous arrival at court.

In 966 Ælfthryth produced her first son, Edmund. The birth, or rather the christening, was celebrated with a great family gathering at Winchester. Eadgifu, Edgar's grandmother, made a rare and last appearance, and his older son Edward, for whom this birth was most ominous, was also present. As in Ottonian Germany, such a demonstration of family unity stressed the continuity of the dynasty, their claims to power as a family. The unity symbolized in 966 was, however, an ideal strained by the divisive nature of Edgar's marriages. Æthelwold drew up a charter whose witness list recorded the event.[20] Ælfthryth and her new-born son were given precedence over the older Edward. The legitimacy of her marriage and of her son, both open to doubt, were stressed. Ælfthryth was to be the first tenth-century queen to play any active role during her husband's lifetime, and her position was strengthened by her coronation as Queen/Empress alongside Edgar in 973.[21] 966 revealed the fissures in family unity which her marriage had opened. The seeds of 975 had been sown.

From 964 onwards monastic reform gathered strength, though the king's patronage remained circumscribed. Its scale increased, but its pattern remained that of earlier tenth-century kings. West Saxon houses, especially royally connected ones, engrossed his largesse with nuns and nunneries high on the list. The traditional motives for patronizing family houses, female as well as male, were the basis of Edgar's involvement in reform (see *The Church*, pp. 190–3). But the presence at court of men like Æthelwold, Dunstan and Oswald transformed this into something more all-encompassing. Edgar gave general backing to all the reformed houses. He presided over the meeting which issued the *Regularis Concordia*, the new rule of life for those houses, and he granted confirmations, if little land, to the new foundations outside Wessex. Æthelwold's houses loom large; it was Winchester, Abingdon and Ely which fared well. The interests of king and bishop met not only in ways which intensified traditional patronage and support for the church, but which combined to extend the reform movement north of the Thames.

Edgar granted to Æthelwold at least three monasteries north of the Thames, Breedon, Barrow and Ely, whilst Æthelwold himself acquired the sites of Peterborough, Thorney, Crowland, St Neot's and Horningsey. Æthelwold's activity in building up the endowments of Peterborough, Ely, Thorney and Crowland was tireless. The northern version of the Anglo-Saxon Chronicle

19. See S. 684 (960); S. 810 (961 × 3); S. 704 (962); S. 721 (963); S. 755 (967); S. 770 (969); S. 795 (974)
20. S. 745
21. Perhaps again with Æthelwold's connivance, see J. Nelson, 'The second English Ordo', *Politics and Ritual in Early Medieval Europe* (1986), pp. 361–74

ascribed to him, under Edgar's orders, the spread of monasticism north of the Thames, the monasteries 'which King Edgar had ordered the holy bishop Æthelwold to institute'.[22] The undoubted role of Oswald at Ramsey and in the Severn valley is ignored but the perception of Æthelwold's role may not be exaggerated. If a single decision actively to spread the movement for reform rather than passively support it was taken, it was at the same council *c*.970 which issued the *Regularis Concordia*.[23]

If Æthelwold was the driving force, Edgar need not be cast as reluctant follower. It is not necessary to argue that he used monasticism as an attack on entrenched noble power[24] to understand why he wished to extend reform to Mercia and East Anglia. A view of England beyond Wessex is a feature of his reign; one of his last land grants was of land in Shropshire.[25] He issued the first tenth-century law code specifically to include North East Mercia and Northumbria, IV Edgar, and his appointments to the ealdormanry and archbishopric of York attempted to draw the area south of the Tees closer into southern control.

The final takeover of York in 954 had left a confused situation in the North. Archbishop Wulfstan I, imprisoned in 952 on suspicion of supporting the Viking takeover, was apparently never allowed to return to York. Oscytel, bishop of Dorchester, was appointed in his place[26] but did not gain control of his archbishopric until 959. The role of the archbishop as a leader in the North made the appointment of a loyal outsider desirable to southern kings, though the crisis of 957–59 posed problems of enforcement. Similar difficulties in ruling the North probably account for the appointment, or acceptance of the rule of Osulf of Bamburgh, lord of England north of the Tees, as ruler of all Northumbria from 954 to 966. In 966 Edgar decided to separate York/Deira again, and put in Oslac, a noble of Mercian, Fenland origin as ealdorman. The choice of a Mercian noble for an ealdormanry was a new departure; the selection of a man with lands and interests south of the Humber was deliberate. Just as Oscytel had retained his southern bishopric along with York, Oslac's southern connections were to commit him to unity not separatism. Edgar continued the pattern in 971. On Oscytel's death his kinsman, Bishop Oswald of Worcester, was given York but did not relinquish his rich southern see. All three of these men were not only from Mercia, but of Danish descent.

Edgar's rule north of the Thames brought northern nobles to his court in e.g. 969 and 970, rare birds of passage last seen occasionally under Athelstan. Complaint from them may have prompted Edgar's strange action in ravaging Thanet in 969.[27] The occasion was local attack on a group of York merchants; the punishment was severe for harrying was a rare answer to the problems of rule south of the Humber. Edgar wished to communicate his readiness to protect

22. ASC MS D 975
23. N. Banton, 'Monastic reform and the unification of tenth-century England', *Religion and National Identity*, ed. S. Mews (Oxford, 1982), pp. 71–85
24. As E John, "The king and the monks in the tenth-century reformation", *Orbis Britanniae* (Leicester, 1966), pp. 154–80
25. S. 975
26. ASC MS B 971
27. ASC MS D 969 expanded by Roger of Wendover, possibly on the basis of lost annals, EHD I no. 4 p. 284

Northerners, and especially merchants. The sort of men who traded between York and Kent were another group of those who were pulling England into a unity of political interests in the tenth century. Edgar was sensitive to them as *northern* merchants, but also as traders.

Edgar continued Athelstan's injunctions on the standard of the coinage and on weights and measures. It was Edgar who finally ensured a uniform and standardized coinage throughout England south of the Tees in 973 (see below, *The Economy*). His motives combined profit-seeking, a desire for high-quality coin for the payment of royal dues and the pursuit of 'good rule'. As his fourth law code shows, the growth of buying and selling could not be separated from its implications for theft, a central question of tenth-century law. Here, as in his concern for royal rights, for the working of the hundred court or the payment of church dues, Edgar continued the trend of tenth-century development (see below, Ruling the Kingdom).

Royal power carried threat as well as promise for the great nobility. The poverty of the sources means that the balance sheet of Edgar's relations with these men can only tentatively be drawn up. In 971 two of Edgar's ealdormen died, Ælfheah and Ordgar, between them rulers of Wessex. No new appointment was made. As in so many reigns the plums of office were distributed in the early stages, ealdormanries were glittering prizes as much as posts needed for administrative reasons and by 971 Edgar may have felt no need to distribute more. Choice of successor could already have posed difficulties: at least four families still powerful at this date had some claim on these two offices. Ælfheah was buried at Glastonbury and his will, with its grants to the king, queen and young princes, shows how far this erstwhile appointee of Eadwig had adapted. Ælfheah and his royally connected wife Ælfswith had done well out of royal patronage; Edgar had added to his predecessors' largesse.

Ælfheah's royal wife, royal office and royal land grants show how far the trend of the tenth century had been to increase links between the king and great nobility at the same time as forfeiture was complicating them. Within individual reigns such trends were worked out in the cross-currents between individuals, in relations not between 'king' and 'nobles' but between, for example, Edgar and particular men. Such politics are ill-served in the sources. Some careers blossomed now, especially that of Ælfhere, brother of Ælfheah and ealdorman of Mercia. Edgar's sensitivity to Mercia may have allowed the re-emergence of an ealdormanry covering all Mercia, a basis for Ælfhere's power; Ælfhere was one of Edgar's early supporters, a good beginning for high favour. His rise, as always in the narrow world of court and patronage, was at someone's expense, at least in the sense that it engrossed gifts. Æthelwine of East Anglia may have seen himself as the loser. This son of Athelstan Half-king never achieved the heights enjoyed by his father and uncles in the 940s. Edgar's coolness to the family may underlie legends of the king's murder of Æthelwine's brother.[28] Edgar was accused of depriving Æthelwine's father of his patrimony[29] and Æthelwine took advantage of the king's death to recover it. A

28. Gaimar, *L'Estorie des Engles*, ed. T. D. Hardy and C. T. Martin, Rolls Ser. (London, 1888–9), vol. I, lines 3601–3966
29. LE Cap. 7 pp. 79–80

festering rivalry between Ælfhere and Æthelwine was another stream waiting to surface in 975.

It has long been recognized that Edgar's espousal of reform might have repercussions for the nobility (see above, n.24). A religious movement which involved breaking the hereditary control of nobles over monasteries might not have been welcome, doubly so if, as has been suggested, the king proceeded to transfer power from ealdormen to abbots. Any interpretation of the reform which involves a deliberate royal attack on the nobility is questionable. Cooperation and consensus rather than conflict and confrontation were the keynotes of relations between king and nobles. Neither king nor nobles may have appreciated the implications of reform (see *The Church*); reform as a movement may appear clearer to us than to them. Rulers then as now could be caught between contradictory aims, both fulfilling traditional roles of patronage and protection of the church and defending their noble followers. It is possible to will an end without the means, especially if neither the full implications of the end nor the details of the means are appreciated. We need not assume Edgar's approval for every harsh deal driven by Æthelwold in East Anglia nor for every extension of territory Oswald made for his Severn valley monasteries. But the king was known as a general supporter of monasteries; protest was inhibited until his death in 975. Then here, too, the floodgates broke.

In 973 Edgar was consecrated king at Bath. It was a second, imperial coronation and his wife Ælfthryth was associated in it. Bath symbolized the Roman, imperial connotations of the occasion. The reform of the coinage and the issuing of the law code, IV Edgar, in the same year drove home the message of power. Edgar journeyed to Chester where six kings of the Welsh and British pledged to follow him and be his allies on land and sea, and Kenneth king of the Scots visited him at his own court. English observers were impressed. Stage-management and planning by reforming bishops does not drain these events of significance as a demonstration of Edgar's power. At the age of 29 he could be presented as ruler of a united England with wider Imperial pretensions. But appearances were deceptive. Kenneth was in fact receiving a cession of territory in Lothian and the Welsh and British kings were seeking an alliance against Vikings in the Irish Sea which mattered to Edgar as to them.

Many of the problems which surfaced after his death are attributable to the limitations of tenth-century kingship and to the politics of his reign. His early death helped ensure his reputation. Had he lived, as his unfortunate son Æthelred did, to approach 50, he would have faced not merely the accumulation of these problems but the revival of full-scale Viking attack. How far he could have dealt with either cannot be known. But we can recognize how far his early death and the events which followed it raised his reign in general and 973 in particular to the status of historical myth.

Edward the Martyr and Æthelred II, 975–1016[30]

The death of Edgar was followed by a struggle for the throne between supporters of his two sons, Edward and Æthelred. 975–78 was not, however, a simple re-run of 955–57. Rivalries at court remained, with the patronage of the new monastic institutions and the prominence of church reforms at court even clearer than in the 950s. Regional feeling may have played a part, but a lesser one than before.The dispute began, as all succession struggles must, in the divisions in the royal family itself. As in the mid century, a woman was at their centre.

Queen Ælfthryth, Edgar's third wife, played the central female role, in this case the classic one of a stepmother working to advance her own son at the expense of her stepson. Arguments about fraternal succession and the rights of brothers may have been used, but questions of division or underkingship were replaced by a straightforward struggle for the throne of the entire kingdom. Doubts about the legitimacy of Edgar's remarriages, arguments about Edgar's own intentions, even of his designation of a son to succeed him, echoed into the saints' lives and legends of later times and are heard especially in the stories which gathered around Ælfthryth.[31]

The death of any tenth-century king was an opportunity to express grievance and particularly to try to undo what had been done in the previous reign. Better documentation of events after 975 can take us closer to the detail of these events in some localities than was possible in 956. Attacks on church property were widespread. From York to Kent and Sussex, from the Severn valley to the Fens the death of Edgar was a signal to those who wished to recover property. 'After the death of Edgar, Leofric tried...to annul all the agreement he had made;...after the death of King Edgar Ælfwold broke the entire agreement',[32] is a constant refrain of the *Liber Eliensis*.

In the North attacks were not simply on land-engrossing churchmen. Here the archbishop was no longer a leader of separatist feeling but was now identified with southern rule and was attacked for that. Reform did play a part here. Archbishops had been judging cases of sin/crime and acquiring forfeit property as a result. Land lost in 975 had been gained by Oscytel in a marriage case,[33] an area of reforming concern. But 975 north of the Humber chiefly illustrated how far this area stood outside southern court politics. Edgar's ealdorman, Oslac, was accused and exiled. We do not know by whom and in what circumstances; whether by a southern king suspicious of the activities of a remote northern ealdorman or as a result of local accusations, it was an ominous sign of the difficulty of ruling the North. Archbishops were seen here as instruments of southern kings, their reforms identifiable as oppression. The new ealdorman Thored may not even have been a royal appointment; Æthelred

30. For recent important work on this reign see *Ethelred the Unready*, ed. Hill; S. Keynes, *The Diplomas of King Æthelred 'the Unready'* and his 'A tale of two kings: Alfred the Great and Æthelred the Unready', *TRHS*, ser. 5, vol. 36 (1986), pp. 195–217; P. Stafford, 'The laws of Cnut and the history of Anglo-Saxon royal promises', *ASE* 10 (1981), pp. 173–90
31. C. E. Wright, *The Cultivation of Saga in Anglo-Saxon England* (1939), pp. 15–74, 146ff and 162ff.
32. LE cap. 8, p. 81 and cap. 10, p. 83
33. EHD I no. 114, p. 565

married his daughter in an attempt to woo him. The patterns of 1065 are already taking shape, England north of the Humber was the most truly separate area of the new kingdom.

Elsewhere the attacks centred on the property of the revived monasteries. The Life of Oswald speaks of an attack on monasticism as such, of neat divisions between a persecutor of monks like Ælfhere of Mercia and a friend of God like Æthelwine of East Anglia.[34] Reality was more blurred. Æthelwine himself used the opportunity to recover land from the abbey of Ely; Ælfhere's attacks were concentrated on Oswald's foundations in the Severn valley where land which once belonged to his office of ealdorman had been diverted into ecclesiastical hands. The line-up of Ælfhere versus Æthelwine, which the life written at Æthelwine's abbey of Ramsey casts into a mould of heroic principle, was determined as much by court rivalry as religious difference. The tensions of Edgar's court including those centred around the queen now surfaced. Ælfhere's brother Ælfheah had been closely connected with Ælfthryth. Little love could have been lost between Ælfthryth and Æthelwine, the brother of her first husband. In Mercia, East Anglia and Wessex the rivalries of court and religious issues meshed; at least as far as its great nobles were concerned England south of the Humber looked more of a unity in 975 than in 956.

The attacks on church land reveal a clash of values which the patronage of monasteries had sharpened and the problems of a movement which was redefining piety. Some churchmen had been high-handed in their efforts to build up an endowment, knocking down prices in the knowledge that they had a king to back them. Even without this their efforts ran up against strong feelings that land and monasteries themselves belonged to the family.[35] Many of those who recovered individual lands were, in other circumstances, the endowers of their family abbeys as was Æthelwine at Ramsey or Ælfhere's family at Glastonbury. Christian reform, by periodically restating the dilemma of the church in the world, shifts the bounds of acceptable conventional piety. Within a generation people who saw themselves as Christian patrons could be recast as devils. Ælfhere and his brother Ælfheah were not irreligious; their family were patrons of Glastonbury where they had a brother in the community, they were connected to Ælfsige, bishop of Winchester. But their brother was a married clerk, Ælfsige a married bishop. Ælfhere's actions after 975 are the product not only of court politics and of loss of land, they are those of a man whose religious habits were under threat.

The divisions of 975–78 were complicated by reform, but not aligned on it. Dunstan and possibly Oswald backed and crowned Edward the Martyr; Ælfthryth held out for her son Æthelred with the backing of Ælfhere and probably of Bishop Æthelwold. Edward sought and won support. At least three new ealdormen were appointed in 975, though there was none of the largesse of the mid century. The crisis of patronage signalled in the build-up of charters in the 940s and 950s was not acute in 975. But Ælfthryth and her supporters did not accept defeat. Edward was murdered at Corfe Castle in 978 on a visit to his stepmother. Ælfthryth was later openly accused of the murder. Though the stereotypes of wicked stepmothers have coloured the accusations, it is difficult

34. EHD I no. 236, pp. 912–4
35. LE caps. 32–3, pp. 105–8

not to see it done by those who felt she would approve. Ælfthryth was a benefactor of churches and an ally of bishops on whom political murder may be felt to sit ill; but arguments based on consistency of character are dubious, never more so than in this period when character cannot be known. The forms of political action open to women were limited to the intrigues of court, survival in that world their only hope. If we cannot know whether she planned the murder, it is certain that she benefited from it.

The murder of an anointed king did shock contemporaries, especially since it was left unavenged and the body dishonoured, facts suggestive of the involvement of Edward's kin. In 980 Ælfhere of Mercia translated the bones with due honour,[36] the action of an elderly man dissociating himself from his allies, or a gesture of conciliation by Æthelred's supporters putting the omission of 978 to rights? By the time William of Malmesbury wrote, these events were seen as hanging over and damning a reign which had come to be regarded as the beginning of eleventh-century troubles. But William conflated and distorted contemporary judgement. The earliest commentators saw the attacks on monasteries as the evils which brought the end of peace and the judgement of God in the form of the Vikings. By the end of Æthelred's reign the murder was being recalled, by Archbishop Wulfstan in the Sermon of the Wolf,[37] but in defeat much is remembered and pinpointed which seemed unimportant in more normal times. The murder must be remembered, but the long reign of Æthelred cannot be dominated by it. In many ways that reign, at least up to AD 1000 if not beyond, was a continuation of tenth-century developments and especially of Edgar. But during this reign the pressures of external attack and finally of defeat tested the pattern of tenth-century politics to the utmost, ushering in the eleventh-century when the established politics of a unified England were reshaped under foreign conquest and rule.

We know more about Æthelred's reign than about that of almost any other early English king, and that knowledge is a major problem. Illumination after obscurity carries the danger that old difficulties will be seen as new. The detailed narrative for the reign was written not on a year-by-year basis, but as a single history at the end of the reign from the perspective of South Eastern England and in the depths of defeat. Its scapegoating of individuals, its obsession with Danish attack to the exclusion of almost everything else, its lack of sympathy or information about the court or about other areas of England and its sense of nemesis have coloured all accounts of the reign. Royal action shorn of context becomes a record of erratic arbitrariness, a basis on which twelfth-century chroniclers expanded. Æthelred's reputation continued to fall as writers after 1066 looked back over the long perspective of two conquests and viewed Æthelred as their origin, an epitome of the sins of the English and their weaknesses. By the twelfth century a story which could be written around individuals was even more popular than in 1016. The end result was at worst a picture of a king who brought about his own downfall and that of his kingdom, at best of an ill-advised monarch surrounded by treacherous and self-seeking men. Yet during this long reign the resistance of the English king and kingdom to the

36. ASC MS D 979 and 980
37. EHD I no. 240, p. 931. The entries in MS D for 979 and 980 are in a York chronicle with connections with Archbishop Wulfstan

Vikings was protracted and often successful, military collapse, when it came, late. England took the brunt of a renewal of Viking raiding not necessarily because it was weak but because it was a desirable prize. For Scandinavians interested in tribute and loot, especially silver, it was the wealth of the English kingdom which attracted. Ironically it may have been the power of the English king to tap that wealth which was the magnet.

During the first twenty years or more of the reign it is the continuity which is striking. No great shake-up occurred at court immediately after 978. Æthelred's supporters sought reconciliation as Edgar and his followers had in 959. Antagonisms with a long history were not simply forgotten: Dunstan's role in the 980s was muted; Æthelwold and Winchester engrossed the king's patronage. But Winchester was the family house of the dynasty anyway. Ælfthryth was at court as queen dowager from 978 to 985 and again in the 990s. Her role was not the paramount one of Eadgifu under her sons, an indication of how much we have lost of the background to the 940s and 50s, perhaps also of how far the ending of dispute in 978 was decisive in a way which neither 940 nor 946, with their legacy of unsatisfied *æthelings*, were.

In 984 Bishop Æthelwold died, the young king came of age and his mother temporarily disappeared from court. The next four or five years have some of the appearance of a new beginning to the reign. A spate of land grants to laymen and changes at court, with some attacks on church property condoned or even undertaken by the king point to a delayed expression of the tensions of 975–78. Ecclesiastical charters later referred to these years as a period of 'youthful indiscretions', of a king misled.[38] But there was more than one acceptable judgement on the ecclesiastical patronage of Edgar's reign, and in other ways Æthelred and his followers were stressing their continuation of Edgar's actions. A new law code and possibly a return to Edgar's attempts to centralize the coinage marked the king's coming of age.[39] If the late 980s stand out in some respects in others they point back into the tenth century.

Æthelred, like Edgar, tackled the problems of ruling north of the Thames. In the North Æthelred first came to terms with Thored and drew him, like Oslac before, to the southern court. When the death of Archbishop Oswald and the death or disgrace of Thored *c.*993 gave Æthelred an apparently free hand in the North, he continued his father's approach. A new archbishop was chosen from Peterborough abbey, a new ealdorman, Ælfhelm from a North Midlands family. Patronage was again extended into Mercia, loyalties across the Humber knitted. The appointment of outsiders as ealdormen had been common since the early tenth century, but there were dangers as well as advantages in putting in men without local connections. No man could rule without such connections, but the making of them could look suspicious from a remote southern court. In 1006 Ælfhelm fell under suspicion and was murdered, his sons blinded at the king's command. By that date internal treachery was coming to be seen as a problem. The harsh treatment meted out to Ælfhelm signalled the failure of tenth-century attempts to rule the North.

A series of deaths of ealdormen like Brihtnoth of Essex and Æthelwine of East Anglia in the early 990s removed the last of the group of men who had

38. S. Keynes, *The Diplomas of King Æthelred the Unready*, pp. 176–86
39. P. Wormald, 'Æthelred the Lawmaker', *Ethelred the Unready*, ed. Hill, p. 63

controlled England since the 950s. Æthelred did not replace them from the same families, in some cases did not replace them at all. The new share-out of patronage was more limited, marked a move away from the large ealdormanries of the mid tenth century. Three marcher areas were placed under the control of ealdormen, York under Ælfhelm, the West Midlands under Leofwine, Essex and the mouth of the Thames under Leofsige. The court of the shire and the raising of local forces was already passing into the hands of royal reeves and high reeves of whom we begin to hear in the reign of Edgar. Ealdormanries had always been appointments determined as much by the needs of politics as of administration, their recipients beneficiaries of royal patronage, their areas drawn by political need. In the 990s Æthelred was choosing to limit the powerbase which ealdormanries had provided for earlier nobles, and at the same time ending the control of families established since the 930s. Such action counts as strong rule, but the disaffection it can leave may make it unwise. Æthelred faced many decisions about the bestowing of patronage during his long reign, and the 'right' answers were not always clear. *C.*1002, for example, Æthelweard, ealdorman of South West England died. Was he to be replaced by his son Æthelmær, a prominent thegn at Æthelred's court, or by the king's uncle, Ordulf, son of the previous ealdorman and another court official? Æthelred chose neither and left the area in the control of high reeves. Both men disappeared from court, and Æthelmær reappears at the end of the reign leading the men of the South West to submit to Swegn in 1013. Patronage could pose dilemmas to which there were no easy answers.

In all this we see continuity and the problems of tenth-century rule fully illuminated. Æthelred's law codes show the same concerns as his ancestors, with the courts and their procedures, with royal rights and in his third law code with the North East Midlands, the area of the Five Boroughs. In this as in so much, he was the son of his father. The detailed knowledge of his reign threatens to show as personal peculiarities what were in reality the problems and limitations inherent in the tenth-century political system. Nowhere is this a greater danger than in relations between king and great nobility.

Æthelred is commonly indicted as a king who could not choose men well nor hold them to loyalty. Murder and exile are dramatic proof of his difficulties with the great nobility: Ælfric of Mercia exiled in 985; Leofsige of Essex in 1002; Wulfgeat in 1006; Ælfhelm murdered and his sons blinded in 1006, Sigeferth and Morcar from the Five Boroughs killed in 1015. In the records of legal disputes the king can be seen depriving nobles of land and profiting from their fall. In addition the Anglo-Saxon Chronicle has its tales of treachery by royal officials, by Ælfric ealdorman of East Wessex in 992 and 1003 and especially by Eadric, ealdorman of Mercia from 1007. For the Chronicler and for most later writers Eadric was the evil genius of the reign. During its last ten years he and his family were made responsible for the betrayal of English military efforts, for counselling capitulation and finally in 1015–16 for the judicial murder of Sigeferth and Morcar and for treachery in changing sides to the Danish invader, Cnut. A king in whose reign such things occurred could be held an outstanding example of failure in the political skills of a medieval ruler.

The judgements passed on men like Eadric are not neutral. Little which is said about him is untainted by hindsight. When the chronicler states that Eadric became ealdorman of Mercia in 1007 he states fact, but since this is the only appointment of an ealdorman he records for the whole reign, it is a fact selected according to the later judgements of the writer. When he wrote Cnut had conquered, or was in the process of conquering the kingdom, and Eadric's role in this was obvious. All the chronicler's remarks about Eadric's earlier actions are filtered through this knowledge. When the Chronicler says that Eadric was responsible for the deaths of Sigeferth and Morcar in 1015 he moves beyond fact to simple opinion. Sigeferth and Morcar were accused of crimes, found guilty, murdered and lost their property. From the king downwards, many individuals were involved in such a process; the chronicler fingers Eadric, boils down a complex series of events to a simple accusation. Lacking alternative accounts of these events we are left to question. Paradoxically it is when the Chronicler indulges most openly in judgement and calls Eadric a traitor that we can trust him most. In the views of this contemporary his actions in 1016–17 appeared treacherous. It is unfortunate that this is the view of a single man, but it is a contemporary judgement of treachery not lightly to be dismissed. Even here we must be aware of the historical need, not felt by the chronicler, to understand Eadric's dilemmas and situation and of the danger of gliding from his definition of treachery into ours. If the judgement of Æthelred is composed of a series of judgements on the actions of men like Eadric, each one of those is subject to interpretation.

The perspective of this single passionate narrative colours most of the incidents involving the king and his nobility. The chronicler was remote in time and space from much of what he records; his exiles, murders and blindings are action without context or explanation. They are recorded as part of a theme, a story of internal treachery, of divisions and dissensions amongst the nobility, of poor leadership which culminated in 1016; they and the theme appeared the most important things about the reign to someone writing at its end.

The exiles, forfeitures, legal judgements and murders should not be argued away, and Æthelred may well be judged a poor practitioner of the art of tenth-century politics. But only by the yardstick of that politics itself. In forfeiture and the pushing of royal rights Æthelred continued the practices of his predecessors, would be adjudged weak had he not. He may well have pursued them more vigorously, though there are other reasons why so many of them are recorded for his reign. The pursuit of legal rights and political action cannot readily be separated. Leofsige, ealdorman of Essex, was banished in 1002 for the murder of a royal reeve; the process was by legal judgement and the result was forfeiture;[40] in 1006 Wulfgeat was deprived of all his property because of 'unjust judgements and arrogant deeds'.[41] Every legal case involving a great noble had a political dimension, entailed a fall from power and a profit to the king. Where do the politics of the court end and the processes of the law begin?

Within such a system norms of acceptable and unacceptable behaviour exist, and Æthelred enforced his rights so vigorously that he was felt by contemporaries to have contravened those norms. When he returned from exile in 1014, it was on condition that he 'rule more justly than he did before'.[42] Cnut's laws

40. ASC MS C 1002 and the *Will of Æthelgifu*, ed. D. Whitelock (Oxford, 1968)
41. ASC MS C and Fl. Wig. 1006
42. ASC MS C 1014

contain specific alleviation of the abuses of power under Æthelred including not only forfeiture and its threat to the rights of widows and heirs but also heavy impositions on the nobility such as large heriots (a form of death tax). But before we accept these as novel oppressions we must examine the context. The opportunity of exile and foreign conquest allowed Æthelred to be blamed for them. Gelds and latterly heavy taxation to pay Danish mercenaries were relatively novel impositions, but in other respects Æthelred was criticized in 1014 and after for conduct which largely followed in the footsteps of his predecessors.

Resentments like those which led in 975 to attacks on church property were aimed in the different circumstances of 1014 at the king himself. It is possible to argue that the entire trend of tenth-century royal power was oppressive (see below, *Ruling the Kingdom*). Æthelred may have been foolish to have stored up resentments by replacing old families in the 990s, raising new men, appointing reeves who caused friction with ealdormen, persevering with difficult northern policies in new circumstances. He may be considered an inept practitioner of tenth-century politics, an unintelligent continuator of his father's actions in inappropriate times. He is unfortunate in that we know too little of his predecessors to tell whether he stands indicted alone. Yet only once, in 1013, was he deserted by the bulk of his nobility. That desertion embarrassed contemporaries. The chronicler's account of the ravagings of 1011/12 is an apologia for the unacceptable crime of desertion of a lord in the face of an enemy, precisely the one of which Eadric stood guilty in 1016. Wulfstan was more forthright. His Sermon of the Wolf castigated the English nobility for their ultimate betrayal. Was Æthelred thus doubly culpable, the man who squandered the prestige of a dynasty which held loyalty for so long? No final judgement on him or his actions can be passed without examination of the Danish invasions themselves. It was these which strained normal political relations to breaking point. Their nature and the question of how soon they have been seen to pose a new and overwhelming danger which might require a rethinking of tenth-century politics are central to the reign.

The first recorded attacks date from the 980s, on the West and South West coasts, originating primarily in the Irish Sea area. They were a continuation of earlier tenth-century attacks on Wales and attack from this traditional direction continued to be important into the 990s. For the king and his advisers, armed with tenth-century experience, it was these, not primarily the new assaults from Scandinavia, which posed the problem. In AD.1000 Æthelred moved against the source of these attacks and against their Scottish allies, with a campaign by land and sea against Man and Strathclyde. The Chronicler, for whom the real enemy was the Danes, is dismissive: 'the enemy fleet had gone to Richard's kingdom that summer'.[43] But the heir of Brunanburh and of the alliances of 973, the grandson of Edmund who had taken retributive action against Viking allies in Strathclyde in 945 would have seen things differently.

The 980s and 990s also witnessed attack from across the Channel, from Viking fleets often direct from Scandinavia who found harbours in Normandy. This was the pattern which dominated by the end of the reign. These were not ignored. Before 991 Æthelred and Richard of Normandy had come to an

43. ASC MS C 1000

agreement about the harbouring of Vikings in Normandy.[44] The agreement was less than effective, as AD 1000 showed. Æthelred's response was to ravage the Cotentin[45] and to renew the alliance by marriage to the count's daughter in 1002. During the 990s military action was coupled with traditional methods of tribute payment and the baptism of the Viking leader Olaf. Æthelred may even have tried the age-old answer of interfering among Viking rulers themselves, supporting Olaf after his return to Norway.[46] The Chronicler remembered only treachery and defeat, but the view from the year 1000 might not have been the same.

What few by the end of the tenth century would have appreciated was the nature and motivation of the attacks from Scandinavia. Kings, would-be-kings and jarls almost indistinguishable from kings led these fleets. Their impetus was the need for loot and tribute to maintain or acquire power in the still volatile North (see below). The well-planned forts of Trelleborg or Fyrkat were not themselves built to train the armies which came to England,[47] but the power which built them and the insecurity which prompted them launched the assault. The Danish kings who constructed them needed to attract personal followings[48] and feared the amassing of loot and followers by nobles like Thorkell the Tall. They, like Thorkell, came to England to meet these needs and in rivalry with each other.

The English response was local rather than national. In 999 the Kentish levies met the Viking army, in 1001 the men of Hampshire, in 1004 East Anglia under Ulfcytel. Larger armies were gathered as in 992 or in 1009, but some of the resentment their assembly produced may be signalled by the fact that it is with these that treachery and disagreement is associated. Although the Chronicler sees the struggle as of the *English* against the *Danes* most of the defence was at the local level, which had been the normal pattern of response to Welsh or Scottish raids in the tenth century. Æthelred recognized the wider nature of the threat and his wider responsibilities in his negotiations with the Norman duke, his ravaging of Strathclyde and especially his raising of national gelds. It is debatable how far the early gelds were universal,[49] but certainly after the recruitment of Thorkell's army as mercenaries in 1012 a general geld to pay them was introduced. General gelds levied from areas not directly affected may have been no more popular than national armies. The costs of his efforts against the Danes may have been among the grievances against Æthelred by 1014.

1006 marked a turning point in political and military thinking. Changes at court and the fall of several great nobles suggest a mood of suspicion, an

44. EHD I no. 230, pp. 894–5
45. William of Jumièges, printed R. Allen Brown, *The Norman Conquest* (1984), p. 5
46. P. H. Sawyer, 'Ethelred II, Olaf Trygvason and the conversion of Norway', *Scandinavian Studies* (1987), pp. 299–307
47. T. E. Christiansen, 'Trelleborgs Alder-Arkaeologisk Datering', *Årboger for nordisk oldkyndighed og historie* (1982), pp. 84–110: N. Bonde and K. Christensen, 'Trelleborgs Alder-Dendrokronologisk datering', *ibid.* pp. 111–52
48. N. Lund, 'The armies of Swegn Forkbeard and Cnut, *leding* or *lið*' ASE 15 (1986), pp. 105–18
49. P. Stafford, 'Historical implications of the regional production of dies under Æthelred II', *British Numismatic Journal*, vol. 48 (1978), 35–51 and M. K. Lawson, 'The collection of Danegeld and Heregeld in the reigns of Æthelred II and Cnut', *English Historical Review*, vol. 99 (1984), pp. 721–38

expansion of the fear of internal treachery which had prompted the massacre of Danes in England in 1002. A rethinking of defences was certainly underway. Uhtred of Bamburgh, victor against the Scots, was appointed to York, and given the king's daughter in marriage. For the first recorded time the entire levies of Wessex and Mercia were called out against Swegn's army. And in 1007 the ealdormanry of all Mercia was revived and Eadric appointed to it. The coordination of military effort on a larger scale was beginning. In 1008 a large fleet was demanded, with one ship to be provided by every 310 hides of land.Its warriors were to be especially well equipped with helmets and coats of mail.[50] The chronicler waxed eloquent on the betrayal of all this effort in 1009 after a quarrel between Eadric's brother and a South Saxon thegn. Behind the personalities lie the problems of a national effort.

In 1009 Thorkell's army arrived in England and the king called out all the people. The level of the English effort and the breadth of Thorkell's movements between 1009 and 1012 indicate a military crisis by this date. And it was fear of Thorkell's successes which brought Swegn back to England in 1013. Thorkell had by now joined Æthelred, been taken into his pay, and fear of that alliance helped move Swegn from a quest for tribute to desire for the crown. Swegn received the submission of England north of Watling Street, of Uhtred and Northumbria, of Lindsey, of the Five Boroughs and of the rest of the army (*here*). He took provisions, ravaged his way to Oxford and Winchester, which submitted, but then failed to take London, where Æthelred and Thorkell themselves led the defence. He turned west to Bath where Æthelmær and the western thegns met him to come to terms. Only now did London capitulate and give hostages. Æthelred fled to Normandy via the Isle of Wight, and both Swegn and Thorkell took tribute and provisions.

Swegn's actions in 1013 invite comparison with the Viking claimants to York in the mid century, and especially the campaign of Olaf in 940 which attempted to reassert control not merely over York but over all England north of Watling Street. These areas of Scandinavian settlement, at a later date termed the Danelaw, appear to shape the aspirations if not the support of would-be Viking rulers. Yet 'Danish England' has no political identity in the tenth century.[51] The Viking settlements were now remote in time and little suggests that they imparted an ethnic unity to these areas even at an earlier date. Deiran kings had sometimes ruled south of the Humber. It was as their successors not merely as Vikings that Scandinavian rulers of York in the late ninth and early tenth centuries exercised power there. Olaf in 940 had been ready to revive them in the realization that rule at York would be strengthened by aggressive expansion south of the Humber.

There is little to suggest that Olaf himself had been attempting to unite 'Danish' England, but in any event Swegn in 1013 was not following Olaf's pattern. He aimed at a conquest of the English kingdom from the North, not merely a revival of the Viking kingdom of York. He did not base himself at York in 1013. The city was a safe haven for him by 1014 when his body was taken

50. N. Brooks, 'Arms, status and warfare in late Anglo-Saxon England', *Ethelred the Unready*, ed. Hill pp. 81–103
51. P. Stafford, *The East Midlands in the early Middle Ages* (Leicester, 1985) and 'The Danes and the Danelaw', *History Today*, 36 (October, 1986), pp. 17–23

there after death,[52] though its leaders may have been more cautious in 1013, remembering the vengeance of southern kings they had suffered before. But Swegn's base at Gainsborough rather than York may show the difference between him and earlier Viking rulers. Gainsborough was more central than York for one whose ambitions lay south into the Midlands and Wessex, were not bounded by the Humber. Gainsborough on the Trent was central not only to York but to the Five Boroughs (i.e. the towns of Leicester, Nottingham, Derby, Stamford and Lincoln and their surrounding areas.) These were all areas of previous Danish settlement. More important, they had trading contacts with Scandinavia throughout the tenth century and Scandinavian merchants may have been established there. It was urban merchants who were the most identifiable groups of Scandinavians in England in the early eleventh century. When Æthelred ordered the St Brice Day massacre of Danes in 1002, it is only in a town, Oxford, that it can be shown to have taken effect.[53] Even if the massacre did not spread to the Five Boroughs, it cannot have endeared Danish merchants here to Æthelred. If Swegn hoped for any Scandinavian support by basing himself at Gainsborough, it is more likely to have been from these recent arrivals than from descendants of ninth-century settlers.

Such traders, along with his own earlier campaigns in England, provided Swegn with the information about the state of English affairs on which he acted in 1013. He may have known of the disaffection of many nobles in the North East Midlands. Those connected with the disgraced family of Ælfhelm played a crucial part in the events of 1013–16. Sigeferth and Morcar, the two nobles accused and killed in 1015, were members of it; the sons of Æthelred's first marriage, Athelstan and Edmund Ironside, were linked to it; the two rival claimants to the English throne between 1014 and 1016, Edmund and Cnut, both married into it. Another potential malcontent was Godwine, the sole survivor in power of the once dominant family of Ælfhere of Mercia.[54] He was ealdorman of Lindsey, the Chronicler singled him out as a man who had led retreat before the Vikings in 993; this hints at his disaffection by the end of the reign. If, as is likely, Æthelred had been responsible for extending the demands of tenth-century rule into the North East Midlands disaffection would have been compounded. Some of the pattern of 1065 (see below, pp. 95–9) is prefigured.

Thus in 1013 Swegn may have hoped to revive residual Viking identity in his support; local or ethnic feeling are not constants, they wax as well as wane and the arrival of a conquering Danish king with a large army could concentrate the mind on ancestry. But Swegn was drawn to the North Midlands by more than its supposed Danishness. It was administrative units not ethnic divisions which submitted to Swegn in 1013; the ealdormanries of Northumbria and Lindsey, the Five Boroughs united under a single court. Through their prominence in the courts nobles became a focus of local identity; the role of those same nobles as military leaders in Æthelred's reign enhanced their local prestige. The attitude of such men in 1013 here, as elsewhere in England, was the key to success. The divisions of early eleventh-century England were not merely the fossils of old kingdoms, nor the result of Viking settlement but the product of the way

52. Encomium p. lvii n. 4
53. EHD I no. 127, pp. 590–2
54. A. Williams, *'Princeps Merciorum Gentis* . . . .', pp. 169–71

tenth-century kings had ruled their enlarged kingdom and in the reign of Æthelred conducted its defence.

1014–16, like the year immediately preceding 1066, are well chronicled. The same desire to describe and explain defeat motivated both and reveals the differences between the two situations. The crisis of the early eleventh century was protracted and expected. It was obvious at least by the arrival of Swegn in 1013 if not of Thorkell in 1009; it was drawn out by Swegn's death in 1014, the return of Æthelred, the rebellion of his son Edmund Ironside in 1015 and the battles between Edmund and Cnut in 1016. 1066 appears out of the blue in English chronicles: reaction came afterwards, spasmodic and delayed. English writers who tried to explain it immediately after went no further back than 1065, could see no deeper roots than recent dissension and the accidental unfolding of tragedy (see below). Cnut's conquest appeared as one event in a long crisis. These differences underlie the contrasts between the aftermath of 1016 and that of 1066. Cnut's conquest was expected. Some had already adjusted to it in 1013, though 1014–15 complicated matters.

Æthelred returned in 1014, on terms. He promised to be a good lord, and his promises were enshrined in legislation. His return had been negotiated by proxy, his representative in 1014 being his ten- or eleven-year-old son Edward, the future Confessor. Edward was Æthelred's son by his Norman wife Emma and it would later be claimed that he had been designated by his father as his successor.[55] This would have increased those tensions in the royal family which were the inevitable result of a second marriage. Æthelred had adult sons, Athelstan, Edmund and others; they were not excluded from public life by the marriage.[56] They continued to be present at court and played a military role in Æthelred's later years, their claims were not forgotten. But open designation or hints at it could only have strained family relations, especially as Æthelred in his 40s had reached an age by which his father, uncle, grandfather and great uncle had all been dead. With a stepmother at court, and especially with the king in exile with her brother in 1013, Æthelred's elder sons would not have felt secure.

The eldest of them, Athelstan, died in June 1014, a few months after his father's return. Neither Athelstan nor his brother Edmund had accompanied Æthelred into exile. Their activity in 1013–14, and particularly after the death of Swegn in February 1014 can only be guessed. With hindsight Æthelred's flight to Normandy looks like temporary exile; in 1013/14 it might have seemed more like abdication. This posed a dilemma for his sons, which the death of Swegn only made more acute. Were they to accept Swegn's rule or resist? In 1014 were they to press their own claims to the throne in opposition to Cnut? Neither action was rebellion against their father, until his return made it so. If the succession had not been an issue before, 1014 would have made it one.

In 1015 ealdorman Eadric acted against Sigeferth and Morcar at an assembly at Oxford. Charges had been involved for the king seized their property. The Chronicler calls Sigeferth and Morcar 'thegns of the Seven Boroughs', a term found nowhere else and one which associates them with all the areas which first submitted to Swegn in 1013. Connivance at Swegn's

55. *The Life of King Edward*, ed. F. Barlow (Edinburgh, 1962), p. 7–8
56. S. Keynes, 'A tale of two kings, Alfred the Great and Æthelred the Unready', TRHS, ser. 5 vol, 36 (1986), p. 215, n.73

conquest is the most likely charge against them, support for the Danish kings then or after; at some date between 1013 and 1016 Cnut married Ælfgifu of Northampton, daughter of the murdered ealdorman Ælfhelm and a member of this family.[57] The fact that the men of Lindsey had joined Cnut's ravaging in 1014 may have enhanced suspicions. Alternatively they were accused of aiding the claims of Athelstan or Edmund. The king's return from exile, no matter how careful the terms, left suspicion and recrimination. Worse than a conquest may be a conquest undone.

Eadric's denunciation of Sigeferth and Morcar had its own motives of which loyalty to Æthelred was only one. Rivalries at court and in Mercia itself could be settled now. From this point if not before Eadric was identified as an enemy of these men and of any groupings to which they belonged. Edmund, Æthelred's oldest surviving son, now carried off the widow of Sigeferth and married her against his father's will. He went north, took the property of Sigeferth and Morcar and received the submission of the men of the Five Boroughs. Edmund called on his own local connections, on the discontents which had played into Swegn's hands and perhaps on his claims to the throne. Æthelred's ravaging of Lindsey in 1014 and the murders of Sigeferth and Morcar would have fanned existing disaffection. A crisis beginning in conquest, exacerbated by the king's return was now complicated by succession. By openly aligning himself with a disgraced family and a dubiously loyal area Edmund rebelled, a fact which was critically to affect English resistance in 1016. He was also openly declaring himself an enemy of Eadric who now had much to fear from Edmund's accession to the throne, imminent since the king (who was to die in April 1016), was old, probably already ill.

In 1015 Eadric collected an army and went over to Cnut. He was looking to save himself, scarcely a heroic motive. Heroism is not normally a yardstick of political action, but 1015 called for heroism in eleventh-century terms. Eadric betrayed not a country or nation but his lord; Æthelred was not yet dead. The disgust of the Chronicler was justified, though judgements by the standards of heroism or epic simplify the quandaries. Eadric could have justified himself as opposing Edmund not Æthelred, as choosing one legitimate successor (Cnut's father had ruled as king) rather than another. It is a feature of the eleventh century with its conquests and tortuous successions that choices became more complicated, that loyalty was often divided and more rarely coincided with self-interest. The standards of heroism may be made for such circumstances, but they pass harsh judgement on the people caught in them.

It is a measure of the crisis of 1013–16 and the effects of conquest and exile that for the first time in the tenth or eleventh centuries a violent succession struggle preceded the death of a king. The explanation of that crisis lies not merely with the unknowable personality of Æthelred. Attack and defeat had tested the politics of the tenth century, revealed the fragility of unity; conquest was to be the eleventh-century crucible which would continue to try them both.

---

57. She had two sons, Swegn and Harold. Both may have been born before Cnut's marriage to Emma, though this cannot be proved since Ælfgifu survived that marriage.

4

Cnut and His Sons, 1016–42

Cnut's is the neglected conquest of eleventh-century England, yet no less important because it proved less permanent than 1066. Its neglect is due in part to the inadequacy of the sources, which provide only the sketchiest outline to compare with the detailed knowledge of 1066 and its aftermath. 1016 appears less traumatic than 1066, the continuity greater, the dispossession less. Some sources create a positive picture of continuity across 1016, like Cnut's two law codes which, far from bearing the mark of an arbitrary conqueror, read as an apogee of tenth-century rule. By contrast a source like Domesday Book points to wholesale dispossessions after 1066. Cnut's laws were framed by Archbishop Wulfstan, the heir of a tradition of law-making dead by 1066. The different effects of 1016 and 1066 on the church accounts for many of the apparent differences between them. No changes in ecclesiastical office or organization followed 1016 and the anguished voices which recorded the results of 1066 may be hushed as a result. Moreover 1016 was too soon undone to stimulate long-term comment. The contrasts between 1016 and 1066 are magnified by differences in the nature of the sources but cannot thus be explained away (see also pp. 108–9).[1]

1016 was not a peaceful takeover. Disappropriation did occur: Worcester, for example, lost lands to Earls Hakon, Ranig and other Danes[2] while Danes acquired lands around the Fens. Cnut was a Christian king in his law codes, but also the murderous conqueror of 1017–19. In both respects English kings had gone before. Worcester lost land to ealdorman Eadric and the reeve Æfic in Æthelred's reign; murder had become a part of politics. Conquest can be royal rule writ large, though scale alters nature. It is in the witness lists of his charters that the enormous changes and instability of Cnut's early years can be measured,

---

1. For recent work on Cnut see K. Mack, 'Changing thegns, Cnut's conquest and the English aristocracy', *Albion*, 16 (1984), pp. 375–87; P. Stafford, 'The Laws of Cnut and the history of Anglo-Saxon royal promises', ASE, 10 (1981), pp. 173–90; A. Williams, 'Cockles among the wheat, Danes and English in the west Midlands in the first half of the eleventh century', *Midland History* 11 (1986), pp. 1–22. Scandinavian background in P. H. Sawyer, *Kings and Vikings* (1982) and E. Roesdahl, *Viking-Age Denmark* (1982)
2. A. Williams, *op. cit.* and *Chronicon Abbatiae Ramesiensis*, ed. W. D. Macray, Rolls Series (1886), pp. 129–43

the traumas of 1016–23 divined. To understand these years conquest must be recognized as a process not an event. Its nature depends on the circumstances in which it occurs, on the motives and situation of the conquerors, on their prior relations with the conquered and on the relative political, social, cultural and economic structures of both sides. Conquests though broadly comparable are individually unique.

1016 was the culmination of two decades of renewed Viking activity. The scale may have differed from that of the ninth century but the nature remained essentially the same. 'Viking' was a response to social and political pressures in Scandinavia,[3] to needs to amass booty to maintain authority. Authority was increasingly expressed through kings and kingdoms though these were still fragile and unstable. 'Norway', 'Sweden' and 'Denmark' are terms which belie the shifting overlordships of the North, as the history of Swegn or Olaf shows. Both were kings, but the authority of their dynasties was relatively recent. In Thorkell the Tall, Eric of Hlathir or Ulf Thorgilsson they faced rivals and equals rather than subjects and subordinates. Saint Olaf rose in Norway with a speed which only a world based on booty and personal loyalty would allow. Olaf began in exile, went 'viking' against Æthelred's England, gathered enough loot to win authority at home and threaten Danish kings to the south. Cnut dealt with him in battle but also by buying his followers with gifts.

From such a society Danish leaders came to England in the early eleventh century for booty and tribute. Although Swegn moved rapidly from tribute-taking to the desire to make the kingdom tributary, booty not land remained his goal. His followers recorded on runestones that they 'took the geld in England', but only when men and geld were back in Scandinavia. Settlement was not the inevitable outcome of Viking activity. After the submission of the English Swegn's first action was neither coronation nor land-taking, but a great tribute, whose scale left memories at Bury St Edmund's and Worcester and prompted Florence of Worcester to brand him a tyrant.[4] How Swegn would have acted had he lived longer cannot be known, but Cnut too saw England as a source of tribute and his followers shared his perception. Most of them returned to Scandinavia in 1018, rewarded by the colossal geld of 82,500 pounds of silver which Cnut had exacted. Such figures raise well-founded doubts about their accuracy.[5] But these were tributes from a conquered people not the taxes of a later medieval king. In his early years Cnut's actions were often contradictory, conciliatory and ruthless by turns. The contradictions were those of a northern king who had decided to stay as an English ruler. Heavy tribute answered the needs of his followers, murder and exile were the weapons to which he was accustomed, but his English ecclesiastical advisers taught him the ways of his predecessors.

Swegn and Cnut were not the only Scandinavians to come viking in England in the early eleventh century. Thorkell the Tall, his brother Hemming and probably Eilaf, the brother of Ulf Thorgilsson had all led armies with

3. P. Wormald, 'Viking studies, whence and whither', *The Vikings*, ed. R. T. Farrell (Chichester, 1982), pp. 128–53
4. Hermann 'De Miraculis S. Edmundi', *Memorials of St Edmund's Abbey*, ed. T. Arnold, Rolls Series, 96 (1890), pp. 35–9 and Fl. Wig. 1014
5. J. Gillingham, 'Levels of Danegeld and Heregeld in the early eleventh century' (forthcoming)

devastating success. These men operating independently were able to gather armies of a size to bring Æthelred's reign to crisis. Their success tempted Swegn back in 1013; fear of them goaded him. The *Encomium Emmae* may exaggerate when it claims that Thorkell ruled most of southern England by the end of Æthelred's reign,[6] but he is the lost counterpoint to the conquest of Swegn and the early years of Cnut. The Danish conquests in England between 1012 and 1017 were not a unity. Nothing suggests that Thorkell or other Scandinavians in England went over to Cnut before 1016 at the earliest. There is every reason to see him carving his own path between 1012 and 1016. Until 1016 that path included loyal defence of Æthelred and the taking of an English wife.[7] Swegn and Cnut faced in England men already important in Scandinavia and now independently established there.

None of Swegn's motives necessarily entailed remaining in England; for other leaders, perhaps especially those without kingdoms at home, staying on was attractive. Cnut in 1015 was in the latter category. At the time of his death Swegn had two sons, Cnut and Harold. Little is known of the latter, not even whether he was the elder.[8] Harold took Denmark in 1014. Thus when Cnut returned to England in 1015, he was setting out to acquire for himself a kingdom which his father had conquered. His aims included the English crown, though possibly as a prelude to an attempt against the Danish one and his brother.

His return led to a series of battles in 1015 and especially in 1016 of which Ashingdon was only the final one. Ashingdon was not a decisive battle, partition not conquest was its immediate result. That it was accepted as final has much to do with the struggle which preceded it. 1016 began with Æthelred still alive, but sick and dying. His son Edmund was in rebellion with the support of the North East Midlands and Northumbria. Wessex had already capitulated to Cnut and ealdorman Eadric. Early in the year Edmund tried to call out the English army (the *fyrd*). The divisive political situation prevented it. With Cnut in Wessex, the attitude of the area between Thames and Humber was critical. The Mercians, reluctant to join a rebellion, refused to fight, claiming that they would do so only if the king himself and the Londoners joined them. They stated that they would not fight against the West Saxons and Danes.[9] Support for Eadric their ealdorman was surely also in mind. There was thus no 'English' resistance properly so-called before the death of Æthelred.

Edmund was then accepted as king by the Londoners and probably Eastern England, but had lost the allegiance of Uhtred of Northumbria, who submitted to Cnut's ravaging. Edmund gained Wessex and fought against an army of Mercians and Danes at Sherston. From then until October London was the crux of the struggle. Edmund received help from the Welsh princes,[10] natural allies to one engaged against the ealdorman of Mercia responsible for raids into south Wales. It was not until late in the year, perhaps only weeks before Ashingdon that Eadric and those who remained with him joined Edmund. Until

6. Encomium, p. 11
7. Encomium, p. 89, Fl. Wig. s. a. 1021
8. Encomium, p. lvi
9. ASC and Fl. Wig. s. a. 1016
10. R. Poole, 'Skaldic verse and Anglo-Saxon history: some aspects of the period 1009–1016', *Speculum*, 62 (1987), pp. 265–98

the eve of Ashingdon the English were divided in their response to Cnut. At some point Thorkell and his army changes sides, probably after the death of Æthelred. The defeat at Ashingdon was attributed to Eadric's treachery: whether true or not the accusation captures the mood of 1016. Cnut's was not a simple Danish victory, but one aided by divisions amongst the English. Edmund's was not an English resistance. At no point did he lead an army onto the field from the whole of England. The nearest he came to it was at Ashingdon, and the disunity of its leaders may have been disastrous. The Chronicler's analysis of a leadership divided amongst itself is an accurate picture of 1016, of an England in which the forces for unity were still balanced by deep divisions.

Ashingdon ended the struggle. The exhaustion of men not necessarily anxious to fight was one factor; the Chronicler numbers the five times the *fyrd* was called out in 1016. Several key local leaders, including Ulfcytel of East Anglia and ealdorman Ælfric of East Wessex were killed. The battle may have provided proof of the unhealable divisions amongst the English nobility. Edmund and Cnut met at Gloucester; Cnut was to have his tribute and the kingdom was to be divided along the Thames. London came to terms separately with Cnut, and he took up winter quarters there.

The English nobility brought to 1016 a long experience of war and ravaging, a legacy of mistrust and a fear of backing the wrong side in a complicated struggle. The divisions, calculations and realizations which succeeded the snap victory at Hastings in 1066 preceded Ashingdon. Cnut suffered less internal opposition than William in his early years, a critical difference in the way their respective conquests unfolded.

How long the division of the kingdom would have held cannot be known; Edmund died before the end of the year. Cnut siezed the whole kingdom, in spite of the existence of Edmund's young sons, his adult brother Eadwig and two half brothers, Edward and Alfred. All were in England in 1016.[11] Cnut took power by sharing it with the two men most likely to oppose him effectively, Thorkell, who was made ealdorman of East Anglia, and Eadric. Cnut's companion in the campaign of 1015–16, Eric of Hlathir, was given Northumbria. The English æthelings were despatched in summary fashion: Eadwig exiled and murdered, Edmund's young sons exiled. Edward and Alfred returned to Normandy. Cnut faced a potential enemy in their uncle, the count of Normandy. In 1017 he offset that threat by marrying Emma, widow of Æthelred, mother of Edward and Alfred and sister of the count of Normandy. The exile and murder of princes and marriage to a predecessor's widow take us back into the kingdoms of the seventh and eighth centuries. Conquest had upset the fragile pattern of the tenth century.

Cnut could not feel secure. An enigmatic reference to Eadwig *Ceorls' king* hints at disorganized resistance. Edmund's sons remained alive and would eventually pass into the hands of the German Emperor, no friend to Cnut. Cnut's army remained in being throughout 1017. It was not paid off until 1018, by which time he had also murdered four prominent English nobles at the Christmas court of 1017. The paying off of his army coincided with his agreement to observe

11. *ibid.* and cf. Thietmar of Merseburg, EHD I, no. 27, p. 348

English law in the guise of the law of Edgar. Seen against the purges of 1017 and the tribute, the gesture was celebratory as much as conciliatory. Archbishop Wulfstan and the surviving English nobles saw themselves committing a conqueror to the laws of the English. Cnut welcomed the stress on his powers as an English king and the opportunity to hark back to Edgar, by-passing Æthelred, the father of dangerous claimants to the throne. At about this date he issued a coronation charter which centred on the vilification of his predecessor, and it was perhaps now that the feast of Edward the Martyr was declared, a reminder of the fratricidal bloodshed in which Æthelred's reign had begun.[12]

In 1019 Cnut returned to Denmark. Such may always have been his intention, or his claim to Denmark may have been raised only by his brother's death. From now Cnut's rule would straddle England and Denmark, and his absences would necessitate regents. Thorkell was the first in 1019–20. He was associated with Cnut in the building and consecration of the church at Ashingdon in 1020. Like Battle Abbey after 1066, Ashingdon minster was an ambiguous symbol; a gesture of conciliation for the dead on both sides, a deliberate reminder that military victory had secured the throne. It did not mark an end to the suspicions of the early years. Thorkell was exiled in 1021, though sufficiently favoured again by 1023 to be entrusted with rule in Denmark.

The translation of the relics of Archbishop Ælfheah in the same year can be read as an indication of continuing uneasiness, of old sores not fully healed. Ælfheah had been murdered by Thorkell's men in 1012 after refusing to allow a ransom to be raised from his own people. His cult had developed rapidly, a criticism of Æthelred's oppressive rule and taxation which Cnut was anxious to stress. Queen Emma attended the translation and brought the infant Harthacnut, her son by Cnut. The claims of her sons by Æthelred, princes across the water in Normandy, were not far from Cnut's mind. The public occasion allowed a reminder of Æthelred's gelds to be combined with a showing forth of Cnut and Emma's new heir. Thorkell had refused to endorse the brutal murder of Ælfheah; it had prompted him to turn from attack to alliance with Æthelred. Veneration of the archbishop's relics in 1023 could underscore the reconciliation between Thorkell and Cnut, but recalled Thorkell's allegiance to Æthelred. 1023 was no unambiguous symbol of a conquest completed.

The Laws of Cnut and the Chronicle speak of 'English' and 'Dane' after 1016; the distinction was not as clear as that between Norman and English in 1066. Cnut's followers who stayed in 1018 were as anxious as William's later to see their position protected,[13] and Cnut's law extended protection to them. But less united the Danes after 1016 than the Normans after 1066. Cnut's was a more personal insecurity than William's. Most of his army returned home and he had reasons to fear as much as to trust many of those who remained.

The charters and their witness lists underline the dramatic discontinuities of these years. The patterns of the tenth century are gone. There is no initial spate of land grants to lay nobles to create a basis of support. From the ealdormen

---

12. P. Wormald, 'Æthelred the lawmaker', *Ethelred the Unready*, ed. D. Hill (Oxford, 1978), p. 54
13. G. Garnett, '*Franci et Angli*, the legal distinctions between peoples after the Conquest', ANS, 8 (1986), pp. 109–37

downwards the court was full of new men. Some were Danes, especially initially the earls – Thorkell, Eric, Eilaf, Ranig and Hakon, and there were Danish thegns, especially in the early years. But it is not the Danishness, even of these first years, which is remarkable, but the instability and discontinuity. There are Englishmen enough, but not familiar ones. At the highest levels there were only two, Leofwine ealdorman in Mercia, the sole survivor of Æthelred's reign, and Godwine, the fastest rising star, the only English earl appointed in the first years of the reign, member of a family whose only previous recorded action was of semi-rebellion in 1009.

A long gap in the charters of the 1020s obscures these important years, but by the 1030s a settled situation had developed. Gone were the Danish earls except for Ranig and a new man, Siward in Northumbria; Danish thegns were now rare, Tofig the Proud and Osgod Clapa prominent in the royal household but exceptional. The court of the 1030s was neither Danish nor Anglo-Danish, but English, yet composed of Englishmen few of whose families were important in the tenth century or even the early eleventh. And already Earls Godwine and Leofric, son of Leofwine, and their sons were well established.

If the the tenth-century nobles had seen the court as a route of advance from father to son the rapid changes under Cnut shattered such expectations. Some profited, one or two spectacularly. Those who rise fast at such times of uncertainty are often the targets for suspicion and criticism. A dangerous isolation of the court nobility may have been the result,[14] though the widespread followings of Godwine, Harold or Leofric as recorded in Domesday belie such a conclusion. Insecurity, however, explains those followings. The wisest course in the eleventh century was to be a client of one of these great survivors. Political changes which shook up relations between king and nobles ironically entrenched the power of a handful of great families. Cnut's insecurity in 1017 led him to recreate enormous earldoms on the mid tenth-century model, and the circumstances of the mid eleventh century did nothing to disturb them. Godwine was later called *dux et baiulus*, earl and office bearer of almost the entire kingdom.[15] The adulatory Life of Edward the Confessor may exaggerate Godwine's uniqueness but not the scale of his power. In such changes lies the importance of Cnut's reign.

A foreign king, involved in the volatile politics of Scandinavia, Cnut was often absent from England. From 1019–20, 1022–23, 1025–26, 1027, 1028–29 the gaps in the charters mark the lack of the king's presence. Cnut's Scandinavian concerns did not exist in a watertight compartment without effect on the English kingdom. 1026–27 is an illuminating crisis. In 1026 Cnut was defeated in Denmark at the Holy River by the kings of Norway and Sweden joined by his brother-in-law Ulf, his regent in Denmark, and by Ulf's brother Eilaf. In the North defeat threatened Cnut's wide but fragile hegemony. In England it exposed the continuing insecurity. In 1027 Cnut was in Rome for the coronation of the Emperor Conrad; he was there to confirm allegiance. The attentions of the Emperors towards Denmark had been far from welcome, and in the aftermath of 1026 were more than Cnut needed. From Rome he sent a letter to

14. Thus K. Mack, *op. cit.*
15. *Life of King Edward*, ed. F. Barlow (Edinburgh, 1962), p. 6

the English, or to his regents. In it he told of the concession gained from the pope, that English archbishops need no longer travel to Rome for the pallium, and of the barriers and tolls on English merchants about which he had spoken with the princes of Europe. Cnut's letter was more than a record of a trading and diplomatic mission; it was a plea for loyalty when he felt threatened on all sides. In it he renewed the promise to rule justly made at the beginning of his reign:

> I have humbly vowed to Almighty God to amend my life from now on in all things, and to rule justly and faithfully the kingdoms and peoples subject to me and to maintain equal justice in all things and if hitherto anything contrary to what is right has been done through the intemperance of my youth or through negligence I intend to repair it all henceforth with the help of God . . .
> I command also all the sheriffs and reeves over my whole kingdom, as they wish to retain my friendship and their own safety, that they employ no unjust force against any man . . . for I have no need that money be amassed for me by unjust exaction[16]

The sort of terms Æthelred accepted in 1014 and Cnut repeated at his coronation were renewed in 1027. The growth of royal exactions and power were continuous themes of the tenth and eleventh centuries; the promises to restrain them were the products of political crises, especially those arising from war, conquest and insecurity in the eleventh century. In England Cnut's response to the crises of 1026–27 was that of an English king. Here that good lordship which brought loyalty meant more than the provision of booty.

In Scandinavia he acted more as a warlord. His brother-in-law Ulf was murdered, the loyalty of Olaf's followers won by gifts. Sighvat the Scald captures the flavour of his Northern politics. 'The king's (Olaf's) enemies were walking about with open purses; men offer the heavy metal for the priceless head of the king'.[17] Sighvat disapproved of the betrayal of a lord not of the distribution of the loot won in battle. 'Cnut, liberal with jewels, asked me if I would serve him as well as Olaf, the generous with rings'.[18] Sighvat was aware that a political world based on loot and gift-giving was distorted by Cnut's acquisition of the resources of England. In England Cnut's exactions fuelled the resentment which his letter sought to assuage.

English æthelings in Normandy or in Europe were uppermost in Cnut's mind in 1027; hence his presence at the Imperial coronation and his abortive attempt to marry his sister Estrith, conveniently widowed by his murder of Ulf, to Robert of Normandy. The Norman threat was real. Robert assembled a fleet on behalf of Edward and Alfred; William of Malmesbury identified it with the rotting hulks still visible in northern France in the twelfth century.[19] The testimony of Jumièges or Malmesbury might be suspect, written after the Normans had incorporated Edward's early life into a story of lifelong Norman aid in gratitude for which Edward offered the English throne. Dudo, writing in the 1020s, confirms Norman designs on England, but speaks not of helping æthelings but of claims based on putative agreements dating back to the early

16. EHD I no. 53, 10–12, pp. 477–8
17. EHD I no. 18, 16, p. 339
18. EHD I no. 18, 7, p. 339
19. William of Jumièges, in R. Allen Brown, *The Norman Conquest* (1984), p. 8 and William of Malmesbury Bk II, cap. 180

tenth century.[20] The conquest of Cnut, like the later conquest of William, opened the way for many claims. The English throne was coming to appear not just a desirable but an attainable prize.

William of Malmesbury attributed Godwine's rise to the gratitude of Cnut after Godwine rallied the English in 1027.[21] The timing is wrong, Godwine was already important. But William's general analysis carries conviction. Cnut's absences, and the problem of handling a delicate English situation during them, were the root of Godwine's as of Emma's power. Emma stressed her own significance as uniter of English and Dane and her descent from a victorious Norman people.[22] Marriage as peace-weaving and the importance of a wife's ancestry were stereotypes in the pictures of early medieval women, but drew their force from their continuing applicability. Emma had knowledge of England and formed a bond with Normandy. Her role at court and in royal patronage was greater than that of any royal woman since Eadgifu. She surpassed Ælfthryth in exercising power during the life of a husband not solely in the reign of a son. The court of a foreign king provided new opportunities for women as for courtiers. Emma's continued power, even more than that of Godwine or Leofric, turned on the succession issue. And that had already taken on the extraordinary complexity which was a characteristic of eleventh-century England.

The partisan arguments and rapidly moving situation which followed Cnut's death have obscured his intentions for the succession. But plans he almost certainly had. A king with three sons, two wives and three kingdoms faced with rival princes from an older dynasty and surrounded by new men who had risen in his reign would hardly have been allowed to neglect succession. His plans were, as the disagreements following 1035 showed, subject to interpretation, perhaps not least because Cnut's own position had changed during the course of his reign and with it the nature of the succession question.

Cnut had married twice, first and before 1017 to Ælfgifu, daughter of the murdered ealdorman Ælfhelm, and second, 1017, to Emma. By Ælfgifu he had two sons, Swegn and Harold Harefoot, probably, though not necessarily born before 1017. Ælfgifu did not disappear after Cnut's marriage to Emma. She and her elder son Swegn were sent to rule Norway in 1030. Emma produced two children, a daughter Gunnhild and a son Harthacnut, the latter born in or before 1023. The status of these two unions and thus of the children born of them was a key argument in 1035. Emma called Ælfgifu a concubine and hedged her bets by stating that Harold was not in any case a son of Ælfgifu and Cnut.[23] Suspicion was not sufficiently widespread to prevent large numbers of the English nobility offering allegiance to Harold. Emma hedged her bet since she and her party must have appreciated the problems of arguing about the nature of marriage in the eleventh century. Emma's own union had been as full and secure as its political importance in 1017 could make it, and she enjoyed the benefits of a wife and queen at court as a result of it. But Cnut had not relegated the children

20. Dudo of St Quentin, *De Moribus et Actis Primorum Normanniae Ducum*, ed. J. Lair, Société des Antiquaires de Normandie (Caen, 1865), pp. 147–8, 158–60 and compare 265
21. William of Malmesbury, Bk II, cap. 181
22. *Encomium*, pp. 7 and 33
23. *ibid.* p. 41

of Ælfgifu to illegitimate oblivion. He had recognized Swegn and his claims on inheritance when he sent him to Norway and Harthacnut to Denmark to rule as his regents. Swegn, though older, was given the acquired land, Harthacnut the patrimony; Harchacnut's greater legitimacy was confirmed. But Cnut's actions point to a hierarchy of claims on family land, not the rigid exclusiveness of legitimacy and illegitimacy.

Emma asserted that at their marriage in 1017 Cnut had promised on oath that he would 'never set up the son of any other woman to rule after him'.[24] Edward the Confessor himself accepted the reality of that oath before and after his return to England in 1041. The problem for Emma was that the Cnut of 1017 was not the ruler of *c.*1030. In 1017 the oath applied to England. In the intervening years Cnut had acquired Denmark and Norway. It was now possible for Harthacnut to succeed to the Danish throne and patrimony, and for Ælfgifu's sons to have the acquisitions of England and Norway. Swegn was despatched to Norway, Harthacnut to Denmark: was Harold's continuing presence in England a sign of his fathers intentions? If nothing more Cnut had opened further the possibility of claims on Harold's behalf. Harold and his mother had family ties and supporters among the English nobility to press them. Earl Leofric may himself have been a kinsman.[25]

Contemporary issues and the rivalries of the nobility once again found expression in dispute over the succession. The costs of a dual monarchy were embodied in the fleet based in London and in the taxation necessary to maintain it. Many English nobles may have seen in Harold a king who, unlike Harthacnut, would detach England from Denmark and the costs of battle there, would rule in person. English disunity again surfaced, with Wessex and Mercia separated as in the 950s. But the role of regional identity as opposed to political faction is as debatable now as then. Rivalry between Godwine and Leofric may already have been surfacing, between the newly risen man and the only representative of the tenth-century nobility. In 1014–16 the relative absence of monolithic earldoms allowed the divisions among the English nobility to express themselves in bewildering geographical patterns. Under Cnut the emergence of great earldoms in Wessex and Mercia in the hands of men exceptionally powerful at court provided a focus for local feeling. Separatism could wax in such circumstances, but the interests of Leofric or Godwine held it in check. Their struggle was for the English throne not for division. Conquest, like unification in the early tenth century, had placed more than one kingdom in a king's hands and strengthened the arguments in favour of providing for all sons. In the events after 1035 the politics of Cnut's reign were revealed: the power of the queen and the earls, involvement in the North and with Normandy, the costs of war and mercenaries, a succession made more complex by conquest and the acquisiton of new kingdoms.

Harold Harefoot and Harthacnut, 1035–42

The death of Cnut on 12 November 1035 precipitated the crisis. Two half-brothers, both backed by a mother and her supporters, faced each other in a classic family drama. In the background stood other claimants, survivors of the

24. *ibid* pp. 33 and 49
25. *The Charters of Burton Abbey*, ed. P. H. Sawyer (Oxford, 1979), p. xliii

dynasty of Æthelred. Fraternal and dynastic rivalry was tortuously entwined in the person of Emma. The widow of Æthelred as well as Cnut, she had three sons, Edward, Alfred and Harthacnut. To compound the problem, Harthacnut was in Denmark in 1035, and did not return to England until 1040. Between 1035 and 1040 political choices were exceptionally difficult, a minefield in which careers and reputations could be blown apart.

Between 1035 and 1037 claims were made on behalf of Harthacnut, Harold Harefoot, Edward and Alfred. A claim was only as good as its support, and in this case Godwine and Leofric were the arbiters of the situation, though the fleet in London and Cnut's housecarls had their role. Edward and Alfred attracted little if any support. Their brief visit to England in 1036 resulted only in the murder of Alfred, a tragedy which cast a shadow across the mid eleventh century comparable to the disappearance of the Princes in the Tower in the late fifteenth. Harold Harefoot made good his claim by 1037, and Emma was exiled to Flanders. Harthacnut resisted the outcome, and had already gathered a fleet to attack England before his brother's untimely death in 1040. His own brief reign did not resolve the tense situation; when he associated his half-brother Edward with him in kingship in 1041, he only underscored his insecurity. The bare bones of these events are provided by laconic chronicle entries which cannot be accurately dated or placed and are fleshed out by partisan account and special pleading. Additional evidence from the coinage is doubly welcome,[26] though its apparent neutrality is no justification for using it to impose our own interpretation. Partisan though it may be, a source like the *Encomium Emmae* forces us to listen to an interpretation current in the mid eleventh century. Its evidence of the arguments, acrimony and suspicion which were the legacy of these years is essential to an understanding of mid-century politics. Unlike 956–59, we have here an almost contemporary account emanating from an actor in the drama.

The division of the kingdom in 1035/6 is the the only dispute of the tenth and eleventh centuries to show up in the coinage. This apparent testimony to the novelty of the situation is in reality a product of the greater central control over the coinage than in the only comparable dispute in 955–57. That control meant that a split in the kingdom sufficiently deep to produce the acceptance of different rulers can be timed and followed at local mints which struck coin in the names of different kings. A division of England followed quickly after Cnut's death. It was between Harold and Harthacnut, and was an agreed one: a new coinage was issued simultaneously in the name of each. The decision must have been made at the meeting at Oxford late in 1035 or early in 1036. At that meeting Leofric, the men north of the Thames and the fleet in London supported Harold, who was in England, Godwine and the chief men of Wessex held out against him. Only Harold and Harthacnut were serious contenders. The Thames marked the boundary of coins struck in the name of each king. But Harthacnut's absence raised the further problem of regency, and Harold's supporters pressed his claim to be regent for his brother's share.[27] Emma and

26.   T. Talvio, 'Harold I and Harthacnut's *Jewel Cross* type reconsidered', *Anglo-Saxon Monetary History*, ed. M. A. S. Blackburn (Leicester, 1986), pp. 273–90
27.   ASC MS E 1035

Godwine opposed it, and Emma took the royal treasure and with it the regency of Wessex, with Godwine and the royal household troop as backing.

The coinage shows that their control was short lived. Even before his accession to the entire kingdom in 1037, Harold's rule was being recognized at mints throughout southern England. The closure of the die-cutting centre at Winchester, which was Emma's stronghold, presumably coincided with Harold's move against her in 1036 and his seizure of the royal treasure. 'Opinion was veering towards Harold' stated MS C of the Chronicle; the coinage does not tell how or why, but demonstrates the fact. The increasing quandary of Godwine can only be guessed.

It was in 1036 that Edward and Alfred were invited to England. The invitation is beyond doubt, its authorship vigorously disputed. A letter in Emma's name could not be denied, but Emma later claimed that Harold forged it. Both had motives: Emma anxious to have a son on the spot in a deteriorating situation, Harold concerned to get other potential claimants into his clutches. Edward went straight to his mother at Winchester, but Alfred journeyed from the South East and came into Godwine's hands at Guildford. Godwine and other great men were later accused of deliberately intercepting him and of the murder of Alfred's companions, and ultimately of the prince himself.[28] Emma told of an attack on them by Harold's men when they were in the evidently inadequate guardianship of Godwine. Godwine was implicated, in turning a blind eye if not in the murder itself as he changed sides to Harold. At no time in 1035–36 can Godwine be seen as a supporter of the sons of Æthelred, but of Harthacnut and Emma.

When Godwine and other great men switched allegiance, Harold gained control of all England. The chroniclers are unanimous in making this a desertion of Harthacnut; the claims of Edward and Alfred were not taken seriously. Emma was exiled and fled, not to Normandy, but to Flanders. She may have judged the turmoil of Normandy during William's minority unsafe; Flanders had been a haven for English exiles since the mid tenth century. Emma had not given up. She summoned Edward, who declined to press claims which had attracted so little backing.[29] Harthacnut was now willing, and temporarily relieved of the problems which had detained him in Denmark. By 1039 he had collected a fleet and sailed to join his mother in Bruges. Harold's death precluded the need for invasion. Embarrassed English nobles hastened to welcome and accept his brother.

Such events could not fail to muddy the politics of the mid eleventh century. By 1041, when the *Encomium* was written, the question of Alfred's death and the involvement in it of Emma and Godwine already crystallized the legacy of these years. Paradoxically it was Godwine and Emma rather than Leofric who had much to explain, first to Harthacnut and then to Edward. Leofric had been consistent in his support for Harold; where Godwine and Emma had been drawn into fancy footwork he at least had led off with steps he could follow. Godwine and Emma had the albatross of 1035–39 around their necks. Had Emma upheld the claims of *all* her sons, and how vigorously? Did she share any guilt in luring one of them to his death? The *Encomium* was her answer. She at

28. ASC MS C 1036
29. Encomium, p. 49.

least was identified with the claims of her sons, was exiled on Harold's accession, carried no incubus from his brief reign. She could claim that the decisions of the English nobles constantly restricted her choices.

Godwine was in more difficulty. He had supported Harthacnut but his attitude to Edward and Alfred in 1036 and his involvement in Alfred's murder embarrassed him with Harthacnut let alone Edward. Godwine was one of those whose choices swung the balance. He had options in 1036/7 closed to Emma. In taking advantage of them he had created a dilemma for himself when Harold died and Harthacnut returned. Edward's association in the kingship in 1041 faced Godwine with two kings, neither of whom he had consistently supported, one of whom had reason to feel betrayed by him, both of whom could hold the death of their brother against him. Godwine has left no *Encomium* to tell his tale; his gifts of fully-armed ships to both kings were designed to erase the past.

Accusations flew thick and fast after 1041. Some of them were obviously strategic. Lyfing, bishop of Worcester, was arraigned for his part in the murder of Alfred. His accuser was the archbishop of York, still trying to recover the Worcester see for his archbishopric. Many men had changed sides in 1036/7, the 'other great men who had power'[30] could be implicated in Alfred's death, though by 1041 Godwine above all others had been singled out. Political murder does not have to be excused to recognize that protracted succession disputes create problems. Choices are made, sides taken, and when one side wins, as in 959 or 978, opponents come to terms with the victor. 1037 was different in that it was so soon reversed. Allegiance must be switched again, with inevitable strains on a political system in which personal loyalty was the ideal. Such an ideal cannot cope with internal conflict or rapid changes of dynasty and ruler.

What is new about eleventh-, as opposed to tenth-century succession, is not dispute, but a protracted period of rapid reversal and doubt over the succession. It was those who came back who posed the eleventh-century problem, Æthelred in 1014, Harthacnut in 1040, Edward in 1041 and, in a different way, Godwine and the other exiles of the Confessor's reign. When a victor emerges only after one or two reversals his original supporters may be the most suspect to him, no one may appear reliable. Over Godwine also hung political murder; more than a simple acceptance of fortune's reversal, a hastening of it on. The significance of the murder of Alfred was determined by the outcome of events, by the return of Harthacnut and Edward. The meaning of action derives from the constant reshaping of the past by the evolution of the present.

> Harthacnut imposed a very severe tax . . . and all who wanted him before were then ill-disposed towards him . . . he did nothing worthy of a king as long as he ruled.[31]

Harthacnut's brief reign (summer 1040 until 8 June 1042) was remembered for taxation. Harold and Cnut had maintained a fleet of sixteen ships, which would have meant an annual heregeld of *c.* £5,500. Harthacnut's invasion fleet was almost four times as big and had to be paid off. Taxation becomes an open

30. ASC MS C 1036
31. ASC MS C 1040

grudge in the Chronicles. The payment of this exceptionally high heregeld is associated with the first recorded instant of price-inflation: wheat rose to 55 pence a sester and even higher.[32] Perception matters as much as economic reality; eleventh-century chroniclers were beginning to mention taxation and to link it with other evils. As rule came to be experienced as oppressive, a sour critical note entered the judgement of kings. Geld and fleets were still in the forefront in 1041. By now Harthacnut had reduced his fleet to 32 ships, still double that of his father. Insecurity led him to retain his fleet, taxation to pay it compounded grumbling insecurity. In 1041 he had Worcestershire ravaged because the men of Worcester had murdered two housecarls collecting tax. The ravaging was carried out by an army led by the earls north of the Thames. In the atmosphere of the 1040s proof of loyalty was necessary.

Faced with such unpopular action, no chronicler tried to gloss or explain Harthacnut. When he dug up Harold's body and threw it into the Thames, it was the vindictive act of an unworthy king.[33] He 'betrayed' Earl Eadwulf of Northumbria whilst he was under his safe-conduct at court which made him 'a pledge-breaker'.[34] Such events are inexplicable without their background. Northern sources make Siward, earl of York responsible for this murder, in quest of power over all Northumbria. Longer perspective would place it in the continuous efforts of Cnut and Harthacnut to establish authority in the far north of England, which had slipped into semi-independence under the house of Bamburgh in the 1020s and 1030s.[35] For the chroniclers they merely proved the nature of a man who came to a fitting end when he died a sudden death, fearfully convulsed as he stood at his drink at the marriage feast of Tofig the Proud.

The one-dimensional representation may seem unfair, but the mood of 1040–42 is recaptured. The chroniclers articulate a readiness to criticize born out of taxation, insecurity and accusation. That mood may, as in 1014–16, have been widely felt. 1014–16 provided an inadequate yardstick to measure the long reign of Æthelred. The reign of Harthacnut was brief enough to be dominated by it.

In this atmosphere Edward, the future Confessor, was recalled to England in 1041 and sworn in as king during his brother's lifetime. Was Harthacnut foreseeing his early death? Or does the invitation belong in the circumstances of 1041? Normandy was a possible threat, Edward's claims a more likely rallying point within England by this time. No ruler could now feel secure with rivals, and associating the remaining one in kingship was an alternative to murdering him. Emma's influence need not be discounted. In 1041 if not in 1035 she was asserting the claims of all her sons. Were there even plans to divide Denmark and England between the brothers, or at least to have Edward as a regent in England while Harthacnut attended to the North? Denmark posed its own problems, and Harthacnut's cousin Swegn Estrithson was in England for some purpose between 1035 and 1042.

32. ASC MS E 1040, M. K. Lawson, 'The collection of Danegeld and Heregeld in the reigns of Æthelred II and Cnut', *EHR*, 99 (1984), pp. 721–38, and J. Gillingham, 'Levels of Danegeld and Heregeld in the early eleventh century' (forthcoming)
33. ASC MS C 1040
34. ASC MS C 1041
35. W. Kapelle, *The Norman Conquest of the North* (1979), pp. 22–6

Emma's hopes were for a trinity of rule, mother and sons together, akin perhaps to the 940s as a way of damping down family tensions. But Emma's past did not fit her to be another Eadgifu. Like Godwine she trailed clouds of doubt behind her, twenty years of her marriage to Cnut, let alone the decisions she had made in 1035/6. She could explain her actions, but to need to do so remained a problem. Harthacnut, Edward and Emma could only be a trinity of suspicion. Despite the accession of both her sons, Emma was never again to enjoy the prominence of Cnut's reign.

It is difficult and dangerous to propose turning points in history. In the political story of the eleventh century there are many candidates for consideration: the later years of Æthelred, with the domination of politics by external attack and internal demands; the rule of a foreign king, cumulating military demands with insecurity and the effects of absence; an exceptionally complicated succession crisis which forced newly powerful men to make difficult political choices, and then with consummate irony reversed them, driving a wedge of suspicion between rulers and their most powerful subjects. Loyalty remained at the heart of the political system, but conquest and dynastic change revealed its fragility and inadequacy as a spring of action. Taxation turned the unacceptable face of kingship at a time when many were ready to see it. If the politics of the mid eleventh century look sordid and calculating that is not solely a function of fuller sources. A strong kingship, one legacy of the tenth century, was deployed at a time of uneasy and rapid political change in a kingdom increasingly involved with its neighbours.

5

Edward the Confessor to Harold II, 1042–66[1]

The historiographical problems which surround all the best-known tenth- and eleventh-century kings are rarely more acute than for Edward the Confessor and Harold. The shadow of 1066 lies across them, not only in the accounts of twelfth-century chroniclers, but in virtually contemporary accounts and in the often partisan work of modern historians. For Norman accounts, and those modern historians who have followed them, the period is a prelude to 1066, a story of promises and undertakings made to William. For an English account like that of *The Life of Edward*, it is a tale of the rise and importance of Godwine and his family. For William of Malmesbury in the twelfth or E.A. Freeman in the nineteenth century it was still both of these. These are not years which can be seen separately from the accumulation of historical controversy.

William of Malmesbury was acutely aware of the problem when he remarked that English and Norman often told a different tale. What he had in mind were not merely the rival interpretations of the Godwine family as dominating or loyal, but flat contradictions, like that between William of Poitiers and Florence of Worcester on the consecration of Harold. Whilst William has a perjured Harold chosen by a minority and consecrated by the unholy Stigand,[2] Florence states that he was nominated by Edward, chosen by the chief magnates of all England and crowned by Archbishop Ealdred of York.[3] What constitutes a majority may be a moot question, who performed a consecration is a simple question of fact. Such contradiction raises the possibility that post-1066 sources not merely selected and judged, but suppressed or even fabricated. Florence and William are not irreconcilable: Harold, like most earlier kings, was probably crowned by both archbishops; each writer chose to mention only the one which

---

1. For studies of this very contentious reign see F. Barlow, *Edward the Confessor* (1970); on the vexed question of the succession compare D. C. Douglas, 'Edward the Confessor, Duke William of Normandy and the English succession', *English Historical Review*, (1953), pp. 526–65, M. Campbell, 'Earl Godwine of Wessex and Edward the Confessor's promise of the throne to Duke William', *Traditio*, no. 28 (1972), pp. 141–58 and E. John, 'Edward the Confessor and the Norman Succession', *English Historical Review*, (1979) pp. 241–67 with Barlow.
2. William of Poitiers, *Gesta Guillelmi ducis Normannorum et regis Anglorum*, in *The Norman Conquest*, ed. R. Allen Brown (1984), p. 26
3. Fl. Wig. 1066, EHD II, no. 2 p. 225

case. But when only one side of the story has survived, as with the Norman claims about promises of the throne made to William the Conqueror or Harold's oath to William *c*.1064, the area of doubt and debate has been wide.

The most recent attempt to put Edward back into his reign and to unfold a narrative unaffected by 1066 is Barlow's biography of Edward the Confessor. He has turned especially to the allegedly contemporary Anglo-Saxon Chronicles and has emphasized the development of the political situation, both in England and among its neighbours, while according central significance to the character of Edward himself. The Anglo-Saxon Chronicles C, D and E, more doubtfully the lost Chronicle believed to underlie Florence of Worcester, are central to any understanding of the reign. Only C and E can be counted as strictly contemporary, and in C the long entries for 1065 and 1066 were written after Harold's death.[4] E is often presented as a Godwinist chronicle, which may point to a retrospective account produced in debate after 1066. As with C, 1065–66 were probably written up after Hastings. But in earlier entries E is a South East England, St Augustine's Kent chronicle not a Godwinist one. Events in Wales, which the emphatically Godwinist *Life of Edward* uses to Harold's credit, are largely ignored in E. Neither Godwine nor Harold are key figures in its account. In 1051–52, Godwine's actions are described because they impinge on Kent, but it is C not E which describes Godwine's warm reception in South East England on his return from exile, while E talks of his ravaging and hostage-taking. If E has any slant on these dramatic years, it is to present them to exonerate not Godwine but rather the men of South East England who provided his foothold for return in 1052. It is an account written soon after the events, perhaps when Godwine's illness in 1053 made the situation worrying for those who had supported him.

D and Florence of Worcester have no status as strictly contemporary chronicles. Though both draw on earlier sources, both were written long after 1066. It is possible that both were influenced by Norman arguments, whether simply aware of them or trying to rebut them. Florence's account of the consecration of Harold in 1066 is a mirror-image of the Norman version given by William of Poitiers. Florence presents the military debates of 1047 and 1048 as straight divisions between Godwine and 'Leofric and all the people'. Florence thought well of Leofric; in an account of debates recollected a generation or more later and after Norman vilification of Godwine, Leofric may have become a hero to Godwine's villain. In 1052 the near-contemporary MS C spoke of *Frenchmen* expelled; Florence made them *Normans* and named them as including holders of castles in the Welsh marches.[5] A Worcester chronicler like Florence was well placed to supply names. But when he turns the neutral 'French' into a Norman party in the events of 1051/2 we must remember that he knew that Normans would take over in 1066, that he was privy to their arguments after that date that Edward the Confessor had been especially partial to Normans.

A chronicle similar to D was one of Florence's sources. These two are alone in mentioning requests for military aid from Swegn of Denmark which Edward

4. see the remark at the end of the 1065, 'Harold was now consecrated king and he met little quiet. . . as long as he ruled the realm'
5. Fl. Wig. 1047, 1048, 1052, EHD II, no. 2 pp. 216–17, 221, 225

refused in 1047 and 1048. But D is a northern chronicle compiled at the end of the eleventh century when Danish claims to the English throne seemed especially important in northern England. What seemed important to its writer may have been less so in the 1040s. D's judgements and insertions often betray a post-1066 northern perspective. It was interested in the family of Edward the Ætheling, whose daughter Margaret was by now queen of Scotland. It waxes eloquent on his return and death in 1057, and laments the failure to choose Edward's son Edgar the Ætheling in 1066; the first was 'to the misfortune of this poor people', the second the reason why 'the worse it grew from day to day'. The fall of Godwine and his family in 1051 is an occasion for moralistic comment on his rise and fall. The fatalism of this chronicler who knew of the dire consequences for northern England of 1066 has tinged many later accounts of 1042–66. When he stresses that Godwine had come to rule the king and all England, he echoes post-conquest comment on Godwine as much as contemporary assessment.

D is the only one of the Anglo-Saxon Chronicles to mention William's visit to England in 1051. Norman sources later associated 1051 with the promise of the throne by Edward to William.[6] Is D merely repeating Norman propaganda? Can it be used as independent corroboration of that visit? The fact that D makes no mention of any promise made to William inspires confidence. So too does the fact that D ignores the story of Harold's oath in 1064, which was central to Norman propaganda. D may be independent witness to the visit. But the visit may only have looked important after 1066, the singling of it out may distort the relationship among a series of events in that year. Neither contemporary account in C or E felt the visit mattered. The present imposes its own patterns of relevance on the past. Every major change in the present taps the kaleidoscope and the pieces reassemble. 1066 and its aftermath were blows which rearranged the story of the mid eleventh century.

The historiographical complexity of these years calls for a clear statement of methodology. I have relied heavily on C and E as giving a pre-1066 view, according a lesser status to the additional details in D and Florence. None of these sources, alone or combined, can provide the full political situation, the gamut of contemporary views or the full range of events seen at the time as significant, let alone those which might have had a bearing on developments. I have thus drawn on comparison with the actions of earlier eleventh- or tenth-century kings. No narrative simply allows the sources to speak. They are prompted by questions in a dialogue with historians who engage as neutral but always as informed participants. I approach the reign of Edward with a knowledge of tenth- and eleventh-century history, especially of that of the 1030s. I have assumed that the facts though not the interpretations, weightings and judgement of post-1066 writers, including Norman propagandists, are accurate. Eleventh-century chroniclers did not understand propaganda in the twentieth-century sense, though they share common techniques in stereotyping enemies, reducing complicated situations to black and white, selecting and interpreting events and motives to fit argument, omitting and suppressing. But mass commmunication coupled with an ability to control what is known have

6. William of Poitiers, *op. cit.*, p. 20 and William of Jumièges, in *ibid.* p. 13

altered propaganda. In the eleventh century those who were to be convinced were usually in a position to know or check. Writers explain and justify, though admittedly often to an audience ready to accept their line. The eclipse of the Old English nobility after 1066 still leaves Norman sources suspect, removing the audience who might have known and could have checked. And Norman arguments were not necessarily produced primarily for an English audience. But in William's early years when the Norman arguments evolved, the Old English nobility were still there, and it is not clear that their total replacement was planned. They, and at the very least English churchmen, had to be provided with acceptable arguments for allegiance to a new king.

Edward the Confessor, 1042–66

Accession and the 1040s

In 1042 Edward succeeded to a crown in which he had already been associated, one of the least troubled accessions of these centuries. Yet William of Malmesbury tells how Edward was so uncertain of his situation that he considered returning to Normandy and was only persuaded to remain in England by Godwine, who offered to bolster his security in return for firm friendship, honour for his sons and marriage with his daughter;[7] Florence claims that Godwine and Lyfing of Worcester exerted their influence to secure Edward's accession, and the *Life of Edward* stresses Godwine's instrumentality.[8] None of these is untinged by later views of Godwine, but all agree that Edward needed support in 1042.

Was Edward insecure, and did that additionally force him into a possibly unwilling dependence on Godwine? There were rivals, though not pressing ones. The allegation of Magnus of Norway's interest in the English throne is based on flimsy evidence, though designs on the kingdom taken by Cnut in 1016 need have had no strong basis. There were Danish claimaints. Cnut's nephew, Swegn Estrithson, had problems in the North, but his brother Beorn and Cnut's niece Gunnhild and her sons were all in England in 1042. Edward however had the advantage of the 1041 designation, and if he lacked support, so, *a fortiori*, did the others.

Edward had been in England for little over twelve months, and prior to that not for more than twenty years. His 1036 sally had proved that there was no automatic party in favour of the old dynasty and his rule had begun in association with Harthacnut, a man whose name was synonymous with taxation. On the other hand, there may have been backing by 1042 for a king who would rule England alone, without the expenses and absences of a Danish connection. For some people military demands and taxation continued to hang over the 1040s, witness the C chronicle's continuing interest in prices, in fleets and their size and in the gradual disbanding of the fleet in 1049–50. Circumstances were not bad enough to force Edward into Godwine's arms, but he could only have welcomed the backing of so powerful a man. Godwine's sons, Swegn and

7.　William of Malmesbury, Bk II caps. 196 and 197
8.　Fl. Wig. 1042, EHD II no. 2, p. 215; *Life of King Edward*, ed. F. Barlow (Edinburgh, 1962), p. 9

Harold, were advanced to earldoms in 1043/4 and his daughter Edith married the king in January 1045. If there was ill-feeling between the king and Godwine Edward had a strange way of showing it.

Edward's attack on his mother and her property in 1043 encapsulates the problem of interpreting the situation at his accession. Emma was a powerful woman, but forty years at court can accumulate more enemies than friends and she above all was linked with the unpopular rule of Harthacnut. Edward rode against her taking the three earls Godwine, Leofric and Siward with him. Formidable Emma may have been, but the degree of overkill suggests a man uncertain of his position. Edward's motives are not given, but his actions point to dislike of Emma's political influence (her appointee Stigand was deposed) and a desire for her wealth and property, assets Edward lacked. Emma was not the first or last dowager seen as an obstacle by her family and deprived by a son anxious to begin marriage negotiations of his own. Edward may also have felt Emma had done less for him than she might. Are these actions to be weighted in support of Edward's insecurity, or used to suggest a capricious and vindictive nature? Personality is unknowable in the eleventh century, and it is difficult to identify any consistent principles or overriding circumstances guiding Edward's actions in the 1040s. Rabid anti-Danishness can scarcely be reconciled with the appointment of Beorn to an earldom in 1045. The evidence for fraught or deteriorating relations with Godwine boils down to suspect statements in Florence of a division of opinion between him and the king over aid to Swegn. Edward tried to act like his predecessors, but in the circumstances of the mid eleventh century he was constrained by the increasing involvement of neighbouring rulers in English affairs and the legacy of the 1030s.

Edward's early years were marked by a series of exiles: Gunnhild and her sons in 1044, Osgod Clapa in 1046, Swegn son of Godwine in 1046–7. Exile was a feature of his reign: Godwine in 1051, Earl Ælfgar in 1055 and 1058, Tostig in 1065. As a political weapon exile dates back at least to Æthelred II's reign. Its importance in the eleventh century was a result of conquest and dynastic change. Exile was an effective but dangerous tool. It was preceded by legal process, accompanied by forfeiture and followed by the distribution of the exile's lands and offices, creating vested interest against return. But return was the danger, and in the reign of Edward became the recurrent problem. Of the exiles listed, only Gunnhild and her sons failed to stage a comeback. The justice of exile, rising from the murky mixture of politics and law, was always arguable. What encouraged attempts to overturn it from the 1040s to the 1060s was not necessarily the feeling that injustice was growing, though that may have entered perceptions, but the realization that it could be challenged.

England's neighbours provided the means for that challenge. Exiles found refuge in foreign courts: Flanders was favoured, but Ælfgar's Mercian connections took him to Wales, the ecclesiastical exiles of 1052 went to Normandy, Harold in 1051 to Ireland while Tostig in 1066 did the grand tour, taking in Flanders and Scotland if not Normandy en route. In these havens exiles could hope to recruit forces to enable their return. On occasion their hosts came with them, as Gruffudd accompanied Ælfgar. More often the opportunity hosts provided was used to recruit ships. Hosts, but especially adventurers, were drawn into the train of returning exiles by the prospect of plunder. Fleets and exiles joined natural disaster and taxation in the Chroniclers' litanies of woe. Successful example encouraged imitators. The ease with which fleets could be assembled and their booty disposed of in Flanders or Normandy unsettled the finely poised relationship between an English king and his great nobility. The English nobility were initiated into a pattern of activity to which many resorted in exile after 1066; little wonder that the reception many of them received in England after 1066 was mixed or hostile.

The refuge they provided made England's neighbours an indirect threat, whilst the harbouring of exiles drew neighbours into English politics and made them aware of its internal problems. The direct threat of foreign raiding grew, whether as an accompaniment to a noble's comeback or as independent enterprise. A pattern going back to Æthelred's reign was again intensified by mid century. Attacks from Wales, by Gruffudd of Gwynedd but also by southern Welsh kings, threats around the English Channel and Thames from Scandinavian adventurers, forays by the Scots show the English kingdom vulnerable and attractive. The response was organization of the marches, and the harbouring of exiles in return. Siward was encouraged into such action in the North (see below). Swegn's appointment in 1043/4 followed by that of Edward's nephew, Ralf in 1047[9], were intended to organize the Welsh marches. It would be surprising if no attempt had been made to reorganize the defences of vulnerable South East England.

The South East coast suffered from no lack of ships as a basis for defence. In 1049 Godwine raised 42 ships from this area and in 1052 he was able to assemble a great fleet by seizing ships from Pevensey, Romney, Hythe, Folkestone, Dover and Sandwich. Edward's experience of raising fleets in the 1040s could have convinced him that his own permanent fleet of fourteen or sixteen ships was unnecessary, especially given the unpopularity of the heregeld which had to be raised to pay for it. The answer to the defence of South East England lay not in an increased royal fleet, but in the organization of marches, akin to those of Wales, in the hands of his own family. It lay also in the use of that family to cut off the bases for exiles or marauders on the southern coasts of the English channel. This is a debatable interpretation of Edward's actions, and entails reappraisal of relations with Normandy and Flanders, but it fits the concerns of the 1040s. His father-in-law Godwine and brother-in-law Harold had been allowed and encouraged to amass concentrations of land in Sussex and Essex.[10] A Flemish marriage for his brother-in-law Tostig was negotiated. Kent remained vulnerable. The shire was dominated by the landholding not of king or earl but of the archbishops. Here perhaps Edward planned to draw in his continental relatives, his brother-in-law Eustace of Boulogne and his nephew William of Normandy with whom he also sought alliance as 'Channel' princes. Both Eustace and William later made claims in England. William's re-reading after 1066 of all promises and negotiations into claims on the throne obscures their original purposes. But garrisons and castles on the south coast, including at Dover where Eustace went in 1051, could lie behind them. They might also explain later claims that Harold had promised to garrison castles for

9. For the date of Ralf's appointment see Barlow, *Edward the Confessor*, p. 93 n. 4
10. See A. Williams, 'Land and power in the eleventh century: the estates of Harold Godwineson', ANS 3 (1980), pp. 171–87 and 230–4 and R. Fleming, 'Domesday estates of the king and the Godwines: a study in late Saxon politics', *Speculum*, 58 (1983), pp. 987–1007

William, why the men of Kent called in Eustace in 1067. Some planned presence of French princes in the South East fits the acquisition of land in the Kent ports by Norman abbeys before 1066.

Edward took his ecclesiastical rights and duties as a king as seriously as his predecessors. He assumed a Christian kingship which entailed responsibility for the church but also powers of appointment, and used ecclesiastical patronage to reward friends and followers as Edgar had done before him. Churchmen figured prominently among the friends he brought to England in 1041 and after and his appointments in the 1040s included Englishmen, Lotharingians and Normans. Like Cnut he appointed an increasing number of men who had served in the royal chapel. Edward was prepared to allow his supporters among the great nobility their say. Godwine was influential in the Canterbury appointment in 1044, as we might expect for an earl of Kent and the king's prospective father-in-law. The tide of reforming zeal had ebbed somewhat since AD 1000, and the English king and nobles appear less able or concerned to tread the thin line between protection and possession, but the differences between Edward and Edgar can be overstressed.

During the 1040s Edward responded to problems similar to those of his father in ways his father, grandfather and great-grandfather would have recognized: organizing defensive marches, negotiating with French princes, using ecclesiastical patronage and calling on family ties. Unfortunately, as his father found before him, old answers do not always solve altered questions. The old answers had had their limitations: exile might not stick, cooperation between king and church could spill into criticism, court politics were dogged by suspicion and family ties were a fragile bond at the best of times. 1049–52 provides a commentary on the 1040s.

The crisis of 1049–52

At the heart of this crisis lie exile and return, especially the exile of Godwine and his sons in 1051 and their return in 1052. It begins with a crucial appointment of Robert of Jumièges, a Norman, to Canterbury. During it both Eustace of Boulogne and William of Normandy visited England. It ended in the expulsion of Robert and other Normans in 1052. It is befogged by the later Norman claims of a promise made to William. At the time the drama drew detailed commentary. It is not merely modern historians who have seen these years as critical.

The detailed account of 1049 illuminates a kingdom assailed by the Welsh, by an Irish Viking fleet and by exiles. Osgod and Swegn, Godwine's son, both returned from exile in 1049. Osgod came to plunder, Swegn to seek the king's pardon. Swegn's family refused to unite behind him. His brother Harold and cousin Beorn had profited from his expulsion, demonstrating that the exercise of the king's right to forfeiture could split a family. Harold may also have judged it unwise to associate with an exile. Beorn agreed to plead for Swegn with the king, and Swegn murdered him for his pains. The motives of his action are unfathomable, it was widely condemned, yet in the following year Edward reinstated Swegn. The full context may be lost, but the extent to which political survival depended on royal favour had been dramatically demonstrated. The question of whether Swegn would recover his possessions in the Welsh marches and elsewhere remained open.

Throughout the dramatic events of 1049 to 1052 the contemporary chroniclers never lose sight of ecclesiastical affairs; in the denouement of 1052, they openly linked them to the crisis. Archbishop Robert was 'most responsible for the disagreement between Earl Godwine and the king',[11] Godwine after his return and reinstatement 'did little reparation about the property of God which he had from many holy places'.[12] Whilst recognizing the interests of ecclesiastical chroniclers we might well begin with their viewpoint.

Church reform in the mid eleventh century was in one of its periodic phases of redefinition. As yet royal control of ecclesiastical appointments, provided it did not involve purchase of office, was scarcely at issue. For the reforming Pope Leo, the abuse of office by lay manipulation and simony and the state of the clergy were central. Noble rapacity was the threat; the desire to improve the clergy the aim. Neither was novel, but the espousal of reform by a pope determined to press papal powers into its service was. It was not yet clear whether kings and princes would work as allies of the papacy. By the late 1040s Leo was making his presence felt in northern Europe. His permission was sought for the reorganizations of the English church Edward undertook, like the amalgamation of the sees of Devon and Cornwall. In 1049 Leo announced his intention of enquiring further into English affairs, and in 1050 at Vercelli came close to quashing the appointment of the Norman Ulf as bishop of Dorchester. In this context Robert was appointed to Canterbury in 1051. A Norman or French appointment to this see at a time when Edward was drawing French princes into the defence of South East England was appropriate. Edward's appointment of Robert instead of a candidate backed by Earl Godwine put him above reproach at a time when Leo was flexing his muscles. Whether Godwine would have seen either the Canterbury affair or the organization of Kentish defences in the same way as the king is doubtful. Reading the runes of royal action for signs of royal intention may have been as difficult in the suspicious mood of the 1040s as for us. It could easily result in over-interpretation and over-reaction.

Robert was not necessarily appointed as a reformer; by the time he returned from Rome in the summer of 1051 his consciousness had been raised. He refused to consecrate Sparrowhawk, the king's choice, to London on grounds of unsuitability, and the question of church property, a root of disagreement between Robert and Godwine, arose.[13] Church property and its defence against lay incursion was close to the heart of all eleventh-century church reform. Robert was well placed to put his case to the king. It was said to be he who fanned into life old ashes of suspicion against Godwine for the murder of Alfred. The division between the king and Godwine which is the central drama of 1051–52 may have begun in a quarrel over Canterbury in the context of south eastern defence, exacerbated by the new archbishop.

The drama was sparked by an incident in Dover. Eustace of Boulogne, after visiting the king, entered the town with military intent and a fracas resulted.

11. ASC MS E 1052
12. ASC MS C 1052
13. *Life of King Edward*, ed. Barlow, p. 19

Eustace told his story to the king and Edward ordered Godwine to punish Dover. Perhaps Godwine felt there was another side to be told, perhaps he was reluctant to alienate his own earldom by ravaging part of it, perhaps he was out of sympathy with Eustace and the king's intentions in Dover. The mix of motives is of less importance than the recognition that they may not have been of long standing. When the earl refused he was called to account. Godwine feared a tribunal which others had already prejudiced. The earl and his sons prepared themselves, and Edward likewise called on Leofric and Siward to mobilize an army. When Swegn joined his father Godwine in 1051, his grievances were drawn in too. The men established in the Welsh marches on Swegn's lands were identified, rightly or wrongly, with Eustace and Robert, becoming the *Frenchmen* whom Godwine and his family increasingly saw as the source of grievance. The situation had escalated and the arguments solidified with great rapidity, not necessarily proof that they had long been festering, but the nature of quarrels in such a climate. The calling of another meeting in London suggests that the situation was not seen as irretrievable, especially if Swegn, who was immediately outlawed, could be separated from Godwine and Harold. Godwine was now too suspicious; doubtless he had knowledge we lack about the circumstances leading up to earlier exiles and forfeitures. Perhaps he preferred to avoid legal judgement. He fled. At this point the king put aside Edith. In 1051 unlike 1049 the family of Godwine facing threat to its head stood together and fell together. The exiles and forfeitures were secured in the usual way. Earl Leofric's son Ælfgar was given Harold's earldom in East Anglia, Odda got the earldom of the South West, and William's presence in England late in 1051 may have been to secure some hold on the eastern parts of Godwine's earldom.

Godwine and his family returned in 1052. It was their coming not their going which inspired the Chronicle accounts of 1051–52. Godwine was not swept back on a tide of popular enthusiasm. His abortive return in late June was successfully resisted by Earls Ralf and Odda, and his later success depended on his rendezvous with Harold and his Irish ships and on the ravaging that both did along the south coast. Edward's failure to resist Godwine stemmed from the same problems of raising fleets and armies which Æthelred had experienced. Reinforcement or aid which Ralf and Odda should have received from the other earls in the summer of 1051 did not materialize. Edward's army gathered slowly even after Godwine's second landing. By the time it had assembled, Godwine had reached London and won support. Even now the king's army was reluctant to fight. The justice of the move against Harold and Godwine in 1051 was debatable. The accusation against Robert and other Frenchmen raised in 1052 was of 'unjust judgements and bad counsel'. Leofric and Siward, who had tried to separate the cases of Harold and Godwine from that of Swegn in 1051, prevailed again. Were these issues sufficient to justify civil conflict which would 'lay the country more open to foreigners'?[14] Hostages were taken, settlement reached, and Archbishop Robert and some of the Frenchmen fled. Those who went were the Norman bishops of Canterbury, London and Dorchester and some of those established in the Welsh marches.[15] A Norman party? Or those

14. ASC MS C 1051
15. Fl. Wig. 1052

who felt, for a variety of reasons, that they had most to fear from a return of Godwine, or who, like Ulf, felt their position insecure? It is not impossible that Edward despatched Robert with Godwine's hostages to ensure his safety.

The crisis of 1051 has often been interpreted as sparked by the succession. Robert of Jumièges is seen as part of a Norman party, William was in England to receive Edward's promise of the throne, Godwine's objections were to a Norman succession and the Frenchmen who fled after Godwine's return become the Norman group associated with these policies. The Normans were later to claim that Archbishop Robert had taken the offer of the throne to William, and that it had been secured by the oaths of Archbishop Stigand, Earls Godwine, Leofric and Siward and by hostages given by Godwine to William.[16] We are moving into the deep waters of post-1066 propaganda.

The alleged promises of 1051 did not play a large part in Norman justifications of 1066. And their story contains inconsistencies and puzzling omissions. A promise made by Archbishop Stigand who did not become archbishop until after 1052 cannot be the same one conveyed to William by Robert in 1051. If these confusions are read as the product of later Norman fabrication, it is an odd fabrication which omitted Harold, already an earl in 1049–52 and the prime object of Norman propaganda after 1066. What we appear to have is a tangled and tantalizing version of actual events rather than pure post-conquest invention.

The succession is likely to have been an issue by c.1050. The king had been married for five years without children. He was approaching fifty and a great nobility which had experienced one crisis over succession would not have relished uncertainty. A promise to William of Normandy was by no means the obvious answer. A new royal marriage could have been canvassed. Edward divorced Edith late in 1051, and later stories of his chastity and her adultery may stem from pretexts used. Non-consummation and adultery of the wife were grounds for divorce in the eleventh century. The timing of the divorce makes it a result rather than a cause of the breach with Godwine, but it could have been discussed earlier and provided another ground for disagreement.

There were other candidates in 1050/51 with stronger claims than William and nearer to hand. Ralf of Mantes, the king's nephew and an English earl, was a grandson of Æthelred II. Eustace of Boulogne was Edward's brother-in-law and Ralf's stepfather, and may have had a daughter whose blood carried claims to the throne.[17] Discussion of the English succession was another question which could have brought Eustace to England in 1051. William's place in the pecking order was not high, but any recognition of it would later be seized upon. Did Robert inform William of the deliberations en route to Rome? Did he remind him of his claims after 1052? Robert in exile in Normandy would have talked up any stake William had in England. Edward could have had Godwine family hostages in his hands from the time of Swegn's reconciliation or from the events of 1051. Giving them into William's safekeeping need have had no connection with the succession, and the fact that Harold felt they could be

16. William of Jumièges in *The Norman Conquest* ed. Brown, p. 13 and William of Poitiers in *ibid.* pp. 20, 24 and 31
17. On this daughter see Barlow, *Edward the Confessor*, Appendix C, pp. 307–8

recovered *c*.1064 argues that they were associated with an old grievance. This dismantling of the Norman case into a series of tenuously related elements is speculative, but has the virtue of recognizing how far cases are made by the selective reassembling of the past and of allowing the succession a role in 1051, if not precisely the one the Normans later claimed.

1049–52 witnessed a conjunction of circumstance, an unfolding in which the legacy of the 1030s, the impact of papal reform and chance interacted. In another sense they were a crisis of relations between the king and the great nobility. Kings who had refined forfeiture and exile in a world of patronage and reward had placed notions of loyalty and justice under strain. Edward's personal position was weaker than his father's, the external situation different. The presence of a foreign element at his court merely made it easier to finger and scapegoat alleged architects of injustice.

1052–1065

At the level of political structures 1049–52 changed nothing, as 1065 would show. At the level of events 1052 was significant. Harold's reinstatement meant that Ælfgar, Leofric's son, lost East Anglia, and although he regained it when Harold succeeded to Godwine's earldom in 1053, resentment remained. Ælfgar was to be twice exiled in 1055 and 1058. Both exiles coincided with the death of earls to whom members of the Godwine family succeeded. In 1055 Tostig, Harold's brother, took Northumbria on the death of Siward, in 1057/8 Harold took over from Ralf in the Welsh marches. Ælfgar could have argued his own claims, in 1055 as a son of Leofric and as a connection of Ælfhelm ealdorman of York until 1006, and by 1057/8 as the earl of Mercia in succession to his father with his own claim to control West Mercia. Argument lay behind his exile in 1055. According to some he was 'outlawed without any guilt . . . having committed hardly any crime' according to others 'a traitor to the king and all the people' whose admission of guilt escaped him in spite of himself.[18] *The Life of Edward* later spoke of 'long-standing rivalry' between the sons of Ælfgar and Tostig.[19] The open disputes between the two families were there in the 1050s.

1049–52 did not cause the dominance of Godwine's children. Edward allowed Harold to succeed to his father's earldom in 1053 and advanced all his brothers during the 1050s and 60s. This continued the 1040s, and Edward also permitted the hereditary succession to Mercia first of Leofric's son Ælfgar then of Ælfgar's son Edwin. Edward did not have, perhaps did not seek the freedom of manoeuvre Æthelred had exercised in the 990s. Heredity succession of families which were trusted was one of the options of tenth- and eleventh-century kings, and Æthelred's troubles warn of a too glib definition of 'strength' as the reshuffling of office. The rivalry of the two greatest families in the 1050s and 60s is more important than any alleged weakness of the king, though it points to ineptitude on his part. Rivalry resulted from the dangerous engrossing of power in too few hands for the restraints of patronage politics to be effective. Similar crises may have occurred in the poorly chronicled mid tenth century

18. ASC MSS C & D 1055 and MS E 1055
19. *Life of Edward the Confessor*, ed. Barlow, p. 50

when the family of Athelstan Half-King came close to rivalling Godwine's later power.

The flight of Robert left a gap but not a vacancy at Canterbury which was filled by Stigand. Stigand had been removed from office in 1043, but had recovered the bishopric of East Anglia by 1044 and in 1047 had received the plum of Winchester.[20] His appointment to Canterbury whilst Robert was still alive was dubious, his retention of Winchester pluralism. Stigand suffered much in post-conquest propaganda and can be no-one's candidate for sanctity. But his insecurity at Canterbury as well as avarice would have led him to retain Winchester. Edward's flirtation with the reforming papacy had ended with a growing realization of what reform now meant. Like William after him and Edgar before, he preferred the old-established relations between the archbishop of Canterbury and the king. But 1051–52 had left a uniquely irregular situation at Canterbury. Only briefly in 1058–59, after he was recognized by the Tusculan Pope Benedict, were English bishops prepared to accept consecration from Stigand. Gone were the days when Dunstan could oust a predecessor at Canterbury, albeit one who had not received his pallium.

If the succession played any part in 1051, Godwine's return threw it back into debate. If divorce and remarriage were an option, that was closed and Edith back in the royal bed. Hereditary claimants with foreign connections now looked unwelcome; arguments against them since the death of Cnut were strong anyway. Ralf was still in England, and after his death his son Harold was in the queen's hands, this special wardship suggesting he was a claimant to the throne.[21] But pressure to find a successor now turned to the son of Edward's brother Edmund Ironside and by 1055 Bishop Ealdred was on the continent searching. In 1057 Edward the ætheling returned to England with his family, but died almost immediately. His children remained at court and his son Edgar was named 'ætheling' by the king.[22] *Ætheling* means throneworthy and by the tenth and eleventh century was a term used only of the sons of kings who had reigned. Edgar did not qualify by birth. His great-uncle's action, if not a straightforward designation, stressed his eligibility.

Perhaps we may catch the mood of the court in the 1050s and 60s in the *Life of Edward*. It contrasts Godwine, the eloquent counsellor, with the restrained secretiveness of Harold and Tostig.[23] Harold sometimes revealed his plans, but sometimes deferred too long; Tostig pondered his plans and would not readily share them with anyone. The reliance on stock types in eleventh-century sources makes their use for the construction of personality hazardous, and Godwine's eloquence is a standard description of a counsellor. But there is no obvious source for Harold and Tostig's circumspect taciturnity. Edith, for it is her interpretation we are hearing, might have thought especially of the misunderstandings which underlay what she saw as the tragedy of 1065. The unexpectedness of Harold's claim to the throne may be at issue. But a mood of

20. On Stigand's career see now N. Brooks, *The Early History of the Church of Canterbury* (Leicester 1984), pp. 304–10
21. DB I, fo. 129 v
22. *Leges Edwardi Confessoris*, printed F. Liebermann, *Die Gesetze der Angelsachsen* (Halle, 1903) vol. 1, p. 665 para 35 1c
23. *Life of King Edward*, ed. Barlow, pp. 6, 31–2

cautious suspicion is indicated, with an ageing childless king, 1035–40 as a warning of the danger of taking open positions, the recent history of noble exile a sign of what could happen if words were allowed to escape which could be construed as treacherous.

The 'words which escaped' Ælfgar in 1055 probably concerned contacts with the Welsh king, Gruffudd. The Scots and the Welsh, Macbeth, Malcolm and Gruffudd, move centre-stage in Edward's reign. In 1066/7 Edith boasted of the achievements of her family and the sanctity of her husband, and stressed above all Harold and Tostig's feats against Welsh and Scots.[24] Gruffudd plundered and destroyed and proved ready to aid an English exile. The military organization of the marches under Ralf and later Harold was against him and his namesake Gruffudd of Dyfed; the statement in the Chronicle that in 1056 he became 'a loyal and faithful underking of Edward'[25] is the wishful thinking of the English court. During the 1050s and 1060s it was Harold's exploits in Wales and the Marches which impressed English Chroniclers. But Leofric and his descendants continued to be active here; Ælfgar's daughter married King Gruffudd, and Edwin and his followers claimed lands stretching along the North Welsh coast by 1066. The rivalries of court into which Gruffudd was drawn were one spur to Harold's prestigious campaigns. His castles, his part in the murder of Gruffudd in 1063, his instatement of that king's brothers as rulers show Harold's aggressive approach. The promises made in 1063 recall Athelstan's day: the Welsh kings would be faithful and ready to follow the English king 'on water and on land' and give such dues 'as before had been given to any other king'.[26] Harold was more active in Wales than any king since the early tenth century. Gruffudd's son, Caradoc, fled to Ireland, and was attacking again by 1065. After the Norman Conquest he would continue resistance to the Norman extension of Harold's and Edwin's advances into North Wales.

Macbeth had proved as ready as Gruffudd to take in English exiles: some of the Normans who fled in 1052 went to Scotland. It may have been in the 1040s and 1050s that English earls extended their control into southern Strathclyde, what is now the Lake District. By 1066 Tostig held lands here as earl. In 1054 Siward capitalized on Macbeth's insecure situation to attack him on behalf of Malcolm, Duncan's son. Everyone could play the game of exiles. If Siward hoped that Malcolm's accession would mean gratitude and peace on the northern borders his strategy was mistaken. Malcolm raided south after the fashion of his predecessors and Malcolm readily extended his hospitality to the enemies of the new English king, William, after 1066. His were not new responses to a Norman king but the old politics of the northern border (see below, England and its Neighbours).

The crisis of 1065–6

In the autumn of 1065 there was rebellion in northern England. In the spring of that year the bones of the murdered King Oswin had been publicly displayed at

24. *ibid* pp. 42–3 and 57–8. Another detailed account of the Welsh wars may have been planned, see pp. 42 and 59
25. ASC MS C 1056
26. ASC MS D 1063

Durham in a call to action rather than a gesture of piety.[27] In the autumn the nobility of Yorkshire and Northumbria rose against their earl, Tostig, attacked and killed his bodyguard in York and chose Morcar, the younger brother of Earl Edwin of Mercia as their earl. They came south to Lincoln, were joined by others north of Welland and Trent before continuing to Northamptonshire, the southern portion of Tostig's earldom. Here they met Tostig's brother Harold, who negotiated with them, renewed the laws of Cnut and carried their demands, which included the outlawry of Tostig, to the king at Oxford. The king reluctantly agreed, and Harold returned as his messenger. In the meantime they had ravaged in Northamptonshire so that 'that shire and many other neighbouring shires were the worse for it for many year'.[28] Tostig, his Flemish wife and followers fled to Baldwin in Flanders.

The revolt of 1065 appeared critical to English writers of the later eleventh century attempting to explain 1066. They speculated on its causes, pinpointing revenge for the murder of prominent northern thegns at the Christmas court of 1064, by order of the queen and at the instigation of Tostig. They spoke of opposition to Tostig's harsh rule, of his robbery of God and of those less powerful than himself, of his heavy tribute, of cruelty and the punishment of men in order to gain their property or at least of attempts to quell the lawless actions of the northern nobility.[29] MS C of the Chronicle and the Life of Edward agree in seeing the tragic division between Harold and Tostig as a key to the events of 1065–66, and the Life claimed that rumour, believed by Tostig, made Harold responsible for inciting revolt against his brother. For C the important battles of 1066 were in the North against Tostig, it was his movements and actions which engrossed this Chronicler's attention in 1066. These English perspectives in the aftermath of Hastings stressed internal troubles dating from 1065 as the reason for defeat.

Less engaged analysis cannot deny the importance of these events. Tostig, the returning exile, was a crucial complication in the military unfolding of 1066. In the winter and spring of 1065/6 his presence in Flanders raising a fleet alerted William of Normandy to the internal situation in England at the time of Edward's death, even if Tostig did not visit William in person.[30] 1065 was a crisis of the politics of Edward's reign if not of tenth- and eleventh-century development as a whole. If Hastings culminated a series of accidents which the murders of 1064 began, these accidents themselves stemmed from the problem of uniting the kingdom. A member of the southern nobility appointed to the North tried to extend there the powers of southern kings. Tostig's appointment had affronted Ælfgar and the rivalries of Edward's court brought Edwin and Morcar into the escalating revolt. Edward's weapon of exile was turned back upon him. Neighbouring rulers played by now familiar parts: Welshmen formed part of the army Edwin brought to Northampton, Tostig fled to Flanders and to Scotland. 1065 echoes 1052. Ravaging by English nobles was a feature of both situations, as was rivalry, exile and return. But the 1050s had taught Mercian earls the possibility of rebellion and the grievances of northern nobles were as

27. Symeon of Durham, *Historia Ecclesiae Dunhelmensis*, ed. T. Arnold, RS 75 (1882), pp. 87–9
28. ASC MSS E & C and Fl. Wig. 1065
29. *Life of King Edward*, ed. Barlow, pp. 50–2
30. As in Orderic Vitalis, vol. II, Bk III, pp. 141–3

much against the results of two centuries of unification as personal. And by 1065 the succession loomed over all.

Tostig felt that Harold had worked against him in 1065 and the succession was the wedge of suspicion and rivalry between the brothers. Between 1063 and 1066 Harold married the sister of Edwin and Morcar, the widow of Gruffudd.[31] If this had taken place by 1065 Tostig could not have relished an alliance between his brother and the family with which he had a quarrel. But the marriage is inseparable from Harold's own plans for the succession, a mark of friendship with Edwin who was necessary to any plans. Harold's secretive caution means that his intentions in 1065 can only be guessed. In 1064/5 he visited Normandy, a visit which assumed special significance and interpretation after 1066. Norman writers claimed that Edward had sent him to bring an offer of the throne to William, and that he took an oath to aid William's claims. Yet their story undermines itself when it admits that Harold had also come to secure the release of his brother and nephew, hostages held by William; and has Harold falling by accident into William's hands. Eadmer, taking an 'English' line, made the hostages the aim of the expedition, but saw such an enterprise as risky, threatening to alert William to the situation in England.[32] Both interpretations read events not from 1065 but with Hastings in mind. Harold may never have intended to visit William before the accident of his shipwreck. He may have been visiting France seeking to understand the plans of the northern French princes about the English succession or their likely reaction to his own. That northern French princes and other neighbours were essential to the political plans of a great English noble by the 1060s is clear. That William was beginning to hatch his own ideas can be the only explanation of the oath he took from Harold: swearing on relics was not an obligatory part of eleventh–century hospitality. Was Harold already planning to take the throne by 1065, as his speedy moves after Edward's death might suggest? Was his decision taken in 1065, even as a result of a Norman escapade which had warned him of William's intentions? Harold would have foreseen claims from Denmark after Edward's death. The first clear signs of a dual threat could have tipped the balance between supporting a minority rule for Edgar the Ætheling, with regency problems, and making a bid for the throne himself. There will always be more questions than answers about the succession in 1066. All that is clear is that the Norman version is the story preferred by the victors, a retrospective and edited one.

In 1066 Harold faced and William and Hardrada utilized the continuing crisis. That crisis raises questions about the unity of tenth- and eleventh-century England which persisted long after 1066. Northumbria, where the revolt began, was the least integrated part of the English kingdom. The methods of rule employed by southern kings appeared at their starkest north of the Humber. Attempts had been made to rule through outsiders, archbishops and ealdormen from south of the Humber, or earls of Bamburgh from north of the Tees. Eleventh-century efforts at tighter control had spawned a series of political murders of which those of 1064 were only the last; the royal court was an

31. *ibid.* p. 139
32. Eadmer, *History of Recent Events in England*, trans. G. Bosanquet (1964), p. 6

unhealthy place for northern rulers.[33] Tostig's appointment in 1055 was the most brutal example of an old pattern of ruling the North, or anywhere north of the Thames through outsiders. 1065 can be read as pure separatism of a region remote from the court, the joining of Edwin and Mercia a repetition of an old pattern. But the Northumbrians chose a Mercian earl to succeed Tostig in 1065, and Edwin was motivated by ambition rather than separatism. Regional identities existed; and the adherence of the North East Midlands which had also submitted to Swegn in 1013 shows there were more of them than simply Mercia and Northumbria. The focus of such identities around leading families, like the earls of Bamburgh or Leofric's descendants, was both a source of power to such men and meant that murders or rivalries which affected them ramified. Regional feeling was exacerbated by royal rule. Tostig and Siward extended the methods of southern kings to the North. Separatism was the product of unification and rule rather than a waning legacy of older kingdoms.

1065 was a rebellion against rule seen as oppression; Tostig was attacked as an agent of royal power. Taxation was widely perceived as the unacceptable face of eleventh-century rule. England north of the Humber may have been especially lightly taxed before Tostig,[34] his impositions a specific and novel grievance, but dislike of growing taxation was general, and from the time of Wulfstan's 'shameful tributes' its justification was debatable. Law and justice were the idealized attributes of rule, but in practice often the excuses for fines and forfeitures. South of the Humber and especially south of the Thames that tension was contained not merely by habits and ideals of loyalty, but by the experience of both faces of the Janus, taxation and patronage, justice and forfeiture, though even here it could spill out as in the crisis of 1015–22. North of the Humber new impositions in the absence of a balance of taxation and patronage, brought an experience of only the oppressive face of rule.

The management of patronage was the prerequisite of royal success. In the tenth century kings had had the advantage of the windfalls of unification; after 1066 William would dispose of a bonanza which dwarfed this. The first half of the eleventh century saw patronage in a cooler climate, with scarcer resources to be distributed over an extended kingdom. In the regions, northern nobles got little of it. At the centre Godwine and his sons created a temporary but critical imbalance which alienated Edwin and Morcar.

Apart from Durham there was apparently no involvement of churchmen in the crisis of 1065. Control over appointments to this northern see had recently been taken into southern hands; monks from Peterborough had been appointed as bishops and their divided loyalties were resented. It was the monks of St Cuthbert not the bishop who utilized their relics against Tostig. But on the whole in 1065 as after Hastings, English churchmen were a force for loyalty to a consecrated king and for unity.

No reading of 1065 can deny that unity as much as regional feeling characterized English politics. The northern rebels asked for a Mercian earl from a family associated with the southern court. As when Edgar was chosen in

33. W. E. Kapelle, *The Norman Conquest of the North* (1979) esp. chap 4. I find his interpretation of an ethnic division between York Danes and northern Northumbrians unconvincing, but his analysis of the so-called northern feud of the eleventh century is enlightening.
34. *ibid*, pp. 96–7

Mercia in 957, political realities guided them. The strength of support from Mercia was necessary, the difficulty of any real separatism by the mid eleventh century underlined. Harold confirmed for them the laws of Cnut. If this stood for anything specific it was for the memory that Cnut had twice promised good government. But like the laws of Edgar after 1017, it was a shorthand for an idealized past, for the good old days. That idealization was of an English past under the laws of an English king. The northern and Mercian nobility in 1065 expressed a desire to be part of the kingdom of the English without the oppression that increasingly meant.

The events of 1065–66 unfolded accidentally, but their roots lay further in the past. It was not inevitable that in 1066 a Norman conqueror would win a succession dispute with the aid of Scandinavian claimants and a noble exile driven out by a combination of court politics and regional response to royal power. What was critical was the uniqueness of the combination, not the novelty of the elements.

The reign of Harold II, January to October, 1066

The briefest reigns are often the most controversial. Their brevity precludes a positive picture of administrative development with which historians are wont to balance the story of caprice and calamity into which monarchical rule so readily degenerates. Their brevity is frequently the result of a violent end, perhaps at the hands of a rival whose subsequent propaganda blackens the loser. If Richard III is the most obvious example, Harold II has suffered even more. His rule, as opposed to his usurpation, is obliterated by a history which moves from Edward to William. By the time of Domesday Book in 1086 the hiatus between the death of Edward and the rule of William had been closed,[35] *King* Harold had slipped out of history, leaving only the perjurer who died with an arrow in his eye at Hastings. We know little of his reign beyond the battles which ended it. The Normans did their job too well.

Edward died on 5 January, 1066 and Harold was crowned next day, probably by Stigand and Ealdred of York. The gathering of the Christmas court, prolonged by Edward's illness, had provided an opportunity for final decision about the succession; the presence on the spot of nobles and churchmen permitted a hasty coronation which political circumstances demanded. As a man without royal blood, Harold was bound to provoke trouble, for there were enough dissatisfied men in 1066. In the aftermath of 1065 opposition in the North was only to be expected; it was allegedly won over by Bishop Wulfstan of Worcester.[36] Elsewhere the legitimacy of his rule was recognized by those who operated royal government: a writ survives in his name, and his coinage covered most of England. Harold had no greater problems than his predecessors in raising an army or fleet. There is a hint of grumbling in the statement that the ones he assembled in spring were larger than ever before,[37] and he experienced

---

35. G. Garnett, 'Coronation and propaganda: some implications of the Norman claim to the throne of England in 1066', *TRHS* ser. 5, 36 (1986), pp. 91–116 and V. H. Galbraith, *Domesday Book, its Place in Administrative History* (Oxford, 1974), pp. 175–83
36. *William of Malmesbury's Life of St Wulfstan*, trans. J. H. F. Peile (Oxford, 1934), Bk I, cap. 16, pp. 34–5
37. ASC MS C 1066

the same difficulty as Edward in keeping an army together until early September, when provisions ran out and the fleet had to be sent to London. At most his position heightened rather than created such problems. Any crowned English king could count on much automatic power.

Tostig returned in the summer of 1066, like other exiles before him. He ravaged in the South and in Lindsey, fled again to the Scots and thence returned with Harold Hardrada, the king of Norway who had decided to capitalize on succession difficulties. Tostig had less success than his father in staging a comeback. Harold had clearly anticipated his return. The army he had assembled in the south was collected against all the external enemies who might take their chance in 1066, not merely against William. Hardrada and Tostig sailed up the Ouse to York in September and defeated a force under Edwin and Morcar at Fulford on 20th of that month. News of the landing and defeat brought Harold north and to a victory at Stamford Bridge on 25 September in which Tostig and Hardrada were killed. But 1066 was the product of the involvement of all England's eleventh-century neighbours in its succession. Whilst Harold was in the North, William landed at Pevensey in late September, grasping his opportunity. Harold marched south to meet him at Hastings on 14 October. The reasons for English defeat have been debated since the late eleventh century; the death of Harold, who had successfully rallied support, ranks high among them. Hastings need not have delivered the throne to William. Many great English nobles were not present at the battle but were gathered in London together with an alternative candidate Edgar the Ætheling. Some supported him[38] and outside London some assumed that he would be made king,[39] but the eventual decision was to offer the crown to William. William's ravaging in the South East may have swayed some minds; the question of regency for Edgar was potentially divisive; the existence of other candidates, including Harold's sons, raised questions which could have split noble counsels, and there were probably those who preferred to give to William as a legitimate king a crown which they feared he would take by conquest. The political lesson of the mid eleventh century had been to spot and back the winner. And there were still possibilities of further fleets arriving from Denmark. The agonizing discussions of late 1066 have been lost. Their outcome was the coronation of William on Christmas day 1066, which transferred to him the advantages Harold had acquired on 6 January and made him the heir of the strengths and problems of the English monarchy.

38. ASC MS D 1066 and *The Carmen de Hastingae Proelio*, eds. C. Morton and H. Muntz (Oxford, 1972), pp. 41–2 and 48
39. ASC MS E 1066

6

1066 and After[1]

1066 is the most famous date in English history. Since the sixteenth and seventeenth centuries the changes which it is alleged to have brought have been hotly debated. Only recently has debate been removed from the political arena where it originated. J.H. Round's contrast between the 'excess of liberty' pre–1066[2] and the strong military rule of William was only the final salvo in a war in which both sides often accepted the reality of the changes, dispute being more about whether liberty or strength was the more desirable good. The legacy of this long controversy has been to set up a strong contrast between England either side of that fateful date. There has been a concentration on the social, legal and institutional effects of 1066: was tyranny introduced or the nature of royal rule changed; did society become more militarized, specifically was 'feudalism' an import in the Norman baggage train; were there changes in the legal system or in liberty? The process of conquest itself has often been relegated to secondary status, even though that process helped determine any changes which followed it. The short-term effects have tended to be downplayed as transient, despite the tendency of chroniclers writing within a

---

1. The debate over the Norman Conquest is vast. On its historical development see D. C. Douglas, *The Norman Conquest and British Historians*, 2nd edn (Glasgow, 1971); C. Hill, 'The Norman Yoke', *Puritanism and Revolution* (1962), pp. 50–122 and A. Briggs, 'Saxons, Normans and Victorians', *1066 Commemoration Lectures* (Historical Association, 1966), pp. 89–112. The ferocity of the late-nineteenth-century phase can be gauged from E. A. Freeman, *History of the Norman Conquest*, which also remains a mine of information, and J. H. Round, 'Mr Freeman and the Battle of Hastings', *Feudal England* (1895), pp. 258–305. These, plus the magisterial accounts of F. M. Stenton, *Anglo-Saxon England* 3rd edn (Oxford, 1971), and D. C. Douglas, *William the Conqueror* (1964) continue to define the parameters of debate. For widely differing views on the military nature of the conquest from a recent generation see E. John, 'English feudalism and the structure of Anglo-Saxon society', *Orbis Britanniae* (Leicester, 1966) pp. 128–53 and compare R. Allen Brown, *The Origins of English Feudalism* (1973). Modern reassessments of most aspects can be found in the collections *Anglo-Norman Studies*, ed. R. Allen Brown, vol. I– (1979–) and in two excellent recent surveys, M. Chibnall, *Anglo-Norman England* (Oxford, 1986) and M. Clanchy, *England and its Rulers, 1066–1272* (1983). For the Norman aspects see J. Le Patourel, *The Norman Empire* (Oxford, 1976) and especially D. Bates, *Normandy before 1066* (1982).
2. Round, *Feudal England*, pp. 302–5

couple of generations of 1066 to place great emphasis here. Twentieth-century historians have moved towards a more balanced view of 1066, observing many elements of continuity. A fuller understanding of Normandy in particular has placed 1066 in a wider northern French context. The time is ripe for a discussion of 1066 not with an eye to the subsequent long term but rather in the light of our changing knowledge of tenth- and eleventh-century England.

The nature of the conquest itself must be a question prior to those about where and why change occurred. The conquest and the events which succeeded it were shaped in both England and Normandy. William's aims and the pressures on him are as important as the responses he met in the earliest years of his reign and the situation prior to 1066.

Rising and rebellion after 1066

1066 was a conquest but also part of a disputed succession to the English throne. It was neither the first conquest nor the first succession dispute of the century. It can be seen as a tenth- or eleventh-century succession dispute writ large, producing the death or exile of some or all of the other side's supporters, as in 956 or 1037, and their forfeiture, as in 956. This helps explain the reactions of English nobles who accepted William in 1066 and his easy acquisition of the allegiances and habits of obedience which meant that from the beginning he ruled England as an English king. The factors which put a rapid term on earlier disputes worked in William's favour. Once he was consecrated king, fine calculations about personal survival made continued resistance unwise.

1066 was not just another succession dispute, it was an exceptionally complicated one even by eleventh-century standards. The range of candidates and would-be candidates was wide, several survived 1066, and some, like Swegn of Denmark, posed a real military threat. In 1066 two men had succeeded whose blood claims on the English throne were nil. It is scarcely surprising that insecurity is a dominant theme of the first reigns after 1066. Despite acceptance by English nobles and consecration, doubt remained, legitimating if not causing rebellions, especially those surrounding the Danish arrival in 1069.

Risings and rebellions are a feature of the years 1067–71, marking 1066 out from earlier disputes and from the conquest of 1016. The fuller chronicles of 1066 may enhance this apparent difference from Cnut's conquest, though even the fullest account of 1016–20, that in Florence, mentions only one rising. This difference was critical, since it determined the ravaging and military responses which characterized William's conquest and which were absent from that of Cnut. The causes of those risings lie in different pressures behind the two conquests.

Since the 1070s the question of why William came to England has elicited stories of claims and promises and of the unfolding of events. The stories answer the question, why England, but ignore that of why conquest. The circumstances which brought William to England may have been in some measure accidental; the pressures which pushed him into conquest were rooted in Normandy. Competition and rivalry between lords and princes for followers and land, the need to sustain a military reputation, a compulsion to follow up all posssible claims were the stuff of the volatile politics of northern France, exacerbated for William by the problems of his own minority. The pressures on Cnut drove him to seek loot and tribute, those on William led to a need for land. William's conquest was thus followed not merely by heavy tribute, but by forfeiture and the distribution of lands. Initially forfeiture applied only to those who had fought against him at Hastings; the consequences were nonetheless considerable.

The effects of these forfeitures were felt widely in England. William directed a writ, for example, to the abbot of Bury St Edmund's requiring him to identify and hand over the land of such men.[3] The writ guaranteed the abbey's own land, but even had such guarantees worked they could not have inhibited the ramifications and impact of the initial forfeitures. Most people in 1066 held land from several lords as well as other lands debatably theirs. Were the forfeitures of 1066 to extend to the lords and followers of those who were at Hastings, to undertenants, to land held by others on which those who had incurred forfeiture had claims? All the dispossession after 1066 raised such problems, as Domesday witnesses. The results of William's takeover were rapidly felt. And their justification was dubious. William was soon to develop the argument that Harold had never been king, that all who fought for him in 1066 were thus rebels against William, the only legitimate ruler.[4] This *post facto* justification cloaked the dispossessions of 1066 in some sort of legitimacy but it was not evolved before the end of 1067. Political forfeiture on this scale for supporting a rival candidate, let alone a duly crowned king, was unknown. Fear of what William had done and might do was a factor in rebellion.

English politics as well as Norman land-hunger were the context of 1066. The rivalries of Edward's reign had spilled out in 1065 and helped ensure the disparate nature of rebellion after 1066. That rebellion was never a unified movement, let alone a unified movement to place another candidate, be it son of Harold or Edgar the Ætheling, on the throne. From the 1040s onwards the great English nobles had shown a readiness to resort to violence to achieve their ends and had regularly used external aid to threaten or ravage their way back to power. The pattern continued after 1066. On the one hand it increased the likelihood of rebellion, which on a limited scale had already become a feature of English political life. The support of Welsh or Scottish kings made William's adversaries more formidable and increased his insecurity and the ferocity of his responses. On the other hand the pattern militated against the emergence of a 'them' and 'us' view of events which might have served to bring resistance together. When Harold's sons returned in 1068 and 1069 they were English nobles backed by a Viking fleet. In 1069 the Norman Brian drove them off, but in 1068 it had been the citizens of Bristol and the thegns of Somerset, led by Eadnoth the Staller. There is little of English nationalism in the aftermath of 1066, though occasionally signs of the habit of obedience to a consecrated king.[5]

3. EHD II no. 238, pp. 983–4
4. G. Garnett, 'Coronation and propaganda: some implications of the Norman claim to the throne of England in 1066', *TRHS* ser. 5, 36 (1986), pp. 91–116
5. S. Reynolds, *Kingdoms and Communities in Western Europe, 900–1300* (Oxford, 1984), pp. 262–7

The rising of 1065 was the immediate circumstance of 1066. It was northern, especially far northern nobles who rose most frequently after 1066, though risings in the South West and the Welsh marches may also point to regional feeling. If royal exactions were a major cause of 1065, they continued after 1066.[6] The rebellions against William were as much rebellions against an English king as against a Norman conqueror. The south-western towns centred on Exeter made their demands, especially 'to pay tribute according to ancient custom'.[7] The turmoil of 1067 may have looked a good time to press an advantage, to seek at local level the sorts of concession promised by Cnut in his laws.

Rival claimants were involved in both the south-western and northern rebellions. Gytha, Harold's mother, was at Exeter, and her grandsons, Harold's sons, tried to land in the South West; Edgar the Ætheling was a recurring figure in the North. In neither case need the risings be seen as primarily attempts to place rival candidates on the throne. The years after 1066 more often saw claimants in search of a rising. Harold's sons were repulsed in the South West, though they arrived too late to gauge how strong their support might have been before William took Exeter. The continual presence of Edgar the Ætheling in the North and the failure to make any attempt to place him on the throne is more telling. The northern revolt began in objections to royal rule, and William's castle building and military responses could have escalated it. But if the northern nobles invited anyone to replace William it was Swegn of Denmark not Edgar. Even this is not certain. Swegn had a fleet, and when that fleet arrived in 1069 it was said to be felt in the North and Midlands that it had come 'to conquer all the country'.[8]

The loyalty of English churchmen to a crowned king was arguably as important as political calculation in preventing northern rebellion coalescing around a rival claimant. Only an archbishop could crown an English king, and Ealdred of York, who might have legitimized Edgar, remained loyal to William.[9] English churchmen had secured the conquest of Cnut, and few of them turned against William. In the far North Bishop Æthelwine of Durham became suspect and was outlawed in 1069 and his brother, a former bishop of Durham, imprisoned. The delicate position of a southern appointee at Durham raised all the grounds of suspicion and conflicts of loyalty which had earlier made ealdormen at York suspect. In general the English bishops and abbots remained loyal. The Peterborough monks made a bad miscalculation in sending their new abbot to be accepted by Edgar in 1066, but were only the more careful to dissociate themselves from later local rebellion.[10]

The disappropriations of English bishops in 1070 were thus as dubious as the forfeitures after Hastings. The depositions or forced resignations of men like Leofwine of Lichfield or Æthelric of Selsey appear blatantly political, associated with the fall of Edwin, Morcar and Stigand with whom they were linked.

6. W. Kapelle, *The Norman Conquest of the North* (1979), chap 4
7. Orderic Vitalis, Vol. II, Bk IV, p. 213
8. ASC MS E s. a. 1070
9. On Ealdred's loyalty see William of Poitiers, in *The Norman Conquest*, ed. R. Allen Brown, (1984) p. 41 and compare Orderic Vitalis, Vol. II, Bk IV, pp. 209 and 217
10. ASC MS E s. a. 1070

The imprisonment of Godric of Winchcombe suggests that some English churchmen took advantage of the situation to extend their own power; Godric was delivered into the hands of the neighbouring English abbot, Æthelwig of Evesham. Reform was the pretext in 1070, and a man like Leofwine of Lichfield was married, but Æthelric of Selsey was a monk-bishop who, if not a saint, would have held his own among the contemporary Norman episcopate. Changes in the church were greater after 1066 than after 1016. Cnut came from a missionary outpost; whatever the state of the Norman church[11] William could present himself as an arm of reform and brought in as archbishop of Canterbury Lanfranc, a man genuinely committed to it. By 1070 William was showing a growing desire to rule England through Normans; the English nobility finally disappear from court *c.*1070. His desire to use the lands of England and not merely its tribute to reward his followers extended to church office.

A simple nationalist interpretation does not capture the variety of cause and motivation of the risings after 1066. That variety and disparity helps explain William's survival. Rebellion was a continuation of earlier patterns as much as a response to William's actions. Accidental difference between the first years of William and Cnut encouraged a different reaction. Cnut stayed in England until 1019, William returned to Normandy in 1067, giving an opportunity for uprisings. The risings altered the process of the conquest. They provoked and justified a wider range of forfeiture of the English nobility and perhaps of churchmen. They may be one reason why, by 1075/6, William was ruling England not with the counsel of the great English nobles but almost exclusively with that of Normans.

The last stand of Hereward the Wake and his supporters in the Fenland in 1071 is a tempting turning point, but it is the stuff of national myth rather than history. There was no sharp ending. William himself faced a further serious rebellion in 1075 in which an English noble and possible claimant, Waltheof, was involved with Norman and Breton nobles. Northern risings continued intermittently throughout the later eleventh century, and together with the threat from the Scots and the presence of Edgar the Ætheling called Rufus to reorganize the northern borders. Rumours of a Danish fleet in 1085 and an obvious fear of the reception it might receive worried William into devastation of the east coast.

Norman tyranny or English royal oppression? (see also pp. 146–9)

The 1075 rebellion had northern French connections and aspects. They recall the earlier dimensions of eleventh-century English history and show the new orientation which joint rule of England and Normandy brought. In 1075 Normans in England revolted, and an English bishop, Wulfstan, put them down. A rebellion involving Earl Roger of Breteuil, son of William Fitz Osbern the conqueror's right-hand man, demonstrates how transient the Norman unity produced by 1066 was. It also casts doubt upon nationalist interpretations of 1066. We witness striking continuity when we see how Norman nobles now in

11. On the Norman church see D. Bates, *Normandy before 1066*

English shoes reacted to the demands of a Norman duke who was also now an English king. William's rule could be seen and was seen as oppressive, by his Norman followers as much as by his English subjects.

William was both castigated and lauded by chroniclers; his son Rufus was heir to the castigation but not the praise. In the case of William the E MS of the Anglo-Saxon Chronicle and Orderic, in the case of Rufus the E MS and Eadmer make critical assessments which adjudge these kings as oppressors. The sources are problematic and it is arguable that their criticism is prompted by the fact that after 1066 churchmen, who were also chroniclers, were suddenly at the receiving end of royal oppression, an experience which made them the temporary mouthpiece for all those who suffered the harshness of royal rule.[12] To think of William as no more harsh than his English and Danish predecessors is illuminating, and an awareness of the unacceptable face of all tenth- and eleventh-century rule is overdue. But we risk an injustice to the Chroniclers' motivations and duck judgement on William himself.

The making of overt judgement in history is unfashionable, and unjustified if the yardsticks applied are ours not theirs. Yet tenth- and eleventh-century England had ideas about just rule by which rulers were judged, and the Anglo-Saxon Chronicler and Orderic criticize William using such criteria. For the Anglo-Saxon Chronicler William was avaricious, made insupportable demands which were extorted from the poor and protected the game of the forest more than the people entrusted to him.[13] Such accusations could have been levelled at any eleventh-century king, but some earlier ones, like Edward the Confessor, had felt it necessary to moderate demands by disbanding the fleet and abolishing heregeld to meet criticism. Orderic picks out not taxation but ravaging, especially the harrying of the North in 1069–70, as William's great sin.[14] The military reaction to the risings after 1066 was harsh; in his constant resort to it and to systematic ravaging William has few precedents in the previous century and a half. Widespread rebellion was novel, the end he pursued, the maintenance of his rule, legitimate, yet the methods William used, the destruction of crops, cattle and farm implements with resulting dearth and famine, contravened contemporary standards of royal behaviour. His forfeitures and dispossessions at the beginning of the reign went beyond what could be expected from a king who claimed to rule as his English predecessors and who had been accepted on such terms by English nobles and churchmen. This behaviour played its part in provoking the rebellions which produced the ravaging. To condone brutality for the sake of long-term gains or out of an uncritical definition of strength is no more acceptable for the eleventh century than for any other period.

If William's rule had its peculiarly harsh side it also shared the long-established oppressiveness of English royal power. At his consecration William took over the rights, lands and authority of an English king. He was heir to their

12. See E. Mason, 'William Rufus: myth and reality', *Journal of Medieval History*, 3 (1977), pp. 1–20 and M. Clanchy, *England and its Rulers*, pp. 52–5 and R. Ray, 'Orderic Vitalis and William of Poitiers, a monastic reinterpretation of William the Conqueror', *Revue Belge de Philologie et d'Histoire*, 50 (1972), pp. 1116–27
13. ASC MS E s. a. 1087
14. Orderic Vitalis, Vol. IV, Bk VII, p. 95 and compare Vol. II, Bk IV, pp. 231–3

problems and limitations and to their method of rule. The monetary system, for example, continued, though not exactly as before. At some point William moved from a regular recoinage and change of type to an unchanging one, and raised and altered taxation on moneyers to allow for this,[15] but most of the moneyers themselves remained English. The king continued to notify his decisions via writs to local sheriffs and holders of sokes, many of whom were still Englishmen. The Norman landholders stepped into the place of their English predecessors and inherited the claims and disputes of those predecessors, which could only be settled by reference to the English past. In these areas 1066 could not have been a sharp break even had the Normans desired it to be.

The record of the trial on Pinnenden Heath exemplifies the continuity which was inevitable despite the intrusion of new landholders.[16] The dispute was between Odo earl of Kent and Lanfranc archbishop of Canterbury, just as that of 1051 had been between Earl Godwine and Archbishop Robert. Both were about the lands of the church and the claims on them of the earl. It was resolved in the old courts, hearing old evidence, according to old procedures. Once in England it was impossible for the Normans to remain a united group. With their lands they inherited the quarrels and the divisions of their predecessors, questions, as here about lay control and ecclesiastical land, which overrode the division of English and Norman. The archbishop took the advantage of the trial to record not merely its outcome, but all his rights, including those *vis-à-vis* the king. The trend of tenth- and eleventh-century rule, with its insistence on royal rights, had given others a need to record theirs, both before and after 1066.

The entire proceedings and its outcome were committed to writing. 1066 was important in enhancing the desire for record;[17] old rights could be seen as under threat, and the rush to record might be taken as another sign of the perception of William's rule as oppressive. But oppression was systemic. During the 1070s many churches complained of the exactions of royal sheriffs, after 1075/6 the complaints were often successful and resulted in repossession. Norman sheriffs like Urse or Picot may have stepped up their activity. But their predecessors had been taking church land since the late tenth century. Churchmen after 1066 were not merely reacting to new dispossessions, but using the uncertainty after conquest to prosecute old claims. In the 1070s William himself seemed to be unclear about the powers in the hands of royal officials and the justice of claims against them. One of the purposes of Domesday in 1086 was to enquire into royal officials whose injustice was debatably Norman, whose powers were emphatically English.

As Pinnenden Heath shows, there were many motives for committing things to writing in the late eleventh century, one of them being that the old knowledge on which claims could be decided was already threatened. The ageing bishop of Selsey, Æthelric, had to be brought to the trial as one 'very wise in the law of the land'. By *c.*1100 this problem was becoming acute, and the spate of documentation in the early twelfth century appears as an attempt to salvage

15. D. M. Metcalf, 'The taxation of moneyers under Edward the Confessor and in 1086', *Domesday Studies*, ed. J. C. Holt (Woodbridge, 1987), pp. 279–93
16. EHD II no. 50, pp. 481–3
17. A. Gransden, *Historical Writing in England, c. 550– c. 1307* (1974), cap. 6

knowledge and expertise.[18] The desire of Norman lords to have all that their predecessors had had made for continuity across 1066, but it was a continuity which when combined with a massive transfer of land and offices brought problems. The king was not certain what were his rights or those of others. Norman lords argued among themselves about claims arising pre-1066 whilst the knowledge to resolve them faded.

Such problems were one motivation behind the Domesday Survey of 1086, that unique account of the lands and rights of the king and lords south of the Tees which is a monument both to continuity and to change after 1066. It was a survey of royal rights and lands, but simultaneously it established the rights of all Norman tenants, both generally by establishing English predecessors whose rights had been transferred, and specifically by resolving disputes.[19] It was a check on sheriffs and all that they administered, from towns to royal lands, part of the general enquiry into royal rights and fruit of the specific build-up of complaints in the 1070s. It was not a neutral, extra-political process. Landholding was so complex in 1066 that doubt existed about who had held what. Which of several possible English predecessors held the land? To which Norman successor were his or her rights transferred? The relative power of the Norman lords arguing in 1086 might determine the answer[20] and in the process affect Domesday's picture of 1066 landholding.

Cnut's conquest had been sealed not by a record of land but by laws. It was captured in I and II Cnut. This conquest occurred at a time when the tradition of law-making in England was strong. Archbishop Wulfstan, adviser to Æthelred and Cnut, saw general legal statement as the way the rights and duties of kings should be expressed. If there is nothing comparable after 1066 this may point less to a contrast between conquests than to the end of the tradition of law-making, largely a tenth-century phenomenon which died with Wulfstan in 1023. Cnut in his laws, like William in Domesday, laid claim to the rights of an English king and guaranteed those of others. The growth of royal power was obvious in both. Cnut's laws brought together royal rights, the tightening of court procedures and other aspects of tenth-century development. Domesday's makers utilized hundred and shire courts, sheriffs and geld lists, records of royal and noble land which were the products of that same development.[21]

But the differences between 1017 and 1066 cannot simply be ironed out as a function of different sources. The difference in sources is not merely fortuitous. Conquest in one case prompted comprehensive legal statement, in the other a comprehensive survey of land and royal rights. Domesday was the record of a conquest which had entailed the large-scale transfer of land, the replacement of an English land-holding high nobility by a Norman one. Domesday is also the fruit of a new, if temporary, balance between king and nobles after 1066. Cnut's laws are marked by reciprocity. The king stated his rights and guaranteed those

18. W. L. Warren, 'The myth of Norman administrative efficiency' *TRHS* ser. 5, 34 (1984), pp. 113–32
19. see J. C. Holt, '1086', *Domesday Studies*, ed. Holt, pp. 41–64
20. P. Hyams, 'No register of title, the Domesday inquest and land adjudication', ANS, 9 (1987), pp. 127–41
21. S. Harvey, 'Domesday Book and its predecessors', *English Historical Review*, 86 (1971), pp. 753–73

of others. Cnut offered benefits as well as asserting powers. The total insecurity of a new ruling group after 1066 was missing. Domesday is a starker statement of royal right. The only reciprocity is the guarantee of secure tenure which this record of landholding offered Norman tenants. In exchange for this Norman nobles accepted detailed enquiry into their lands. From king to undertenant the new Norman lords were united in fear for their claims to the land they had taken. That fear worked in the king's favour. In the decades immediately after 1066 it was only ecclesiastics, bolstered by institutional continuity and records, who could afford to demand their rights against the king. For the moment the nobility preferred to see their *possession* underwritten. This change in the balance was not permanent. By 1100 Henry I was being called to promises in his coronation charter analogous to those of Cnut. The shift should not be exaggerated. Cnut was not in the hands of his nobility, nor could William ride roughshod over his. But beyond the continuities, 1066 did effect some immediate changes in the structures of power.

Relations between king and nobility after 1066 have always been linked to possible military and social changes. One landholding, military ruling elite replaced another; in fundamental ways little changed. That elite continued to draw sustenance from peasant rent, its family structures and organization were comparable across 1066, its ideals remained essentially the same. Debate still centres on whether the transfer of land took place in such a way as to constitute a major reorganization or revolution in landholding, and whether a military conquest produced changes in military organization which either altered the nature of the nobility or increased royal demands. Was the temporary shift of balance after 1066 accompanied by a more permanent one?

1066, a revolution in landholding or in noble society?

Normans stepped into the shoes of their English predecessors on a scale sometimes masked by Domesday's inconsistent recording of English land-holders in 1066. In many shires Domesday records the 1066 undertenant, but the transfers after 1066 were from tenant-in-chief to tenant-in-chief. To assess the takeover accurately we must first establish the English tenant-in-chief. If we attach English undertenants to these English overlords, the estate structures and pattern of land exploitation appears more continuous across the conquest.[22]

Computer analysis of some shires, however, has shown that the changeover could be revolutionary.[23] Each Norman lord did not take over from a single English predecessor. Land was rearranged and reorganized, the holdings of several English tenants were often divided and amalgamated so that new estate patterns had been formed by 1086. The shape of some estates was altered so fundamentally that individual villages were disrupted, resulting in some cases in falls in land values between 1066 and 1086.

Full computer analysis of Domesday may resolve this debate, though the two arguments are reconcilable. Disruption and continuity coexisted. Undertenancy

---

22. P. Sawyer, '1066–1086. A tenurial revolution?', *Domesday Book, a Reassessment*, ed. P. Sawyer (1985), pp. 71–85
23. R. Fleming, 'Domesday Book and the tenurial revolution', ANS, 9 (1987), pp. 87–102

was undeniably important in 1066, the English nobility no less than the Norman were the lords of other landholders and of military followers. The complications produced by undertenancy account for some of the disruptions after 1066. Many English undertenants were the men of several lords, holding land from several. In the rapid land transfer there was room for much debate. Norman lords were inclined to claim all the land held by their predecessors, even if those predecessors had held it as tenants of someone else. Such claims could be successful. Moreover the transfer of land after 1066 occurred in stages, and different principles and needs determined the result in different places and times. In the Welsh marches, for example, the pattern of landholding of the earls of Herefordshire after 1066 differs from those in Shropshire and Chester.[24] William Fitz Osbern was made earl of Hereford in 1067. No compact block of land was created for him; he and other men like Walter de Lacy took over English estates, succeeding to specific predecessors, in this case the lands of Earl Harold, sheriff's land and royal demesne. Shropshire and Cheshire were organized four years or so later. The estates of the marcher earls here were from the first compact, the earl dominating the landholding of his shire, the pattern of pre-conquest land-holding ignored to achieve that end. The situation had changed since 1067. By 1071 William was abandoning his attempt to rule the Midlands with the cooperation of English nobles. Edwin and Morcar had forfeited, as had Eadric the Wild, giving William a freer hand. The problem of defence against the Welsh was clearer. Even the view of a transfer of land whose principles altered over time is too simple. Both straightforward succession to all a predecessor's land and the disregard of former patterns to achieve specific ends operated simultaneously and from the beginning. Along the south coast, William was as aware of the problem of defence in 1067 as Edward had been. Compact estates grouped around castles like Pevensey and Dover were William's immediate pattern here,[25] following moves in this direction under Edward.

Too many factors influenced the transfer to allow a simple picture. Many Normans were allotted the forfeit land of a named English owner. With it they inherited all the disputes and possible claims against it, all the possibilities of pursuing a predecessor's claims to the utmost and perhaps fewer inhibitions about doing so. The forfeiture of English nobles occurred in stages as rebellions progressed. New opportunities arose with every forfeiture. Defensive needs had to be met, some clear in 1067, others emerging more gradually. William himself vacillated between acting the legitimate king, transferring specific English estates to a successor, and the nervous conqueror, remodelling blocks of territory around castles. Between 1066 and 1086 some Norman tenants died, some left England or forfeited, many maximized or reconstructed their estates, others continued the work of English sheriffs, using royal office steadily to augment their holdings. Domesday freezes one frame in this moving picture, just as it froze another in 1066.

24. C. Lewis, 'The Norman settlement of Herefordshire under William I', ANS, 7 (1985), 195–213
25. J. F. A. Mason, 'William the First and the Sussex Rapes', *1066 Commemoration Essays* (1966), 37–58

The greatest danger lies in arguing about the disruption or continuity of a landholding pattern which is seen as static and immemorial up to 1066. The estates of 1086 were the products of the previous twenty years; those of 1066 could have a short pedigree. The concentrations of land in the hands of the Godwine family date back no further than fifty years. They had been constantly added to and altered.[26] The estates held by Harold and Tostig in 1066 were no older than the 1050s. No-one who has tried to follow the fate of late tenth-century noble families or of the landed estates of the monastic revival can fail to be struck by the enormous changes in land-holding which are a feature of the eleventh century. No-one who has followed the build-up of noble and ecclesiastical estates through the grants, office-holding and forfeitures of the tenth century could argue that the situation was new after AD 1000. The problems so many Norman tenants experienced in establishing their rights to land were in part the result of forfeitures, gifts and changes in the years prior to 1066. The lands they took over were already disputable. If 1066 was a tenurial revolution it had its precedents.

Changes in military organization and their effects on nobles and king have been bogged down in the labyrinthine debates about 'feudalism'. That term has served as a Platonic form for many medieval historians, to which individual societies imperfectly approximate, or else as a teleological end towards which all were struggling.[27] Early medieval Europe produced a variety of social formations broadly comparable because formed from similar elements: an agrarian basis, family structures normally ego-based and limited to three or four generations, a military elite whose ideals derived from family and battle, and combinations of landholding and service throughout society, some of which go back to prehistoric communal dues to ritual centres and chiefs, others to notions of gift and reciprocity.

By the first half of the eleventh century in England the nobility was a military elite, increasingly marked out from the rest of society by specialized fighting methods and expensive equipment.[28] An English fighting force of this date would be formed both of paid men and of those whose duty to fight with a lord had in many cases become connected to their right to hold land; some would have been personally summoned by the king, others served in the contingent of a lord.[29] Earls like Siward and Tostig had bands of household troops, housecarls, sometimes, as in the case of Edmund Ironside, called *cnihts* or knights.[30] English churchmen owed some form of military duty to the king. In 992, 1016 and 1066 abbots and bishops were involved in battle; they may not always have fought, though they were sometimes killed, as were the bishop of

26. R. Fleming, 'Domesday estates of the king and the Godwines: a study in late Saxon politics', *Speculum*, 58 (1983), pp. 987–1007 and A. Williams, 'Land and power in the eleventh century, the estates of Harold Godwineson', ANS 3 (1980), 171–87 and 230–4
27. E. A. R. Brown, 'The tyranny of a construct, feudalism and historians of medieval Europe', *American Historical Review*, 79 (1974), 1063–88
28. Of central importance is N. Brooks, 'Arms, status and warfare in late Saxon England', *Ethelred the Unready*, ed. D. Hill (Oxford, 1978), pp. 81–103; on the use of horses and fighting on horseback, J. Kiff, 'Images of war: illustrations of warfare in early eleventh-century England', ANS, 7 (1985), 177–94
29. R. Abels, 'Bookland and fyrd-service in late Saxon England', ANS, 7 (1985), 1–25
30. ASC MS D s. a. 1054 and MS C s. a. 1065, and R. 74

Dorchester and the abbot of Ramsey in 1016. Bishops and archbishops paid heriots, death duties in military equipment to the king: Archbishop Ælfric left in his will a warship with sixty helmets and coats of mail as his heriot, and two further ships to the people of his dioceses in Kent and Wiltshire. The payment of a heriot in cash and arms already guaranteed the landholding of a noble and ensured the inheritance of his wife and children. The universally paid geld was justifiable on the ground that it was part of the military service owed by all (see *Nobility, Ruling the Kingdom*.)

The situation in 1066 was the result of long evolution, and especially of the needs of the new kingdom of the English. Its notions of personal duties based on standing in society and landholding and its military nobility were comprehensible to Normans if not identical with their system. William, like English kings before him, worked with what he had to meet his needs. His armies consisted of a core of household warriors and men who fought for pay, reinforced by the troops of his close followers, and increasingly of other English landholders. The castles he built to hold a conquered country were new, as were the uses to which he put them, though this response to a new need is comparable to the *burh* building of the later ninth and early tenth centuries. The extent to which he relied on his own followers after 1066 may have forged a stronger bond of personal obligation among a small group. But Henry I's coronation charter, with its worries about inheritance and death dues, shows that none of the tension between the nobility's duties to their own families and those to their lord had been resolved. The strength of the royal lord's demands, in 1100 as in 1016, was the fruit of tenth- and eleventh-century development not merely of 1066. Changes after 1066 must however have been felt by Norman nobles who now found themselves and their lands open to the pressing demands of an English king.

The Norman Conquest did not permanently alter the political balance or the political system of England. William greatly extended the royal lands from their size in 1066, but the royal lands had always fluctuated.[31] Their scale on the eve of 1066 had been depressed by the rise of the Godwine family, which held many of them. There may be no-one as mighty as Godwine, Leofric or Harold after 1066, though William Fitz Osbern and Odo of Bayeux could pass as imitations, but Godwine, Leofric and Harold were products of the mid eleventh–century situation not structural parts of the English kingdom. William appointed earls especially in marcher areas in a way Æthelred would have understood. Kings had moved gradually away from large ealdormanries in the second half of the tenth century, others had recreated them in the eleventh. William's changes were more sudden and brutal but not an entirely new option, and he was certainly ready to create powerful noble estates with the spoils of victory. If the dual rule of England and Normandy produced nothing like Harold, it was more than the dual monarchy of England and Denmark which had facilitated his rise. The failure of history to exactly repeat itself is no proof that the structure of the political system was altered in 1066. William, like Cnut, had increased military needs. The problem of ruling England and Normandy lay

31. P. A. Stafford, 'The *farm of one night* and the organization of King Edward's estates in Domesday', *Economic. History Review*, ser. 2, 33 (1980), pp. 491–502

behind many twelfth-century developments, but here 1066 must take its place alongside 1016, 1106 and 1154 as a date of debatable significance, and none of them may have the importance of 927 or 954.

The need to place 1066 in a long perspective is clear in the final case of changes in the church. William moved bishoprics, separated the church courts from those of the hundred and, allegedly, brought reform to England. He is sometimes accused of enforcing augmented royal control over the church or alternatively of defending his rights against the reforming papacy. The reorganization of bishoprics was an eleventh-century trend which brought them in line with eleventh-century reality. A conqueror may be more ruthless in his readiness to change, but Edward had already moved and amalgamated English sees. Archbishop Wulfstan had been fully aware of the distinction of God and king in the courts, though like many after 1066 he felt God needed the king's backing if he were to get his rights. English reform had continued since the tenth century, episcopally led, as was widely the case in Europe. Wulfstan had his successors in the North both in his concern for the way of life of the clergy and in his view of a bishop's role in his diocese. The law of the Northumbrian Priests was written after Wulfstan's death[32] and Ealdred of York carried out reorganization of his diocese.[33] Lanfranc was not the origin of English reform. The breath of papally-led reform had touched England *c*.1050, and after an initial dalliance with it Edward's aim was that of William, to retain his rights to appoint and maintain bishops.

The reform which had moved falteringly on since the ninth century was altered in the late eleventh when a reformed and active papacy provided it with leadership and with a court of appeal over and outside lay power. The uneasy coexistence of sacred and secular had been apparent by AD 1000. Rising taxation in eleventh-century England did nothing to allay it. The growth and regularization of all courts between the tenth and twelfth century brought the separation of church jurisdiction. The eleventh century in Europe was critical for these developments, but 1066 was not a crucial date. Some things were changed, especially in the short term by a prolonged military takeover. Some things were changing already in the long perspective. But the structures of personal monarchy, landed nobility and Christian church were altered, if at all, more by unification than by conquest.

32. H. P. Tenhagen, *Das northumbrische Priestergesetz* (Dusseldorf, 1979)
33. J. M. Cooper, *The Last Four Anglo-Saxon Archibishops of York*, Borthwick Papers, 38 (York, 1980)

7

England and Its Neighbours[1]

Two centuries of English history which began with Viking attacks and saw two external conquests cannot be seen in isolation. Both the broad sweep of development and the detail of internal politics were affected by the neighbours of the new English kingdom as well as by the actions of its own rulers. Since England itself was built up by conquest and was ruled by non-English kings in the eleventh century, the definition of 'neighbours' changed throughout the period, involving at one date York's Viking rulers, at another the German emperor or the French king. At the margins of England itself the distinction between neighbour and subject was blurred, especially in the North where the earls of Bamburgh faced in two directions. The eventual boundaries of England still appeared far from inevitable: in the early tenth century their extension into Wales seemed likely, whilst northern England was being drawn into a Viking Irish Sea kingdom. The growing power of the king of the Scots throughout these centuries meant that no area north of the Mersey or the Tees could have been deemed inevitably English. Relations among neighbours shifted through a spectrum from opportunistic welcoming of each other's exiles, passive hostility, raiding for booty to invasion and conquest; from the securing of prestige or aid by marriage and alliance to submission and the acceptance of lordship.

By c. AD 900 a century of Viking raiding had produced a sense of common purpose among the rulers surrounding the North Sea and English Channel. The view that the Vikings were the common enemy and that defence against them rather than their use for internal political advantage was the function of a king had been slow in growing and was still not unanimous. Vikings were not beyond the pale of civilized life, as some sources present them. They shared too many

1. Further detail on the areas covered in this chapter can be obtained from J. Dunbabin, *France in the Making, 843–1100* (Oxford, 1985); E. James, *The Origins of France* (1982); P. H. Sawyer, *Kings and Vikings* (1982); E. Roesdahl, *Viking Age Denmark* (1982); A. A. M. Duncan, *Scotland, the Making of the Kingdom* (Edinburgh, 1975); A. Smyth, *Warlords and Holy Men, Scotland AD 80–1000* (1984); W. Davies, *Wales in the Early Middle Ages* (Leicester, 1982) and H. Loyn, 'England and Wales in the tenth century: the context of the Athelstan charters', *Welsh History Review*, 10 (1980–1), pp. 283–301

values and practices with their European neighbours. In the 860s Ceolwulf was prepared to treat with Viking armies to gain his own ends in Mercia, and Alfred's nephew, Æthelwold, would do the same in the early tenth century. But many rulers shared a desire to present the Vikings as different and pagan, a common interest in fighting against them. Alfred and his descendants, the West Frankish kings and the counts of Flanders were joined in a web of alliance sealed by marriages. Wessex and Mercia, hitherto hostile neighbours, had moved towards cooperative action, again confirmed by marriage, a combination which incidentally helped pull southern Welsh princes who suffered from Mercian raiding to Alfred's court. The search for prestige played its part in the links between the counts of Flanders and Alfred, and in the later marriages of West Saxon royal women to kings and princes in Ottonian Germany and northern France. The court of Athelstan and its learning appears European as much as English as a result. Success had already broadened Alfred's horizons within England. His effective power was often limited, but his aspirations were already wide. West Saxons, by producing the Anglo-Saxon Chronicle, had located their own history in an *English* frame. Some of Alfred's followers called him 'king of the English'. The idea was not new, if the espousal of it in Wessex was.

The settlement of the Viking armies posed new dangers to rulers of Mercia and Wessex. Edward the Elder and Æthelflæd responded with military conquests. That same settlement removed the immediate pressure which had brought together West Saxon kings and continental rulers. The marriages which had tied the knot of earlier alliance and friendship had left wives, widows and heirs as cause and opportunity for later interference. When Charles the Simple and his son Louis d'Outremer were ousted from the throne of western Frankia, Louis and his mother Eadgifu sought refuge at the court of Athelstan, their uncle and brother. In 939 Athelstan sent a fleet to ravage the southern coasts of the Channel on Louis' behalf. Realignments within northern France cut across old lines. The counts of Flanders saw Herbert of Vermandois and his kinsman King Ralph as the rising stars and gave no help to Louis. In the 940s Edmund ravaged Flanders and received Flemish exiles: in the 950s the counts of Flanders reciprocated by welcoming Dunstan when he fled from Eadwig's court. English æthelings were as quick to utilize the new situation as Æthelwold had been to ally with the new Viking rulers. In 933 Athelstan's younger but more legitimate brother Edwin was shipwrecked and drowned en route into exile. He was on his way to Flanders where his body was washed up and given the honourable burial of a kinsman by Count Adelolf, his cousin.[2]

When Alfred died in 899 he was ruler of Wessex with some control of Mercia; by 927 Athelstan was ruler as far north as the Tees if not beyond. The speed of that transformation was another factor changing relations among the rulers of Britain and North Western Europe. It threatened others as much as it added to the prestige of the English dynasty. Athelstan's court attracted exiles and friends from Brittany and Scandinavia; the Ottonian King Henry I sought a bride there for his son Otto. Welsh princes came there regularly to reap the

2. Acts of the abbots of St Bertin, EHD 1, no. 26, pp. 346–7

benefits but run the risks of alliance with an English Charlemagne. To the Scottish kings and the Viking rulers, especially those with claims on York, it was the threat which was most apparent. At Brunanburh in 937 they united against Athelstan and were defeated. The victory enhanced the image of successful warrior leaders which the English dynasty now enjoyed, but it did not destroy the rulers of northern and western Britain. Between Athelstan's death in 939 and the final submission of York in 954 the activities of Strathclyde Britons, Scots and Dublin Vikings raised constant doubt about whether the kingdom of York would be assimilated to southern England.

Edgar's coronation as emperor of Britain in 973 is an indication of the aspirations of southern English kings towards hegemony. It is also a warning against seeing the tenth century in Britain solely through southern English eyes. Edgar was crowned at Bath as a ruler of many peoples, English, Danish and British. Soon after he travelled to Chester, where the kings of the Welsh met him and 'gave him pledges that they would be his allies on sea and on land'.[3] Later English sources associated Kenneth of Scotland and the ruler of Strathclyde in the submissions to Edgar. Yet 973 was no simple affirmation of the power of the English king. Alliance among the rulers around the Irish Sea such as produced Brunanburh in 937 or the events of 973 was no more natural and long-lasting than earlier alliance around the English Channel produced by Viking menace under Alfred.

Rulers who still relied on raiding for booty readily returned to it, and the Viking rulers of Man especially had been ravaging along the coasts of Wales if not of northern Britain. The kings of Strathclyde like the people of York had a history of contact with Viking rulers to their west. Strathclyde was to the Scottish kings what York was to Wessex. In 972 Kenneth ravaged Cumbria/ Strathclyde as far as the Dee, that is as far as Chester.[4]

Edgar in 973 sought renewed alliance with Welsh kings with whom he now had common interests. Strathclyde kings were desirable friends for an English king concerned with Irish Sea Vikings: an English king a prestigious ally for a Strathclyde ruler asserting independence against the Scots. Edgar and Kenneth were successful and expanding neighbours. Chester was a meeting on boundaries, between Edgar and the Welsh at the point of common threat from the Irish Sea, between Kenneth and Edgar near what Kenneth might now claim as the southerly tip of his power. Peace and friendship were sworn, boundaries recognized with Kenneth as beneficiary. Scottish kings' control over Lothian, once part of the English kingdom of Northumbria, was accepted. Only English eyes could see this as a simple imperial triumph.

At the end of the tenth century attacks direct from Scandinavia were renewed. The impulse to them lay in changes within Scandinavia itself, especially in Denmark. Overkingships had been established, often on an impressive scale, but they were still subject to challenge. To present a history of Scandinavia at this date as a history of the kings of Denmark, Norway and Sweden is to oversimplify a situation in which many rulers still coexisted. Harold Bluetooth had had a long reign, and his great building works at Jellinge testify to

3. ASC MS D 973
4. A. O. Anderson, 'Anglo-Scottish relations from Constantine II to William', *Scottish Historical Review*, 42 (1963), pp. 4–5

his power and his aspirations. But it is his forts at places like Trelleborg and Fyrkat which bear witness to his power and its insecurity. They were constructed at the end of his reign against internal enemies and challengers, including his son Swegn but extending beyond his own family. Power in the North was still intimately linked to military prowess, the capacity to overawe and exact tribute. Harold's southern neighbours, the new Ottonian kings, were equally subject to these compulsions and their attacks northward did nothing to raise Harold's prestige. The Vikings who came south in the late tenth century came for tribute to use in the northern world. The responses to them were often equally traditional. Æthelred stood godfather to Olaf in 994 after negotiating peace with him, seeking an answer in personal ties. When Æthelred later sent Olaf missionaries[5] he was not merely maintaining contact and friendship but attempting to play off northern rulers against each other in a way Louis the Pious would have recognized over a century and half before.

The renewed threat of the Vikings did not automatically reactivate the friendships of the late ninth century, though it did turn the attention of English rulers back to the Channel and the southern end of the North Sea. Viking armies were able to take winter refuge in ports in Normandy, and the agreement between Æthelred and Richard in 991 renewed by the marriage of Æthelred and Emma in 1002 did not prevent it. During the eleventh century traders-cum-pirates from Scandinavia continued to gather fleets or dispose of their loot in Normandy or Flanders. In the late tenth and eleventh centuries the princes of northern France shared no common perception of the danger with English rulers. Norman counts had a long history of contact with Scandinavia in the tenth century and kept some memory of their origins there. But ethnic links are less important than the recognition that in the eleventh century as in the ninth Viking presence could offer opportunities rather than threat and was readily assimilated into the European world. Pirates in England were traders in Flanders. They were available mercenary forces: Arnulf of Flanders had Danes in his service in the early eleventh century, as did Æthelred in England. By AD 900 a century of raiding had been necessary to produce a by no means unanimous view that Vikings were an overwhelming political fact, a more or less common threat. But *c.* AD 1000 attacks had only recently revived and were limited in geographical impact. Scandinavians were not seen necessarily as Vikings and their attacks followed the familiar pattern of one ruler on another. There was no basis for even the most superficial perception of a common threat. What was central to Æthelred's England was peripheral to the concerns of northern French princes.

During the eleventh century Norman and Flemish counts were drawn into English politics. In the case of Normandy the context was specifically Viking, but in both cases their links with England were an extension of the politics of northern France. This was a highly competitive world in which marriage alliances, claims of lordship and wardship, step-relationships and the reception and use of exiles were used to extend territory, secure loyalty and as pretexts for intervention. None of these methods of personal politics was new, though the

5. P. H. Sawyer, 'Ethelred II, Olaf Trygvason and the conversion of Norway', *Scandinavian Studies* (1987), pp. 299–307

small size and fluctuating fortunes of the units involved intensified resulting struggle. The tenth century had shown how far and how fast personal power could be extended, or lost in these ways. They were tactics not strategic game plans. Each prince or ruler found himself at the centre of a web of alliances which was the product of a multitude of specific and transient needs and constantly shifting. Like players in a game they acquired cards and chips, including the wildest of possible claims. Only if the opportunity presented itself were the cards played or the chips gambled in any particular direction.

Neither Flanders nor Normandy were simple enemies or friends of England. The Flemish counts were ready to take English exiles and back them: Emma in 1037–39, Osgod Clapa in the 1040s, Godwine in 1052, Tostig in 1065, Æthelwine of Durham in 1070, Cospatric and Edgar the Ætheling in 1072. English politics ensured that exiles and opportunities to use them came thick and fast. The counts formed only one tenuous link with the English dynasty in the marriage of Tostig and Judith *c.* 1052. The Norman counts gathered more usable English cards. The marriage of Emma, the exile there of Æthelred in 1013 and of his sons after 1016, the accession of one of those exiles in 1042 produced a long and continuous interest. 1066 was the opportunity to play the cards but not an inevitable result of having collected them. Other rulers across the Channel and in Scandinavia held some of the English suit. Edward the Confessor's sister Godgifu had married first the count of Mantes and later Eustace of Boulogne. Ralf of Mantes, her only son, was brought to England in the 1040s; Edward may have preferred to keep his rival claimants close to home. Eustace of Boulogne's appearance in England in 1052 and his equivocal attitude to William after 1066 were attempts to play his hand.

The relationships between eleventh-century northern French rulers and English kings recall earlier ones between Frankish and English rulers, complicated perhaps by the greater number of French rulers by this date. Viking attacks were now concentrated on England, resulting in conquest and Danish rule from 1016. Danish rule was not an interlude in eleventh-century history. It left Danish kings with claims on the English throne more powerful than those accumulating in the hands of French princes. From 1042 onwards Swegn Estrithson, Cnut's nephew and king of Denmark, had such claims which the Danish historian Adam of Bremen presents as plans for the English succession. Adam, like other post-1066 apologists, may exaggerate, but that does not detract from the continuing importance of Danish claims. After 1066 William certainly took them seriously.

Between 1016 and 1042 kings of England who were also kings of Denmark found they had new neighbours, not only among the Scandinavian rulers in whose struggles English resources were not committed, but in the person of the German Emperor. The link with the Ottonians formed by the marriage of Athelstan's sister in the early tenth century had not been forgotten later in that century. The inspiration of the imperial coronation of 973 was less the remote events of Charlemagne's crowning in AD 800 than the recent coronation of Otto II in Rome. Cnut's experiences, however, were not of remote ties with imperial prestige, but of Ottonian attacks and raiding. It was the emperor who received and helped the sons of Edmund Ironside, fleeing from England after Cnut's takeover. When the Ottonians were replaced in 1024 by Conrad, a descendant of Otto I in the female line, Cnut may not have relished having a descendant of Edward the Elder, a remote kinsman of the native English dynasty on the imperial throne. His attendance at Conrad's coronation in 1027 was less a masterstroke of diplomacy than a gesture of self-preservation after the defeats of 1026.

The emperor sent gifts and ambasssadors to Edward the Confessor's consecration in 1043. Ambassadors of the emperor had been in England in the 940s. The ties had been renewed by eleventh-century developments, but they were still not close. The emperor was the remotest of neighbours to a king who no longer ruled in Scandinavia, though it must be remembered that Edward's claim on the Danish throne was no wilder than many eleventh-century claims to the English one.

The story of England and Scandinavia can be read as one of victim and attacker; of England and northern France as one of exile, alliance and claims; of England, Carolingians and Ottonians as one of prestige and gift exchange and all can be contrasted with the relation of England to Wales as one of domination and between England and Scotland as one of aggression. There is truth in such contrasts but they simplify. Exile, alliance and marriage were common relations used in many of these, and in any case ideas of stable relationships, whether of friendship, enmity or domination are inappropriate to the flux of politics of personal rule. That flux operated, however, under deeper compulsions, such as the needs for tribute or land which impelled Danish or Norman attackers and geographical proximity. The expansion of their overlordship which early medieval rulers so readily achieved was immediately over their closest neighbours.

Wales

'Wales' *c.* AD 900 is a misnomer applied to a series of kings and kingdoms: Gwynedd, Dyfed, Morgannwg/Glywysing, Gwent, Brycheiniog and Powys. The tenth and eleventh centuries can with some justification be described in southern Britain as the 'rise of Wessex', and in northern Britain as 'the rise of the kingdom of the Scots'. It is tempting to describe the history of western Britain as the 'rise of Gwynedd', but that parallel would suggest a symmetry which hampers understanding of Welsh history.

South-east Wales was united for much of the tenth century, *c.* 930–74, under Morgan Hen, of the dynasty of Glywysing. Before and after this its political history was fragmented. Threatened by the ravaging of Rhodri the Great and his son Anarawd of Gwynedd as well as by Mercia, the kings of this area sought the alliance of Alfred at the end of the ninth century. The threat of such ravaging continued to bring Welsh kings to the English court in the first half of the tenth century. In the late tenth and eleventh centuries Gwent was often separate from Glywysing, sometimes ruled by a member of the dynasty of Dyfed, sometimes directly from Dyfed, sometimes by Gwynedd. In 1015 its king was a man called Edwin, a son of the king of Dyfed, but whose English name is witness to the long-standing contacts of this area with Mercia and Wessex.

South-west Wales, i.e. the kingdom of Dyfed, and north-west Wales, i.e. Gwynedd, are interwoven in their history during these centuries. Rhodri the

Great in the third quarter of the ninth century enforced his overlordship on Powys and Ceredigion, and as a result of marriage alliances his descendants ruled both Gwynedd and Dyfed for most of the tenth and eleventh centuries: Rhodri's grandson, Hywel Dda, married a daughter of the king of Dyfed. As the history of Western Europe in the early Middle Ages demonstrates over and again, the fact of a common dynasty did nothing to produce peace and unity. Members of the dynasty sought to acquire control of the other kingdom and all claims were complicated by the practice of shared kingship, under which the claim of brothers and cousins remained strong. Members of this family established a series of temporary hegemonies over much of Wales: Hywel Dda of Dyfed took Gwynedd from *c.*942 to 950; Maredudd of Dyfed held Gwynedd from 986 to 999. Gruffudd ap Llywelyn in the mid eleventh century is thus only the most spectacular example of the trend. His father married into the Dyfed line. In 1039 Gruffudd took Gwynedd, killing its king, Iago; in 1055 he went on to take Dyfed, killing Gruffudd ap Rhydderch, its ruler, and also the south-east Welsh kingdoms. From 1055 to 1063 he was ruler of all the kingdoms of the Welsh. It was the struggles of the two Gruffudds in the 1040s and 1050s and the harrying of Gruffudd ap Llywelyn in the late 1050s and 1060s which stimulated Edward the Confessor to organize the Welsh marches defensively. These temporary warlords are a feature not only of Welsh but of all early European history. That they did not give rise here to a kingdom of the Welsh is no sign of primitive political development, but a result of many factors, most notably the extreme difficulty of the Welsh terrain.

In relations between these Welsh and English kings cooperation, marriage and alliance coexisted with hostility and ravaging. The greater resources of the English kings by the tenth century distorted them, but did not necessarily entail dependence for the Welsh. There was ravaging in both directions, as each used their frontiers as the time-honoured source of booty. In the tenth century the ravaging was usually by English rulers into Wales, as in 942, 949, 967, 978, 983, 990s, 1012 and 1046. By the mid eleventh century the raids were largely in the opposite direction, in 1049, 1052, 1053, 1055. The lack of sources from Mercia means a probable underestimate of all raiding throughout the period. Tribute, punishment and deterrence were the motives, but few of these raids were simply of one side against the other. In 983, for example, Ælfhere of Mercia led an army with Hywel of Gwynedd against Einion of Dyfed; in the 990s Edwin son of Einion led English forces against Maredudd of Dyfed; in 1049 Ealdred, bishop of Worcester had Welsh forces on his side when he fought against Gruffudd ap Rhydderch. Records are incomplete but the most common pattern up to the early eleventh century is of an English earl or ealdorman and a Welsh king or claimant fighting against another Welsh king; at this date open struggles which could be utilized were mostly among Welsh kings. In the eleventh century open struggle was a feature of politics on either side of the border, and the situation was often reversed. In 1016 Welsh fought alongside Edmund Ironside against Cnut and in the 1050s Gruffudd ravaged with Earl Ælfgar, son of Earl Leofric, against Earl Ralf.

It was ealdormen or earls of Mercia rather than kings of the English who were actively involved in Wales, continuing the concerns of eighth- and ninth-century Mercian kings. To describe their actions as 'border defence' misses the importance of borders as lands of opportunity as much as problems in the early Middle Ages. The question, who got the spoils of Welsh ravaging, cannot be answered, but it is legitimate to speculate that much of it was distributed by Mercian ealdormen. Wales for them was an area where a military reputation and the following that goes with it could be built up. Harold made his name here in the 1050s and 1060s, Ælfhere's great renown as 'prince of the Mercian people' may have rested on a similar basis. It was also across borders that alliances and contacts were made which could be used to establish power and independence. Mercian earls in the tenth and eleventh centuries do not normally appear to have used such opportunities, a tribute perhaps to the pull of the patronage of the English court. But our knowledge of events here is woefully inadequate, and the full lineage of Edwin son of Einion would make interesting reading. If tenth-century ealdormen did not feel the need to use their opportunities, Earl Ælfgar in his quarrels with the English court in the 1050s did. The marriage of his daughter, the sister of Edwin and Morcar, to Gruffudd shows that his alliance with Gruffudd went beyond ravaging together.

When Ælfgar returned from exile in 1058, he came with the help of Gruffudd and with a fleet under Magnus of Limerick. It was from Dublin that rulers of York in the early tenth century came. Gwynedd was ravaged by the rulers of Man in the second half of the tenth century, with Anglesey/Môn constantly attacked. Maredudd, king of Gwynedd bought them off in the later tenth century. Æthelred was aiming at the Isle of Man in his campaign of AD 1000. After Gruffudd's death at Harold's hands in 1063, a death connived at by his half-brothers, his son fled to Ireland. From there he returned in 1075 to claim Gwynedd and successfully to resist Norman expansion into North Wales. It is the Irish Sea as much as the Viking connection which links them all.

Scotland and the North

Scotland and North Britain is a simpler political story to tell. The tenth and eleventh centuries saw the rise of not one but two large kingdoms in Britain, that of the Scots and that of the English. During the first half of the tenth century the kingdom of York was linked by dynastic ties to that of Dublin, and Scandinavian rulers controlled much of the periphery of the Irish Sea and the Western Isles. The fate of Britain north and west of the Humber and the Dee was no foregone conclusion in AD 900.

By the 870s the kingdom of Strathclyde, which extended from the Clyde region at least as far south as what is now the Lake District, was coming to be dependent on the kingdom of the Scots to the east. 'Dependence' is a strong word for relations which were more like those between tenth-century Dyfed and Gwynedd or early tenth-century Wessex and Mercia. Kings of both kingdoms were drawn from the same family, but stable peaceful relations were not thereby guaranteed. In 945 King Edmund ravaged all Cumbria and 'granted' it to Malcolm, king of the Scots in exchange for alliance and friendship. Thus did the English seek to present what is more likely to have been joint action on the part of Malcolm and Edmund to put down a situation which each for his own reasons found unacceptable. Malcolm was the immediate beneficiary, and throughout the tenth and eleventh centuries the kings of the Scots drew

Strathclyde into ever closer relations. In 937 Constantine of the Scots and the king of Strathclyde fought alongside each other at Brunanburh. Attempts by the kings of Strathclyde to use Scandinavian rulers or English kings to maintain their independence account for the help they gave to Vikings in the 940s, for which 945 was a punishment, and their attendance at Chester in 973. Yet by the eleventh century Strathclyde was a sub-kingdom used to resolve some of the tensions caused by the system of succession among the Scots: either to provide a kingdom for the segment of the family not holding the throne (the Scots practiced alternating succession between segments of the same family),[6] or as a sub-kingdom for future heirs. The parallel between Mercia and Strathclyde is instructive; Duncan was king of Strathclyde during the reign of his grandfather Malcolm II, and Duncan's son, the future Malcolm III, held it under his father and during the period when Macbeth ruled the Scots. As in Mercia, such action would foster continuing independence as much as quell it.

East of the Pennines the earls of Bamburgh stood between the Scots and the English and to their south lay the Scandinavian kingdom of York. Until 927, and again between 940 and 954, the old kingdom of Deira from the Humber to the Tees retained its identity under Scandinavian rulers whose ties were often with Dublin. Geographical remoteness and the existence of this powerful rival dynasty with the military capacity to make good its claims to York rather than the extent of Danish settlement made York difficult for the southern kings to conquer. The rule of Scandinavian kings at York had reopened the old division of Northumbria along the Tees. Bernicia, or northern Northumbria, was now ruled by a noble family associated with the stronghold of Bamburgh, that is with the old royal centres of Bernicia between Yeavering, Bamburgh and Lindisfarne south of the Tweed. The lords of Bamburgh are referred to in southern English sources as earls or high reeves, as subordinates, but the Annals of Ulster, unaffected by the aspirations of southern English kings, call Eadwulf of Bamburgh a king in 913[7] and in 920 when Edward the Elder met the rulers of northern Britain at Bakewell, Eadwulf's sons were among them. The presence of Scandinavian rulers at York had not driven them into alliance with Alfred and his successors as Viking rule in eastern Mercia had driven Æthelred and Æthelflæd. Bernician rulers were well placed in the far North to act independently, and they had always faced north towards Fife and Strathclyde as much as south. Lothian was still a part of Northumbria at the beginning of the tenth century.

Strathclyde was a kingdom which was absorbed into Scotland as the northern border was defined. Deira and Bernicia became part of England. Scandinavian rulers at York were a threat and tenth-century English rulers had not lost interest in loot and tribute. York/Deira was a candidate for southern ravaging and conquest especially in the period 940–54. In 940 Olaf had taken not only York but north-east Mercia as far as Watling Street and Welland. He may have been attempting to control all those areas taken by the Great Viking Army in the 870s; he was following in the footsteps of earlier kings of

6. Here cf. Smyth, *Warlords and Holy Men*, pp. 218–22 and A. A. M. Duncan, *Scotland* (1975), pp. 112–14
7. *Annals of Ulster*, ed. W. M. Hennessy, vol. I (Dublin, 1887), pp. 424–7

Northumbria and acting, like Athelstan or Edmund, as a warlord who would extend his control as far as proved possible. York had to be conquered to remove the likes of Olaf as much as to unify England.

Relations with Bamburgh were different. The earls of Bamburgh occasionally turned up at the English court in the tenth century, in much the same way as Welsh kings. They maintained an unbroken hereditary control of the far North until 1041 and their importance long survived 1066. There is none of the waxing and waning of power associated with southern noble families dependent on royal patronage. Southern kings sometimes extended the power of this family, but until the reign of Cnut never limited it. Osulf of Bamburgh was given the rule of York from 954 to 966 and Uhtred held York from 1006 until his death. In 954 it was not clear that York could be successfully controlled from the south. In 1006 Æthelred sought to reorganize the defences of England by appointing ealdormen with power over large areas, a practice which Cnut and his sons tried to retain. In 1041 Eadwulf was murdered at the court of Harthacnut and Siward became earl of all Northumbria, the first attempt to replace this family by a southern appointee. Siward tried to link himself with them by marrying into the house of Bamburgh, but Tostig, appointed in 1055, was an unreconstructed southerner. Political murder remained the major way of dealing with the northern nobility. In 1063 Tostig had Gamel and Ulf assassinated and in 1064 Cospatric was murdered at court. Cospatric and Gamel were members of the Bamburgh family, Ulf was connected with them. After 1066 William tried to use some of these northern discontents in his early appointments of northern rulers. By turning to the house of Bamburgh to rule in the North he was reviving a long tradition. But the problems of ruling the far North from southern England had now been exacerbated by the murders and taxation of the mid eleventh century. William like Edward attempted more direct rule: the Norman bishop, Walcher was brutally murdered at Gateshead in 1080 by members of the Bamburgh family.

When Siward and Tostig took over as earls of Northumbria they inherited the concern of northern rulers with Scotland. The rapid and spectacular development of the kingdom of the Scots defined the political geography of the British mainland as much as did the kingdom of England. The nub of the Scottish kingdom was formed in the mid ninth century when the Scottish kings of Dalriada/Argyll took control of the eastern kingdom of the Picts with its centres at Perth, Scone, Dunkeld and St Andrew's. Its kings were as concerned with overlordship, tribute and conquest as their English counterparts, westwards towards Strathclyde and south to Lothian and Bernicia. Attacks, raids, marriage, the use of exiles and claims were the familiar methods. Constantine II during the 920s and 930s married his daughter to Olaf of Dublin, struck a friendship with Athelstan in which Athelstan became the godfather of Constantine's son and attacked and was defeated by Athelstan at Brunanburh in 937. In such fluid relations neither friendship nor defeat were final and lasting. Lothian had been taken into Scottish control by 973, only to be lost again. In 972, 994–95 and 1006 Scottish kings raided south. Malcolm II (1005–34) took advantage of the problems surrounding Cnut's takeover to recover Lothian, and probably played a role in stirring the events of 1026 (see above, pp. 74–5). Cnut retaliated with an attack on the Scots by land and sea.

The power of these rulers made eleventh-century English kings apprehensive. The earls of Bamburgh never attended Cnut's court; Cnut's murder of Earl Uhtred at the beginning of his reign is only part of the explanation. The appointments of Siward and Tostig were motivated by a growing desire to control the far North in the face of Scottish successes. Durham too was brought into closer southern control with the imposition of a Peterborough monk as bishop. The previous incumbent had died at Harthacnut's court in 1042; the climate of the South proved unhealthy for northerners in the eleventh century.

Expansion into Strathclyde and Lothian was only part of the story of the kingdom of the Scots. The survival of the Scottish kings was as insecure as any overlord's and they faced threats from rivals. To the north this produced a marriage with the Jarls of Orkney, re-cemented when Malcolm married his cousin's daughter in 1057. It also explains the feud which brought Macbeth to the throne. The Mormærs, or great Stewards of Moray, held power in north-eastern Scotland. A feud within this family in the 1020s and 1030s was possibly stirred by Malcolm himself. Macbeth's father and cousin were killed in the feud, and Macbeth married his cousin's widow, Gruoch. Gruoch was a granddaughter of Kenneth III. The claims to the throne which she gave her husbands and sons may lie at the heart of Malcolm's fears, especially if he had broken the alternating succession in Scotland to hand the throne to his grandson Duncan rather than to a descendant of Kenneth III. In 1039 Duncan attacked Macbeth and in 1040 Macbeth killed Duncan and became king. Duncan's sons, including the future Malcolm III, took the path of exiles, south to claim Strathclyde and to seek the protection of their uncle Maldred, who was married into the house of Bamburgh. Siward used Malcolm as the pretext to attack Macbeth in 1046, and in 1054 he led an army into Scotland to set up Malcolm as king. It is not surprising that Macbeth's court proved a haven for some of the Norman lords driven out of England in 1052.

If Siward hoped to set up a Scottish king beholden to him, as Harold tried to do in Gwynedd in 1063, he was disappointed. Alliance, raid and the harbouring of exiles remained the unstable pattern. Malcolm became Tostig's 'sworn brother' and visited the English court in 1059. But whilst Tostig was in Rome in 1061 Malcolm raided south and from 1065 onwards welcomed a procession of English exiles: Tostig in 1065, northern nobles after 1066, Edgar the Ætheling and his sisters. In 1070/71 Malcolm married Margaret, Edgar's sister and a granddaughter of Edmund Ironside. The claims on the English throne which he acquired could never be ignored by Norman kings and merely added to the existing compulsions on English kings to concern themselves with their northern neighbours.

The rise of the Scottish kingdom meant that these centuries could not be read as a simple story of increasing control by English kings over the rulers of Bamburgh. The latter might visit the English court and sometimes be preferred royal patronage and office, but poised between English and Scottish rulers they could use their opportunities to remain independent. In 918 Eadwulf fled north not south to escape the advance of Ragnald from York; in the eleventh century his descendants married into both the English and Scottish royal families. Those links could easily have meant Scottish domination; northern English boundaries cannot be assumed as inevitable – witness the loss of control over

Lothian. Developments in the North, like relations among all the rulers of the British mainland, are obscured by Anglocentric interpretations. In particular a series of meetings, alliances and peace negotiations have been seen as a steady advance of English hegemony, not least by later English and Norman kings anxious to cloak their own expansion in precedent. As late as the fifteenth century English chroniclers would celebrate Edgar as a ruler of Britain. The problems of interpretation and perspective begin in the sources from the tenth and eleventh centuries themselves.

Interpreting the language of British relations

According to Asser Æthelwulf of Wessex in the mid ninth century was helping Burgred of Mercia devastate the Welsh and submit them to his authority.[8] He alleges that Alfred ruled southern Wales, whose kings had submitted to him or had sought his lordship and defence. Furthermore Anarawd of Gwynedd came to Alfred, was received with gifts, became the king's son in confirmation and submitted to Alfred.[9] In 918 Edward took control of Mercia and the kings of the Welsh 'sought him as their lord'.[10] In 920 at Bakewell Edward was chosen as father and lord by the Scottish king, by Ragnald of York, by the king of Strathclyde and by the sons of Eadwulf of Bamburgh, and all the Northumbrians, English Danes and Northmen, bowed to him. When Athelstan took over York in 927 he went on to Eamont Bridge and there met Hywel Dda, Constantine of the Scots, Owen of Strathclyde and Ealdred son of Eadwulf 'and all the kings of this island were brought under his rule . . . and made peace with oath and pledge, to live in peace and to give up all heathen worship'.[11] William of Malmesbury claimed that Athelstan took tribute from the Welsh. The meeting of kings with Edgar in 973 is a pledging of oaths and common action on land and sea in the tenth-century chronicles, but by the time Florence of Worcester wrote at the end of the eleventh century this had become the symbolic rowing of Edgar on the Dee by Welsh and Strathclyde kings who showed their subjection to him.[12] The Scottish king is claimed to have 'placed himself in his (Cnut's) hands and was his man' though he stood by it only a short time.[13] In 1056 Gruffudd of Gwynedd was defeated and swore oaths that he would be a 'faithful underking to Edward and would not attack him',[14] and in 1063 after the making of peace and giving of hostages, Gruffudd's half-brothers swore oaths and gave hostages that 'they would not harm him in any way, and would be everywhere ready for him on land and water, and would give the king whatever had been given from that land before to any other king'.[15] In 1073 Malcolm came and 'made peace with William and was his man and gave him hostages and afterwards went home with all his army'.[16]

8.   Asser, *Life of Alfred*, ed. W. Stevenson (Oxford, 1959), cap. 7, p. 7
9.   *ibid.* cap. 80, pp. 66–7
10. ASC MS A 918
11. ASC MS D 927
12. Fl. Wig. 973
13. ASC MS D 1027
14. ASC MS C 1056
15. ASC MS D 1063
16. ASC MS D 1072

A history of constant and growing subjection seems to be signalled, most fully of the Welsh kings, more questionably of the Scots. But the sources are English interpretations, sometimes long after the event. William of Malmesbury and Florence of Worcester saw the tenth century through eyes which had already seen Norman advances into Wales and north Britain. MS D of the Anglo-Saxon Chronicle, which recounts many of the 'subjections' is a northern chronicle of the late eleventh century particularly interested in relations with the Scots and other neighbours. Even the accounts of 973 are not strictly contemporary, but date from the beginnings of the mythologizing of Edgar's reign. The accounts of Edward the Elder's takeover of Mercia and his relations with the Welsh and Scots are heavy with suggestions of submission and overlordship; but they were produced close to the West Saxon court and are only one, partial view of actions which could have appeared more as alliance and peace-making from the other side. The submissions of tenth-century kings of Britain to English overlords may have been consistently overplayed. The variety of rulers involved in 927, for example, is itself a warning that different types of relationship may be run together in descriptions of such meetings, and the subsequent history of these rulers has already showed that their outcome was not the inexorable rise of England but depended on the unfolding events in Britain.

In a political world in which kings were accepted but faced constantly by rivals, where the need for tribute or land led to raiding and counter-raiding relations between rulers show little consistency. Raids, the reception of exiles, the backing of claimants, the pursuit of a personal claim: the making of peace or alliance, after battle, in the face of a common enemy, under threat, whether from the new ally or others – such relations were expressed in a language of actions which like all languages carried symbolic but ambiguous meanings. Gifts were given and accepted, including the gift of women in marriage; kinship ties were created through marriage or through the fictitious bonds of baptism and confirmation; rulers attended each other's courts, met each other, within or on the edges of each other's territory, swore friendship with oaths, with oaths and pledges, with oaths, pledges and hostages, bound each other by the ties of friend- and lordship. Some of these actions carried a message of submission. To accept another king as father and lord was to accept two relationships which implied benevolent protection, but also domination. To give gifts which were not reciprocated was to create obligations. To attend a meeting in the heart of another's territory was not only a physical risk, but carried connotations different from one on a common boundary. Some actions denoted equality, such as the exchange of oaths, hostages or gifts. When the sources record actions which carry a mixture of meanings we must be wary of deliberate misinterpretation. When Edward met the rulers of northern Britain at Bakewell in the Peak he met them on the bounds of his territory: their acceptance of him as father and lord is at most a temporary recognition of his power, wishful West Saxon shorthand for several different relationships. Edgar's meeting at Chester in 973 was on the borders of Wales, England and Strathclyde, at a point which symbolized the direction of the common threat from the Irish Sea. All pledged to work together on land and sea. Gestures of ritual submission in the rowing on the Dee are later accretions.

The actions were symbolic, and could be reinterpreted as events changed. Their contemporary meaning depended on the context. Malcolm might have become William's man in 1072. Whatever the accuracy of the account, the significance of such an action is lessened when we recognize that it came at the end of a hostile campaign, but against a longer history in which the advantage had swung from one side to another. Constantine's son became Athelstan's godson, but the tie was made in the hope of friendship not the immediate expectation of subjection. The sequence of actions and the relative powers of both sides are critical. The Welsh kings, after repeated ninth-century raiding, were brought to submissions to Mercia. Each repetition reinforced the meaning. These kings on their own initiative appeared at the court of Alfred seeking protection against Mercia and other enemies. Protection from the powerful is dangerous, doubly so when the ruler of Wessex becomes the lord of Mercia. When Welsh kings went on to seek English patronage in the first half of the tenth century and to attend the English court, they did not become *ipso facto* dependent, though the continuation of an earlier pattern tended in that direction. If tribute was also paid, the Welsh kings came close to becoming subject to English kings in the first half of the tenth century. But whilst power was as much personal as territorial such a state of affairs could prove temporary. The problems of the mid and late tenth century upset the sequence of events. When Gruffudd raided England in the mid eleventh century he was not a subject king throwing off domination but an independent ruler.

Was England inevitable?

The eventual shape of the kingdoms of Britain can thus appear more accidental than predetermined. Cornwall in the ninth century was as much an independent Welsh kingdom as the familiar ones of Wales. Is the more thorough absorption of it by early tenth–century kings primarily a result of the fact that they were kings of Wessex, heirs to its concerns and priorities? Had Mercian kings become kings of the English might the southern Welsh kingdoms have been a priority? Had England been built up by a dynasty based at York rather than south of the Thames, might the northern boundaries of England have been different and the Welsh left in greater independence?

Lothian was not particularly Scottish in the ninth and tenth centuries. Northumbrian control here was long-established, the church of St Cuthbert held lands here, it was on the doorstep of the old Bernician kingdom. It was also an obvious area to be raided by Scottish kings now based just beyond the Forth. If Lothian was not inevitably Scottish, was Northumbria inevitably English? Could the Scottish kingdom have expanded to the Tees if not to the Humber in the east; to Stainmore and Rere Cross in the Pennines if not to the Dee in the West? Were Æthelflæd's defences along the Mersey and the Dee solely against the Vikings, or also against a Strathclyde which stretched this far south? Archbishops of Glasgow later claimed jurisdiction as far as Stainmore and the Scottish chronicle which records Kenneth's attack on Strathclyde in 972 makes Strathclyde stretch to the Dee. Edgar in 973 had more than the Vikings to think of. English kings granted huge rights north of the Mersey and west of the

Pennines. Wulfric Spott and his brother held unspecified lands 'between Ribble and Mersey' by 1004; Athelstan endowed the archbishopric of York with Amounderness. Such grants look like later Norman licenses to border lords to take what they could get, an encouragement to expand rather than an indication of territory controlled.

The boundaries of kingdoms are formed externally by the pressure of neighbours and internally by political perceptions. One definition of an eleventh-century kingdom is a community of the consenting powerful under the rule of a king: the area where the king's rule was effective with the cooperation of the nobility. On such a definition England comprised the area south of the Humber and east of Offa's Dyke, more dubiously south of the Tees, and only tenuously south of the Tweed and west of the Pennines. The limitations of Domesday, of the attendance of nobility and bishops at the southern court and of royal control over bishoprics point to these boundaries.

Kingdoms are also what their kings aspire to rule, aspirations the fruit of long traditions. Tenth- and eleventh-century kings were determined to draw into their kingdom Cornwall, Mercia, East Anglia and Northumbria. In Cornwall they acted as kings of Wessex, but north of the Humber they aspired to be kings of the English. York was conquered with a determination which may be explained by the threat of its Scandinavian rulers. Yet seen alongside the pursuit of control of Bernicia other motives appear important. Athelstan was prepared to leave his relations with Welsh kings as the loosest hegemony, yet he patronized the cult of St Cuthbert, went north and gave gifts to Durham, granted Amounderness to York, actions which have no parallel in his links with Wales. Eleventh-century kings did not seek to control Welsh bishoprics as they sought to appoint to Durham and York.

The English kingdom cannot be explained in any simple way. Athelstan's wide hegemony threatened to engulf the Welsh kings and *c.*939 the boundaries of England could still have been drawn further to the west. Mid eleventh-century rulers went north for reasons of defence as much as to unite the kingdoms of the English. In the North especially the final border fell short of encompassing the historical kingdoms of the English, further south than Northumbria at its widest extent, limited by the rise of the Scottish rulers. The tenth and eleventh centuries drew the boundaries of England in the context of kingly aspiration, external development and accident.

Part II

Introduction

During the later tenth century the abbey of Ely put together an estate at Downham in Cambridgeshire. Ely was a religious house refounded during the tenth-century movement for reform, an especially dynamic example of the process of land acquisitions by the revived abbeys. The acquisition of Downham involved a series of exchanges, sales and gifts. Individual transactions were disputed and considered in courts from the royal court itself to those of local hundreds: they were discussed and witnessed by groups of men ranging from ealdormen and bishops to peasant landholders. Bishop Æthelwold recorded the acquisitions, and the problems they entailed in his 'Little Book'.[1] He recorded the world of tenth-century England in microcosm.

At the apex stood ealdorman Æthelwine of East Anglia and his brother Ælfwold, men who straddled national and local politics. Their family had held royal office since the 930s and they came frequently to the royal court, as in AD 989 when they attended a meeting in London where bishops, abbots, ealdormen and king's thegns surrounded the king[2] and gave judgement. Within East Anglia itself they were pre-eminent, leaders of local society as well as a bridge between centre and region. Æthelwine as ealdorman presided over local courts like that of the eight hundreds which met at Wansford, attended by the 'great men' (*primates*) of Northamptonshire and East Anglia.

Among such 'great men' were king's thegns and men linked by clientage to Æthelwine or his brother. An exchange of land at Downham and Chippenham was transacted in a meeting to the west of Cambridge, before twenty-four judgement finders, and with the witness of Eadric, Æthelwine's man, of Ælfhelm Polga and his kinsman, Leofsige. Ælfhelm was a king's thegn who paid his heriot or death duty directly to the king. His will reveals a substantial landholder, his possessions largely in eastern England, a local noble. He was a wealthy man, who could make substantial bequests including a longship which he left to the abbey of Ramsey. He had companions who rode with him, to whom he left half of his stud of horses. Ælfhelm may have been primarily a local noble,

1. LE caps. 11 and 11a, pp. 84–91
2. R. 63

but he was sufficiently important to have attended the royal court on occasion, and to have received a grant of land at Wratting from the king.[3] He was a *king's* thegn who made his will with the king's permission and made play with his loyalty and service. 'Now I pray you, dear lord, that my will may stand and that you will not permit it to be wrongfully altered. God is my witness that I was obedient to your father as ever I could be and thoroughly loyal in thought and deed'.[4] Royal influence reached down into local society, not simply mediated through officials like Æthelwine, but directly to benefit and affect men like Ælfhelm.

As the king's representative and a rich local landholder Æthelwine attracted his own followers. Eadric, a witness at Cambridge alongside Ælfhelm, was his man. He, like Ælfhelm, may also have been a king's thegn, but for others the ealdorman stood as their sole lord. When Siferth of Downham wanted to make his final bequests, including leaving land to Ely, he called for Abbot Brihtnoth and other local men, including Æthelwine's man Eadric. His will was drawn up in three copies and one was sent to Æthelwine, requesting that he grant permission that the will might stand. Siferth and Eadric were both Æthelwine's 'men', though not equal. Eadric was a *procer*, a man of substance with a weighty voice in the courts, Siferth a lesser local landholder. Æthelwine's links with him were as lord and as royal official, his office as much an attraction as his wealth. Æthelwine and his brother Ælfwold drew many such followers, and the influence they wielded in the courts was a powerful magnet. When a certain Ælfwold and his wife feared to lose out in a deal with Ely they appealed to their lord, Ælfwold, Æthelwine's brother. The brothers assembled the great men of East Anglia and Cambridge at Freckenham and at Hinton Hall and there the case was settled, in Ely's favour, but with additional compensatory payments secured for Ælfwold and his wife. Even at the local level the benefits of royal favour, whether expressed in land grants to Ælfhelm or through the advantages of a royal office like an ealdormanry, were not to be lightly foregone.

Lordship and family were the ties which bound this society. The man whose exchange of lands was witnessed by Ælfhelm Polga was called Ælfric: he had his own man Brunstan. Like Eadric, Æthelwine's man, he acted on his lord's behalf in the courts. Eadric was his lord's witness at the making of Siferth's will; Brunstan witnessed the final handing over of the land which his lord had exchanged. Ælfhelm Polga acknowledged the king's own lordship as well as the bonds with the companions who rode with him. But the bulk of Ælfhelm's will was concerned with bequests to his family: to his son, his three brothers, his nephew, his kinsman, Leofsige, and especially to his wife and daughter. Family ties run as threads throughout the Downham case. Two brothers held land there jointly; widows, heirs and heiresses disputed land and had it claimed on their behalf. Brothers, fathers and sons and kinsmen appeared together in court; Æthelwine and his brother Ælfwold frequently acted together.

We see the working of society through the records of courts and legal cases: from the deliberations of the king and the great men of England in London; through provincial meetings of local landholders down to the hundred and the village. Three purchases of 110 acres and houses at Chippenham were made

3. S. 794
4. W. 13

with the witness of the hundred, but the final handing over of the land itself took place in the village of Chippenham. Now the villagers themselves appeared, two of them forbade the sale of seven acres, and here their own hierarchy can be briefly glimpsed. Judgement and witness was the function of 'all the better folk of the village'.

To see a society at its moments of litigation may not be to see all its day-to-day workings. But it is to see its power structures and the mobilization of its bonds of mutual aid. In this case it is to witness how far we are from dealing with a series of closed societies, how far royal power and external influences had penetrated even to the level of the village community itself. The legal cases show people turning outwards for help, witness or judgement as well as inwards to family and community. The meetings of courts are not merely a window into that world, but a dynamic part of it, creating their own ties and alliances. It was already an unequal world, stratified even at village level, one too where women, as widows, wives and heiresses, played an important part. It was a Christian society where the church was subject to change and reform, where its needs for land could be disruptive; litigation over church land drew many into the courts. It was already a world of buying and selling, from village land sales to a king's thegn raising cash to pay his heriot to the king, an agrarian society based on the land, but one already permeated by markets, turned outwards by their needs. During the tenth and eleventh centuries all this had developed in the context of growing royal power. East Anglian society at the end of the tenth century had its own structure, its own great men, its own internal links, but it was touched at point after point by the hand of the king.

8

Ruling the Kingdom

In the tenth century the kingdoms of the English were brought together under one ruler, in the eleventh the resulting kingdom was twice conquered. It would be no surprise if the rule of Alfred were different from that of Henry I. Yet the continuity across these centuries is as important as the contrasts. Neither continuity, nor the impact of unification and conquest can be understood apart from the question of the aims and nature of rule at this date, from what was expected of kings, from what kings sought to do and from the mechanisms through which rule was made effective.

By the time of Alfred kings were expected to rule, which meant first to judge and thus to preserve order. In the lengthy preface to his laws, Alfred quoted extensively from the Old Testament. Its picture of the king as judge ordering human society so that it might please an interventionist God was an ideal model for a late ninth-century king. The king was expected to judge difficult cases or those brought to him, to guarantee that all his people could obtain just settlement. In the tenth and eleventh centuries this would mean especially guaranteeing the working of the courts and procedures which brought people to justice and ensured that cases were heard. The king's interest in law and justice was influenced by Christianity, Alfred's making of *written* law testifies to such influence, but it met with the consent and approval of his noble followers. Alfred selected and rejected rulings 'with the advice of my counsellors', and the final result was shown to them for their approval.[1]

The roles of the king as judge, guarantor of order and lord of followers reinforced each other. King Edmund called on all to swear him loyalty 'as a man should be faithful to his lord . . . loving what he loves, shunning what he shuns';[2] Edgar promised to 'be a very gracious lord to you as long as my life lasts'[3]. Rule was the exercise of lordship, criticism as well as acceptance of it was framed in these terms. When Æthelred was recalled from exile in 1014 the counsellors of the English sent a message to him saying that 'no lord was dearer to them than their natural lord, if he would govern them more justly than he did before' and

---

1. Alfred, Intro. cap. 49.9
2. III Edmund 1
3. IV Edgar 16

his reply was to reiterate his father's promise 'that he would be a gracious lord to them'.[4]

A lord was an arbitrator among his followers, a protector and defender; the Old Testament kings were warriors as well as judges. This aspect of lordship had already produced reciprocal duties, most notably the requirements to repair fortifications, bridges and roads laid on all landholders. Such duties built on ancient foundations, demands for forced labour which may go back to the building of prehistoric works. But they had been developed during the battles of the eighth and ninth centuries.[5] They are an indication of how important the needs of war were in transforming a king or lord's demands on his followers.

The upkeep of fortifications and roads for the movement of armies may not have been popular, though men expected to fight with their king as a lord. Alfred's battles against the Danes were fought by king and ealdormen with their followers: Æthelwulf ealdorman of Berkshire and his followers fought at Englefield in 871; in the same year Alfred and his ealdormen 'with their men' fought innumerable skirmishes; at Wilton Alfred fought with a few men, just as he went into retreat in 878 'with his small band of nobles'.[6] General demands for military aid grew from the long-accepted duty to fight with a lord.

Kings ruled as their Christian followers expected and in accordance with tradition. Kings had long protected vulnerable merchants who brought scarce and prestigious goods to their courts. Trading centres like Southampton (*Hamwih*), York, even London, had developed under royal auspices, sometimes around a royal centre. When Alfred built his *burhs* he was generalizing from the defence of such sites to general defence against the Vikings. Protection can be one face of control. Royal control over the minting of coin was already established, though not monopolized. When Alfred captured the town and mint of London his issues of coinage were propaganda as much as finance.[7] Traders needed both protection and a guaranteed coinage of acceptable weight. Even here rule was part ruthless royal fiat, part consensual meeting of interests.

In the absence of a paid bureaucracy or a monopoly of force, rulers must work with a degree of consent, through the structures of society, here local community, lords and kin. Counsel determined what was acceptable; social structures limited what was possible. Coercion is always present in rule, but to be dominant it requires a strongly developed central administration and paid officials. Even the most optimistic estimates of literacy and the growth of central institutions in tenth- and eleventh-century England leave it short of the mechanisms of a coercive, centralized state. Rulers could still harry and devastate, occasionally in the tenth century, as when Eadred ravaged Northumbria in 948 or Edgar Thanet in 969, frequently after 1066. But ravaging is not ruling. Northumbria, the area most frequently attacked, was always least effectively ruled. Ravaging is

4. ASC MS C 1014
5. cf. N. Brooks, 'The development of military obligations in eighth- and ninth-century England', in *England before the Conquest*, eds. P. Clemoes and K. Hughes (Cambridge, 1971), pp. 69–84 and J. Campbell, 'The age of Arthur' in his *Essays in Anglo-Saxon History* (1986), pp. 121–30 and M. Jones, *England before Domesday* (1986)
6. Asser, Life of Alfred in *Alfred the Great*, eds. S. Keynes and M. Lapidge (1983), pp. 78, 81 and 83
7. S. Lyon, 'Some problems in interpreting Anglo-Saxon coinage', ASE 5 (1976), pp. 181–3

an alternative to ruling, and even if systematic and constant, rarely the case at this date, is a poor basis on which to construct it. Rule had to be through mechanisms by which society itself was organized,[8] though those mechanisms were as coercive as they were consensual. Community, kin and lord demanded and imposed as well as helped and protected, and the gross inequalities of society cut across all ties.

The most widespread local community at this date was the agrarian one of village, hamlet or vill. When Domesday was compiled in 1086, the vill was called to supply information, represented by its priest and six others.[9] When a tenth-century legal case came down to boundary definition, to land on the ground, the proper place to take it was the village, where the final stages of the Chippenham dispute were resolved.[10] But units as small as this were not the basis of ruling, not least, perhaps, because nucleated agrarian villages were far from the norm. The lowest level of *enquiry* in the Domesday survey was the hundred court, where representatives of a group of local settlements attended. The Chippenham village enquiry was finally resolved at Hinton Hall in the presence of three hundreds.

The hundred appears in the tenth century as the community of a court, a grouping which is the product as much as the basis of royal power. Such groupings of settlements together may be regularized by kings, but they have a long organizational history for the satisfaction of many needs, including royal ones. In some areas they centred on a king's hall and its requirements for labour and service. West Saxon hundreds were normally centred on a royal estate.[11] In others agricultural need may be the basis of grouping, the needs of transhumant agriculture, once widespread in early England, being only the most obvious example. Crimes like theft and cattle rustling, the determination of pasture rights would always have necessitated meetings and arbitration over a wider area than the immediate settlement. Whatever the varied factors in its origins, it was this community and court which tenth-century kings chose to reaffirm and whose responsibilities were repeatedly stressed. The tenth-century laws are full of attempts to regularize their courts and procedures, to reinforce their involvement in pursuit and bringing people to court, to extend royal control over them and to do this beyond the bounds of Wessex. North of the Thames some redrawing of hundred boundaries occurred, though it is still unclear how far they rode roughshod over older patterns. From the Welland to the Tees they were known as wapentakes not hundreds: the functions were the same. The reshaping of older units into wapentakes was not complete in the East Riding of Yorkshire by 1086. The interest of kings in such groupings continued into the eleventh century.

Hundred and wapentake were to meet every four weeks and their function included raising the hue and cry and witnessing buying and selling. The

8. Excellent discussion of the working of local courts in *The Settlement of Disputes in Early Medieval Europe*, eds. W. Davies and P. Fouracre (Cambridge, 1986), pp. 214–40
9. EHD II, no. 215, p. 946
10. LE Cap. 11a, p. 89
11. H. M. Cam, 'Manerium cum Hundredo: the hundred and the hundredal manor', *Liberties and Communities* (1963), pp. 64–90 and P. H. Sawyer, 'The royal *tun* in pre-conquest England' in *Ideal and Reality in Frankish and Anglo-Saxon Society*, ed. P. Wormald (Oxford, 1983), pp. 273–99

regularity of common action reinforced their nature as communities. The shire was the other local grouping used by tenth- and eleventh-century kings. It was larger and its court met only twice a year. South of the Thames shires were already old units, north of the Thames they were redrawn during these centuries. The midland shires grew out of defensive needs, grouped around the *burhs* from which they take their names, *Warwick*shire, *Leicester*shire. Further north in Yorkshire the boundaries of the old kingdom of Deira were preserved, first in the Viking kingdom of York and later in the shire, and the ealdormanry and later the shire structure of East Anglia did the same. What combination of respect for local loyalties, marcher defences, special patronage for ealdormen was involved in such cases cannot now be recovered, but it is a reminder that loose notions of hegemony coexisted with the aspiration to unification and uniformity in the tenth century. The shires, first under ealdormen, later under shire reeves, were the key to royal rule. The shire was both a court and a political grouping, a gathering of the local nobility and their point of contact with royal rule. Land disputes were resolved here, royal decisions communicated here, announcements of royal patronage in the form of land grants made here, all under the presidency of a royal official. The fact that England did not fragment into semi-independent groupings of such shires is an indication of how far the nobility who presided and met here saw themselves benefiting from the king.

In the laws which emphasized the importance of the hundred tenth-century kings recognized the power of local lords. In redrawing of administrative boundaries the property of lords could be respected. In the Severn valley the hundreds were carefully designed to accommodate and separate the lands of the churches of Gloucester and Worcester.[12] Lords, along with the hundred, received a share of the fines from those they were encouraged to bring to court. The nobility were essential to the functioning of rule throughout the Middle Ages, so much so that their ideals and structure are dealt with elsewhere (see *The Nobility*). King Athelstan had involved both lord and kin in standing surety.[13] The bond of kin was so old and ubiquitous that the laws scarcely refer to it, except to deplore the protection it might offer an accused. In this society a series of ties, of family, lord and community overlapped but were never coterminous. The king could seek to utilize each, but they were unlikely in turn to coincide in ways which would encourage or facilitate action against him or against the lords who ruled locally in his name. England at this date was not a land of tightly knit communities of interest.

Tenth-century kingship has been characterized as theocracy, less starkly as 'pastoral kingship'.[14] Edgar began his second law code by stating that he determined to rule 'with the advice of his counsellors, for the praise of God, for his own royal dignity and for the benefit of all his people'. 'The praise of God' here joins the pursuit of royal rights, rule with advice and the attempts to improve the procedures of justice which are so evident in theory and practice. Kings who surrounded themselves with churchmen, and by the late tenth century with

---

12. C. S. Taylor, 'The origin of the Mercian shires', in *Gloucestershire Studies*, ed. H. P. R. Finberg (1957), pp. 17–52 and H. P. R. Finberg, 'The ancient shire of Winchcombe', in *The Early Charters of the West Midlands* (Leicester, 1972), pp. 228–35
13. II Athelstan 1 and III Athelstan 7
14. P. Wormald, 'Æthelred the Lawgiver', in *Ethelred the Unready*, ed. D. Hill (Oxford, 1978), p. 75

churchmen whose reforming ideals stressed the role of kings in protecting the church, were not untouched by these ideas. Their laws contain decrees on tithe payments, on witchcraft, incest and many moral questions. One of the aims of rule was the furtherance of Christianity, one of its instruments churchmen, in central royal counsel and in the local control of land and hundreds.

The aims and methods of these kings were those of an early European kingdom, of personal monarchy in a largely pre-literate, agrarian, Christian society. The tenth and eleventh centuries were to bring a new framework and new problems: unification and conquest, new military needs, the rule of two kingdoms, the growth of towns and trade, the difficulties and opportunities of ruling a large kingdom. But the rule of Alfred or of Æthelred was not different in kind from that of Henry I or even Henry II. The latter were the products of long tradition and not merely of 1066.

The laws of Cnut issued between 1018 and 1023 are the most complete codification of tenth- and eleventh-century English law, specifically of the king's concerns in it. They culminate a century of active royal law-making and show the impact of the first conquest. They are the most comprehensive guide to the concerns and powers of an English king *c.*AD 1000 and of the limitations on his rule.[15]

Cnut's takeover was marked by a series of legal enactments. He probably issued a coronation charter in 1017 itself, offering mitigation of abuses of royal power under Æthelred. At least two other meetings at Oxford and Winchester considered relations between Danes and English and Cnut's position as an English king. When I and II Cnut were finally drafted by Archbishop Wulfstan they contained elements of all these, incorporating much of the laws of Edgar and Æthelred, and tenth-century decrees back to Alfred's day. Insofar as they are a codification, it is of tenth-century development in particular. Cnut offered, if he did not always uphold, a mitigation of the harsher aspects of tenth-century rule, whilst claiming the rights which his predecessors had acquired and guaranteeing the position of his own followers in England.

It is chiefly due to Archbishop Wulfstan of York that the crisis of 1014–20 was expressed in legal form. Wulfstan was the last expression of the tenth-century English phase of the alliance between church and king, a phase similar to the Carolingian model in which law was seen as the fundamental instrument of ruling. Between 1008 and 1023 Wulfstan saw English society faced with an all-encompassing crisis. He offered the all-embracing analysis and answer of the legal traditions he represented. In the law codes V to VIII Æthelred and I and II Cnut he embraces sin and crime, morality and legal procedures, the rights of the king and the duties of different ranks of society in comprehensive statements. To castigate these laws as 'loquacious and futile'[16] is to fail to recognize that they are a statement of a legal and religious philosophy. Wulfstan's analysis underlies all tenth-century law-making, but is nowhere so fully expressed. He was the last of a series of tenth-century archbishops who

15. On these laws and their date and purpose see P. Stafford, 'The laws of Cnut and the history of Anglo-Saxon royal promises', ASE 10 (1981), pp. 173–90
16. H. G. Richardson and G. Sayles, *Law and Legislation from Æthelberht to Magna Carta* (Edinburgh, 1966), p. 27

influenced kings to produce *written law* to tackle specific problems: Athelstan and Archbishop Wulfhelm, Edmund and Archbishop Oda, Edgar and Archbishop Dunstan. For Wulfstan the scale of the problem, a country facing defeat, called for an articulation of the ideas behind the written law: that moral collapse, and the injustice of a world turned upside down were at the root of it all. The peculiar circumstances produced a particular type of statement which can easily obscure how far the drift of tenth- and early eleventh-century development forms the basis of English common law and royal rule.

Surviving laws give only a partial picture of that development since their committal to writing was originally in the hands of churchmen and often haphazard, or reflecting their especial interests. Thus, for example, the reform of the coinage in 973, or Athelstan's earlier attempt at uniformity in the 930s must have been enshrined in enactments now lost. The organization of shipsokes and payments of military equipment recorded by the Anglo-Saxon Chronicle in 1008 would have required individual directives. A specific decree about the coronation of Queen Ælfthryth in 973 has survived only by chance in a rubric in a coronation order.[17] Such decisions were never copied into collections, perhaps never elevated to the level of general pronouncement in the first place. But they give a picture of kings dealing with specific problems and events which the more general laws obscure.

Reforming ecclesiastics may have distorted our picture of rule at this date not only by selection, but by couching the royal laws in so general a way as to hide the problems and diversity of the new kingdom. Kings aspired to rule all England, and in their laws may have tried to give effect to that aspiration, but there are hints of particular difficulties in particular areas, sometimes even casting doubt on the universal applicability of earlier laws. Wulfstan himself recognized in Æthelred's fifth law code that some abuses were more prevalent in particular areas of the country.[18] More significant are the fourth law code of Edgar and the third of Æthelred which are concerned with Danish areas and the North-East Midlands. Each recognizes the distinctive nature of legal practices in these areas in ways ignored by earlier laws. Æthelred specifically extends to the North-East Midlands the notion of the king's peace and its protection which had been central to much tenth-century development, though this area had been technically a part of England since the reign of Edward the Elder. When considering what the laws tell us, we must be aware of what they may hide.

Even so their content suggests substantial continuity in the development of English law and ruling. Many are addressed to the local officials who will implement them, as in I Edward, Athelstan's ordinance on charities or IV Edgar. There is attention to local enforcement, even a dialogue between the king and localities, as in III and VI Athelstan, which are replies by the great men of Kent and London to Athelstan's demands about the keeping of the peace and the suppression of theft. IV Æthelred, a statement of London customs, shows that central enquiry and local response continued into the eleventh century.

17. J. Nelson, 'The second English *ordo*', in her *Politics and Ritual in Early Medieval Europe* (1986), at p. 372
18. V Æthelred 32, version in CCCC MS 201

From the beginning of the tenth century a major concern of the laws was the tightening of procedures for bringing people to justice, making the courts and their decisions acceptable and binding. By the end of the century this had progressed to the point where detailed consideration was given to particular questions. Most of Æthelred's first law, for example, was a detailed working out of the law of surety, a form of bail and guarantee for bringing people to court. The second half of II Æthelred does the same for vouching to warranty, the system for witnessing buying and selling.

This may not be a royal law but what is termed a 'private' fragment, that is, a compilation of decrees and procedures made by or for some ealdorman, bishop or similar court president, akin to a series of such fragments which date from these centuries, giving guidance on the performance of ordeals, the law on arson and its treatment, on the payment of *wergelds* (the compensation due to kin if a person were murdered). Such fragments speak as eloquently as the royal laws of the widespread interest in the courts and their procedures and of the differences which royal intervention in them was making. From the early eleventh century if not before some private collections of royal laws were being made. Wulfstan's collections are well known, but give only a partial picture. The collection which lies behind the twelfth-century Textus Roffensis was probably put together now. Its author was less concerned with sin and penance than Wulfstan, more interested in procedures and towns.[19] There was more than one attitude to the law in early eleventh-century England. The early twelfth-century collections so often said to mark new development have their ancestors.

Courts were to meet regularly, majority verdicts and amicable settlement were to be as binding and acceptable as unanimity or the full process of litigation.[20] Theft is the recurrent concern, always a problem between communities and perhaps especially in a society where buying and selling were more frequent. The tenth-century coronation oath promised not only to judge with justice and mercy, but also to forbid and repress robbery. The laws of Æthelred and Cnut show that violent attack, assault on the king's highway and other crimes of violence against the person were also important.[21] But it is enforcement, apprehension, bringing people to court, coping with refusal or failure to attend, proving theft, or dealing with aiders and abettors, receivers of stolen goods and the powerful protection of lords and kin which recur time and again.

The methods used to tighten enforcement consistently draw in an ever wider group. Everyone must be in a tithing, a sworn group of ten who will be accountable for each other. Everyone must have a surety who will bring him or her to court and pay fines if necessary. Kin and lord must not only protect but be involved in bringing people to justice. The hundred especially must pursue suspects and make enquiries about stray cattle and other possibly stolen goods. Underpinning the system lay the oath which all adults over the age of twelve were to take. By Cnut's day the taking of such an oath was seen as a proof and consequence of freedom.[22] Few elements were new; their combination and reiteration were.

19. The *Textus Roffensis* is based on a compilation made in the early eleventh century. It begins with a genealogy which goes no further than the accession of Æthelred II in 978
20. III Æthelred 13.2 and 13.3
21. P. Wormald, 'Æthelred the Lawgiver', pp. 65–6
22. II Cnut 20

The penalties for failure grew increasingly heavy. By the end of the tenth century it was not criminals alone who paid for their crimes, but failed sureties, lords, kin, accomplices, aiders and abettors, receivers of stolen goods, hundred members who had refused to follow thieves. The accounts of legal cases which survive from this date show most of these penalties in action. The king was providing justice, and there were losers and beneficiaries in the process. It was the king and his officials who received fines and forfeitures: the lord and hundred took their share. Edgar in his third code was already recognizing the dangers of false accusations by over-zealous royal agents and others. We cannot assume that the system worked perfectly and everywhere, and the problem of the powerful who could resist it always remained. But the records of disputes leave us in no doubt that it could work, and that the chief beneficiaries of it were the king and his officials.

The original motivation may have been simply the provision of justice, but by the second half of the tenth century if not before the benefits were obvious to the king himself. King Æthelred claimed jurisdiction over all who held land by charter.[23] A man's lord took his share of the fines and forfeitures, and the king was making it clear that the nobility were *his* men, the profits of the courts as well as heriots and other dues coming to him. 'The king shall have his rights everywhere as his father had'[24] stated IV Edgar, and Cnut's laws defined them: 'These are the rights which the king possesses over all men in Wessex'. They were the crimes which carried heavy fines, which were punishable by outlawry and which resulted in forfeiture, 'if he has bookland [land held by charter] it is to be forfeited into the king's possession no matter whose man he be'.[25] These were not marginal questions for Cnut, but the issues he returned to time and again in his law.[26]

Royal rights included rights over the coinage, which again can be traced back to the early tenth century and beyond. The spur to the intensive legal development was the aspirations of kings who ruled England. In the coinage too Athelstan speaks the language of unification, one he might have learned from the tentative moves in this direction of his grandfather Alfred. There was to be only one coinage, and money was to be minted only in towns, with each mint assigned a number of moneyers. The regulations of the coinage comes in a section of his laws which deal with the related issues of trade, towns and military questions. Fortresses were to be repaired, shields to be of good quality, two well-mounted men (to aid in the defence of the boroughs?) to be provided from every plough, and no horses, essential military equipment, were to be sold across the sea. Royal interest in trade and coinage was old, but military needs, especially the building of fortified *burhs* in the early tenth century, had added a new dimension and urgency. Fortifications must be maintained, attracting trade there made them more viable and provided a population for their defence.

It is possible that Athelstan was here referring to the first of the two tenth-century reforms of the coinage in the 930s. The second, Edgar's in 973, is known only from the coins themselves, which demonstrate it to have been more

23. I Æthelred 1.14 and compare IV Edgar 2a
24. IV Edgar 2a
25. II Cnut 12 and 13.1
26. II Cnut 13.1 and e.g. 30.6, 31.1, 31.2, 33.2, 57, 83, 83.1, 83.2

permanent and successful than the earlier attempt. Athelstan tried to bring in a uniform penny with a high silver content, stamped with the king's head and guarantee and carrying a mint signature to allow checking. It was short-lived, and apparently never observed in the Mercian mints.[27] Edgar's reform seems to have coincided with the imperial coronation in 973. All coins were now to be of the current type, and no obsolete or foreign coin was to circulate in England; the king's head was to be struck on all coins, and each would carry the name of the mint and moneyer who struck it. Many new mints were opened, but all moneyers were now to collect their dies from a central point, probably Winchester. Centralized die-supply, if it was meant to be permanent, was abandoned under Æthelred and Cnut. Otherwise the reform worked, though draconian punishments laid down by Æthelred and Cnut suggest resistance.

Such a barely concealed tax on the use of coin was certain to be unpopular. Æthelred exploited the requirement to use no foreign or obsolete coin by regularly changing the type, forcing constant reminting. There was profit for the king in the sale of dies, perhaps also in a regular tax on mints; if the latter was not part of the original reforms it was a potential which had been realized by Edward the Confessor's day.[28] New mints were opened in excess of economic need. And the king's dues were paid in good coin. But as in the case of royal rights developed in the area of justice, the increase in royal profit was accepted not simply because of harsh penalties but because there was more here than a mere imposition of taxation. Traders and moneyers might object to recoinage, but they welcomed guaranteed coinage.

Athelstan's laws on trade and coinage were bound up with those on fortification and defence. In the early tenth century military needs were still pressing, and even after 954 the threat from the Irish Sea was still alive. Edgar may have kept a fleet and employed foreign mercenaries.[29] In the face of renewed attack in the reign of Æthelred military demands grew apace. Embedded in the moral exhortations of V Æthelred are specific decrees about defence: military duties were to be performed, fortifications to be kept in repair, ships to be supplied every year by Easter, strong penalties were laid down for desertion. In 1008 hundreds were grouped in threes for the provision of ships and every eight hides was to provide a helmet and a coat of mail. Rising demands on his nobles included rising heriots.[30]

Kings expected to meet military needs in two ways: by demanding general aid, the repair of fortifications, provision of ships and equipment; and by personal service from their nobles. Alfred had built *burhs* and fought with his own followers. The acceptance of the right of the king to aid and service justified the huge gelds and tributes levied during Æthelred's reign, one-off payments like the £36,000 paid in 1012 or the £22,000 raised in southern England to pay off the Scandinavians in 994.[31] The size of such sums has

27. C. E. Blunt, 'The coinage of Athelstan, 924–39: a survey', BNJ, 42 (1974), pp. 35–159
28. D. M. Metcalf, 'The taxation of moneyers under Edward the Confessor and in 1086', in *Domesday Studies*, ed. J. C. Holt (Woodbridge, 1987), pp. 279–93
29. ASC MS D 959, William of Malmesbury Bk II, caps. 148 and 156 and cf. K. Leyser, 'Die Ottonen und Wessex' *Frühmittelalterliche Studien*, 17 (1983), p. 93
30. V Æthelred 26 ff; ASC MS C 1008 and cf. N. Brooks, 'Arms, status and warfare', in *Ethelred the Unready*, ed. Hill, pp. 81–103
31. ASC MS C 1007 and II Æthelred 7.2
32. J. Gillingham, 'Levels of Danegeld and heregeld in the early eleventh century', forthcoming

provoked scepticism.[32] They are unequalled in the period after 1066 and are high even by the standards of thirteenth-century England. The volume of the English coinage at this date, however, indicates a capacity if not a readiness to pay. The £80,000 tribute paid in 1017 was paid during a coin issue, Quatrefoil, whose total output topped 45 million pennies, over £187,000.[33] The extraction of almost half that sum would be a breathtaking level of taxation. Such sums were rarely repeated, but may be credible in view of the nature of Cnut's conquest and the tenth-century background of a growth of royal rights which verged on the brutal.

In 1012/13 Æthelred took a mercenary fleet under Thorkell into his pay and instituted a regular geld taken on all land to pay it. Mercenaries had been in his pay before 1002 and the tax was probably not unprecedented, but its regularity was. Its yield of perhaps £4,000 p.a. was a large sum against a value of currency in circulation of between £8,000 and £33,000.[34] It proved especially onerous. There were no exemptions from a tax which seems to have been taken as a form of commutation into cash of widely recognized duties laid on all land and nobles.

Tenth-century kings even profited from their responsibility for Christianity. They concerned themselves with tithes, dues and sanctuary, but, at least in the surviving legislation, Æthelred and Cnut were the first to be extensively concerned with marriage, incest and the related areas of personal morality which were a major interest of tenth- and eleventh-century reformers.[35] Failure to pay church dues or to hold by the Christian sexual ethic incurred fines and forfeiture, which were normally divided between king and bishop. Already the bishop gave judgement in such cases[36] and took forfeitures. But problems over who got such fines, what would later be called problems over ecclesiastical and secular spheres of jurisdiction, were already occurring. Wulfstan lamented that the fines were not always divided as they should be. Here too the Midas-touch of tenth-century kings turned their legitimate concerns into cash.

I and II Cnut codify precisely these tenth-century developments. Ecclesiastical payments, lay morality, legal procedures and royal rights are brought together in a comprehensive statement of how society should be ordered which is also a gloss on what Edgar meant by 'the king's dignity'. They were issued by a Danish king and recognize differences between English and Dane. Cnut was giving recognition to his own followers, but also continuing the interest of IV Edgar and III Æthelred in the local differences within England, between Wessex and Mercia as well as between both and the Danes.[37] But these are treated as local variants in a code for all England. The unity imposed by royal rule overrode diversity.

Cnut's laws emanated from his consecration and contain elements of a coronation charter offering alleviation of grievances brought to the fore since 1014. It is the act of a conqueror but against a tenth-century background. Edgar in his fourth code, associated with his consecration, had asserted his royal dignity, but also guaranteed that of his thegns. Consecration had been

33. D. M. Metcalf, 'Continuity and change in English monetary history, 973–1086, Part II', BNJ, 51 (1981), p. 56
34. *ibid.* p. 65
35. II Cnut 51 and 52; Edward and Guthrum 4
36. Edward and Guthrum 4; II Cnut 53.1
37. II Cnut 15

developing as a ritual which symbolized rule, including the reciprocal, consensual aspects of it. English kings had been consecrated at their accessions since the ninth century if not before.[38] By the tenth, anointing and formal investiture by two archbishops was the normal ritual confirming that a king had taken power. The ceremony stressed the religious basis of his rule, that he was the lord's anointed, but also the importance of the tie between king and nobles. The ceremonies included a feast at which king and followers ate together. Even the choice of site was symbolic. From Edward the Elder to Æthelred this was normally Kingston-on-Thames, a royal manor central to a kingdom which comprised Wessex, Mercia, East Anglia and Kent, appropriately close to the tidal limit of the Thames for kings who claimed the loyalty of their followers 'on land and sea'.

The mid tenth century had seen changes which already stressed the definition of royal duties[39] alongside the rights which kings were extending. It became normal for the archbishop to preach to the king and people on the duties of a Christian king. The three commands which the king had hitherto issued to his people at the end of the ceremony were transformed into the three promises, or coronation oath, which he took at the beginning. The advance of political ideas during the intellectual revival of the tenth century is one reason for this shift of emphasis towards the duties of office. The hagiographers of Dunstan and Oswald picked out the alleged behaviour of Eadwig and Edgar at their consecrations as symbolic of their respective rule. Eadwig absented himself from this expression of unity between king and nobles withdrawing to the private joys of the bedroom: contrast Edgar and his wife in 973, presented as dutifully devoted to the communal delights of the table. Eadwig's wanton wilfulness, ignoring his duties at precisely the moment when they were defined, epitomized his unfitness for power.

By 1017 consecration was the obvious occasion to elaborate the relations between king and people. As in 1066 a foreign conqueror associated himself with previous practice and established his own legitimacy; as in 1066 the archbishops in the name of the conquered asked for a promise that the conqueror would uphold rights and stand by duties. The management of this takeover by an archbishop, or group of ecclesiastics, trained in traditions of written law, ensured the production of I and II Cnut. As insecure conquerors both Cnut and William attacked the reputation of the supplanted king with an eye to his surviving heirs. Faced with the brief rule of a noble, it was not difficult for William to construct an interpretation which denied the legitimacy of his rule and expunged him from the list of kings[40] without endangering the rights William claimed as passing from Edward. Cnut's predecessor, Æthelred, had ruled for thirty-eight years and his son Edmund had forced a partition of the kingdom in 1016. The attack had to be on the nature of Æthelred's rule, much as Henry I attacked his brother Rufus, but without denying the rights of kings.

38. Nelson, 'The earliest royal *ordo*: some liturgical and historical aspects', in her *Politics and Ritual*, pp. 341–60

39. J. Nelson, 'The second English *ordo*', pp. 361–74. The shift to threefold promise is as likely in the reign of Edgar as in that of Eadwig.

40. G. Garnett, 'Coronation and propaganda: some implications of the Norman claim to the throne of England in 1066', *TRHS* ser. 5, 36 (1986), pp. 91–116

Cnut, like Henry, met existing grievances half way. A tissue of spurious accusations would have served little purpose, and Æthelred had already suffered criticisms of his rule in 1014. The circumstances of defeat and exile, like those of foreign takeover, are abnormal and can allow the articulation of grievances accumulated over time. Grievance grows in the telling, but the ideas expressed in 1014 and 1017 are criticisms not solely of Æthelred but of the trend of tenth-century rule, just as in 1100 the need to attack Rufus led Henry to highlight developments which dated back to 1066 if not before. Tenth- and eleventh-century rule had its unacceptable face which political circumstances could scapegoat on particular kings. It could be arbitrary, bordering on tyranny, and those aspects of it were to the fore between 1014 and 1017. But it was constantly mitigated in individual cases by the problem of enforcement and the consequent need to rule as the nobility expected.

Appointments to ealdormanries show the constant pull of politics on administrative development. Ealdormanries fluctuated in number and size throughout these centuries. Enduring policies can be glimpsed: the appointment of Midland nobles to York in an attempt to bind it more closely to the South, the use of West Saxon nobles to rule north of the Thames, a tendency to dispense with large-scale ealdormanries as the tenth century advanced and replace such provincial rulers by shire reeves.[41] But political change constantly disrupted policy. Eadwig in 956, Edward the Martyr in 975 made a string of new appointments, which in 975 at least included carving out some new ealdormanries. In a succession crisis each shared out patronage. During his long reign Æthelred promoted and exiled ealdormen, dispensed with and recreated ealdormanries in response to changing political and military need.

An ealdormanry was a plum of royal patronage, subject to the political pressures of relations between king and nobility. But it would be a mistake to separate politics and administration, and to place coinage, law, hundreds and shires in a separate sphere of unbroken and unruffled development. The rigid centralization of die-cutting in the coinage, for example, was relaxed to allow a return to local centres, a recognition of the difficulties of enforcement and the provision of an interest for ealdormen and reeves who could take their own share of the profits.[42] Even the apparently arbitrary lines of shire and hundred can be shown, at least in the Severn valley, to have been bent to accommodate local interest (see above, n.12). The pre-modern system of rule was based on cooperation between king and those lords who held power locally. Royal power could be nudged forward, the range of what was acceptable enlarged; the fact that nobles could share in the profit of court or coinage helped. The nobility accepted royal rule as legitimate and only peculiar circumstances, like the exile of a king, gave their grievances any cohesion and expression. But the longer tenth-century kings exercised and extended their powers the more they trespassed into the rights of other men, the dignity of his thegns which Edgar guaranteed.

41. See e.g. P. A. Stafford, 'The reign of Æthelred II: a study in the limitations on royal policy and action', in *Ethelred the Unready*, ed. Hill, at p. 29
42. P. A. Stafford, 'Historical implications of the regional production of dies under Æthelred II', BNJ, 48 (1978), pp. 35–51

In 1014 and 1017 the grievances concentrated on the abuses of lordship, especially at the expense of family. Death duties were too high and when widows and heirs failed to pay they suffered; liability for crime and forfeiture was passing on after death and leading to disinheritance; widows and heiresses were being married off without their consent. The overlapping claims of lord and family would continue to cause trouble for centuries. A lord who was also king had extended his powers of lordship at their expense. Here was an ideal issue for the clemency of a coronation charter. But Cnut's mitigation begins with protection against the demands of royal officials, against the noble wearing his other hat. It was difficult for nobles who were both gainers and losers from royal power consistently to oppose it. The long loyalty to Æthelred through the military problems of his reign is as significant as the grievances expressed at the end of it.

The circumstances of defeat and conquest offered a unique insight into tenth-century rule. Conquest led to rule over two kingdoms, with problems of absence and growing military needs. The conquests of the eleventh century produced disruption and change, but also continuity. Cnut may have promised mitigation, but not at the expense of his royal rights. He continued to take land from his nobles as a consequence of crime or treason.[43] William used the principle on a large scale in his vast disappropriations after 1066; his officials implemented it in day-to-day administration. In the political debacle of 1066 the family of Godwine lost all, a certain Wulfric in East Anglia forfeited a mere 68 acres in a legal judgement.[44] Eleventh-century wills show a nobility increasingly anxious to tie up bequests in such a way that they precluded forfeiture. Ælfhelm Polga had protested his loyalty to the king's father as a blanket plea that his bequests might stand. Thurketel Heyng by the mid eleventh-century granted land to his daughter with reversion to St Benet Holme, stating that she could not forfeit.[45] The concerns of the king and his officials remained the same. Cnut's laws began by stating the rights of the church and followed them by those of the king. In the early twelfth century the author of the *Leges Henrici Primi* was instructing the sheriff to open the meeting of the shire court with the rights of the church and then enquire into royal ones.

Cash continued to prompt the greatest sophistication in government. Royal lands had always been the core of royal resources. The unification of several kingdoms had increased them, loss through patronage and acquisition through forfeiture meant constant fluctuation. By the eleventh century the management of the royal lands allowed for constant reorganization to accommodate these changes. Rents and renders from them were paid in ways which ensured that changes in the weight of the coinage did not affect their yield. Central supply of dies for the coinage was resumed in the later years of Cnut. The Confessor's attempt to change the coin type every three years or so maximized profit, and William increased the impositions on moneyers to allow for the loss of income when he abandoned regular type changes. The reassessment of geld payment, envisaged in 1086, would only have been the last of many.[46]

43. Writs 48
44. DB I fo. 214 R
45. W. 25
46. S. Harvey, 'Taxation and the ploughland in Domesday Book', in *Domesday Book, a Reassessment*, ed. P. H. Sawyer (1985), pp. 86–103 and cf. C. Hart, *The Hidation of Cambridgeshire* (Leicester, 1974)

Insofar as rule is traditional, formed by the expectations of kings in the framework of possibilities determined by a particular society, continuity could be expected. But the tenth and eleventh centuries were not static. Unification enhanced royal wealth, aspiration and prestige; conquest brought new problems, especially military and financial needs. From 1012 to 1051 the employment of permanent mercenary forces was a fact of English life which had to be paid for in a regular tax, the heregeld. As England's neighbours became more involved in its history, defence played a larger part in internal organization, in the marcher ealdormanries whether of Æthelred, Edward or William. Changes in the coinage are a continuation of tenth-century development but also a response of kings anxious for cash.

Financial need and royal rights went hand in hand to stimulate greater central development and sophistication. By later standards royal government at the centre was still rudimentary, but money called forth change. Winchester had been a collecting point for royal dues when Edgar took its standard for weights and measures as that at which all royal dues should be paid.[47] The Winchester mint consistently struck heavy pennies; royal payments were to be taken at the highest rate. By the 1030s a royal treasury was established at Winchester.[48] Royal income had already passed the point where it could follow the king round in a box to be stored under his bed.[49]

Rule over two kingdoms, or over kingdom and duchy, meant constant absences. Individuals benefitted from the regency this entailed: Godwine and Emma under Cnut, William Fitz Osbern and Odo of Bayeux under William. Any more permanent development was halted after Cnut by the end of Danish rule, and even after 1066 took long to appear. The mechanisms of coinage, law and royal dues could already function without the king's continual presence, though prolonged absence or succession problems would still disrupt the relations of king and nobles on which they depended. Long-term foreign rule after 1066 may have had another result in the eventual loss of the English expertise which ran the system at local level, a problem which was surfacing by AD 1100.[50]

In 1086 William ordered the Domesday survey of England to be made. It is the fruit of conquest, of the king's need to know about the kingdom he had taken over, of his success in persuading a still insecure nobility to cooperate. The Survey was to be an enquiry into royal rights, a judgement on difficult disputes over landholding which the transfers after 1066 had produced. It would set the seal of legitimacy and title on new Norman holdings. Its comprehensiveness and its combination of functions were unparalleled in earlier royal surveys, and individual lords recognized this when they kept copies of the Domesday record for their own use.[51]

The Survey is also evidence of massive continuity. William's priorities were those of earlier kings; he set out to discover his rights and check on the activities

47. III Edgar 8.1
48. ASC MS C 1035
49. D. M. Metcalf, 'Continuity and change in English monetary history, 973–1086, part I', BNJ, 50 (1980), at p. 24
50. W. L. Warren, 'The myth of Norman administrative efficiency', *TRHS* ser. 5, 34 (1984) pp. 113–32
51. See e.g. J. C. Holt '1086', in *Domesday Studies*, ed. J. C. Holt (Woodbridge, 1987), pp. 41–64 and H. B. Clarke, 'The Domesday satellites', *Domesday Book, a Reassessment*, ed. P. H. Sawyer (1985), pp. 50–70

of royal officials. Many shires begin with a statement of 'local custom' which closer inspection shows to be local demarcations of royal rights agreed in previous reigns. Shire town and royal lands follow, taking pride of place as sources of royal profit. Both were administered by royal officials, especially by the sheriff, whose activity required constant checking; in Edgar's third law code, in 1017 and 1027 the need to restrain agents of royal power had been recognized. After royal lands come the holdings of the tenants-in-chief, listed tenant by tenant in each shire. Should those lands be forfeit to the king or fall into wardship, they could be accurately assessed and managed by the local sheriff. Lands of some English and Norman widows were recorded in 1066 and 1086 because such women were royal assets at both dates. Control of widows and heiresses was already a grievance in 1017; when William exercised his right to marry off the widow of the English sheriff of Gloucestershire he was only acting as an English king.[52] And within every holding in Domesday, on every manor, the assessment to the king's geld was noted. William had stepped into Edward's shoes. There had been little need to measure him for a bigger pair.

Domesday can be hailed as the first document of English administration, a written record of central government, bringing in its train the seeds of bureaucracy. It was more than this: an awe-inspiring royal progress by proxy, a fearsome sacred book of judgement,[53] no mere equivalent of a modern land register. As a written record, it is the product of a trend not a new departure. The information it contains and the speed of its compilation argue the existence of a range of documentation on which it was based: lists of tenants-in-chief and their lands for 1066, geld-rolls, lists of tenants and dues from towns, records of royal lands and the farms due from them.[54] The records of Old English rule, written in the vernacular, may have disappeared where chronicles, laws and charters, preserved in religious houses, have survived. There are dangers in inferring the existence of too many of them. Some of the attitudes of early English rulers suggest a carelessness about central records which is a world apart from the habits of mind of bureaucracy. There were written laws in the tenth century, but a surprising indifference to their final written form. Different versions of Æthelred's legislation survive, and oral promulgation, the word of the king, never lost its force.[55] Little attention was paid to the preservation of royal laws. No central collection was kept, at least it has left no trace.

There is great debate about the existence of a royal chancery or writing office in the tenth and early eleventh centuries,[56] a fact which itself indicates that it can have been no more than embryonic. The king may have recruited a writing office from major religious scriptoria by the mid tenth century, but it was still fluctuating, and its existence did not prevent some beneficiaries of royal largesse securing a record of the royal grant elsewhere. No central record of charters

52. See P. A. Stafford, 'Women in Domesday', forthcoming
53. J. Nelson, 'The rites of the conqueror', ANS, 4 (1981), at p. 131 and M. Clanchy, *From Memory to Written Record* (1979), at pp. 18 and 121–2
54. S. Harvey, 'Domesday and its predecessors', *English Historical Review*, 86 (1971), pp. 753–73
55. P. Wormald, '*Lex scripta* and *verbum regis*: legislation and Germanic kingship, from Euric to Cnut', in *Early Medieval Kingship*, eds. P. H. Sawyer and I. N. Wood (Leeds, 1977), pp. 105–38
56. Compare P. Chaplais, 'The Anglo-Saxon Chancery: from the diploma to the writ', *J. of the Society of Archivists* 3 (1966), pp. 160–79 and S. Keynes, *The Diplomas of King Æthelred the Unready* (Cambridge, 1980)

granted or writs sent out was maintained. It was individuals anxious to record their rights and settlements who prompted the development of new forms of written title in the tenth and eleventh centuries. The chirograph was a two or three fold copy of a document cut and kept for checking by the parties concerned. It grew up as a private record. Even the shift from charter to writ can be traced to the needs of the beneficiary and what he or she wished to have recorded. In the litigious world of the later tenth and eleventh centuries the record of the king's notification of a grant to the shire court (the writ) was more useful than the ponderous record of the royal meeting where the grant was made (the charter). It would normally be in the shire court, not before the king, that future trouble would be resolved.

This cavalier attitude to certain types of central record keeping survived the eleventh century. The conquest of 1066 and Domesday are not the origins of bureaucratic rule. But Domesday has much in common with the first regular records of central rule, the Pipe rolls and exchequer system, and it is here that a lost lineage of documents can be supposed. The Pipe rolls and Domesday are not concerned with general statements of law and procedure, they do not require the central copying of many documents, though the Pipe rolls argue the need for some central record of royal grants. Their obvious preoccupations are royal rights and income and a check on the local agents of the king. Edward, Cnut, Æthelred and Edgar shared these concerns; it is unlikely that they left them entirely unrecorded.

Domesday implies not just central but local records. The shire customs it lists are more accurately defined as what the king could and could not take from the shire. They record especially local variation and exemption, which must have been the subject of grant and agreement between king and individuals, shires and towns. In Kent the king forewent his normal share in fines for adultery on the lands of Holy Trinity, St Augustine and St Martin; here and in Nottingham-shire and Derbyshire his rights to take heriots were defined, in Oxford twenty burgesses were to go with the king on his expeditions, or to pay twenty pounds.[57] Behind such statements lie negotiations, agreements and privileges, conducted sometimes not by individuals, but by towns or shires with the king or his representative. And with the king so attentive to his rights it would be well if others saw to the record of theirs.

Concern for royal rights produced records. It provided opportunity for a new form of patronage, not just the grant of office but the individual arrangements and agreements which led to the eleventh-century beneficial hidations (a reduction of hidage assessment) for individuals and areas, to the grants of right to take the ever more profitable fines and forfeitures in the courts which are given in the writs of Cnut and Edward the Confessor. Royal rule treated not only with individuals but with groups. From Athelstan in the early tenth century calling for action from the bishops and thegns of Kent to the lost agreements which lie behind the rights and exemptions of Domesday, kings reinforced the existence of collective action even as they utilized it.[58] Domesday stands as a record of two centuries of advancing royal power and of the patronage, agreement, consultation, cooperation and compromise which had been its necessary corollaries.

57. DB I fos. 1 R, 280 V and 154R
58. On which see S. Reynolds, *Kingdoms and Communities in Medieval Europe* (Oxford, 1984)

9

The Nobility

The social group of whom we are best informed at this date is the nobility, especially the great nobility. In the political history of these centuries they are undoubtedly the most important group, central too to the mechanisms of royal rule. Their values, their structure as a group and changes which affected them are of wider interest. Describing them, however, like describing any social group, is not simple. We are faced on the one hand with contemporary legal classifications which carry the dangers of simplification and of a description of society largely from the king's viewpoint, on the other with our own classifications in terms of wealth, occupation or relationship to power which may have been less important at the time. Detailed description is an apparent answer, though even it must select its material and utilize terms such as 'noble' and 'peasant' which entail conscious definition or unconscious assumptions. To understand a society fully we need not only to be aware of such problems, but to have a range of material available which will allow us to explore how people saw themselves as well as how contemporaries defined them. The lack of such a range for the tenth and eleventh centuries means that social analysis brings difficulties even greater than those for later periods.

The Book of Ely is tantalizing on the question of status distinctions and social description. It uses some specific terms, *dux* for an ealdorman, but more often a variety of almost interchangeable terms, *primates*, *proceres*, *satrapes*, which seem to indicate nothing more precise than 'great men'. We know from other evidence that Ælfhelm Polga would have counted as a king's thegn by some tenth-century definitions, but he is never given such a title. Clearly much has been lost in the twelfth-century translation from the Old English to Latin, but the distinctions between this text and the legal documents is still remarkable. It identifies people by descent, relationship, place of origin or where they held land; its distinctions are between 'the great men of the province', the 'better folk of the vill' and the rest.

By contrast the general legal statements about society employ a precise terminology and envisage a clear hierarchy of social divisions. In Cnut's laws different heriots were laid down for earls, king's thegns and lesser thegns in

Wessex and Mercia, king's thegns and lesser thegns among the Danes.[1] For each group a heriot was prescribed, for lesser men cash only, for king's thegn, earl or the lesser thegn in Wessex, cash and military equipment. Wulfstan, in his tract 'On wergelds and dignities'[2] echoes the alliterative jingles of literary texts, *eorl* and *ceorl*, but also specifies exactly how a ceorl could once prosper to be a thegn, a thegn to an earl, how a thegn who has other thegns holding of him has a different status. These clear statements belong especially to the pen of Archbishop Wulfstan but not exclusively so. Domesday can make distinctions, as in Nottinghamshire and Derbyshire, between thegns who hold six manors or more and those with less.[3] The charter of liberties of Henry I with its barons, other men of the king and those who hold of barons is still part of the same world.[4]

All classifications simplify heterogeneous reality and impose their own selective criteria. The purposes for which a particular classification was made must always be recognized. Most of our classifications at this date are in royal documents or laws, or produced by those anxious to define legal standing in the courts. It is scarcely surprising that most of them envisage a hierarchy in which relationship and service to the king are a major distinguishing criterion, or that they list precise and measurable criteria such as quantity of land as a means of qualifying or disqualifying people from particular rights and duties.

Wulfstan's classifications are subject to all these caveats: he was a man interested in the law, in rights and obligations, a royal counsellor. Like many of those who comment on society he was also a man who felt its current state was a cause of contemporary woes. The moralist as social commentator is a familiar figure. For Wulfstan the 'good old days' were past: '*Once* it used to be that people and rights went . . . ' Remembering the past with nostalgia embalms and rigidifies it. Nothing was ever really as simple as Wulfstan's nostalgia suggests.

This does not mean that classifications emanating from these sources are useless. Status determined many things in tenth- and eleventh-century England, some of them precise. The value placed on your oath in court, the heriot paid at your death, your life itself depended on status. All had wergelds or values placed on their lives which were paid in compensation if they were killed and determined other fines and compensations. Wulfstan still divides society by wergeld.[5] Whether or not you were a baron decided the just relief in Henry I's day just as whether you were a king's thegn determined your heriot under Cnut. These may be imperfect descriptions of society, but they were not matters of idle social speculation. They were the descriptions of a ruler not of a neighbour, a ruler whose influence was felt increasingly in the lives of many people. Classifications used by governments are not neutral descriptions of society, they affect it. When demands are made according to status, people need to know where they fit. If eleventh-century people had been asked to describe themselves and their society they would have talked, like the Book of Ely, of kin, clients, greater and lesser men, but they would have been increasingly aware of

1. II Cnut 71–71.5
2. EHD I, no. 51, p. 468
3. DB I, fo. 28 V
4. Ed. W. Stubbs, *Select Charters from the Beginning to 1307* (Oxford, 1870), pp. 118–19
5. EHD I, no. 51, p. 469

free and unfree, ceorl or thegn, king's thegn or earl, with or without jurisdiction; aware, that is, of the language of royal government and of lordship.

Wulfstan tells us that a ceorl might thrive to be a thegn, and a thegn to an earl. An earl in the eleventh century, or an ealdorman in the tenth, was an appointed royal official. He was also a great noble, and his office made him wealthier, but he was easy to define and recognize because of his official position. Not so the thegn, who worried Wulfstan more. He too should perform royal service, should have a seat and special duty in the king's hall, if he were of higher status he might ride in the king's household band, on royal messages and missions and have other thegns under him. Wulfstan's thegn, like the *minister* of the charters, means 'servant', a royal servant in a society where service was dignified by the rank of those for whom it was performed.

'Thegn', like that other term 'noble', had none of the precise meaning of earl or ealdorman. Wulfstan recognized this. Thegns were men set apart by a certain life-style. They would have fives hides of land, a bell(tower), kitchen, church and fortified place, the accoutrements of a later lord of the manor. A thegn would not live by agricultural labour, and would have the means to exercise hospitality and liberality. Excavations at sites such as Goltho[6] have confirmed the reality of that lifestyle. Wulfstan gives priority to the landed basis of such a life-style; he wanted a measurable qualification in face of the muddy uncertainties of status distinctions. If a ceorl prospered so that he possessed a helmet, a coat of mail and a gold plated sword, if he had not land he was still a ceorl.[7] The irony is heavy; only the wealthiest, certainly not the simple holder of five hides of land, could afford such equipment. Wulfstan may have been coping with a problem of his own day. Military demands on the nobility were rising, with Æthelred demanding larger heriots in military equipment.[8] Perhaps a military life-style was becoming a more important aspect of noble status, but Wulfstan wished to avoid such loose criteria.

The legal statements suggest that a noble or thegn was distinguished by landholding sufficient to maintain a non-agrarian life-style, was a member of a military elite, a person whose local standing gave him an influential voice in the courts and over whom the king sought lordship. Such statements seek to draw the difficult base line for the differentiation of noble and non-noble. They give little indication of the enormous differences within the nobility, none at all of the values they shared or the way they saw themselves.

By the mid tenth century and before a great nobility was marked out by its wealth and power. Ælfheah, ealdorman of West Wessex who died in the early 970s, held land amounting to some 700 hides, on a par with if not exceeding the holdings of the richest followers of William I after 1066.[9] During the 940s the family of Athelstan, aptly named 'Half-King', had a stranglehold on the English ealdormanries comparable in nature if not in scale to that of the Godwine family

6. G. Beresford, 'Goltho manor, Lincs.: the buildings and their surrounding defences', ANS, 4 (1981), pp. 13–36
7. Norðleoda Laga, EHD I no. 51, p. 469
8. N. Brooks, 'Arms, status and warfare', in *Ethelred the Unready*, ed. D. Hill (Oxford, 1978), pp. 81–103
9. A. Williams, '*Princeps Merciorum Gentis*: the family, career and connections of Ælfhere, ealdorman of Mercia', ASE, 10 (1981), pp. 143–72

in the 1060s: Athelstan held East Anglia, his brother Æthelwold Kent and perhaps south-east Mercia, a third brother, Eadric, east Wessex.[10] At the height of its influence, Godwine's family controlled all England except Mercia, but family concentrations of power were not new in the eleventh century. The ealdormanry was to the tenth century what the earldom was to the eleventh, a key to further advance.

The great nobility were characterized by the geographical spread as much as by the scale of their landholding. These families acquired much of their wealth through the exercise of royal office. They rarely originated from the area where they held office, so that land acquired in this way combined with patrimony to produce a wide scattering. Ælfheah's land stretched from Buckinghamshire and Middlesex to Somerset. Those of Wulfric Spott, member of a north Mercian family, went as far north as the land between Ribble and Mersey, as far south as Gloucestershire, fanning out from the concentration in Staffordshire, Derbyshire and Warwickshire. Wulfric himself never held royal office, but his brother Ælfhelm was appointed ealdorman at York, and his family had been wooed by a series of royal land grants throughout the tenth century. The lands of Earl Harold or of Earl Leofric's descendants were even more extensive. By 1066 Harold had land in almost every county south of the Trent, some 1,900 hides, 500 carucates and 3 sulungs, not to mention a quarter as much again held by his men.[11] The comparison with Ælfheah is not straightforward since Domesday gives a more total picture than Ælfheah's will, and includes land attached to Harold's office. Rather we should recognize that unification and the growth of royal power had produced the conditions for the rise of a great nobility, whilst the politics of the eleventh century allowed some to utilize those conditions to the full.

Below the level of this great nobility distinctions are difficult to follow in the inadequate sources. Ælfhelm Polga had more than twenty pieces of land in Cambridgeshire, Essex, Suffolk, Bedfordshire and Huntingdonshire. His heriot would make him a king's thegn and he attended at the royal court where he appears as a witness of charters. He stood out as a great man within East Anglian society in much the same way as Siweard and Sigered did in Kent *c.*AD 1000. These two brothers were king's thegns, and when they attended the royal court were of sufficient importance to be recorded as witnesses. Siweard is called on one occasion 'of Kent'.[12] In local records they act in the company of Kentish nobles, Wulfstan of Saltwood,[13] Lyfing of Malling, Leofstan of Mersham, Leofwine of Ditton, Sidewine of Paddlesworth, Ælfnoth of Orpington.[14] The use of a place-name to identify such men cannot easily be interpreted. There are too few documents to know whether, for example, it was permanently attached to them.[15] It cannot be used simply to associate them with a single estate or family seat. Leofric of Brandon in the Book of Ely held land in

10. C. Hart, 'Athelstan Half-King and his family', ASE, 2 (1973), pp. 115–44
11. A. Williams, 'Land and power in the eleventh century: the estates of Harold Godwineson', ANS, 3 (1983), pp. 171–87 and 230–4
12. R. 63
13. R. 62
14. R. 69
15. J. C. Holt, *What's in a Name, Family nomenclature and the Norman Conquest*, Stenton Lecture, 1981 (Reading, 1982)

at least three places.[16] At the same time it suggests a local nobility, lords of a handful of places, men who needed more precise identifications than a Siweard of Kent or an Ælfhelm Polga. Contemporaries saw a difference between such men and those of the importance of Wulfric *Spott*, recognizable by a nickname or by the fame of his descent, Wulfric *Wulfrune's son*.

The ties of lordship enmeshed all these men, and some women, from the king downwards. They shared the values implied by that bond. The *Battle of Maldon* was a poem written to commemorate the fight against a Scandinavian army in 991 in which ealdorman Brihtnoth and others fell. Loyalty to a lord, taking vengeance for his death, an honourable fate on the battlefield, protection of one's people and land are the ideals voiced by Brihtnoth and his followers. 'Here stand a noble earl with his troop who will defend this land, the home of Æthelred, my prince, my people and my land'.[17] The ultimate proof of loyalty was death with a lord on the battlefield, 'near the prince he lay low, as befits a thegn', but the bond between lord and follower was expected to function in more mundane circumstances. A lord was expected to protect and help his men in court; Ælfwold, brother of Æthelwine, was appealed to as a lord in the Chippenham case. In the real world beyond the poems, protection was bought and sold. Archbishop Dunstan received land from Ecgferth 'in order that he might act as guardian for his wife and child'.[18] The warm sentiments of Brihtnoth and his men were ideals, but no less important for that. Loyalty, protection, mutual benefit characterized the idealized relationship of lord and man, which encompassed that between king and noble. Such ideals bound the nobility to the king and provided a yardstick by which abuse and tyranny could be measured.

In the *Battle of Maldon* Ælfwine spoke for the ideals, for those who had not fled ignominiously. He exhorted them to bravery and loyalty, but he also declared his lineage. He would fight to save his honour, not merely as the man of his lord but as a member of a distinguished family. He greatest grief was that Brihtnoth had been his lord and his kinsman. His fight is presented as the pursuit of a family feud and vengeance. The bond of kin was as important as that of lordship. Birth and blood mattered. The rise of Godwine and Harold, like that of Athelstan Half-King or Ælfheah was the rise of a family not merely of individuals. Godwine advanced his daughter, sons and nephew, Harold his brothers, Athelstan and Ælfheah both held office alongside siblings. Any rivalry between Godwine and Leofric was rivalry also between their families for office and royal position. Edward the Confessor marked Godwine's fall in 1051 by giving an earldom and abbacy to Leofric's son and nephew. Commitment to the family, particularly to the three-generational family, the descendants of common grandparents, was strong (see below, chapter on *Family and Women*).

Family and lord overlapped in their claims and functions. Overlap could mean clash, as was the case in wardship and marriage (see below). The Maldon poet felt that the bonds were strongest when lord and kinsman were identical. Kings shared his opinion about such reinforcement. From Edward the Elder marrying the daughter of an ealdorman of Kent to William I joining his niece Judith to

16. LE caps. 8, 20 and 35, pp. 80–1, 82–4, 110
17. EHD I, no. 10, p. 320
18. R. 44

Earl Waltheof, kings sought to add the belt of family to the braces of lordship in their relations with great nobles. With the nobility as a whole they could not avoid the problems of being royal lords whose powers were extended at the expense of noble families.

These values moulded noble patronage to the church. Prayers for the family dead and the maintenance of family foundations motivated land grants to a God who was also seen as a lord with rights and claims. In Edgar's fourth code the Christian God avenges the non-payment of tithes and church dues as a lord would punish those who withhold rent. Yet Christianity added its own values, and transformed others through the belief in an afterlife. Wulfstan uses moral exhortation indiscriminately in sermons and laws: 'Let us love God . . . zealously honour one Christian religion . . . and loyally support one royal lord'.[19] Nation-wide penance and fast were enjoined in 1009 as part of the response to attack, and a penitential ordinance was imposed c.AD 1070 on all who had fought in the battle of Hastings. Those to whom such ideas were addressed paid more than lip service to the Christian ideals they mobilize. Obedience to one God and one king were parallel.

A reconstruction of English society which included wills, records of disputes, poetry and sermons as well as legal definitions would certainly emphasize divisions by wealth and landholding, even more so than Wulfstan's tracts. It would see more separating than uniting a humble thegn with five hides and an ealdorman like Ælfheah. It would recognize that the king played a large part in the lives of the greatest nobles and that many of them were touched by his power in the local courts. It would see the military side of the noble life-style, but not emphasize it at the expense of the pursuit of influence and prestige as the lord of followers. Birth and family would not be ignored alongside king and lord and the values emanating from both would be acknowledged as deep, though sometimes conflicting.

During the tenth and eleventh centuries the power of English kings grew at the same time as the economy was marked by developing trade, a market in land, town growth and a less provable agrarian upswing. In the eleventh century military needs became more pressing again. Noble society experienced a period of rapid social mobility, with a burgeoning lesser nobility and the emergence of an exceptionally powerful greater one. The former was largely the result of changes in economy and land-holding; the latter was effected primarily by unification. To speak as if the English nobility were a unified group is unwise, though many, in varied ways, felt the impact of royal power.

Wulfstan's remarks indicate social mobility. He spoke of thriving ceorls who could become thegns by acquiring five hides of land, who acquired thegns' rights by the earl's gift.[20] Wulfstan's tone is rhetorical and he had his own reasons for stressing social mobility. In his attempts to enforce the celibacy of the clergy he offered thegns' rights to those priests who held to the ideal. He needed to suggest that such rights could be gained. Conversely his bait would have been meaningless unless such rights could be gained. Social mobility through the

19. VIII Æthelred 43–4
20. Quoted from CCCC MS 201 in F. M. Stenton, 'The thriving of the Anglo-Saxon ceorl', in *Preparatory to Anglo-Saxon England*, ed. D. M. Stenton (Oxford, 1970), pp. 388–9

acquisition of land and other forms of wealth must have been familiar to his audience. Other evidence points in this direction. Many English place names take the form of a personal name coupled with a naming element *by* or *tun*, e.g. Woolstone = Wulfric's tun, where *tun* or *by* means settlement and the name indicates its owner. These names are increasingly dated to the tenth and eleventh centuries and can sometimes be traced to a change of ownership of the land which occurred at this date.[21] On occasion it is the owner of the land in Domesday who is recorded in the place name, as at Blackmanstone, earlier *Blacemannescirce* in Kent.[22] This phase of English place name giving, which laid so much stress on ownership as the way to distinguish settlements, is linked to changes in estate structure, in the land market and in notions of property. The increasing use of a place name as a way of distinguishing individuals also suggests a tendency to identify people with the land they held. A group of small-scale lords, owning and associated with a few estates, was apparently growing in number. Social mobility is not new in the tenth and eleventh centuries, but the changes in place names at this date suggest that some factors were accelerating it.

The emergence of a great nobility in the aftermath of unification is a clearer social change. Men like Ælfheah with his 700 hides scattered throughout southern England are not found among the ninth-century nobility. He is one of a small group of families who profited from the way kings chose to rule their enlarged kingdom, from royal gifts of office, land and marriage partners. Ælfheah was the recipient of a series of land grants from the late 930s onwards.[23] By 940 he had married Ælfswith, a kinswoman of the royal house. The gift of an ealdormanry in the late 950s culminated his rise. Godwine in the eleventh century exaggerated but did not create the trend. His ascent, like that of Eadric of Mercia under Æthelred, was vilified retrospectively as a result of political developments. But neither represents a new phenomenon.

During the tenth century especially the great nobility were connected among themselves and with the royal dynasty. Ealdorman Brihtnoth of Essex died at the Battle of Maldon. Kinship connected him to his contemporaries ealdorman Æthelweard of west Wessex and his son Æthelmær, who held office at the royal court; to Ealhhelm, former ealdorman in Mercia and father of ealdorman Ælfheah and his brother Ælfhere. Brihtnoth had married the daughter of his predecessor, Ælfgar of Essex and his sister-in-law was the widow of King Edmund. His kinsmen Æthelweard and Æthelmær were descendants of King Æthelred I, Alfred's older brother, and Ælfheah and Ælfhere were related to King Edgar.

These links cannot be read simply as indicating a closely knit and cohesive group. They are the result of kings advancing their own kin but also of royal attempts to secure loyalty through marriage. They are the ties of faction at court and of the search for local support. They were a basis for a group sense and especially for an identification with king and kingdom rather than regional feeling, reinforced by widely scattered lands and the hope and need for further royal patronage. The extent to which these men shared common ground is

21. M. Gelling, *Signposts to the Past* (1978), pp. 181–4
22. A. Everitt, *Continuity and Change* (Leicester, 1986), p. 203
23. See e.g. S. 440, 475, 494, 564

emphasized by their role as major patrons of the reformed monasteries of the late tenth century, espousing a movement centred on the court. But they were divided by rivalries and their desire to establish family claims to office ran counter to the king's need to use patronage. They owed much of their position to royal gifts of land and ealdormanries, but once established in office their ties with the local nobility became an additional source of power, their position as local lords an additional motive for action. Their relations to the king and kingdom combined loyalty and tension.

As a social group these people were a result of unification, but their individual rise and fall depended on the flux of politics. The family of Athelstan Half-King achieved its highest status in the 940s and 950s. Athelstan's sons continued to control East Anglia and to figure among the great until 992, but the engrossing position they enjoyed under Edmund and Eadred was never recovered.[24] The death of ealdorman Æthelwine in 992 ended their importance as a noble family of the first rank. Æthelwine had sons, but none of them play a significant role in eleventh-century politics. Æthelwine's contemporary, ealdorman Brihtnoth, suffered a similar fate. After his death at Maldon his descendants continued to be important in East Anglia, where they are still identifiable in Domesday, but were no longer in the top ranks of English noble society. The new great nobility were wealthy and powerful, but their position was also precarious and dependent on continuing royal favour.

Some ealdormen were removed from office: Æthelred especially is known to have exiled or murdered several. But natural death rather than deposition was their normal fate and kings, including Æthelred, did not lightly remove men who had built up local power. Nor did men lightly rebel who owed so much to the king and hoped for so much more. But patronage fostered rivalries. The rise of Ælfhere of Mercia in Edgar's reign could be seen as taking place at the expense of Æthelwine of East Anglia. As the tenth century wore on more families had competing claims to the same office. An obsessive concern with the succession was the product of a situation where these men judged access to and influence with the king as crucial, where the identity of a new monarch could be an opportunity as well as a threat. Two things stand out from Æthelred's relations with his great nobles: a tale of sporadic individual disloyalty and exile alongside an overwhelming general loyalty through setbacks to the end of the reign. The values and the development of the tenth-century nobility explain the conundrum.

The tenth-century nobility were southern English rather than English. The dominant group of families from the 930s to the 990s was West Saxon in origin, and the lands and offices they acquired gave them interests no further north than Mercia. They came constantly to court and their rivalries developed and were often played out there. Beyond them were other families less attached to king and kingdom. And the eleventh century saw the rise of new families and an altered pattern.

The structure, values and changes outlined above are based on a study of documents concentrated in southern and eastern England. The extent to which any of this analysis would apply in the north Midlands, north of the Humber or Tees or west of the Pennines is doubtful. Domesday or Durham sources show a

24. W. 21 and R. 63

similarly landed nobility, reveal its military and family values, the ties of lord and man among the nobility and between them and peasant cultivators. But Domesday itself fails as a source north and west of Yorkshire, in precisely the area which lacks any evidence of substantial penetration of cash, of a market-oriented economy or towns and, as Domesday's coverage demonstrates, where the impact of royal power was least. York was the most northerly mint, the most northerly town and Yorkshire the most northerly shire in eleventh-century England. The far north is also the area from which we have the least information. The changes in landholding which accompanied royal power and the use of cash further south would not be expected here and these may have been precisely the changes producing a burgeoning lesser nobility. The balance of gains and losses involved in royal patronage and the working of the royal courts was not felt here. From the North Midlands north and west the nobility rarely came to the southern court, rarely received royal office. The story of two families who were drawn to varying extents into southern politics show some of the differences which being on the peripheries of England made.

The North Midlands family of Wulfric Spott owed some of its importance to southern kings.[25] From the time of Edgar if not earlier grants of land to them marked the attempt of kings to extend their influence northwards. Members of this family came regularly to the royal court during the second half of the tenth century until their fall in 1006. In 993 one of them, Ælfhelm was given the ultimate royal patronage, an ealdormanry at York. In 1006 Ælfhelm was murdered at the king's command and his sons blinded. Far from disappearing from history this family became an important factor in eleventh-century politics. It was considered a key to the North Midlands at the end of Æthelred's reign, and both Cnut and Edmund Ironside married into it. The marriage of Cnut was one key to its continued influence. Harold Harefoot was not only the son of Cnut but the grandson of Ælfhelm. The support he gained from Leofric of Mercia in 1035 may derive from a connection between the two families, or may be the source of that connection via the probable marriage of Leofric's son Ælfgar to Ælfhelm's great-niece. It is not the rise and fall of the family which sets it apart from the experience of southern nobles, but its continued importance after its fall. This may spring from its local power independent of the king, a function of the distance from royal control. But equally it is a result of the turbulent politics of the first half of the eleventh century in which a noble family which had fallen under one king could use the subsequent turns of fortune to its own advantage.

The house of Bamburgh is an unequivocal example of the history of a family never integrated into the politics of southern England.[26] From the early tenth to the late eleventh century this family was associated with England north of the Tees. They maintained a hereditary control over the area as high reeves and earls until 1041. Even after the murder of Eadwulf at the court of Harthacnut in that year its influence remained. Two members of this family became earls soon after 1066. The house of Bamburgh owed little of its power to southern kings. On two occasions an ealdormanry further south was granted to them, between 954 and 963 and from 1006 to 1016 when the family controlled all England north of the Humber: on the second occasion King Æthelred married his

25. P. H. Sawyer, *The Charters of Burton Abbey* (Oxford, 1979), pp. xxi–xxiii and xxxviii–xliii
26. Writs pp. 419–23 and 562, and W. Kapelle, *The Norman Conquest of the North* (1979)

daughter to Earl Uhtred. But except briefly and occasionally they were not drawn to the southern court. If we define England as the area whose nobility were effectively pulled into royal politics it would end at the Humber.

As the family of Wulfric Spott showed, the eleventh century offered opportunities for independent action on the part of the nobility: this might be seen as a contrast with the closer ties between king and nobles in the tenth. The exile and return of eleventh-century nobles and the rapid rise to great influence of Godwine and Leofric suggest the same interpretation (see above, chapters on *Cnut* and *Edward the Confessor*). The number of great families certainly became more restricted. But the mid tenth century had witnessed comparable trends reversed under Æthelred. Edward the Confessor's apparent inability to do this owed less to a novel structure of the nobility than to the political situation of the 1040s and 1050s. The royal court was no less a magnet for Godwine and Ælfgar than it had been for Æthelwine and Ælfheah. It was rivalry there rather than entrenched local power which precipitated their rebellions. The existence of a great nobility by the mid eleventh century is a social fact, continued in an exaggerated form from the tenth; the domination of too few people at court is a political fact peculiar to its own time. William's conquest and redistribution altered the situation, at least in the short term.

The development of royal power and rights (see chapter on *Ruling*) touched all nobles, especially where it conflicted with notions of family. The tenacity with which claims to forfeit lands were pursued shows how deeply forfeiture offended feelings of family right in hereditary land. A case in which land first changed hands early in the reign of Edward the Elder when ealdorman Sighelm borrowed £30 was only finally settled in the reign of Edgar when the land in question passed to the church. The family had reopened it at every intervening opportunity.[27] The precariousness of land held after forfeiture gives insight into the disturbances and plots surrounding successions to the throne, which provided ideal opportunties to revive old claims. The fact that decisions on forfeiture could be reversed indicates how political they might be. In 956 a thegn, Wulfric, lost all his lands for crimes under King Eadwig; in 960 Eadwig's brother Edgar restored Wulfric. Either he was not guilty of the crimes in the first place, and the forfeiture was political, or he was guilty, and the restoration was political. The advance of the king's rights is the other side of royal patronage. The evolution of noble wills in the tenth century recognizes the significance of both.

The making of pre-mortem arrangements to take effect after death was a tradition before AD 900. It is only at the end of the ninth and in the tenth century that these develop rapidly among churchmen and nobles into something like a regular form covering a wide range of bequests. The typical tenth-century will was addressed to the king, specified the due heriot often along with other bequests to the king and royal family, asked for royal permission for the bequests to be made, and then detailed them, usually emphasizing those to churches and to women, wives and daughters. Their tone sometimes hints that the king's intervention was as much feared as sought: Ælfhelm Polga protested his loyalty to Edgar and Æthelred. The will can be seen as a response to royal

---

27. Harmer SEHD 23

rights. A wise person fixed heriot and agreed it with the king before death. The prudent or those with cause to fear, sweetened it with additional offerings. The heriot was a key to inheritance, failure to pay it resulted in loss. Heriots were rising, no doubt in an inflationary spiral stoked by royal demand and desperate noble offerings. The problems surrounding inheritance and forfeiture meant it was wise to specify bequests, and the preponderance of grants to women and churches is not accidental. A wife's dower had long been considered as exempt from the crimes of her husband. Tenth-century kings did not always observe this, indeed the succession of a widow was sometimes the point at which they chose to raise an old crime. To specify dower in a will was to try to give it the maximum protection. Grants to the church may have carried the same moral exemption from forfeiture. In addition the testator acquired powerful guarantors for the will. At the same time a will guaranteed by the king enabled a testator to circumvent traditional family arrangements for land, perhaps especially those which cut out women or inhibited grants out of the family to the church.

The will cannot be understood outside the development of royal power and reaction to it. Ealdorman Ælfgar of Essex left his lands to his daughters, specifying that they pass on to offspring and to churches where prayers would be said for him and his ancestors. By doing so he provided for his daughters, but simultaneously tried to guard against the marrying-off of heiresses which threatened to carry family land into other men's hands.[28]

To see the will as a dialogue between nobles and royal power is to raise again the problem of that power and how it was extended. The answers, as shown in the chapter on Ruling, lie in a balance of loss and gain and the extension of accepted duties and rights. The evolution of the will shows nobles responding to royal power with moves to protect individual inheritance. It need not imply that they interpreted the entire enterprise as a concerted attack upon them, which it manifestly was not. Defeat and conquest produced statements of grievance, (see above, pp. 144–6), but such statements are no more a complete picture of noble reaction to royal power than was their failure to articulate opposition at other times, though the escalation of demands in the eleventh century in response to attack and to the needs of conquerors threatened to upset the balance.

As the wills show, royal demands if not economic changes were combining to produce a more pressing need for the nobility to raise cash. Signs of the use of cash and the problems it could produce are common. Ælfhelm Polga proffered his heriot to the king in his will, but also made arrangements for the sale of land at his death to cover the cash payment. Sighelm, the father of Queen Eadgifu and ealdorman of Kent had to borrow £30 from a thegn called Goda and to give him one of his hereditary estates as surety of it. In the Downham case a man called Ælfric was driven to sell his land in order to raise the cash to pay a tribute.[29] There was recurrent pressure on nobles in the form of geld and at the point of inheritance. Cnut promised fixed heriots at the beginning of his reign: the sums he specified were still huge, 200 gold mancuses (one mancus = thirty pennies) for an earl, fifty for a king's thegn, and the wills of the later tenth century show that they had regularly been exceeded. It is impossible, however,

28. W. 2
29. LE cap. 11, p. 88

to demonstrate that such demands ruined individuals and unlikely that they produced deep structural change in the nobility. They were, however, a feature of an increasingly cash economy. Regular demands for cash were one of the factors stimulating the economy. This together with royal power, a growing land market and the demands for land of revived monasteries were factors which produced the strong statements of hereditary rights and inheritance which run through tenth-century legal cases. The more the claims of family were threatened the more they were defined and stated. It is time to examine the role of family in more detail.

10

Family, Marriage and Women[1]

It has become normal to speak of the family, kin or even clan in early Europe, though not always to define those terms precisely. The family is a universal human institution and therefore a varied one. Our modern word confuses two different things: a kin, that is a group of people connected by blood and marriage, and a household, a group of people who live and sometimes work together, which may include members not related in any way. The word *familia* originally meant a household not a kin group. Most historians who speak of the ties of family as important in the past mean the ties of kin, though if they slip into terms such as clan or lineage they are implying something more precise, a particular type of kin group which is enclosed and exclusive, which has a clearly defined membership and can act as a social unit. Neither England nor much of Western Europe had such clans by the tenth century, and kin must be thought of as a looser if still potent tie. Neither kin nor household were closed to external pressures, from king, lords, village or other communities. Marriage especially was the point at which they were demonstrated. Marriage continues and extends the kin, may create a new household and unites two individuals. It is personal and public and susceptible to both moral and social pressure. The study of kin and marriage is essential to the understanding of any society, doubly so if we wish to understand women, whose horizons have arguably been more bounded by these institutions than those of men.

The English kin group was bilateral and ego-centred; insofar as it still functions as a group it still is. Each individual (ego) had a kin group peculiar to

1. Little has been written specifically on these topics for Anglo-Saxon England though see B. Philpott, *Kindred and Clan in the Middle Ages and After* (Cambridge, 1913) which is still important, L. Lancaster, 'Kinship in Anglo-Saxon society', *British Journal of Sociology*, 9 (1958), pp. 234–48 and 359–77, H. Loyn, 'Kinship in Anglo-Saxon England', ASE, 3 (1973), pp. 197–209 and J. C. Holt, 'Feudal society and the family, parts I to IV', TRHS, ser. 5, 32–5 (1982–85). On family and on women, C. Fell, *Women in Anglo-Saxon England* (1984), and P. A. Stafford, 'Women in Domesday Book', forthcoming. Work on other periods is illuminating, see especially M. Anderson, *Approaches to the History of the Western Family, 1500–1914* (1980); R. Fox, *Kinship and Marriage* (1967); L. Mair, *Marriage* (1971); L. Stone, *The Family, Sex and Marriage in England, 1500–1800* (1977); G Duby, *Medieval Marriage* (1978) and *The Knight, the Lady and the Priest* (1983) and J. Goody, *The Development of the Family and Marriage in Europe* (Cambridge, 1983)

him or herself since kinship was counted bilaterally (that is on the father's and mother's side). Both the mother's and father's kin could be called on and played a part in the life of an individual. Since each couple is unique the children of each couple had a unique set of kin, grandparents, aunts, uncles, cousins. Cousins, for example, shared only half their kin. Such a system precludes the development of an exclusive social grouping. Feud or vendetta becomes difficult to pursue, especially since marriage will have pulled an individual into more than one kin group.[2] In such a society the kin is unlikely to form the major or sole social group, the potential importance of other communities, and of lord or king is enhanced.

This did not mean that kin were unimportant. Royal laws assumed that they would be responsible for protecting and answering for their own. The second law code of King Edmund, issued in the 940s, dealt with murder and killing. It would be the relatives of slayer and slain who would pursue the feud to the point where compensation or wergeld (the price of an individual) were paid. It was they who might succour and protect the killer, who needed restraining from escalating the feud.[3] The laws rarely specify who the kin are; this was precisely the sort of customary practice which they did not cover. But when compensation was sought or paid, the kin group had to be defined. It was bilateral, but with a strong bias towards the father's kin (patrilineal). Compensation payments were divided between a mother's and father's kin, with one third going to the first and two thirds to the second.[4]

Different sources give different answers to the question of how far the kin group stretched, an indication among other things that kin are counted differently for different purposes. The author of the *Leges Henrici Primi* felt that in default of direct heirs an inheritance should pass back to the kin. These should be traced in the order father/mother, brother or sister, father or mother's sister or brother on to the fifth joint or degree.[5] Archbishop Wulfstan used a similar calculation when defining the prohibited degrees of marriage in the early eleventh century: no marriage was to take place within the sixth joint of kinship. Interpreting the meaning of joints or degrees of kinship is not easy, but these calculations suggest that for some purposes kin were the descendants of a common set of great-great-, or great-great-great-grandparents.[6] The inheriting kin of the wills from the ninth to the eleventh centuries was much smaller. At most a three- or four-generation family is indicated, the descendants of the same grandparents or great-grandparents. King Alfred in his will calculated no further back then his grandfather Egbert, and included the generation of his children and nephews, a four-generation family;[7] a century later ealdorman Ælfheah recognized the claims of a kin group no wider than the descendants of his own father, his brother, sister, nephews and their sons.[8]

It is not unusual to find that the kin group varies in size for different purposes. The group which was considered to have strong claims on inheritance was more restricted than that which could be called for protection or liability in the courts.

2. M. Gluckman, 'Peace in the feud', *Past and Present*, 8 (1955), pp. 1–14
3. II Edmund 1–1.3
4. Alfred 30 and cf. Ine 57
5. *Leges Henrici Primi* cap. 70.16 ff
6. Goody, *The Development of the Family and Marriage in Europe*, pp. 134–46
7. Harmer SEHD 11
8. W. 9

In practice these distinctions are blurred by individual circumstance. One tenth-century noble, Wulfgar, apparently childless, recognized a wide section of his family when he stated in his will that he left his lands 'to such of my young kinsmen who obey me best...if they show due obedience'.[9] To be kin for one purpose, protection and wergeld, could imply hope of some share in the inheritance, though only if a choice were exercised. Wulfgar had no children and was searching more widely for heirs; the relish with which he dangled expectation before his young kinsmen was an attempt to use the perennial power of an older generation over a younger via inheritance. But the overwhelming message of the wills is a preference amounting to a binding tradition for leaving land within the three- or four-generation family, and the claims of any person's own offspring were paramount.

Alfred, Ælfheah and Wulfgar also demonstrated a preference for the male line in inheritance, echoing the dominance of the male kin in the share of fines. At the end of the ninth century the two factors which strengthened a claim were being of closer kinship (*gesibbre*) and of the male sex (*wepnedhadnes*).[10] Maternal kin inherited, though normally the males among a mother's relatives. Women could and did inherit. They were often of closer kinship than other heirs, and fathers exercised choice in their favour (see below). But their inheritance was most often a life interest, its future destiny frequently controlled in their father's will. The tenth-and eleventh-century kin was already strongly patrilineal and male dominated.

At the heart of overlapping groups of kin was the conjugal family of wife, husband and children, which was also the core of the household. When Athelstan laid down rules for dealing with men who were too rich or of too powerful a kindred to be easily brought to justice, he demanded that they be led out of the district, their wives and children with them.[11] When laws on theft sought to demarcate responsibility especially in the case of receiving stolen goods, they had to deal with the question of the household. A man (*sic*) would often bring stolen goods to his house: the assumption was that the other occupant of it would be his wife. She was exonerated from any responsibility for the stolen goods since she must obey her husband.[12] No wife could forbid her husband to deposit stolen goods within their cottage, thus the responsibility of her and her children for the husband and father's crime was limited.[13] The conjugal family was taken to be the normal core of a household. Noble households included servants, like the *hired*- (household) women to whom Wulfwaru left a chest in her will,[14] and perhaps a chaplain or military followers. Sparse as the evidence is, none of it suggests that the residential household normally comprised an extended family or kin group. Many bequests in wills assume that children and grandchildren will need the wherewithal to set up a household of their own. Wynflæd left chests, beds and bedding and tapestries to her grandsons and granddaughters.[15] In these wills it is the conjugal family of

9. R. 26
10. Harmer SEHD 10
11. IV Athelstan 3
12. Ine 57

husband and wife who own and bequeath such property. Movable household property was most frequently left in women's wills, pehaps indicating their primary responsibility for it, though it must be remembered that the women in question were widows.

Marriage joined together husband and wife to form the conjugal couple. Marriage was an affair for the individuals concerned, but also for their families. Marriage linked two families who continued to have an interest in and responsibility for the man and woman and their children. The legitimacy of children, guaranteed by the public forms of marriage, meant the right of children to call on the aid of or to inherit from not only parents but a wider family. In addition both families provided for the couple in land, dower and dowry. Marriage could not simply be a personal affair. Since it created a new household which would be part of a productive group, agrarian village or similar, it was also of concern to that wider group, and to anyone with control or interest in it, lord or king. It draws in those with other claims on the individuals, especially their lord. And being the sexual union of two people, at a time when sexuality was a central moral question, the Christian church as arbiter of morality could not but become involved. Marriage straddles the public and the private; it is a social institution and an individual passion; it not only expresses strong feeling but has long been a way of regulating its potentially disruptive influence.

Marriage at this date was arranged between families rather than individuals, with friends and peers of the couple playing a part. A man who wished to betroth a woman approached her and her kinsmen through third parties or advocates, and arrangements of property were finalized before the woman's kinsmen set about betrothal.[16] The woman was represented by the male head of her family, be it brother or father: when Wulfric married the sister of Archbishop Wulfstan it was with the archbishop that he negotiated terms.[17] The family group involved in negotiations was the narrow one of parents and siblings, but from the early eighth century till the eleventh sureties and pledges drawn from the community took part in negotiating and guaranteeing the union. When Godwine married Brihtric's daughter, eleven men acted as surety.[18] Witnesses to the terms were needed, varying in status according to the standing of the couple. Wulfric's marriage agreement with an archbishop's sister was witnessed by an ealdorman, a bishop, an abbot, a monk 'and many good men besides': Godwine and Brihtric's agreement had the witness of King Cnut, an archbishop, an abbot, a sheriff, six men of standing, two religious communities 'and every trustworthy man in Kent and Sussex, thegn or ceorl, is aware of these terms'. Then as now marriage not only confirmed or enhanced social status, it was an opportunity to demonstrate it.

These marriage, or more correctly betrothal, agreements record the arrangements of property between families: at this stage in marriage-making the family role took priority. By the tenth and eleventh century the lord too could have his say. Cnut acknowledged the reality of that power when he repudiated abuses of it which resulted in the forced marriages of widows and heiresses.[19] Two English

16. EHD I, no. 50, p. 467
17. EHD I, no. 128. p. 593
18. EHD I, no. 130, p. 596
19. II Cnut 74

lords in Domesday, Bishop Wulfstan of Worcester and Queen Edith, had found husbands for daughters of their followers; the treatment of widows in the Domesday survey suggests that many of them were considered to be in the king's hands and gift.[20] The lord, like friends and neighbours, acted as a guarantor of marriage arrangements. If a woman at marriage was taken into the jurisdiction of another thegn, additional assurance of her future had to be sought.[21] The lord had an interest both in the peasant household and in the fines paid by men and women and was thus unlikely to ignore marriage. Throughout the East Anglian Domesday the continuing claims of a lord over a wife after marriage are recorded. Many a woman was listed only so that it could be specified that she had a different lord to her husband. Two later peasant fines paid to the lord, *legerwite* (literally a fine for laying down, or deflowering) and *merchet* (a marriage fine) cannot be precisely dated in their origins.[22] It is tempting to see them as an early acknowledgement of the lord's claim to interfere in peasant marriage.

The documentary evidence on marriage inevitably stresses the property arrangements and payments. The husband gave his wife a morning-gift, a sort of virginity payment delivered at the time of marriage and consummation, a dower to keep her in her widowhood, and remunerated those who had reared her. There were general rules about dower. It was to be a third of a husband's property in Wessex, a half in Nottinghamshire and Derbyshire by the time of Domesday;[23] the *Leges Henrici Primi* speak of a third of all jointly acquired property, plus clothing and a bed.[24] In practice dower varied enormously, as one would expect when dower was the result of a bargain between two parties whose relative positions varied. The wills of the tenth and eleventh centuries show an increasing tendency to name a few estates as dower, and this happened in the case of some Norman widows after 1066. Yet some widows got all of a husband's lands, some a lion's share, others held jointly with sons. Dower was the result of the original agreement, but of many other factors during marriage as well as the precise situation at the time of death.

The stress on a husband's provision for his wife and careful guarantees of it is consistent with a society in which the wife normally left her kin at marriage to live with her husband and rely on him. The new household provided for both, and her share in it needed affirmation. But the wife and her family made their own contributions to husband and household. Domesday has many cases of a *maritagium* or dowry given with the bride by her family, held by the husband during his lifetime but passing to the widow at his death. This was not a Norman innovation. Thurcytel left to his wife all the lands he acquired when he married her.[25] He may be referring to the fact that she was an heiress, but it was clearly dowry which Edward the Priest had received with his wife, or that Bishop

20. P. A. Stafford, 'Women in Domesday', forthcoming
21. EHD I, no. 50, p. 468
22. J. Scammell, 'Freedom and marriage in medieval England', *Economic History Review*, ser. 2, 27 (1974), pp. 523–37 and 'Wife–rents and merchet' in *ibid*. ser. 2, 29 (1976), pp. 487–90 and E. Searle, 'Freedom and marriage in medieval England, an alternative hypothesis', in *ibid*. pp. 482–6
23. DB I fo. 280V and Ine 57
24. *Leges Henrici Primi*, cap. 70.22
25. W.24

Ælfmær had got when he married.[26] Both husband's and wife's kin created an interest through property arrangements in the new household. In 1086 this continuing interest was often expressed as lordship: the husband holding his wife's dower as his father-in-law's man. Kinship and lordship could reinforce each other as well as clash.

The property arrangements agreed at the betrothal did not all come into effect at the point of marriage. Even those settlements made immediately on the bride were usually in the hands of her husband during his lifetime. Others like dower were only implemented at the death of the husband. There were opportunities for rearrangement and for interference between marriage and death, whether by the husband's kin at the wife's expense or by the wife's kin to protect her. The tract 'On the betrothal of a woman' had reason to fear for a woman who at marriage was taken far from the surveillance of her family and friends.

Of the marriage ceremonies themselves we know little. The Old English words used to describe it are a rough guide, though words have a long life and often survive the circumstances they once described.[27] Feasting and celebration (*færmo, symblu, brydealu*) and the formal escorting of the bride to the groom's home (*hæman, hæmed*) are probable. The most common Old English word for marriage was *sinscipe*, meaning a permanent state, or condition; the word is used regularly from the ninth century. The property arrangements indicate how permanent a condition it was hoped marriage would be, a stability which was the goal of laypeople as well as of churchmen.

Churchmen played no necessary part in the making of a marriage; both it and its ceremonies were always largely a lay affair. By the end of the tenth century if not before it was felt proper in some circles for a priest to bless a marriage,[28] but the blessing did not *make* the marriage, then or later. Nonetheless churchmen, especially reformers, took a lively interest in marriage. It had always been a part of the Church's concern with morality and with the mores of the Christian community. The laws of the late tenth and early eleventh centuries were more detailed on this area than any before. Incest, i.e. marriage within the prohibited degrees, was defined,[29] concubinage was forbidden,[30] monogamy was paramount and divorce unacceptable,[31] the importance of a woman's consent in marriage was stressed.[32]

The concern of tenth-century reformers with the laity was primarily with sexual morality and a clarification and reiteration of Christian ideas on marriage, *viz.* lifelong monogamy between partners who were outside the proscribed degrees of kinship and who consented to the match. Earlier inconsistencies in the Christian viewpoint were being ironed out throughout Europe in an atmosphere of strong pastoral concern. Claims to ecclesiastical jurisdiction over this area of life had been assembled, though secular aid in their enforcement was still sought.

26. DB II fos. 431V and 195R
27. A. Fischer, *Engagement, Wedding and Marriage in Old English* (Heidelberg, 1986)
28. EHD I, no. 50, p. 467
29. VI Æthelred 12–12.1, I Cnut 7 and II Cnut 51
30. II Cnut 54.1
31. I Cnut 7
32. II Cnut 73–4

C.AD 1000 church peace in England was defined to include marital affairs.[33] Church peace, like the king's peace, had a long history. At first it meant the peace or sanctuary required and guaranteed in the presence of a particular person. It was gradually extended to include buildings, occasions, meetings, and other individuals or groups to which that special protection had been extended. Protection meant payment for infringement, so that 'peace' carried with it notions of jurisdiction, rights to fines and forfeitures. In cases of *unriht hæmed*, a catchall phrase which included many sexual and marital offences, the king was to have the male offender, the bishop the woman.[34] How generally these rulings were applied is unknown but applied on occasion they were. Archbishop Oscytel acquired land at Helperby in Yorkshire in the mid tenth century after a judgement of *unriht hæmed*;[35] in the mid eleventh the bishop of East Anglia had a woman in his hands because she had married within a year of her husband's death.[36] The division of fines and lands was sufficiently common in these cases for privileged churches to have gained the right to the king's share by 1066.[37] There may have been a growing feeling that these matters were properly the sole concern of churchmen. When William and Lanfranc separated the church courts they were merely taking the logical next step.

The public faces of marriage and of the working of the kin group can be charted, however incompletely. Their inner workings and the emotional ties which bound them cannot be so easily recovered. In practice the workings of family are matters of preference as well as obligation, though obligations determine the range of people who may be preferred and inhibit the free play of choice. Wulfgar would choose among his young kinsmen according as they were dutiful, obedient and pleasing to him. But like most tenth- and eleventh-century testators, it was among kinsmen and not among friends that he chose.

The bonds of family, albeit the restricted three-generation one, appear strong in the wills. They are evident also in the naming practices of families who often retained the same name element through the generations. *Athel*stan Half-King was the son of *Æthel*frith, grandson of *Æthel*wulf, brother of *Æthel*sige and *Æthel*wold, father of *Æthel*wold, *Æthel*sige and *Æthel*wine.[38] Brothers often acted together. Æthelwine ealdorman of East Anglia and his brother Ælfwold attended courts together; Wulfric Spott and his brother Ælfhelm came to the royal court together, like many brothers, often along with Ælfhelm's sons. Royal patronage was extended to families as well as to individuals: Godwine and his sons are an obvious example, but Ælfheah and Ælfhere in the 950s, Athelstan Half-King and his brothers in the 930s and 40s, and Edwin and Morcar in the 1060s demonstrate how often kings were moved to recognize the ties between such men. Family ties were as important as lordship as a route to advancement. Sons succeeded fathers and brothers in office. Ecclesiastics often preferred their own nephews: Archbishop Oda advanced his nephew Oswald, who went on to distribute Worcester land to his

---

33. VIII Æthelred 4
34. Edward and Guthrum 4
35. R. 54
36. DB II fo. 199R
37. DB I fo. 1R
38. C. Hart, 'Athelstan Half-King and his family', ASE, 2 (1973), pp. 115–44

brothers and kinsmen (see below, chapter on *The Church*), Archbishop Wulfstan was eventually succeeded at Worcester by his nephew, and when Ælfric moved to be archbishop of Canterbury he secured his former abbacy of St Albans for his brother Leofric.

Feeling and duty cannot readily be separated in such cases. The emotional ties between husband and wife, parents and children are unfathomable. The importance of the conjugal family encouraged the strongest ties here and the frequent reiteration of prayers for parents and concern for widows in wills should be taken literally. To go beyond this is to encounter not only problems in the sources but in our own definitions and ideas of romantic affection. The words used to describe various relationships may be called into play, and Old English usage sometimes seems to deny uniqueness to the tie between husband and wife. A *freond* may be the partner of the marriage bed, as in the *Wife's Lament*, but ealdorman Ælfheah uses it as a synonym for all his kin in his will, and it can mean a lord or protector, like those sought by the unjust steward in Ælfric's translation of the biblical story.[39] But to assume a specific correlation between a feeling and the word used to describe it is dubious, and literature may be a poor guide to reality.

At the same time we must be wary of the priority we now give to a set of emotions which in other times and places have been labelled as disruptive lust or dangerous infatuation. Feelings between husbands and wives, parents and children need not have our exclusiveness and intensity to qualify as genuine and strong. Old English poetry, prose and language had a sharp eye for the pleasures of the flesh; a complete study of the Old English words for sexual intercourse, fornication and adultery would require a full-length thesis.[40] But the needs of both lay society and Christianity invoked the representation of marital love as chaste and restrained. In the *Life of King Edward* commissioned by Queen Edith, the restrained affection of father and daughter is taken to characterize the relationship.[41] Edward was dead by now and passion recollected in widowhood may not be comforting, whilst the barrenness of the marriage of Edith and Edward may have made the image especially appropriate. But a similar picture is given of the marriage of Tostig, faithful to his wife and chaste in body, [42] and of the church as mother, dear to Christ her husband because of her fecundity, but joined chastely to him in her embraces.[43] It was not merely this author who expressed such ideas. Two centuries earlier Alfred and Asser interpreted the king's illnesses within a similar framework. Piles, the illness of Alfred's youth, was a God-sent remedy for the king's fear of his bodily appetites, and his second, life-long illness, also of the bowels[44] first struck him on his wedding day. Alfred's afflictions were presented as an aid to chaste restraint. In his additions to Boethius' *Consolation Of Philosophy* he was more eloquent on the

39. *Homilies of Ælfric, a Supplementary Collection*, ed. J. C. Pope, vol. II, EETS 260 (1968), no. 16, p. 548
40. A. Fischer, *Engagement, Wedding and Marriage*, p. 24
41. *Life of King Edward*, ed. F. Barlow (Edinburgh 1962), pp. 59–60 and 79
42. *ibid.* p. 32
43. *ibid.* p. 48
44. Asser, Life of Alfred in *Alfred the Great*, eds. S. Keynes and M. Lapidge (1983), caps. 25, 74 and 91 and p. 270 n. 220

emotions between husband and wife, though the language was not that of passion or lust.[45]

Questions about emotional relationships in the past are not questions of the existence or non-existence of sexual appetite, rather of where and how it was felt appropriate to express it, how large a part it should play in the formation or continuation of given relationships. In the meagre fragments of literature which cover this question, marital restraint was often the ideal. In poetry wives especially were given the stronger expression of feeling. Both partners were presumed to suffer from separation, but it was the wife who was made desolate, ill with longing for her husband.

Neither marriage nor kinship could be immune to royal power and its agents, to ecclesiastical reform, to economic and social change. A more cash-orientated economy had repercussions for inheritance, one of the bonds of family. Land was bought, sold or changed hands for loans of cash. At the end of the tenth century ealdorman Æthelmær left only three estates in his will, but large amounts of cash.[46] Cash could mean more choice in the making of bequests, though Æthelmær's follow a traditional pattern. Buying and selling land, or giving it to the church in the rush of patronage in the second half of the tenth century may have strengthened as much as undermined notions of family and property. The notion that land belonged to the family rather than the individual to dispose of was tenacious. Claims on family land were being brought against Ely in the 970s which were already two generations old. The gifts made to the church in the tenth century were usually in return for prayers for kin. When Wulfric Spott founded Burton on Trent abbey *c.*AD 1004 he called on his brother Ælfhelm to be its protector. It was difficult to extricate the church and its lands from family control (see chapter on *The Church*).

The emergence of a great nobility could refresh parts of the kinship structure. It is at this social level that we see the widest ties of kin in operation. When Archbishop Oswald founded Ramsey he was able to mobilize remote kinsmen in East Anglia to assemble land for his new foundation. His wider kin can be traced both here and in the south-west Midlands. Information is concentrated at this social level, but it may be unwise to generalize from it to the rest of society. The kin, as we have seen, were not a fixed group. Kinship was claimed, remembered and pursued, the more so when the kinsman in question was an archbishop with influence at the royal court.

The king himself as lord and ruler affected this social group in particular. It has already been argued that the will was a response of individual nobles to royal power (see above, pp. 159–60). The will gives clear evidence of the strength of family feeling, but it also encouraged and allowed a limited scope for personal preference within the family, a fact which worked in favour of women's property (see below). Nobles sought in their wills to gain from as well as to respond to royal power. The king was to be a guarantor of their bequests, against his own intervention but also against that of their families. Some of the earliest wills, like that of ealdorman Alfred, deliberately sought royal intervention in family inheritance to secure a particular outcome which traditional practice alone might

45. Quoted Fell, *Women in Anglo-Saxon England* p. 73
46. W. 10

have made difficult. Alfred wished to use his limited freedom of manoeuvre with royal protection to ensure that his wife and daughter got, if not outright control of land, at least some profit from the sale of it and even the power to choose to which of his paternal kinsmen they sold it.[47] The laws of Cnut referred to grievances over the king's interference in family inheritance, but the will of Alfred suggests that that interference had not simply been the result of brute force and royal fiat.

Tenth-century kings utilized kin, lord and local community in their efforts to enforce the apprehension of suspected people, recourse to the courts and acceptance of the courts' decisions. In so doing they strengthened the hands of lords and confirmed the importance of the hundred. Kin often emerge as the villains of the piece, powerful kindreds protecting their own members[48] against whom the hundreds must stand. It is easy to read tenth-century law as an attempt to replace or curb them by encouraging lord and hundred to extend their responsibility. It was rather an effort to call all social forces into play to achieve its ends in which the fundamental roles of kin scarcely required stress. Kin remained part of a person's sureties and protectors, alongside lord and a group of associates in hundred and tithing. Kin never had been the all-engrossing social formation in early England, and the tenth-century laws merely confirm this fact.

When churchmen passed from moral exhortation and penitential demands to legal enforcement backed by fines to king and bishop, they brought a need for precise definitions into the area of marriage. As incest regulations required the following of kinship ties to the fifth or sixth degree, awareness of family must have been sharpened. As divorce, concubinage and adultery were attacked, the need to know what was and was not a marriage became insistent. Christian suspicion of sexuality and a consequent desire to bring all consenting sexual unions into the sphere of binding marriage was to cause endless problems in the search for a provable definition of marriage throughout the Middle Ages and beyond. The seeds of future difficulty were already sprouting. Consent was emphasized, though it was only one of a range of public ceremonies which started at betrothal and ended on the wedding night. Consent was the least public and provable of them, yet proof of the nature of a sexual union was essential to any definition of marriage. The public ceremonies, especially the fully witnessed property transactions, were the firmest ground and the ones developed by laypeople who had their own concern with legitimacy. Of these ceremonies, morning gift was the one which best fitted the church's needs. It passed from husband to wife and its acceptance could readily signify her consent. It was handed over on the morning after marriage, a virginity or consummation payment which left no doubt that the union had gone beyond projection to fulfilment. Tenth- and eleventh-century wills contain increasing references to written documents, usually concerning the wife's lands, made at marriage. They were the clearest proof of the nature of the union.

Definition in this difficult area was not to be so easily achieved. There was room for argument about which of the many stages from wedding to bedding

47. Harmer SEHD 10
48. III Athelstan 6, IV Athelstan 3, VI Athelstan 8.2 and 8.3

172 Unification and Conquest

tied the binding knot.[49] Mere performance of lay ceremonies was insufficient as long as churchmen stressed consent. Incest prohibitions opened a loophole to escape from marriage at the same time as other definitions were seeking to tighten the indissoluble knot. The familiar Christian marriage ceremonies were evolving in France at precisely this time to try to cope with these problems.[50] We cannot follow each stage of development, but the end result was elegant. As churchmen had become the arbiters of marriage and legitimacy, they had taken over surveillance of the key ceremonies. An enquiry into incest and relationship preceded marriage, the consent of the parties before witnesses was then sought and the exchange of property effected. It was as close to an answer as the eminently practical pastoral bishops of the ninth to eleventh centuries could produce.

The reaction of the laity to clerical ideas is hard to gauge and is unlikely to have been uniform. Information is fullest about the impact of ecclesiastical decisions at the top of society. They may have been most effective here, especially in the glare of the royal court itself, though the spread of parishes and local priests would have permitted more clerical supervision of marriage and checking on incest. It would certainly be wrong to see churchmen imposing ideas of binding, legitimate marriage on a reluctant laity. Some laymen had always sought greater security for their daughters during and after marriage, all wished for certainty about the legitimate claims of inheritors and kin. Indeed the wide area of doubt opened up by ecclesiastical ideas on consent and incest will have worried many. Churchmen had not closed the door on divorce, though they called it nullity on grounds of incest, and were embarrassed by earlier excuses Christian views had condoned and which were still circulating in the penitential literature. Uhtred of Bamburgh married three times, including once to the daughter of a bishop, and set two wives aside. His pretexts are unknown. Not so those of kings. Henry VIII was not the first king who conveniently forgot incest at the point of marriage, but piously remembered it later. In the case of Eadwig it was others who remembered it for him, separating the king and his wife in 958. Edward the Confessor when he thought of divorcing Edith, toyed with older ideas of non-consummation and adultery.[51] The first was a favoured ploy at royal level where few would dare to check. The latter was weak ground by the eleventh century, though the fact that Edward had the backing of the archbishop of Canterbury in his actions reveals how confused the ecclesiastical stance still was.

As always, we know more of the theory than the practice when it comes to the population at large, though if practice followed theory to any extent women would have been among the beneficiaries. Divorce was of wives by husbands, not vice versa, and consent gave a woman some say in negotiations normally undertaken by her male kin. Information, scarce enough about men and marriage, dries up almost completely for women. How control by kin worked in practice, how far it was preferable to that of lords, whether lords and

---

49. See e.g. S. Wemple and J. A. McNamara, 'Marriage and divorce in the Frankish kingdom', in *Women in Medieval Society*, ed. S. M. Stuard (Pennsylvania, 1976), pp. 95–124
50. J–B. Molin and P. Mutembe, *Le rituel du mariage en France du XIIe au XVIe siècle* (Paris, 1974)
51. P. Stafford, *Queens, Concubines and Dowagers, the King's Wife in the Early Middle Ages* (1983), p. 82

churchmen provided welcome alternatives for some women can only be speculated. This does not mean that women are completely hidden. A series of great women political actors and landholders have led some to see this period as the last phase of female power and influence ended at the Norman Conquest.[52] Women could and did hold land, both before and after 1066. They played political roles which the Empress Mathilda and Eleanor of Aquitaine would continue in the twelfth century. They acted, however, usually within the confines of family and filled few roles in the social or political community, though to treat them as a homogeneous social group may itself be as misleading as it is helpful.

In the making of marriage we saw women as part of a society in which men were the public actors. Negotiations between families, meetings of the courts of king, shire and hundred were all in the public sphere and women are conspicuous by their absence. The queen, or king's spouse, was alone among women in being of sufficient public moment to be listed among witnesses of royal charters: royal daughters, abbesses, noblewomen never appear. In recorded legal disputes women feature regularly only as defendants. They were not lost in their husbands' public identity to the extent of losing responsibility for their own crimes or actions. When the case involved a woman they might also act in the court as oath helpers: in the lawsuit between Wynflæd and Leofwine, Wynflæd called twenty-four people to support her case, thirteen of whom were women, including two abbesses and the queen, Ælfthryth, who spoke for her.[53] Women were not excluded by their sex from the normal methods of proof and trial. Two women in Domesday Book offered the *judicium*, judicial proofs, in cases involving land, another called the king to warrant her holding.[54] Women were not public non-persons, but they played no role in the public life of local communities. We search in vain for them among the lists of witnesses, sureties, judgement finders and beaters of bounds in the Book of Ely and elsewhere.

Women were consequently less directly affected by some of the political and social changes of the tenth and eleventh centuries than men. There are relatively few royal grants of land to women, the exceptions being almost all royal women and nuns. Grants to them are part of provision for the royal family or patronage of the church not of the patronage of nobles which is so significant at this date. No woman received royal office as reeve or ealdorman. Ironically, given the belief in a deteriorating situation after 1066, the only example of a woman sitting as president of a court is William I's wife Mathilda, who acted on at least two occasions as a court president in her function as regent.[55] Emma may have played such a role in the absence of Cnut, but no records as full as Domesday survive for this date. Whereas both men and women lived in a society in which family and kin played an important part, women were more or less confined to the roles and possibilities they provided. Men had some opportunities elsewhere and they alone played an active part in the groups and communities which debated and implemented society's rules.

52. D. M. Stenton, *The English Woman in History* (1956) and cf. J. C. Holt, 'Feudal society and the family in early medieval England: 1. The revolution of 1066', *TRHS* ser. 5, 32 (1982), pp. 193–212
53. R. 66
54. DB II fos. 137R, 277V and 125R
55. DB I fos. 238V and 48V

Yet given the importance of family and household, roles within them must be examined not dismissed. It was here, both before and after 1066, that women could gain access to property and its control and with it a voice both inside and outside the family. The great women landholders of the tenth- and early eleventh-century wills are women who had acquired and disposed of substantial property. Important though that fact is, it can obscure how often that property was an aspect of family provisions and hedged around with limitations. Moreover female landholding on this scale is apparently a transient phenomenon, which itself requires explanation.

The bilateral nature of English kinship is not a simple pointer to power in the hands of women. A mother's and father's kin were both counted, but not equally, and it was the male kin on each side who acted or had claims. The wills of King Alfred and his namesake, ealdorman Alfred were of men who had inherited from father's and mother's kin. It was not exclusively the case that land passed from male to male whether through the maternal or paternal line. Land inherited from women was sometimes used to endow women, though the person making the endowment was usually a man through whose control it had passed. Bilaterality is nonetheless significant when considering the status of women. A woman did not lose her ability to call on her own kin at marriage. She remained responsible for her own crimes and her kin retained an obligation and desire to help her in the payment of compensations.[56] The contributions her family made to the new household symbolized their continuing interest in it, in her and in her children. Women did not pass entirely under the control of husband and husband's family. The laws stressed her obedience to her husband and her consequent absolution from complicity in his crimes (see above, p. 164), and we should certainly not assume that a woman's kin offered her independence, a doubtful commodity in any event at this date. But they gave her a potential leverage within the household *vis-à-vis* husband and children. How far that leverage could be used depended on conjunctions of economic situation, the relative status of the two families, personality and much else. It may be one of the factors behind the endless variety in provision for widows we can see in Domesday.

Variation was the keynote of women's inheritance and control of property, though variables operated within defined limits. In the ninth century men made provision in their wills for women, but usually only for life, with reversion to male kin if a daughter died childless. Ealdorman Alfred made extensive but temporary bequests to his wife and daughter. His paternal kinsmen retained claims on the land left to his daughter. If she had no children they might have the land but had to buy it back. As in the twelfth century, a woman here held land as the mother of future heirs, especially male heirs.[57] Even in the women's wills of the tenth century, and in spite of a variety of individual situations, women's landholding was usually temporary or heavily circumscribed by the

56. Alfred 18.1–18.3; Be Wifmannes Beweddung cap. 7, EHD I, no. 50, p. 468; Leges Henrici Primi, 70.12 and 82.9
57. J. C. Holt, 'Feudal society and the family in early medieval England: IV The heiress and the alien', *TRHS* ser. 5, 35 (1985), pp. 1–28 and especially S. Milsom, 'Inheritance by women in the twelfth and early thirteenth centuries', in *On the Laws and Customs of England* ed. M. S. Arnold *et al.* (Chapel Hill, 1981), pp. 60–89

continuing claims of her male kin. Ælfgifu, the widow of King Eadwig [58] had no children: she left most of her land to siblings, reverting back to the direct male line. Leofgifu had only a daughter.[59] She left lands to her, but recognized and placated male claims by bequests to her brother-in-law and nephew. Wulfwaru had children, sons and daughters.[60] She left land to all of them, but a lion's share to her sons.

The fact that women were able to make wills is, of course, an indicator of some control over property. But since we rarely have a sequence of family wills, and most of the women concerned were widows, there must be a strong suspicion that these women are often doing little more than implementing arrangements made by husbands and fathers. This is provably the case in the one set of family wills which have survived, those of Ælfgar ealdorman of Essex and his two daughters Æthelflæd and Ælfflæd. Perhaps fearing losses through the exercise of wardship by the king, perhaps recognizing how property in women's hands could be lost to her husband's family, perhaps merely following customary practice, Ælfgar carefully tied the bequests he made to his daughters. Their own wills progressively implement their father's wishes.

But not entirely. Both Æthelflæd and Ælfflæd altered the directions of individual bequests, and added other lands which show that they had acquired property in other ways. Leofgifu and Wulfwaru both left land to daughters, and all women's wills leave land to the church. Even the limited manoeuvre left by ealdorman Alfred should not be underestimated. His daughter was able to choose to which of her male kin she should sell the land if she were childless. Only a blinkered obsession with absolute property rights, which are a question of debate in any age, would ignore the importance of choice and sale. Lifetime possession enabled a woman still to choose from a pool of heirs, to exercise influence within her family and gain necessary protection in her widowhood. Wulfgar used his ability to choose his heirs in his will to require the obedience of his young kinsmen. The fluid possibilities opened by cash as opposed to the immobilities of family land existed by the tenth century.

Women acquired land in several ways. A bequest to a daughter might be a share in the inheritance as dowry, in which case her husband would control it for life and it would be hers only in widowhood (see below), but it might be a gift to her as heir, especially in the absence of sons. The laws of Henry I in the early twelfth century stated that if there were no direct heir (male or female not specified) property should go to father, mother, brothers, sisters, father's kin, mother's kin in a fixed order which did not relegate all women as secondary to all men. Ealdorman Alfred's principles are recalled: heirs should be *wepnedhad* (male) but also *gesibbre* (of closer kin). A society which stressed the tie of blood did not allow gender entirely to extinguish it.

A woman also stood to gain the land earmarked for her at marriage, the dowry from her own family and the morning gift and dower from her husband. Ealdorman Ælfheah left far more land to his wife than to his male siblings and their sons. If his bequests implemented the marriage agreement they are a

58. W. 8
59. W. 29
60. W. 21

reminder that marriage was a bargain between often unequal sides, in which a woman's status could outweigh her sex. Ælfheah had received a wife from the royal kin, one of a handful of women in the tenth century important enough to receive grants of land directly from the king. Such an asymmetrical marriage entailed careful provision for the wife, both by her own family and in the lands guaranteed to her by her husband.

A woman gained the lands promised at marriage in widowhood. Married women had little power of disposal over their lands. The Book of Ely frequently notes gifts made with the wife's consent, or joint gifts by husband and wife. A wise abbey took care to secure and record the consent of a wife who had claims as a potential widow or as the heiress whose lands these originally were. These gifts do not prove that women held land during their husbands' lifetimes, they rather suggest the opposite. The women who make wills, who appear as landholders in Domesday are in the majority of cases widows. This was the time of greatest risk, but paradoxically the stage of the household cycle when they could expect most control of property. Morning gift, dower and dowry could now become theirs. The risks for widows were real. The care with which husbands provided for them in wills betokens the threat from male relatives, from sons and grandsons as well as brothers-in-law. Godgifu, widow of Earl Leofric, had lost lands to her grandsons Edwin and Morcar before 1066. But the rewards could be proportionately great. Gytha, widow of Earl Godwine, held land in most shires south of the Thames by 1066; her nine manors in Devon alone had a capacity for 385 ploughs.

The upper-class female landholders of the tenth and eleventh centuries have a high profile: women have been so ill-served by history that any activity by them can attract disproportionate attention. Their powers and rights have been exaggerated, their prominence has masked the paucity of their numbers. Domesday is an incomplete record of women's landholding, but women landholders are conspicuously absent from it, whether the wives and daughters of the English nobility or the Norman. These few outstanding women are also a recent phenomenon in English history, linked in some way with social changes. They are the female aspect of developments which had raised their husbands and fathers into the great nobility at this date. Their powers over land look greater than the temporary usufruct of many ninth-century wills, and this too is recent. Royal and ecclesiastical changes which had resulted in the making of wills and the recording of matrimonial property arrangements worked in their favour. The greater fixity and capacity for proof of written title helped them, as it had aided seventh- and eighth-century noble women in the aftermath of conversion. The courts in which title could be proved were more regular and formal and these women especially could have recourse to the royal court where the king, and increasingly the queen, could lend a sympathetic ear. Widow's land was part of the old family provisions which nobles successfully exempted from royal forfeiture. Whether or not this encouraged larger dowers, it contributed to the increasing desire carefully to specify what widows were to get.

These developments affected especially great noble women as daughters, wives, but especially as widows. The family roles of such women cannot be judged from the standpoint of modern household drudgery. They were the basis on which the series of political women seen in earlier chapters could build:

Eadgifu as a mother and especially as a dowager queen mother influencing the royal succession, which was a matter of family inheritance writ large; Emma and Mathilda as regents, dependable female members of the family who could not mount a challenge for the throne in their own right, ideal as rulers in the king's stead; Edith a daughter and wife, the power of her family securing her royal marriage, its fall almost carrying her down, but her status as royal wife transcending her origins and carrying her safely across 1066.

The vicissitudes of Emma, Edith and Eadgifu showed the limitations in family roles for women. In the *Encomium* and the *Life of Edward the Confessor* Emma and Edith revealed the significance of family as well as of women in the high levels of eleventh-century politics. Both women sought to advance their own cause and ambitions, each did it through stressing her family, in one case husband and son, in the other father, brothers and husband. Neither woman could succeed for herself; ambition was a face they did not choose to wear. The objects of their vicarious ambition and attempts at self-preservation, husbands, sons and brothers, were doubtful quantities. These women travesty the precariousness of the personal nature of politics which affects both men and women. It is with other counsellors and courtiers that their position must be compared. But confined at the same time within the family, from which they derived their status, and denied access to the security provided by more formal positions, the plight of women in such politics could be particularly harsh.

The family roles which appeared to unite women in a common lot were themselves transformed by distinctions of status. A role as wife which entailed sitting in judgement over the bishop of Worcester, as did Mathilda's role as regent, cannot be identified with that which entailed working in the fields. The high-ranking women who left wills cannot stand as examples of the property claims of all women. When Edith, abbess of Wilton, was taken to task by Bishop Æthelwold at the end of the tenth century for her splendid clothes she retorted that as incorrupt a mind could be found under her gold raiment as beneath his tattered dress. The pride and confidence of her reply were those of a royal abbess, where birth and role were more important than sex.

The tradition of ignoring women in forming the historical canon justifies singling them out for special attention, though political and religious women have been dealt with elsewhere. Singling them out, however, implies a particular social analysis in which women are perceived as a distinct group, sufficiently united in their disability or situation to make this justifiable and useful. The common experience of women in public life, and in the stages of the household cycle from daughter to wife to widow invite such justification. However, at every stage important differences emerged. Wife, widow and daughter themselves had very different experiences of, for example, property holding. The structure of particular families, some childless, some producing only daughters, some the products of serial marriages or asymmetrical unions, defy glib generalization. Social class cut across all. The widows in Domesday,[61] the largest group of women in the Survey, are a very varied bunch. They hold land varying from a handful of acres to huge estates comparable with the highest nobility. Sometimes they hold their land alone, sometimes jointly with a son or son-in-law,

---

61. See Stafford, 'The women in Domesday' for these and other examples.

sometimes as the tenants of a son. Sometimes they retain all their husband's lands, sometimes a few named properties. These differences were produced by the working of economic need and opportunity, personal preference and personality on families in different stages of wealth or poverty, rise or fall in the social scale. It is the function of social history to refine the tools for describing this complexity, and gender is a useful one. It is not its function to produce sweeping generalizations which collapse this diversity into 'the condition of widows' who may have had little in common but their weeds.

Few families and their women can be traced across 1066. One such is the Lincolnshire family of Eadgifu the widow of Tope, her sons Ulf and Halfdan and Ulf's wife Madselin. They occur in the pages of Domesday and in the will of Ulf.[62] Eadgifu was already a widow in 1066, and her dower, six carucates and more, was shared with her younger son. His total holding of thirteen carucates was much smaller than that of his older brother Ulf. Eadgifu had certainly not received half her husband's lands in dower and the family holding had been divided in a way which gave priority to the eldest son. Ulf clearly feared the immediate consequences of 1066. If, as seems likely, he was a relative of Abbot Brand of Peterborough who spectacularly miscalculated the outcome of that year by referring his consecration to Edgar the Ætheling not William, his fear may be explicable. He and his wife Madselin left England on a pilgrimage which appears to have become exile. Before leaving they made a will. Madselin herself made bequests, but Domesday lists all her lands as if they were her husband's. Women had claims on land, but in some eyes, including the important ones of local courts and royal surveys, that land was under the control of their husband. By 1086 the family's lands were scattered. Eadgifu's dower was in the hands of Erneis of Burun, perhaps falling into his hands whilst he was sheriff of Yorkshire exercising the king's right as lord over the wardship of widows. Halfdan's lands had passed to the bishop of Lincoln. Ulf's were mostly in the hands of Drogo de la Beuvrière, who claimed as successor to Earl Morcar. Ulf had held land of Earl Morcar, but also of Earl Waltheof and Waltheof's widow, Judith, was disputing some of them in 1086.

Different types of document give different views on society. The wills present it as organized around kin and family; Domesday and documents like it start from the perspective of lordship. Both were part of social reality whether in the tenth or late eleventh century. The disruption of this family's lands is a stark testimony to the impact of 1066 on the English nobility. They dispersed along lines of lordship because 1066 was about a transfer of lordship from one group to another. But 1066 did not create the intrusion of lord into family, nor did it introduce into England a nobility novel in the priority it gave to lordship and its ties. The Norman nobility came from an area of France where competition for land had become acute. They had evolved, though only recently, systems of patrilineal primogeniture and a strong attachment to central family holdings which were to pass exclusively in the male line.[63] These changes had taken the claims of men, especially of eldest sons, further than those we can trace in

62. W. 39
63. J. Holt, 'Feudal society and the family in early medieval England, II: notions of patrimony' *TRHS*, 33 (1983), pp. 193–220 at p. 213

pre-1066 England, though similar tendencies to succession in the male line and preference for eldest sons existed there also. That development had not extinguished the claims of all children, including daughters, and the tenacity of the idea that families provided for all offspring, including women, caused it to surface again in the twelfth and thirteenth centuries, though in the same limited way it had existed in ninth- and tenth-century England. The nobility who came to England after 1066 were, in the most important respects, like their predecessors. They shared a strong commitment to family, in neither case to the exclusion of all other ties. In 1066 Norman dukes took over the powers of English kings. Once the initial stages of conquest were over, Norman nobles acted like their English predecessors, and in similar circumstances they could press parallel grievances. The languages of Cnut's law code and of Henry I's coronation charter may be different; but both sought to resolve the familiar conflict between lord and kin.

11

The Church

Many sources from the ninth to the twelfth century invite an interpretation of the English church as progressing from decline to decline via a temporary upsurge of reforming monastic zeal. Alfred lamented the state of the mid-ninth-century church in the preface to the *Pastoral Care*, the Latin language decayed, the parlous state of learning in general, the English possessing 'only the name of Christians, and very few...the virtues'.[1] Bishop Æthelwold of Winchester, writing in the late tenth century, stressed how few monks there were in early tenth-century England, how the holy places needed cleaning of men's foulnesses, especially of the negligent clerks and their abominations.[2] Wulfstan writing in 1014 claimed that Gildas' portrayal of the sins of the British, 'the sloth of the bishops and the wicked cowardice of God's messengers who mumbled with their jaws what they should have cried aloud...the foul wantonness of the people' applied to his own day, when worse deeds had been done among the English.[3] And William of Malmesbury looked back on Church and people on the eve of 1066 to see an unlearned clergy scarcely able to stammer out the words of the liturgy, over-indulgent monks and a nobility given up to luxury and wantonness, hearing matins and masses from a hurrying priest in their own chambers amid the blandishments of their wives.[4] This gloomy picture of a church in decline and decay after the glorious age of the conversion would be relieved only by the light of the monastic movement of the tenth century, whose achievements were celebrated in saints' lives like that of Æthelwold, in the pages of the monastic authors of the twelfth-century Book of Ely, Chronicle of Ramsey and Hugh Candidus' history of Peterborough, or by the great monastic chroniclers, Florence of Worcester, William of Malmesbury and the like. In the later tenth century and the reign of Edgar in particular William and others could see an oasis when 'the light of holy men was resplendent again in England....great monasteries like Ely, Peterborough and Thorney were raised from

1. EHD I, no. 226, p. 889
2. *ibid.*, no. 238, p. 922 and *Regularis Concordia*, ed. T. Symons (Edinburgh, 1953), p. 2
3. EHD I, no. 240, p. 934
4. William of Malmesbury, Bk III, cap. 245

their foundations, the servants of God increased. But alas, after Edgar's death, the state and hopes of the English met with a reverse'.[5]

The problem with this picture is the nature and purposes of the sources from which it derives. Both Alfred and Wulfstan wrote history as moral commentary, seeing the Viking invasions in each case as a punishment for sin and negligence. Sin and negligence are always with us, but they are highlighted at times of danger and emergency especially in the writings of moralists. A strong tradition of pessimism and of castigating sin as the cause of current woes developed in eleventh-century English monastic writing. The English monastic chroniclers' response to the Norman Conquest was deeply coloured by it. They saw it as a defeat brought on the English by their own vices. It was a mood which readily fused with the Norman justification of 1066 which stressed the decadence of the English church and its need for reform. William of Malmesbury in this as in so many ways, speaks with an Anglo-Norman voice. The English church had its share of problems and warts in these centuries, but moralistic commentaries on disaster are not the place to begin study of them.

These sources are also almost exclusively monastic. We should not look to the reforming monk Æthelwold for a record of the achievements of the secular church, the canons and the clerks. For him and his late tenth-century contemporaries through to William of Malmesbury, a monk who saw himself as a descendant of their revival, the state of monasticism is the index of the state of the church, its triumphs and vicissitudes identified as those of the church as a whole. The state of monasticism is of undoubted importance at this date, beyond the boundaries of the monasteries themselves, but the almost exclusive concern of many sources with it is a distortion. It exaggerates not only the significance, but the nature and extent of the so-called 'monastic revival' of the tenth century. This is especially so in the pages of late eleventh- and twelfth-century chronicles of houses like Peterborough, Ely or Ramsey whose splendour and wealth by the late eleventh century is no guide to their tenth-century status, though later authors inevitably date it from then. It underplays the importance of bishops and priests, of developments in parochial provision and of episcopal attempts at reform much wider than the monastic. It may even have affected our view of relations between kings and ecclesiastics.

By the late ninth century the English church had a structure based on dioceses and minsters. The conversion and establishment of Christianity had taken place within the political framework of the seventh century and the dioceses still reflected kingdoms and their organization. Thus Mercia had five ealdormen and five bishoprics, Lindsey, Lichfield, Leicester, Worcester and Hereford. There were two bishoprics in East Anglia, at Elmham and Dunwich, for the North and South Folk, one at Selsey for the South Saxons, two in Wessex at Winchester and Sherborne mirroring the division of Wessex east and west of Selwood. York served the old kingdom of Deira. In the far north and in the south-east the patterns and divergent developments of the conversion era were still apparent. Augustine's mission had established bishoprics at Canterbury, Rochester and London. The north had been heavily influenced by Celtic

5. *ibid.* Book II, caps, 148, 149 and 160

Christianity. The monk-bishop of Lindisfarne was associated with the old heart of the Kingdom of Bernicia and its predecessors,[6] but his colleague at Hexham had no such obvious political link. Hexham is a warning that a more detailed investigation of the political history of the seventh and eighth centuries would uncover other political units and a reminder that the shape of bishoprics at the end of the ninth century is the end product of the rise of large kingdoms. Some bishops' sees were sited in important centres, York, London, Canterbury or Winchester. All were in places significant at the time of their establishment between the seventh and ninth centuries.

The bishoprics were disrupted by the Viking invasions. Episcopal lists show that by the 870s Elmham, Dunwich, Leicester and Lindsey had ceased to function. The bishop of Leicester had fled to Dorchester on Thames by the 890s. The monks and bishop of Lindisfarne had left their exposed island and sought refuge at Chester-le-Street. Hexham had disappeared. The situation at Lichfield is not clear, though some disruption of the succession of bishops seems to have occurred. Eastern and northern England had lost much of its crucial organization of dioceses.

The importance of bishops to the life of the church meant that this situation was critical. Bishops were required for the ordination of clergy, for many of the liturgies of Holy Week including the blessing of oil and water for the ceremonies of baptism. Their pastoral functions were large. The life of Wulfstan II, written at the end of the eleventh century, shows an ideal bishop still as one who travelled his diocese preaching, baptizing and ministering to his flock.[7] Ideal may have been remote from reality in 900 as in 1100, but the lack of bishops in any guise was serious, though the survival of minsters in these areas, as we shall see, means that they were far from denuded of Christian service.

The bishoprics were reorganized in the first half of the tenth century. The shift from attack to settlement by the Scandinavians followed by their rapid conversion to Christianity opened the way for some re-establishment of bishoprics in eastern England. The new political situation uniting first Wessex and Mercia, then Wessex, Mercia and Northumbria made possible ecclesiastical change. The nature of the actual changes throws extra light on political realities.

Edward the Elder and Athelstan reshaped bishoprics primarily in Wessex; their actions were those of southern rather than English kings. In 909 Edward and Archbishop Plegmund reorganized the two large West Saxon dioceses of Winchester and Sherborne to produce five new ones, Winchester, Ramsbury, Sherborne, Wells and Crediton. Athelstan further divided the bishopric of Crediton to give a bishop to the West Welsh, Cornwall, at St Germans. In Wessex bishoprics had come almost to follow the shire system, an argument for thinking that the shire remained the sphere of office of an ealdorman in the poorly-recorded history of early tenth-century Wessex. The emphasis on units small enough for the bishop to exercise pastoral care may indicate how far bishops were seen as the primary agents of Christian advance and reform.

6. See N. Higham, *The Northern Counties to AD 1000* (1986), pp. 46–8 and 266–7
7. See e.g. E. Mason 'Change and continuity in eleventh-century Mercia: the experience of St Wulfstan of Worcester', ANS, 8 (1985), pp. 154–76

Yet north of the Thames little was done. Western, or as it was *c.*900, 'English' Mercia continued to be served by bishops at Hereford, Worcester, probably Lichfield and Dorchester. As the conquest of the Danish settlements continued no new bishoprics were created or old ones re-established, though Lindsey had a bishop by the late tenth century. Dorchester and London assumed control over the East Midlands and East Anglia respectively, though it would be more correct to say that in each case the respective bishops exercised occasional functions within these wide areas. By the end of the tenth century bishops of Dorchester were actively involved in and around the Fenlands. The bishops concerned were connected with the Fenland abbey of Ramsey, but this alone does not explain their involvement. Bishop Oscytel of Dorchester/York had earlier heard ecclesiastical cases in East Anglia. Any control exercised by the bishops of London in East Anglia was short-lived. Part of this area, probably Suffolk, was still under London in mid century,[8] but there was a bishop of Elmham by 956 and the bishops of Elmham would later control much of East Anglia.[9] Athelstan had certainly tightened his control over East Anglia, especially with the appointment of ealdorman Athelstan Half-King in the 930s, and some parallel attempt to re-establish a bishopric here is possible.

The doubt over the organization of the English church in the first half of the tenth century is instructive. If Lindsey was revived as early as this it would be from York rather than from the South. The vast and indeterminate diocese of Dorchester symbolizes the tenuous rule of southern kings. North of the Thames there was none of the division which was designed to provide better pastoral care in Wessex, or to draw Devon and Cornwall more closely into the West Saxon orbit. Loss of land, disruption of episcopal estates, lack of royal land to endow them are all answers to the difference, as they are keys to the superficiality of royal power here. In addition Athelstan may have preferred to let Mercian sensibilities lie, making no changes in the surviving bishoprics of west Mercia. The archbishops of York were wooed with grants in Amounderness in 934 and of Southwell in 956.[10] At Southwell an extension of the diocese south was granted or sanctioned. By the 950s southern kings were attempting to control appointments to York, though with limited success (see above, p. 49 on Oscytel and his appointment). The history of the English bishoprics in the first half of the tenth century is that of control of the kingdom: closest and fullest south of the Thames, especially in Wessex, more careful and cautious in Mercia, a question more of aspiration than fact in eastern and northern England. The diocesan structure by the eleventh century was thus only partly created by religious need. It had been an evolution in a political situation. It remained largely unchanged until the late 1060s, partly through inertia, partly perhaps because of the engrossing concerns of monastic reformers, more likely because the powers and attitudes of southern kings in and towards these areas had developed little.

The history of bishoprics is difficult to reconstruct, the detailed picture of minsters almost impossible. For the late ninth-century translator of Bede a

8. W. 1 and notes
9. F. Barlow, *The English Church, 1000–1066* (1963), pp. 216–17
10. S. 407 and 659

'minsterplace' (*mynsterstowe*) was a familiar part of the landscape and associated in his mind with important, populous places: he uses the term to translate *urbana loca* (urban places).[11] *Minster* derives from the Latin word, *monasterium*, and minsters were communities of priests or monks.[12] The term would once have covered both recognizably monastic communities, i.e. having monks and/or nuns who had taken vows, normally celibate and under an abbess or abbot, and communities of married priests. The distinction is over-rigid, though any emphasis on monastic reform was bound to sharpen it, whether the spread of Carolingian reform and the Rule of Benedict in the ninth century or the triumph of both in tenth-century England. These communities could provide for the spiritual needs of people outside their walls, serving areas many times larger than later parishes. Many early ones were situated at royal or episcopal estates and ministered to the needs, and took the ecclesiastical dues, of those living on them.

The definition of minsters became more narrow and precise under the critical eye of those who had their own view of what a community of religious should be. Asser felt that the monastic life had virtually died out of England 'even though quite a number of monasteries which had been built in that area still remain but do not maintain the rule of monastic life in any consistent way'.[13] The preface to the *Regularis Concordia*, rule of life for monastic houses, *c.*970, shared the view that monasteries had declined, and that the sign of it was the negligent clerks and their abominations. It set out to enforce the Rule of Benedict, celibacy and uniform observance. Neither Asser nor the *Regularis Concordia* denied the existence of communities; both found them wanting in the nature of their rule and observance. Asser may have had Celtic houses in mind as a yardstick: by the 960s and 970s it would be the reformed abbeys of the continent like Fleury. The sort of men who made these judgements played a large part in determining the direction the articulate strand of the English church was to take in the tenth and eleventh centuries, and they already indicate how far that direction would be inspired from beyond the frontiers of England. Their views should not blind us to the continuing importance of the minsters throughout this time, an importance attested by the substantial lay patronage they continued to attract.

The late ninth and tenth centuries saw reform and change through much of the west European church. These movements were not isolated phenomena but continued the impetus of the ninth-century Carolingian reforms and led directly into the better-known movements of the mid and late eleventh century. Their common links with the Carolingian era are notable in three areas: the inspiration for most of them lay in the canonical collections begun in the ninth century and continued in the tenth; as in the Carolingian period bishops were the spearhead of reforms; but as in the ninth century, neither bishops nor reform should be isolated from monastic developments. Monastic reform was itself a major strand, continuing attempts to regularize monastic practice and enforce common standards which go back beyond Louis the Pious and Benedict

11. *The Old English Version of Bede's Ecclesiastical History*, ed. T. Miller, EETS, 95 (1895), p. 161
12. Excellent general discussion in J. Blair, 'Secular minster churches in Domesday Book', *Domesday Book, a Reassessment*, ed. P. H. Sawyer (1985), pp. 104–42
13. Asser, Life of Alfred in *Alfred the Great*, ed. S. Keynes and M. Lapidge (1983), p. 103

of Aniane. In retrospect, with the Gregorian dichotomies of religious and secular, church and state in view, the degree of independence which these movements claimed from lay power has often seemed the most important aspect of them. Cluny especially has been seen as representing a demand for total separation from lay control, whilst the English and Ottonian variants of monastic reform have been considered to preserve an older, Carolingian alliance of church and king. To approach them from the eleventh century in this way is to distort their concerns and the common ground.

The Carolingian traditions, on which all fed, contained potential tensions between religious and secular. Organized Christianity had always known them, though they could be more or less muted. The major aim of all was reform, but many things were understood by that term: the extension of Christianity itself, since conversion was still superficial, thus superstition and heathen practice were to be eradicated; an increasing concern for lay morality, specifically for sexual morality, marriage, incest and fornication; the strengthening and defence of the church and its ministers for the achieving of these ends, with a consequent interest in the life-style of the clergy, in clerical discipline and celibacy, their correct performance of rituals, the defence and augmentation of church property, the payment of tithes, the sanctity of the church building and sanctuary; and finally the role of bishops in organizing the church and society at large for these ends.

Such concerns inevitably impinged on lay power, on lay society as a whole. They would lead to a growing awareness of the separation of the sacred and the secular, a new demarcation of the 'holy' which increasingly excluded the laity, and a re-emphasis on the church and its bishops as a group necessarily separate from the laity. But in their origins and aims they were not revolutionary. It was easy for Alfred to agree with Asser that Wessex needed monasteries, for Edgar and Æthelwold to unite and drive out married clerks. It would be harder for Rufus to agree with Anselm, but by then the implications of two centuries of reform were becoming clearer, as they arguably were even before 1066. It is easier to understand the progress and patronage of tenth-century changes if they are recognized as evolutionary stages of long-accepted developments.

Carolingian influence was reaching England by the late ninth and early tenth century if not before, in some cases via Celtic links.[14] Canonical and penitential literature of the type which inspired much tenth-century episcopal reform was arriving in Winchester and at the court of Athelstan from places such as Brittany and Rheims. Some arrived in a form already shaped to the tenth-century path. The canonical collection known as the *Hibernensis*, for example, had already been excerpted to focus on questions of lay morality, especially marriage, and on the grades and life-style of the clergy. These Celtic and Frankish books together with earlier English penitential literature, were studied at the court school of Athelstan, that crucible of tenth-century reform. Here future archbishops and bishops like Oda, Dunstan and Æthelwold were trained in the royal

14. See e.g. A. Frantzen, *The Literature of Penance in Anglo-Saxon England* (New Brunswick, 1983); M Wood, 'The making of King Æthelstan's empire: an English Charlemagne', in *Ideal and Reality*.., ed. P. Wormald *et al.* (Oxford, 1983), pp. 250–72, and S. Keynes, 'King Athelstan's books', in *Learning and Literature in Anglo-Saxon England*, eds. M. Lapidge and H. Gneuss (Cambridge, 1985), pp. 143–201

chapel, men crucial to later developments. Already their interest lay in monasticism. Dunstan's uncle, Bishop Ælfheah of Winchester, encouraged him to take monastic vows and he acquired the abbey of Glastonbury at this date. But equally these men were, or went on to become, bishops. And they were only a small minority of the English church by the 940s.

It must be doubted whether Athelstan saw himself as spearheading a great reform movement, especially a revolutionary one. Charlemagne and his own grandfather Alfred provided examples of kings who had gathered a court school. His law codes show him as a king in their mould, who had imbibed and digested Christian views on how a king should act. But like them he belongs in a society in which holiness and power fed on each other. Athelstan collected and exchanged not only books but relics. Together they provided an understanding of the will of God and an ability to influence it. The king who sponsored a learned palace chapel also opened the tomb of St Cuthbert. His aunt Æthelflæd had moved the relics of Mercian saints to amass power and loyalty to herself; his brother Edmund would later bring south the bones of northern saints as a loot which drained the northern kingdom. Athelstan did what great kings had always done, and his rule of all the kingdoms of the English would inspire him to see himself as a great king.

In Athelstan's palace school men like Oda and Dunstan imbibed an equally traditional lesson from the books they read. When Oda was appointed archbishop of Canterbury he produced a set of *Constitutions*, or rules, which inspired King Edmund's ecclesiastical law code. His concerns were those of European tenth-century bishops as various as Atto of Vercelli, Burchard of Worms or the assembled synods envisaged in the German *Pontifical Romano-Germanique*.[15] The church itself and all its property and buildings were to be holy and protected; kings ruled, but had to heed the admonitions of bishops; bishops had clear duties to their rulers and their dioceses; the behaviour of priests must be carefully regulated, whilst the laity should espouse Christian marriage, avoid incest, correctly observe feasts and fasts and pay their tithes. The first stirrings of reform, in England as on the continent, came from the bishops fed by Carolingian traditions. They were not confined to monastic issues[16] but began from a brief for the whole of church and society.

Dunstan had also been trained at Athelstan's court and by the 930s had been inspired to take monastic vows and had become abbot of Glastonbury. Dunstan's subsequent career cannot be read either as the simple saint's life of his later biography nor yet as a tale of political manoeuvring and intrigue in which religion played only a secondary role. Dunstan was to be twice exiled from court, and only narrowly escaped banishment on a third occasion. There may have been about him something of the uncomfortable prophet painted in his later Life. Yet he was happy to accept a bishopric when he returned from exile in 957 and not averse to adding another and to ousting an archbishop of Canterbury and accepting appointment in his stead in 959.[17] Oda and Dunstan

15. See e.g. *Le Pontifical Romano-Germanique du dixième siècle*, eds. C. Vogel and R. Elze, *Studi e testi*, 226 (Rome, 1963) and S. F. Wemple, *Atto of Vercelli* (Rome, 1979)
16. R. R. Darlington, 'Ecclesiastical reform in the late Old English period', *English Historical Review*, 51 (1936), pp. 385–428
17. On events at Canterbury in 959 see N. Brooks, *Early History of the Church of Canterbury* (Leicester, 1984), pp. 237–44

were closely involved in the court factions of the mid tenth century and subject to the vicissitudes and rewards of their politics. We have lost the detail which would allow us to see how far religious issues helped form the factional groupings of this date, but we need not assume that Oda or Dunstan did not seek to use their position at court to further reform. What is more debatable is how far that reform was conceived of primarily in monastic terms.

In the exiles of the 950s Dunstan went to Flanders, to be received by a count whose own exiles Edmund had welcomed, and Oswald, Oda's nephew, went to Fleury. Oswald's later monastic biographer claimed that he went voluntarily, out of disgust at the luxurious and unreformable habits of the clerks in his house at Winchester. But if Oda were an opponent of Eadwig in the 950s [see above, pp. 49–51], Winchester would have been no place for his nephew. Fleury was at best a self-imposed exile until Oswald, like Dunstan, could return to England on Edgar's accession. At Fleury and at Ghent in Flanders Oswald and Dunstan came into contact with continental monastic reform. That reform was like the English still in its earliest incoherent stages. The deliberate creation of a monastic reform movement in the mid tenth century by men who sought specific inspiration from continental monasteries is a construction imposed by historians from the late tenth century onwards. But contacts between England and the continent which these exiles utilized were crucial to the history of the English church throughout the tenth and eleventh centuries.

In the 960s and early 970s an impressive tide of monastic foundations or reformations included the Old and New Minsters Winchester, Worcester, Evesham, Pershore, Ramsey, Ely, Peterborough and Thorney. The Life of Oswald later claimed that at a royal council in 970 it was decided to found forty abbeys in Mercia alone; the number may be exaggerated, but a large number of foundations north of the Thames have been shown to belong to about this date.[18] At about the same date a new rule of life for English monks was approved in a royal council and given the backing of the king. A monastic movement was under way, yet recognition of that fact leaves unresolved the questions of its nature in the 960s and 970s, of how deeply and how quickly it changed the nature of the communities involved and of how far its nature and implications were grasped by the royal and noble patrons who espoused it so enthusiastically.

For later monastic chroniclers and writers the changes in monasticism appeared to have been the most important developments of the tenth century. Their significance should not be underestimated. The communities founded and refounded now played a major role in the intellectual and religious life of the eleventh and twelfth centuries. Their products dominated the English episcopate until the mid eleventh century. An estimated nine out of ten bishops between 970 and 1066 were drawn from the monasteries, an interesting contrast to the worldly noble-dominated Norman episcopate.[19] A golden age of manuscript production and artistic development flowered in their scriptoria. And the endowment of the dozen or so richest abbeys by 1066 rivalled that of

18. N. Banton, 'Monastic reform and the unification of tenth-century England', in *Religion and National Identity*, ed. S. Mews (Oxford, 1982), pp. 71–85

19. D. M. Knowles, *The Monastic Order in England* (Cambridge, 1966), pp. 699–701 and C. N. L. and R. Brookes, 'I vescovi di Inghilterra e Normandia nel secolo XI: contrasti', in *Le Instituzioni ecclesiastiche della 'societas christiana' dei secoli xi–xii. Diocesi, pieui e parrochie* Universita Cattolica de Sacro Cuore, miscellaneo del centro di Studi Medioevali, VIII (Milan, 1977), pp. 536–45.

most great nobles and far surpassed that of most bishoprics. This glowing picture, however, ignores the possible ill effects of the unbalanced share of wealth and patronage between bishoprics and abbeys as well as the restricted geographical spread of the movement which never affected England north of the Humber and was very localized south of it. It obscures how far the monasteries developed between the mid tenth and the mid eleventh centuries in consequence overestimating the late tenth-century phase and its perception by contemporary patrons. Concentration on it has hidden the greater diversity of the late tenth- and eleventh-century church and the wide range of lay patronage.

The *Regularis Concordia* or rule of life approved *c*.970 gives the clearest indication of the nature of reform by this date. Existing communities of clerks were to be replaced by monks and new communities of the latter were to be founded. The difference between monk and clerk is not spelled out, and the systematic abuse of the clerks by monastic writers makes it difficult to discuss their way, or ways of life. The *Regularis* suggests that reformers were particularly concerned to impose a uniform way of life, the rule of St Benedict, and strict sexual morality, implicitly celibacy. Contact between communities of men and women was frowned on; there was no way open for any of the older double houses which might have survived into the tenth century to flourish. Monks were discouraged from much contact with the secular world and a round of daily prayer and liturgy was laid down for them. Long-standing aims were restated, though the liturgical emphasis was part of a common tenth-century trend.

The relationship between the reformed monasteries and the lay powers of king and nobility has been made central to the interpretation of the tenth-century reform. At one point the *Regularis* specifies the need to end 'saecularium prioratus' which had been the ruin of the monastic life in earlier times.[20] What the authors meant and the audience understood by this term is not clear. 'Secular domination' could be its meaning, a wholesale attack by reformers on the noble control of monasteries.[21] It may be little more than a reiteration of the theme of non-involvement in secular affairs. In either case it is given little prominence in the document and it would have been easy to miss the full, long-term implications of such a potentially novel idea amid the general thrust of the reform programme. Patronage and protection by the king were more than acceptable, he could even intervene in the choice of abbot.[22]

If the communities were to be separated from worldly concerns and at the same time maintain a continuous existence endowment and its nature were important questions. At the end of the *Regularis* the king made the important concession of remitting the heriot or death payment for abbots and abbesses, who were thus discouraged from developing a personal treasure and from the idea of personal property in the abbey's lands. Abbots and abbesses were not to give gifts to worldly rulers and they and their relatives were to have no claims on abbey lands.[23] The growing danger of forfeiture in the tenth century meant that abbey lands needed protecting from the personal claims or losses of

20. *Regularis Concordia*, ed. Symons, p. 7
21. E. John, 'The king and the monks in the tenth-century reformation', *Orbis Britanniae* (Leicester, 1966), pp. 154–80
22. *Regularis Concordia*, p. 6
23. *ibid.* p. 69 and EHD I, no. 238, pp. 922–3

individual abbots or abbesses. This fact was most apparent to Æthelwold when he wrote his *Old English account of the foundation of monasteries* after Edgar's death, his awareness sharpened by the use of legal means to attack monastic lands after 975. The realization of the need for full community of property and the dangers from patrons and from the processes of tenth-century law may have grown gradually. By the time Wulfric Spott founded Burton Abbey in 1004 they were clear. Wulfric placed his abbey under the lordship of the king and solicited the advocacy of the archbishop of Canterbury and of his own brother, ealdorman Ælfhelm. It was advocacy and protection not possession which he sought. The line between the two may be implicit in the *Regularis Concordia*; it was now spelt out.

Corporate endowment as opposed to family possession was a key to the longevity and success of the Benedictine communities. They not only attracted patronage but retained it, though rarely without problems. The differing fortunes of an apparently unreformed house, or minster, Stoke-by-Nayland and neighbouring Ely is instructive. Stoke was generously endowed throughout the tenth century by ealdorman Ælfgar of Essex and his daughters Æthelflæd and Ælfflæd.[24] Ælfflæd and her husband, ealdorman Brihtnoth, were also lavish patrons of Ely. The patrons were drawn from the same strata of society, but the fortunes of the houses diverged. By the time of Domesday Stoke held none of its tenth-century acquisitions, while Ely had prospered to become one of the wealthiest houses in England. But the contrast is not merely between 'reformed' and 'unreformed'. Wulfric's 'reformed' foundation at Burton had lost most of its original endowment by 1066.[25] At Ely it was the capacity of the late tenth-century abbots to make good use of the invigorated local courts which helped them retain property. At Ely and Peterborough the dynamism of eleventh-century abbots played a major role, indeed the pattern of monasticism in 1066 owes as much to eleventh-century patronage and abbots as to the tenth-century reform.

Family interference continued to lead to loss of property for reformed and unreformed houses. The community of clerks at Horningsey lost land because its leaders and their families were involved in local society and were punished for, among other things, receiving stolen goods.[26] The local bishop, Oscytel was not so committed to the idea of inviolable ecclesiastical property that he was not prepared to take payment in such cases. Oscytel may not have been a reformer, but on any normal definition his nephew Oswald was. Yet Oswald endowed his kin with Worcester lands, leasing them in ways forbidden as early as ninth-century synods.[27] Eleventh-century abbots were not divorced from family and political considerations. Wulfric of Ely used abbey lands to enable his brother to make a good marriage [28] and the Leofric who made Peterborough great acquired it, and the other houses he held in plurality, through family connections. It is difficult to see the monastic movement conceived as an overt and swingeing attack on lay power in the tenth-century origins or developing as one in the eleventh.

24. W. 2, 14 and 15
25. P. H. Sawyer, *Charters of Burton Abbey* (Oxford, 1979), pp. xliv–vii
26. LE caps. 32–3, pp. 105–8
27. e.g. S. 1370, 1361, 1355, 1348, 1345, 1340, 1326, 1315, 1308
28. LE cap. 97, pp. 166–7

Doubts must thus be raised about how tenth- and eleventh-century patrons saw their patronage, and especially whether they identified a clear movement with stated aims. Their serious religious motivation is beyond doubt. Only the most cynical could dismiss the words of will after will as clerical misrepresentation of the patrons' intentions. Prayers for the souls of ancestors, spouses or self are cited over and again as the reason for benefactions. Benefactors secured a place of burial and prayers for their souls. Vicarious salvation or more accurately communal salvation was central to early medieval Christianity. Ealdorman Æthelwine and his brother Ælfwold were claimed to protect monks 'who by the help of God maintained all the Christianity in the kingdom...by whose prayers we can be snatched from our enemies'.[29] If there is distortion here it is in the exclusive virtue and protection attributed to monks. Noble and royal patronage were spread more widely.

The newly founded abbeys did attract much patronage but alongside other, often older institutions. At court charismatic reformers like Æthelwold were successful in convincing some patrons that the prayers of celibate monks were more efficacious than those of clerks. The role of reforming bishops themselves must never be underestimated. The great houses of the Fenlands and East Anglia or of the Severn valley owed more to Bishops Æthelwold and Oswald than to any individual noble. For many of the latter the reformed monasteries shared rather than engrossed their patronage. A picture drawn largely from the twelfth-century chronicle-cum-cartularies of Ely, Ramsey or Abingdon inevitably makes the new abbeys appear dominant. One derived from the charters and wills of the tenth and eleventh centuries is different, remarkably so given the fact that most such documents owe their survival to the reformed abbeys. Far from the new houses enjoying a monopoly of noble patronage, old established centres such as the Old and New Minsters Winchester and Christ Church Canterbury, and non-reformed minsters and nunneries remained favourites. Particular houses, whether reformed or not, were identified as family foundations and fostered, and this was as true of royal as of noble patronage. There are significant individual differences between learned men like ealdorman Æthelweard and his son Æthelmær who had important links with the scholar and reforming monk Ælfric or ealdorman Ælfhere and his brother Ælfheah, whose connections were with non-reforming ecclesiastics like the married bishop of Winchester. The date of patronage is also significant, and the relationship of patrons to court circles. Blanket support for a clearly perceived reforming movement is far from the true picture.

In the mid tenth century, for example, the houses of the so-called reform movement played little role. Bishop Theodred of London left land to three minsters, at Mendham and Hoxne in Suffolk and at the future Bury St Edmund's, not to be reformed until the eleventh century.[30] Ealdorman Ælfgar in the late 940s also patronized the community at Bury with its important relics of St Edmund, but most of his patronage went to Stoke by Nayland for his soul and the souls of his ancestors. His daughters continued to make this family house the major beneficiary of their wills until *c.*AD 1000, although there is no evidence that it was part of the reform movement [see above, n.24]. His eldest daughter,

29. EHD I, no. 236, p. 914
30. W. 1

Æthelflæd was the widow of King Edmund and her royal connections drew her into patronage of the royal house of Glastonbury, his younger daughter Ælfflæd left land to her husband's family house at Ely. At least seven minsters and the nunnery at Barking received land in the wills of these two women. Patronage of Shaftesbury nunnery was prominent in the will of Wynflæd who was connected with the community in the mid tenth century,[31] though it was not only women who left land to nunneries.

These wills were early, before the thrust of the movement, or in the case of Ælfgar's daughters arguably enacting the wishes of father or husband formed before the major development of reform. But the will of ealdorman Æthelmær dates from 971-983.[32] His was the patronage of a great southern noble at the alleged height of reform. Æthelmær was a pious man and he spread his bequests widely. His will left money rather than land, giving him the greatest freedom of manoeuvre. The Old Minster Winchester got the bulk of his cash, with the reformed, but also royally connected Glastonbury second. He left bequests to three other reformed houses, but also to two bishops, four nunneries and two or three communities of clerks. Æthelmær's patronage may have been that of a politically active man. What is clear is that the reform had only marginally affected his perception of the church.

The new monasteries did not even cease to be seen as family houses. The endowment of Ramsey came from the family connections of Archbishop Oswald and ealdorman Æthelwine. Ely was the favoured house of ealdorman Brihtnoth and his successors, his wife Ælfflæd, his daughter Leofflæd and her husband Oswy, Oswy's two brothers and Leofflæd's daughter. A son and nephew of Oswy became monks there. Abbots and bishops displayed some of the same motivation. A proprietary attitude was not confined to the 'lascivious clerks'. Archbishop Ælfric was abbot of St Albans before promotion to a bishopric and his brother succeeded him there.[33] Archbishop Wulfstan of Worcester continued Oswald's practice of leaving Worcester lands to his kin,[34] and when his nephew succeeded to the bishopric a decade or so later he made grants to family which were still causing Worcester trouble after 1066.[35] When such activity recurs in the mid eleventh century it is branded as nepotism and a sign of decay, yet it was already apparent in the generation of 'reform'. Stigand abused an established pattern, and one which was an inherent part of a society in which family connection was an expected route of advancement. It must be doubted how far reformers launched a head-on attack on such values, how far they hoped rather to draw a line between protection and patronage on the one hand and control and domination on the other, a line to be held perhaps by trust in individual patrons, perhaps with the backing of the king.

Even the king's own patronage cannot be seen as indiscriminate support for reform. Edgar was generous to the church in the manner of kings before him, though the scale of his generosity argues the influence of bishops at his court and not merely the continuation of tradition. Three quarters of Edgar's patronage,

31. W. 3
32. W. 10
33. W. 18
34. S. 1384
35. Barlow, *The English Church, 1000-1066*, p. 174

however, went to West Saxon houses mostly connected to the royal family, a full quarter of it to the old established houses of Winchester. North of the Thames he was far less generous, reflecting in part the spread of royal land itself. Most houses claimed a general confirmation charter from Edgar, few north of the Thames claimed more. Æthelwold's houses did especially well, Winchester and Abingdon in the south, Ely in the east. And within Wessex nunneries fared as well as places like Malmesbury or Muchelney. Edgar's patronage can be read in many ways. It is both continuation of traditional family patronage and support for the monastic reformers, more precisely support for Bishop Æthelwold, whose dominance within the monastic reforms is crucial.

Shorn of the later perspective the pattern of the late tenth century appears differently. It was still the old-established houses of Winchester, Glastonbury and the royal nunneries which stood out. Abingdon already looked important, sufficiently so for ealdorman Ælfric to gain its abbacy for his brother in the 980s,[36] but the great Fenland stars would not have shone as brightly as in 1066. There were still many small houses of clerks, some, like Wolverhampton, founded or refounded as late as this. Æthelwold acquired several of them at Barrow, Breedon and St Ives. Eleventh-century empire building by Ely or Peterborough swallowed these up, but at the end of the tenth century they were still comparable in size to some of the 'reformed' houses, and the differences between the two may be more apparent to us than to many contemporary patrons. At Winchester Æthelwold, with royal backing, dramatically expelled the clerks in the 960s. His ferocity was not repeated everywhere. The Worcester community under Oswald changed its nature only gradually; the changeover at Christ Church Canterbury was so piecemeal that it is difficult to date.[37]

The story of the nunneries underlines the distortions of a twelfth-century monastic perspective on the tenth-century church. Grants to religious women and to royal nunneries continue throughout the tenth century. One or two new foundations were made, as at Chatteris.[38] Shaftesbury encouraged and maintained an important royal cult of the murdered King Edward into the eleventh century and Wilton's wealth and importance as a house of royal women was still marked after 1066.

The story of the nunneries is also a tale of the ultimate success of the ideals developing throughout the tenth and eleventh centuries, a reminder that if the successful rewrite history it is because they have succeeded. However slowly they grew, however obscurely they were perceived at the time, those ideals contained new elements. The idea of family control had been undermined, celibacy and an ideal of communal property had been established, uniformity of rule and observance encouraged. The nunneries, along with the minsters, looked increasingly anomalous. There were organized communities of women in 1066, but there were also nuns [*nonna, monialis*] holding individual property.[39] The

36. S. 876
37. P. H. Sawyer, 'Charters of the Reform movement: the Worcester archive', in *Tenth-Century Studies*, ed. D. Parsons (Chichester, 1975), pp. 84–93 and Brooks, *The Early History of the Church of Canterbury*, pp. 255–66
38. LE cap. 71, p. 141
39. e.g. DB I, fo. 170 V, DB II, fo. 26 V

larger houses were usually associated with royal women, a close association which had brought losses as well as gains, as Barking had found to its cost.[40] Some individual nuns were attached to Benedictine houses like Ely or Worcester, but not as the abbesses of great double houses as in the sixth or seventh century. Brihtnoth's granddaughter, Æthelswith, was given a small amount of land close to Ely where she lived as a nun and became known for her embroidery.[41] Unlike his contemporaries in Ottonian Germany, Brihtnoth had chosen to make his family house a monastery not a nunnery. That choice was determined by the pattern of English reform. Despite a continuing lay interest and demand female monasticism did not become a significant strand in English reform at this date. Monasticism has an inherent emphasis on celibacy, on sexual morality and on dualism, on those aspects of Christianity which are at best neutral, at worst actively antifeminist. Its charismatic individualism and its communal structure adaptable to family needs allowed the development of female monasticism in certain situations in the early Middle Ages. But monasticism does not encourage female participation and in the tenth and eleventh centuries that participation was marginalized.

If the monasteries should not engross our picture of the church, we should nonetheless be aware of how far the monastic movement altered the English church. In the first half of the eleventh century monasticism dominated its learning. It was not isolated from wider ecclesiastical concerns. Three of its products, Archbishop Wulfstan of York, Abbot Ælfric and Byrhtferth of Ramsey were interested in the parochial clergy and their education. English bishops drawn from the monasteries could achieve high standards and if Cluniac bishops are taken as an index of reforming zeal and excellence in the continental church, products of tenth-century Winchester should rank high in the English church. The dominance of a monastic pattern in the thought of a man like Wulfstan of York may have sharpened his awareness of the separation of cleric and lay as it was producing similar changes in eleventh-century Europe.

The centres of wealth and influence in the mid-eleventh-century church resulted in large part from a century of monastic endowment. Many bishoprics fell outside them. The wealthy bishoprics, places such as Canterbury, Winchester and Worcester, were those with a long history of importance and also those which had become monastic chapters. The income of most bishoprics would have placed their incumbents low down the social scale in comparison with an abbot of Peterborough or Ely, or with a late-tenth-century ealdorman or mid-eleventh-century earl. The abbess of Wilton was as wealthy in Domesday as the bishop of Wells or Exeter, or as those of Ramsbury or Sherborne before they were united. The bishop of Thetford's annual landed income would have placed him on a par with the smallest monasteries and well below many a king's thegn. The situation was recognized by some of Edward the Confessor's bishops, men like Leofric who built up the endowment of Exeter, or Hermann, for whom Ramsbury and Sherborne were united.

The tenth century had begun with the division of the southern dioceses by Edward the Elder and his archbishop and with the losses of ecclesiastical land

40. 'La vie de Sainte Vulfhilde par Goscelin de Canterbury', ed. M Esposito, *Analecta Bollandiana*, 32 (1913), pp. 21–2
41. LE cap. 88, pp. 157–8

in the turmoil of the Danish settlement north of the Thames. Both factors helped impoverish the English bishoprics. The intention of early tenth-century reformers was to achieve widespread renewal through the pastoral activity of bishops, an ideal retained actively by Archbishop Wulfstan in the early eleventh century but difficult to realize in the small poor or overlarge dioceses. Monasticism may not have engrossed patronage, but it diverted significant amounts of it. Moreover the monk-bishops who took over many sees from the late tenth century onwards often retained as much loyalty to their old monasteries and their endowments as to their new sees. The enlargement of the tenth-century kingdom brought great wealth into the hands of kings and lay nobles; its final ecclesiastical resting places were monasteries and minsters not bishoprics.

Medieval Christianity had two inseparable faces: the call to individual salvation and the demand that all be saved through missionary and pastoral activity. The first had been institutionalized in monasticism, though the difficulty of separating the two had drawn monasticism into concern with the world beyond the abbey wall. The integration of monasticism into the family and communal world of the early Middle Ages had enhanced that concern; and tenth-century patrons, and the monks who recorded their patronage were aware of the integration. For Æthelwine and his brother Ramsey was not merely a mausoleum for their family dead but a monastery committed to the salvation of the Christian people. The earliest English communities had had pastoral functions, still continued in the tenth and eleventh centuries by many of the minsters. Such communities, serving large areas, provided most of the thinly spread pastoral care in early England. 'Reformed' monks like those at Ramsey, however, were encouraged to remain within their monasteries. Although this did not prohibit a concern for the parish priest and for local churches, as an ideal it confined the monk to prayer for the community rather than active pastoral involvement in it. Although there are claims that monasteries founded local churches, we must look beyond the abbeys for the growth of pastoral provision.

Ninth-century Carolingian bishops had made parish and pastoral provision a priority [42] and the tenth- and eleventh-century English bishops working in the same traditions echoed them. These centuries saw a rapid growth in the numbers of local churches, if not always in parishes. Architectural remains show a heyday of church building and especially by the eleventh century of stone buildings; with them came regular provision of services. Domesday Book shows that in counties like Suffolk and Surrey there was a church and priest in almost every village in 1086.[43] Domesday is a patchy source on churches and similar full provision is probably hidden in other counties by inadequate recording. Church reformers showed a growing interest in local priests and churches, in contrast with earlier English synods and penitentials. Even royal laws of the late tenth and early eleventh centuries suggest the urgent need to fit new churches into the existing framework of tithes and church dues. Edgar differentiated between old minsters and the churches thegns had built on their own bookland, some with

42. R. McKitterick, *The Frankish Church and the Carolingian Reforms, 789–895* (1977)
43. J. Blair, 'Local churches in Domesday Book and before', in *Domesday Studies*, ed. J. C. Holt (Woodbridge, 1987), pp. 265–78

graveyards, others without.[44] None of this evidence taken in isolation would prove that such churches were relatively new and growing in number at this date. Cumulatively it points to a significant growth of local religious provision.

New churches do not mean that a parochial system had sprung fully-fledged into being. Parish formation may be a relatively late phenomenon in Europe.[45] But by the late eleventh century, many local churches in England show signs of parochial status, with an endowment of land, tithes and a defined territory. In the tenth century a variety of local provision is identifiable. Old minster communities remained, and some lesser churches were founded as daughters from them. Other local churches were lay foundations. In the burgeoning towns this sometimes involved groups of people supporting a priest and church; in other cases individual townspeople or nobles founded urban churches. In Lincoln the dedication stone of St Mary-le-Wigford records that Eirtig built the church, whilst Earl Siward founded a minster at Galmanho in York.[46] Rural foundations by groups of people were made in eastern England, though inevitably it is local churches founded by thegns which are most often chronicled. Sometimes a noble household had its own priest or even group of household chaplains, sometimes a permanent church was established separate from the household. In the early eleventh century Archbishop Wulfstan thought that the possession of a church was one sign of noble status.[47] His reformer's concern that the rituals be performed correctly in a consecrated building with the proper vessels may have led him into wishful statements. William of Malmesbury's scathing comments on the 'chamber priests' of the late Old English nobility [48] suggests that religious provision attached to the household lived on, though his lack of sympathy for the pre−conquest church probably overemphasized it and its abuses. By 1086 English churches appear varied in their status and in their endowment, a variety which reflects their differing origins.

With local churches, in some cases perhaps even before them, came local priests. Those who framed the Domesday survey expected them to be everywhere and incorporated them into the mechanisms for information gathering. The reformers of *c.* AD 1000 were very interested in them. Two bishops, Wulfsige of Sherborne and Wulfstan of York, both former monks, sought the advice of Ælfric of Eynsham, himself one of the greatest products of the tenth-century monastic movement, on their pastoral duties. Ælfric's advice dealt with the perennial problems of performance of the liturgy and rituals by isolated and barely literate clergy: how the mass should be said, the altar and its vessels cared for, the holy oils kept and used, the sacraments administered. Archbishop Wulfstan's own work is primarily that of a reforming bishop. The bishop himself is the central figure for Wulfstan, the key to reform and the health of the church. He is the vicar of St Peter, God himself the 'bishop of all bishops'.[49] Bishops must speak out, counsel the powerful, preach, hold synods,

44. II Edgar 1.1–2.1
45. S. Reynolds, *Kingdoms and Communities in Western Europe, 900–1300* (Oxford, 1984), chap. 4
46. ASC MSS D and E 1055 and P. Stafford, *The East Midlands in the Early Middle Ages* (Leicester, 1985), p. 186
47. EHD I, no. 51, p. 468 n. 7
48. William of Malmesbury, Bk III, cap. 245
49. *The Homilies of Wulfstan*, ed. D. Bethurum (Oxford, 1957), nos. 15 and 17, pp. 236 and 243

guide and admonish their clergy. The life-style and education of their own clergy must be their constant concern. Wulfstan himself drew up a rule of life for his clergy, the *Canons Enacted under King Edgar*, he wrote homilies on the subject of negligent priests and others on basic instruction – on baptism, on the fundamentals of the Christian life along with English translations of the *Pater Noster* and the Creed. Wulfstan aimed to improve the standards of the local clergy through regular synods and basic instruction and preferably through celibacy. For those priests who observed celibacy he held out the carrot of noble status and its legal privileges. In this last concern, as perhaps in many others, he echoed the lost injunctions of Dunstan.[50]

The sheer practicality of Wulfstan's work, its recognition of problems and its tackling of basic questions of instruction mark it out as active pastoral concern and not merely scholarly speculation. The anonymous author of the *Northumbrian Priests Law*, written in the first half of the eleventh century has a similar engagement with immediate problems. Not for him the call for celibacy, but rather that a priest should live with one woman and not take another. His primary aim was to organize the priests into a gild, so that corporate identity could replace the ties of family and the world, a common rule and group overcome the problems of the isolated cleric.[51]

Penitential literature, too, was developing in ways which made for easier use.[52] Between the seventh and the ninth centuries penitentials, whether in England or in Frankia, had become lengthy, cumbersome, complex documents, adapted and transmitted in an academic tradition. Tenth-century English penitentials, by contrast, were remarkable both for the speed with which they changed and developed and the increasing practicality of their organization. They were true handbooks for confessors, adapted to use. The list of sins was reduced to those most likely to be committed, penance was simplified, practical advice given to the priest. Aimed at the priest, these penitentials were part of the pastoral reform of the tenth and eleventh centuries. When penitential development resumed again in the twelfth century its emphasis would be individual, for the use of the sinner seeking to repent rather than the priest concerned with corporate salvation. Wulfstan and other English reformers at this date were preoccupied with the role of the organized church in salvation, with the place of priests and bishops within that church. In tenth-century England the emphasis was not on individual repentance but on public penance, in which the bishop's role was paramount. In the Northumbrian Priests' law as in the early tenth century it was a case of episcopally led reform, parallel to, encompassing and drawing on the better-known monastic one.

Whether in local churches or in monasteries the net result was a growth in the size and organization of the clerical element in society. At the royal court the bishops were joined by an increasing number of abbots. It is not clear that they met separately to debate on the ecclesiastical legislation which was increasingly recorded in separate law codes, but the court itself provided the opportunities for the development of that group cohesion for which Wulfstan called. If gilds of

50. V Æthelred 9 and 9.1, *Canons Enacted under King Edgar*, ed. R. Fowler, EETS, 266 (Oxford, 1972), cap. 68c, p. 17
51. EHD I, no. 52, pp. 472–6
52. Frantzen, *The Literature of Penance in Anglo-Saxon England*

priests were formed and synods met as demanded they provided further opportunity for the clergy, especially the higher clergy, to develop a sense of identity. The monasteries physically separated monks; reforming bishops called for a different life-style for the priests and emphasized the holiness of the church building and its sanctuary. Reform sought, if it did not always produce, clerical identity and separation; it drew lines and made divisions, around the clergy, the church building and its rituals, between cleric and lay.

Simultaneously churchmen were drawn into structures of power themselves developing rapidly. They played their role in the advance of royal rule. Abbots and bishops sat in local courts, in shire meetings, had responsibility for weights and measures. The priest collected tithes and dues, information for the Domesday Survey. Church and king still cooperated. In the increasing concern for penance, for example, especially for public penance specified by the bishop, religious discipline and secular law combined. From the time of Alfred and Athelstan the confession of sin led to the remission of secular punishment, including the penalties for false oaths.[53] Kings encouraged penance, but simultaneously required its public performance. The alliance with power was actively sought, and for motives which included the highest Christian ideals. The hundred courts of the Severn valley, controlled by the bishop of Worcester, allowed him to draw profit from the developments in tenth-century law and to protect and extend church property. Kings and bishops shared fines and enforcement in marital and sexual offences, bringing secular aid to moral discipline in an area of increasing ecclesiastical concern.[54]

Developments in lay piety as well as royal power heightened the potential tension in the role of churchmen. Lay piety is never easy to measure in the Middle Ages, but there is much to suggest that the stage of technical conversion was already giving way to a deeper religious commitment. The foundation of local churches is one sign of this, and simultaneously a cause of its further development. The sacraments and rituals of the church were provided on a more regular basis, hence Wulfstan's growing worries about their performance. Christian funerary sculpture was manufactured in workshops catering for lay tastes.[55] Relics were used in ways which show their function in popular piety, whilst contact with them enhanced their significance[56]. Rulers like Æthelflæd, Edmund and Cnut translated relics as political symbols, a religious analogy to the amassing of secular power, but it is the processions with relics, ordered for example by Æthelred in 1009 to combat the Danish threat, which speak more of mass piety. Tenth-century kings ordered that oaths be taken on relics and the regularization of the courts made oaths more frequent. Local communities committed to their relics opposed the translations or thefts undertaken by abbeys like Ramsey.

The meeting of popular piety and episcopal reform parallels the movement known as the Peace of God on the continent. The Norman synods of the 1070s

53. Alfred 1.8 and II Athelstan 26
54. VIII Æthelred 36–38 and Edward and Guthrum, Prol. 2.4
55. R. Bailey, *Viking Age Sculpture in Northern England* (1980), pp. 254–5 and J. T. Lang, 'Anglo-Scandinavian sculpture in Yorkshire', in *Viking Age York and the North*, ed. R. A. Hall, CBA Research Reports (1978), pp. 11–20
56. D. Rollason, 'Relic cults as an instrument of royal policy, *c.* 900–*c.* 1050', ASE, 15 (1986), pp. 91–103

with their attacks on clerical marriage, their affirmation of lay marriage, their demands for correct performance of the liturgy and their stress on the power of bishops would not have been out of place in Wulfstan's England. The wide tenth- and eleventh-century concern with clerical and lay morality, with penance and sanctuary, with the inviolability of church property and the utilization of relics and mass piety encompassed the English church. The seeds of the Gregorian confrontation can be discerned. Bishops and priests combined many roles. They stood for their local communities, could speak for and influence them, but exercised royal powers over them. They were encouraged to see themselves as separate, even to castigate the powerful, yet were deeply involved in politics. They possessed and manipulated the relics which focused popular piety yet used those same relics to take oaths in the increasingly onerous royal courts. The recurrent tensions of a church in the world, called to be not of the world, had sharpened again. Confrontation was not inevitable. It remains to explore the relations between kings and ecclesiastics before the state of the English church in the kingdom can be fully understood.

Neither the church nor churches were immune from the growth of royal power charted elsewhere in this book. Church land was not exempted from the increasing gelds of the eleventh century and loss of land was one result of them.[57] Forfeiture applied to ecclesiastical land as to lay, as Æthelwold's attempts to stress its immunity show. Heriots, developed and inflated now, pressed on bishops even if Edgar exempted abbots and abbesses.[58] The making of such a payment so closely identified with inheritance and the royal control of appointments raised the spectre of simony.

Kings had not systematically exempted the church from the burdens of increasing royal demands. They had, however, taken increasing control of ecclesiastical office. Most bishoprics and abbacies had already come into royal hands in England by 899, and the new sees and abbeys created during the following two centuries followed the same path. York and Durham were only acquired during the tenth and eleventh centuries. The imposition of Oscytel as archbishop of York in the 950s was the first appointment by a southern king to that see. From then until the 1020s York was regularly held in plurality with a rich southern see, usually Worcester, in an attempt to compensate for its poverty, and also to reduce the temptation to unilateral action on the part of the archbishops. From the 970s the most forceful men in the English church were regularly appointed to York. Chester-le-Street/Durham was a survival of the Celtic pattern of monastic bishops. Appointment here was in the hands of the community, its secular relations with the earls of Bamburgh. *c.*AD 1000 Uhtred of Bamburgh was married to the bishop's daughter. The monks of St Cuthbert never showed the independent tendencies of the archbishops of York in the 940s, but the first southern-imposed appointments of southern monks as bishops in the reign of Cnut were ill received.

The extension of royal control over bishoprics did not constitute the construction of a deliberate system of political control through the church, nor yet an attack on local noble power. That it could be resented is clear from the

57. M. K. Lawson, 'The collection of Danegeld and Heregeld in the reigns of Æthelred II and Cnut', *English Historical Review*, 99 (1984), pp. 721–38

58. W. 18 and 26

attacks on the property of the archbishop of York on Edgar's death. But controlling the church and securing the loyalty of local nobles went hand in hand rather than meeting head on, especially since neither church nor nobility were a monolithic grouping. Church appointments were rather drawn into the web of royal patronage, used to reward friends and followers, to manipulate, or succumb to factions. Edgar advanced Dunstan and Oswald not merely or primarily as reformers but as political supporters. Edward the Confessor allowed Leofric of Peterborough, nephew of Earl Leofric, to accumulate a monastic empire in the Midlands. The powers of royal appointment were also used throughout the period to advance men we judge as having the interests of the church at heart, Wulfstan to York in 1002, his saintly namesake to Worcester in 1062, later still Anselm to Canterbury. The contrasts apparent in these appointments raise questions about the kings who made them and about the churchmen and the church they involved.

Our pictures of tenth- and eleventh-century kings have been deeply affected by their relations with churchmen. The holy Edgar advancing good bishops and abbots, giving to the church contrasts with the evil Rufus, a foul incarnation of immorality, living off ecclesiastical vacancies and tormenting the saintly Anselm. Such judgements were contemporary. It is tempting to replace them with a new Edgar and a new Rufus, the first using the church to advance royal power, the second rightly scornful of the unjustifiable claims of a priestly class.[59] Contemporaries presented Edgar and Rufus in alliance or confrontation with saints, extending religious and moral judgement to both. Present-day historians have preferred to make political expediency the yardstick encompassing not only kings but saints who become political, manipulative and successful or mulish, stupid and failures. Both views are oversimplified. Neither we nor contemporaries have found it easy to make judgements where the institutionalized ideal which is medieval Christianity is concerned. It was precisely at periods of reform as in the tenth and eleventh centuries that institution and ideal came most frequently into conflict.

Piety then, as now, was subject to some fashionable or expedient redefinition. Leofric of Peterborough, an undoubted pluralist, was lauded by the chronicler of his house for his defence and extension of Peterborough's wealth.[60] Such men were necessary to the survival of a church in the world. But ideals, even when institutionalized, have limits to their interpretation. The contradictions were enacted over and over again. A bishop of Worcester might sit in his local hundred court and pocket the fines, whilst in 1012 an archbishop of Canterbury, Ælfheah, accepted martyrdom rather than allow his people to be taxed to ransom him. Corruption and sanctity are only the two extremes of a spectrum within which individuals explored their personal limits of compromise.

Learned English bishops in politics were well aware of the contradictory messages about the nature and legitimacy of secular power carried by the Christian tradition. In England archbishops especially took on the role of defining royal duties and occasionally of articulating criticism of kings, in laws,

59. See e.g. E. John, 'The king and the monks in the tenth-century reformation', *Orbis Britanniae* pp. 154–80; E. Mason, 'William Rufus, myth and reality', *J. of Medieval History*, 3 (1977), pp. 1–20 and F. Barlow, *William Rufus* (1983)
60. *The Chronicle of Hugh Candidus*, ed. W. T. Mellows (1949), pp. 65–7

sermons or consecration rituals (see above, *Ruling*). As leaders of the church and counsellors of the king they were uniquely placed to do so. Standing at the point where value-systems met and overlapped they could offer a critique of power as well as a defence. If a note of self-interest or special pleading can often be heard the message is not thereby invalidated. Only in the world of stereotypes can human beings be neatly divided into politicians and prophets, courtiers and saints.

In the tenth and eleventh century kings and churchmen operated in a world in which the reality and legitimacy of royal power, the religious roles of kings and the involvement of the church in the world were all accepted. Yet during these same centuries changes occurred in that acceptance. Movements of reform raised the question of the separation of lay and ecclesiastic and by the end of the eleventh century the papacy emerged actively as an external court of appeal over and if necessary against kings. In England royal power grew and increasingly trespassed on ecclesiastical property and the transmission of church office as on other areas of secular life.

The result was that Wulfstan II's demand that bishops speak loudly in the face of the powerful hardened into Anselm's intransigence. An archbishop of York in the mid tenth century could be suspected of treachery and imprisoned, a bishop of Durham in 1088 would appeal against trial to the pope himself. When William of St Calais made that appeal, Lanfranc, archbishop of Canterbury, stood alongside Rufus in refusing him clerical immunity. For many, even the learned, the old alliance remained tenable. But William argued against Lanfranc on the basis of a canonical collection which Lanfranc had himself compiled, a descendant of those canonical collections which had inspired tenth-century reform at the court of Athelstan. The scene was ironic, and a final reminder of how far the changes of the tenth and eleventh centuries had derived from the bishop's study via the monastic scriptorium.

12

The Economy

England in the tenth and eleventh centuries had a primarily agrarian economy in which the major producers were peasant farming households paying rent and dues to lords and king. It was not a purely subsistence economy. Towns and markets already existed and were growing in importance. They were centres of production but especially of exchange. Peasant farmers had been drawn into exchange by the demands of king and lords if not by their own needs. Steadily rising taxation, intermittent requirements for Danegeld, the scattered estates of nobles and churchmen all contributed to the pressures to raise cash. The role of king and lords was as significant as that of the primary producers in shaping the economy, which owed much to political factors as well as to the hidden mechanisms of impersonal forces.

England at the end of the eleventh century was, to quote Lennard, 'an old country'.[1] Just how old its landscape and settlement patterns may be is only now becoming apparent. Environmental archaeology has opened a long perspective on the development of the landscape which puts the documented historical period, let alone the tenth and eleventh centuries in proportion.[2] The reduction of the Wildwood and its replacement by managed woodland is now to be dated to the prehistoric period, as is the creation of moor and heath and the essential pattern of arable and pastoral farming. The boundaries of landholding may themselves go back beyond the beginning of the Christian era. A boundary such as that at Woolstone, Berkshire, first delineated in documentary form in the tenth century seems to have prehistoric origins.[3] Neither the historical period in general nor the tenth and eleventh centuries in particular were ages of agrarian pioneering. We must be ready to see not so much a fundamental reorganization of the landscape as changes within an established pattern.

This is an important corrective to a view of constant change which fails to grasp the longer-term continuities in relationships between humans and their environment. The result is not, however, a static picture. Change still occurred as a result of population movement and land control. Ownership, estate

1. R. V. Lennard, *Rural England, 1086 to 1135* (Oxford, 1959)
2. M. Jones, *England before Domesday* (1986)
3. M. Gelling, *Signposts to the Past* (1978), p. 181 and cf. Jones, *op. cit.* p. 84

structures, political change have effects on patterns of agricultural exploitation as well as on the generation and trading of surpluses and thus on towns, markets and social structures. The open fields of parts of England, for example, with their endless variety played a large part in altering the landscape, not to mention the social organization of the English countryside. The role of landlords in the creation of these may not be negligible. In the West Midlands, for example, they had grown up especially on the estates of great landlords,[4] who alone had the power to enforce such reorganization, the detachment from local quarrels to mediate it, perhaps even the supply of ploughs and plough beasts to encourage and necessitate it.

Population should be the starting point for any study of a pre-industrial economy; unfortunately few areas are so obscure at this early date. By the time of Domesday estimates of total population and regional comparisons can be made, as long as the many incalculables in the figures are recognized. England's population in the late eleventh century is estimated at between 1.5 and 2.5 millions. That should be compared with estimates of 4.5 to 6 millions in 1348 on the eve of the late medieval population fall, perhaps 2-2.5 million at the nadir of that fall in the mid fifteenth century and something over 2.5 million by the early 1520s.[5] However debatable this figure may be, the major problem with it is its isolation. Its place in longer-term population trends cannot be established. Such trends were likely to be part of the cycles of population which are observable in England up to the eighteenth century. Given the fact that the twelfth and thirteenth centuries are normally seen as times of population growth, the tenth and eleventh may well have been the beginnings of the upward stage of that cycle. But the debatable nature of every stage in the above argument makes it difficult to argue for rising population pressure at this date and dangerous to found theories of economic change primarily upon it.

Population distribution is clearer, though again the vagaries of the Domesday evidence on which we are reliant has to be remembered. According to Domesday figures the densest populations were in the East; in East Anglia, in eastern Kent and in parts of Lincolnshire. The apparent density in coastal Sussex may be accounted for in part by the recording of the population of the Weald here. The lowest densities were in Yorkshire, the Pennines, Cornwall and other upland areas and in the North West Midlands. Neither set of figures can be taken at face value. In eastern England a large and important free population forced itself on the attention of Domesday commissioners who elsewhere may have ignored such groups. But this is not a fatal flaw in the picture. It was the scale of the free peasantry of this area which led to its recording in Domesday. Had they existed in large numbers elsewhere Domesday is unlikely to have ignored them. Yorkshire and parts of the North West Midlands had suffered badly at the hands of William's armies at the beginning of his reign, a ruthless harrying which must have affected the population densities of these areas. These are likely to be peculiarly depressed in 1086. Yet

4. B. Campbell, 'Commonfield origins – the regional dimension', in *The Origins of Open-Field Agriculture*, ed. T. Rowley (1981), pp. 112–29 and D. Hooke, *The Anglo-Saxon Landscape: The Kingdom of the Hwicce* (Manchester, 1985), pp. 191–7
5. J. Hatcher, *Plague, Population and the English Economy, 1348–1530* (1977), pp. 68–9 and H. C. Darby, *Domesday England* (Cambridge, 1977), p. 89

the long-standing division between upland and lowland England is also apparent here.

Dense populations often coincide with inheritance practices which allowed many children a share. Such 'partible' inheritance practices may lie behind population growth, allowing more children the means to marry and produce offspring; they could be a sign of available wealth, of possibilities of land clearance, additional income from fen and sea which encouraged the division of property rather than its conservation by 'impartible' inheritance of a single heir. Partible and impartible inheritance may complicate the simple use of Domesday to chart population densities. Domesday's lists of tenants are usually converted into population sizes by multiplying by a notional 'household size'. But household sizes may have differed in line with inheritance practice, smaller in partible inheritance, larger in impartible, but the same multiplier is used for both. Both overestimation and underestimation may have resulted.

The population patterns certainly do not coincide in any simple way with the indicators of agrarian wealth in Domesday, that is with land values, arable estimates and so on.[6] The richest lands calculated by value were in the south and south-east, though if plough-teams are included as an indicator, large areas of the Midlands and East should be added. The richest areas in 1086 according to Domesday were not necessarily the most populous. Densely populated areas were far from being the poorest, though some of their land values were lower than appears at first sight if value is calculated per head rather than by acreage. Domesday values have been vindicated as real measures of resources[7] and cannot be dismissed. But it is the lord's resources which are measured. There is a danger that the free peasantry in these populous areas were not included in calculations of plough-teams and other indexes of arable wealth, unlike, for example, the villeins of Warwickshire on whose ploughs and capacity the lord could call. The lack of information about the peasant holding as a productive unit in Domesday is a limit on its utility.

These problems in the use of Domesday to gain an overall picture of agrarian England in the eleventh century may be overcome in the future by the increasingly sophisticated analyses which the computer allows, though our limited knowledge of, for example, household size, will be intransigent. Even before such analyses the importance of noble, royal and ecclesiastical estates in the economy is clear. Estates consisted not simply of land but of rights over its peasant holders. A typical tenth-century charter granting or confirming land specified the grant of a named place, as for example land at Aspley Guise, Bedfordshire 'with all its useful appurtenances, fields, pastures and woods'.[8] The boundary delineated the land on the ground, often making it clear, as here, that the grant of working fields was involved: the boundary points at Aspley included the 'heafod æcer' or head acre of an open field. The peasants who farmed the land and who used the pastures and wood were tacitly included. Wynflæd made this explicit when she left land to Shaftesbury abbey complete with the *geburs*.[9]

6. Darby, *op. cit.*, pp. 130, 132, 224, 228, 229
7. J. McDonald and G. D. Snooks, *Domesday Economy: A New Approach to Anglo-Norman History* (Oxford, 1986)
8. S. 772
9. W. 3

These were not slaves or chattels but rent payers. However varied the organization of individual estates, landlords and rent-owing peasants were constants.

Payment of rents and dues seems almost as old as the farmed landscape itself. The most universal and perhaps the oldest were rents in kind and basic labour on the lord's house or for the upkeep of his hunting. Traces are found throughout England and beyond the eleventh century. At Stanhope, Co. Durham, as late as the end of the twelfth century, peasants carted, rode on missions for the bishop, carried venison and built a kitchen, larder and dog kennel; at Whickham they made payments in cattle, hens and eggs.[10] At Tidenham, Gloucestershire, in the mid eleventh century, peasants rode, carried and transported for their lord, repaired the fences of his house, gave yarn for fish nets as well as honey and malt, whilst at Hurstbourne Priors, Hants., they provided ale, wheat, barley, wood, fencing poles and two ewes with two lambs.[11] Such payments were more widespread than the familiar 'manorial' services of agriculture labour on the lord's land, though labour services were already in regular use. At Tidenham and Hurstbourne regular weekly services were taken on the lord's home farm. How far such development had increased the ancient demands of lords depended on estate structures and the lord's needs.

Lords and their estates determined peasant dues, the pressure on peasant surpluses, the need for cash and marketing, even peasant organization itself. The lord's needs were for survival, a word which rarely means keeping body and soul together. Nobles and ecclesiastics maintained households and communities appropriate to their status and function in society. They sought to hand on inheritance to their heirs or successors. Status and function were not static: the increasing military needs and the changes in monastic organization discussed elsewhere in this book are only the most obvious examples of developments affecting both in this period. The political milieu within which noble or bishop sought to maintain position made its own demands: for gifts to the king, for expenditure on fashionable patronage, monastic or other, for favours to followers. When the king required escalating payments and in cash, when luxury items were available for silver pennies new pressures were felt. Lords sought to meet their varying needs from their lands, utilizing the powers they had over others, acquiring more land where possible, reorganizing what they had. The estate structures of the tenth and eleventh centuries are the result, their variety a testimony to diverse origins and pressures, to politics and farming practices.

The local economy and the differing fortunes and organization of large and small estates, lay and ecclesiastical are obvious variants. Equally if not more important were the differences between those estates which were in the hands mainly of subtenants and those held entirely by the tenant-in-chief, those held by static religious communities and ones managed to provide for the different needs of a bishop, between the compact and those which comprised scattered holdings, between estates consisting primarily of large or small agricultural units. Some estates were relatively old, others formed during the tenth and eleventh centuries themselves. And after 1066 there was the added complication of new Norman management in some cases. The differences which could arise from

10. *Boldon Book*, ed. D. Austin (Chichester, 1982), pp. 40–1, 48–9
11. EHD II nos. 173 and 174, pp. 879–80

these variables have been well illustrated from the West Midlands in the late eleventh century.[12] Here marked differences of estate management were visible. On royal estates, for example, the maximization of rents in cash was a major aim and proved feasible given large units and a prosperous peasantry. On small, subtenanted lay estates, by contrast, the emphasis was much more on the home farm and its production, with consequently greater demands for peasant labour rather than rents. The differences between those lords who had access to the additional income provided by the profits of wood, meadow, pasture and jurisdiction and those who relied almost exclusively on the farming of their own land was marked. The largest proportional investment in the home farms was made by the smaller lay tenants. In Kent too small-scale proprietors were an especially productive group of farmers.[13]

Domesday provides a unique opportunity to study estates, not merely to reassemble them but to compare their incomes, varied management, and resources, though sophisticated study like that of the West Midlands or Kent is still in its infancy. The problem as with population, is to delve back beyond Domesday, to see its patterns against longer-term change or stability. Occasionally this is possible. The royal estates are exceptionally well surveyed in Domesday; scarcely surprising given that one of its primary aims was to uncover royal rights and income. Study of these has revealed a dynamic estate management stretching back beyond 1066 into the early eleventh century.[14] The royal estates in some southern shires had been constantly reorganized into large units capable of providing a large rent in cash and or kind called 'the farm of one night'. This was theoretically capable of supporting the royal court, but may well have been more of an accounting device by this date. Not only were the royal lands constantly regrouped to take account of losses and acquisitions but the value of the farm itself was periodically reassessed. The working of the system confirms the view that the sheriff was the man locally responsible for the royal estates; variation occurs on a shire basis. Elsewhere in England, in for example East Anglia, the royal estates' managers utilized the same opportunities which a large-scale estate offered for overall organization of resources. And the treatment of a variety of rents, dues, jurisdictional payments and very old renders as components of a working system is obvious. The managers of royal revenue had made provision to prevent the fluctuations in the weight of the coinage from affecting royal revenue.[15] The sophistication of the system dating well back into the eleventh century shows how wary we must be of assuming a static and traditional approach to estate management at this date.

It is possible that similar studies of other estates in Domesday will reveal the same dynamism. The precise patterns of 1086 are certainly not old. The changes in the structure of estates after 1066 is obvious, and it has recently been

12. J. Hamshere, 'Domesday Book: estate structures in the West Midlands', in *Domesday Studies*, ed. J. C. Holt (Woodbridge, 1987), pp. 155–82
13. S. J. Harvey, 'The extent and profitability of demesne agriculture in England in the late eleventh century', in *Social Relations and Ideas*, ed. T. H. Aston *et al.* (Cambridge, 1983), pp. 45–72
14. P. A. Stafford, 'The *farm of one night* and the organization of King Edward's estates in Domesday', *Economic History Review*, ser. 2, 33 (1980), pp. 491–502
15. S. Harvey, 'Royal revenue and Domesday terminology', *ibid.*, 20 (1967), pp. 221–8

argued that those changes disrupted land-holding down to individual village level producing often catastrophic falls in land values as even the most basic units of resource managment were disturbed. The extent of this disruption is debatable but the reality of great changes between 1066 and 1086 undeniable. Such disruption was not however new. The estates of the Old English nobility in 1066 were not necessarily old. To take an extreme example, those of the Godwine family can have dated no further back in many cases than 1017. Changes produced by political fluctuations, forfeitures and royal grants affected many other families. Not even ecclesiastical estates were stable. The history of grants to ecclesiastical houses from the mid tenth century to Domesday has two marked features: the remarkable number of grants, showing how rapidly these estates themselves were built up, but also the discrepancy between grants claimed and holdings in Domesday. Both loss and acquisition is the story on ecclesiastical estates over this century. Indeed given the constant changes in the structure of both lay and ecclesiastical estates it is tempting to look here for one explanation of the widespread preference for rents over direct farming in the eleventh century.

Whether this constant disruption affected the productivity of estates is a difficult question. A key issue here is the productive unit itself and the extent of disruption at this level. The arguments for falls in value after 1066 cited above are derived from study of a county where most villages contained several manors and many individual freeholders over whom lordship after 1066 changed. In such an area the wholesale transfers of land after 1066 would do maximum damage. In places where the manor and the village, the unit of production and the lord's holding, were one and the same, the transfer would be of entire agricultural units and the consequent disruption less. Moreover the bulk of reeves and similar local officials who organized agrarian production at this level were English and survived the Conquest unchanged. Again our documentation limits the extension of this question back into the pre-1066 period.

This lack of documentation cannot be taken as a sign of a static approach to estate management. Were it not for the accidental record in Domesday the constant changes in the royal estates would have been lost. Oral forms may themselves sustain complex societies, though many estate records have been lost. A handful of estate surveys, records of loans of stock, equipment and seed from one abbey to another survive. The poor state of the document which records the loans made by Ely to Thorney at its foundation is witness to the chanciness of survival.[16] The documents of estate management are far more ephemeral than the chronicles and religious texts which libraries preserved. Since most of them were in Old English their chances of survival were even smaller. These documents may never have existed in the quantities we have for the twelfth century, though greater documentation is no simple sign of greater efficiency at that date.

Some estates have left records, of food farms at Ely, of leases at Worcester. The primary concern of this early as with later estate documentation is with checks on farmers and lessees. Again we must be wary of arguing from this to a static, uneconomic mentality in estate management. A desire to maximize profits

16. R. Appendix II, 9

whilst minimizing the risks of direct farming was widespread. By 1066 the trend was away from demesne farming (i.e. the landlord's direct involvement in agricultural production) and towards the leasing of estates for a fixed rent. These attitudes became so well established that they continued into the twelfth century, with land leased and rents raised until such time as price inflation made some landlords think again or the capacity of tenants to pay dried up. The latter was an inherent problem in the estate management techniques of the eleventh century. Short-term attention to profit and convenience was paramount. It carried the danger, especially when combined with harsh royal taxation, of destroying the very peasant resources on which it relied.

These attitudes to rent and farming are not mere conservative traditionalism. Estate managers were able to deal with the changes in structure with which the politics of the tenth and eleventh centuries constantly presented them, even if they were not especially foresighted as economic planners.

Peasant farmers are the group best hidden by the sparse sources. Traditionally historians have unearthed them to discuss peasant freedom and the origins of serfdom in early English society. But freedom cannot be divorced from questions of production and agrarian exchanges, prosperity from lordship. If the peasantry were drawn into the market, it was often by the pressure of lord or king.

Contemporary descriptions of society use a bewildering variety of terms to cover the non-noble groups: ceorl, gebur, villanus, bordar, cottar, sokeman, servus/ancilla, theow, are only the most significant. *Ceorl* is often applied to all the non-noble, eorl or ceorl is a common jingle. In other circumstances it denotes a potentially prosperous peasant farmer, the ceorl who thrives to be a thegn or noble, whilst it may also mean a person who performs labour services and pays rents and dues, as at Hurstbourne Priors.[17] It is the tenth- and eleventh-century equivalent of terms like 'the common man', 'the people' with the same imprecisions and ambiguities. Other terms are used more precisely. A *gebur* is always a person who pays substantial rents and dues, a relatively prosperous peasant but one burdened by the lord's demands, the equivalent of Domesday's *villanus* or *bordar*. *Sokemen* are distinguished often by lighter services, or no service at all, and by their frequent ability to buy and sell their land freely, but they do have a lord who can take some customary payments from them and has their fines in court.[18] A *theow* belongs to his or her lord, may be bought or sold or granted freedom. By 1086 *theows*, referred to in Domesday as *servi* and *ancillae* were listed along with the plough-teams as a lord's possession and asset. They normally worked for the lord on his land and were provided for by him, though a few had ploughbeasts of their own.

None of these terms provides more than the roughest of guides to social structure. They are as debatable and their edges as blurred as modern definitions like 'working class' or 'bourgeois'. At what point did work for a lord cease to define a slave/theow and instead indicate a gebur? How far did birth or quantity of land-holding make that distinction? How light did service need to be to indicate a sokeman rather than a villanus? What combination of other

17. R. 110
18. See F. W. Maitland, *Domesday Book and Beyond* (1960 edn.), pp. 95–109

freedoms in the courts separated the two? Domesday's magisterial division of
the population into a series of categories hides endless variation. Like most of
our documents, it is at best a royal and landlord's view of society. But along with
those other documents it indicates the criteria used by lords to make distinctions: service to a lord, economic standing, status in the courts.

Wealth was a significant divider. Domesday's basic terminology of villanus,
bordar and cottar points to substantial and middling landholders and cottagers.
Where Domesday gives more detail, as in Middlesex, the villanus holds
anything from half a virgate, fifteen acres, to a full hide, 120 acres, though most
have between fifteen and thirty. Bordars hold up to fifteen acres, though
averaging five or a little more, cottagers have a garden and a few acres of land. A
villanus normally had one or more ploughbeasts, a share in a team, and some
bordars possessed these valuable animals. Individual, regional and estate
variation was wide. The small peasant holdings of eastern England contrast
with the larger ones of the West Midlands, with some of the richest and best
equipped peasants in this last area found on the royal and large ecclesiastical
estates. In this as in the relative uniformity of size of peasant holdings the hand
of the lord appears as significant as the local economy in peasant prosperity.

Sources like Domesday measure at best household not individual wealth. It
would be necessary to know more of the size of peasant households and variation
among them to make accurate assessments and comparisons of prosperity.
Information here is non-existent. The household unit is invariably treated as the
working unit of the peasant economy. Some church dues, like the hearth penny,
were paid by the household. Domesday and the earliest estate surveys list
households not individuals for the payment of dues, though they normally treat
with or record the head of the household, usually male. The twelfth-century
estate surveys from Durham recognize the division of labour between the
housewife and other members of the household. A peasant performs labour
services 'with all the household of their dwelling except the housewife'.[19] The
head of the household was clearly responsible for its members. Tenth- and
eleventh-century laws faced this problem when attempting to limit the liability
of wife or heirs for the crimes of husbands, treating its members as individuals.
Landlords dealt with this economic unit and in so doing perhaps confirmed its
structure. (see above, *Family, Marriage and Women*).

Relations between lord and peasantry were wider than narrow discussion of
serfdom as a legal term suggests. Serfdom is not a useful concept to apply to
tenth- and eleventh-century society. This was a later medieval legal construct
which even then sat uneasily on social realities. Freedom and the constraints
upon it is a more appropriate line of enquiry, though such a value-laden word
must be handled with care. If rents demanded for no return are a sign of a lack
of freedom, few if any early medieval peasants were entirely free. Marc Bloch's
famous dictum would apply to all: 'In social life is there any more elusive notion
than the free will of a small man'.[20] We must distinguish freedoms *to do* certain
things, from freedoms *from* impositions and demands and be aware that
political and other developments constantly create new freedoms, redefine or
restrict old ones.

19. *Boldon Book*, ed. D. Austin (Chichester, 1982), entry for Boldon, p. 12
20. M. Bloch, in *Cambridge Economic History of Europe*, vol. 1, 2nd edn. (Cambridge, 1971), p. 268

Demands by lord and king were increasing. The profits of the estates were made and increased by raising the rents and services of peasants. Increasing military needs, the wants and possibilities opened by a widening market economy, the creation of larger monastic communities, church building were among factors creating these pressures. How universally demands were being increased only a fuller study of the estates of Domesday will show. But the preliminary answer is – widely.

The rising costs of warfare, and especially the demand for fuller military equipment during the tenth and eleventh centuries confirmed the key medieval social division between those who fought and those who laboured on the land,[21] reducing the relative standing of the latter. Royal responsibility for local courts and procedures was tightened and with it the need to define social status. With the oath of a thegn/noble worth so much more than that of a freeman, with a thegn now an essential part of many legal procedures, the interest in social definition in the late tenth century was far from academic. The new courts created in the tenth century in North East England were called wapentakes, a term which refers to the brandishing of weapons or at least the showing of them. Weapons may once have been regarded as a mark of adult status. By now their possession was probably restricted. Yet they are shown as a proof of court-worthiness at a time when courts were increasingly regularized. The hundred or wapentake court became another place where divisions within society were clarified at many peasants' expense. Tenth-century laws constantly recognized and confirmed the role of lords in protecting, controlling and bringing peasants to justice. The laws of Athelstan show the various processes at work. When the hue and cry was raised in the hundred those who had horses were obliged to follow it; those who did not stayed behind and worked for their lord.[22] The possession of an expensive animal of military use was used to define a person's standing expressed in performance of a communal legal duty. The distinction between those who can perform that duty and those who will work for a lord turned on a military criterion. Many peasants were the losers thereby.

Many but not all. The legal developments may appear more or less universal but they hide local variation. The control of the courts and the implementation of royal laws was not necessarily England-wide (see chapter on *Ruling*). Changes were also at work in the opposite direction. Wulfstan, interested in defining thegns, wrote of prospering *ceorls*, substantial peasant farmers.[23] It has been argued that the impact of Danish settlement in parts of eastern England produced an increase in peasant freedom, whether as a result of significant migration or the disruption of local landholding.[24] Serious questions surround the scale of the Viking settlement here, but the disruption of existing estates is probable and the Danish takeover may have played a role in stimulating trade and markets (see below). The freedoms of the free peasantry of eastern England were specific: freedom to buy and sell land and freedom from the more developed demands of landlords. They are the freedoms of an area where the

21. N. Brooks, 'Arms, status and warfare in late Saxon England', in *Ethelred the Unready*, ed. D. Hill (Oxford, 1978), pp. 81–103
22. VI Athelstan 5
23. EHD I, no. 51, p. 468
24. See e.g. H. Loyn, *The Vikings in Britain* (1977), pp. 132–3

land market had become significant and where the nature of most local estates neither required nor permitted the development of heavy labour services.

Slaves were the most sharply defined group of the unfree. They belonged to their lord, worked in the household or the home farm, could be bought and sold. At Lewes in 1086 a 4d toll was paid for the purchase of a man, $^1\!/_2$d for an ox and a penny for a horse.[25] Slavery was a legal punishment and could result from an inability to pay fines. The heavy fines imposed in tenth-century law codes seem almost designed to produce slavery if regularly imposed. The terms 'witetheow' or 'witefæstne mann' (wite = fine) are often found in wills.[26] The ætheling Athelstan in his will refers to *witefæstne mann* acquired *on spræce*, that is as a result of a legal case. A northern document probably to be dated to the tenth century speaks of those 'taken for their food'[27] in evil days, i.e. people who had given themselves into slavery in return for food. The frequent natural calamities and warfare of early medieval society produced their own consequences. There were at least two pestilences in the brief reign of Edgar alone.

We hear most about slaves in documents of manumission or in wills where they are being freed. The freeing perhaps especially of slaves acquired through the legal process was a work of charity in the tenth century. Athelstan required his reeves on all his estates to free one witetheow every year.[28] How many slaves were freed through such action is unquantifiable. Other sources apparently show lords exerting pressure towards slavery. In a Bodmin manumission a man had been claimed as a slave and had had to buy himself off; at Ely in the late tenth century the abbot threatened to claim a man's wife and child as slaves (or bondpeople) – a rare reference in English documents of this early date to the transmission of status through the mother.[29] Putrael, who bought himself free at Bodmin, gave eight oxen and 60 pence for the favour. He was no poor man. In the fifteenth century landlords pursued prosperous villeins who had fled in order to secure fines from them, often ignoring the poorer fugitives. A man like Putrael was worth the effort of an accusation. The Ely threat was only made to secure the abbey's hold on land being disputed, to twist the arm of the man bringing the case against Ely. There may have been many such instances, but these two alone cannot be used to argue that this was a period in which landlords exerted particular pressure to produce slavery. In view of their practices of estate management only certain lords had a strong economic interest in advancing slavery. Where the tendency to rent applied, the pressures would have been the reverse. The operation of the law may thus have produced a continuing supply of slaves and in the 'war zones' along the Welsh, Scottish and Cornish borders a more traditional source of supply was maintained. But as a group they may not have grown in importance. Social mobility clearly raised some, others were freed. The role of slavery in tenth- and eleventh-century England was not necessarily great.

25. DB vol. I, fo. 26 R
26. W. 3, 8 and 20
27. EHD I, no. 150, pp. 610–11
28. Athelstan, Ordinance on Charities, 1
29. EHD I, no. 147, p. 609 and LE cap. 10, p. 83

The nature of estate management affected the peasantry as well as landlords' income. The relative prosperity of the peasantry on royal and some ecclesiastical estates was the prerequisite for a rent-oriented approach. That prosperity may be a result of the actions of these same lords, by, for example, restrictions on the fragmentation of holdings through sale or inheritance, or even the provision of ploughbeasts and equipment. The heavier demands on peasant time and resources on estates with large home farms could conversely have acted as a drag on prosperity. In the West Midlands it was on small lay estates that the peasantry had fewest ploughs of their own and where the emphasis on demesne farming resulted in greater proportions of slaves. The demand for rent in cash by some lords made its own inroads by forcing the production and perhaps the sale of surpluses. The combined onus of rent and taxes could reach crippling levels by the end of the eleventh century. Whether they were maximizing rents or the output of the home farm, most large-scale landlords by the eleventh century were managing their estates in ways which encouraged buying and selling, by peasants to pay dues or by lords who had created surpluses.

Towns, trade and cash played an important part in economic life. About 10 per cent of the population lived in towns by 1086. The archaeological evidence for towns is clear and growing apace. Excavations at York, Lincoln, Winchester and at a host of lesser sites have revealed the size and complexity of tenth-century towns and pointed to their growth during these centuries. Most of these places had features which we would unequivocally accept as urban. They were centres for the manufacture of pottery, boneworking, leather production. They had inhabitants who specialized in the storing and marketing of food stuffs and engaged in both local and long-distance trade. Unlike fairs or other more transitory market places, they were permanent settlements engaging in these activities. Their internal organization was often specialized, with industrial areas at York and Lincoln for example, a cattle market with a permanent site in Canterbury.

In some cases in southern England towns bear unmistakable signs of planning. The grid plans and other features, such as a continuous street behind the walls, suggest military functions and link at least some of these urban settlements with the burh building of Alfred and his son Edward the Elder. In the North and East there is no evidence of such planned development though many towns here burgeoned at places like Nottingham, Stamford or Leicester chosen as defences during the wars between the Danes and the West Saxons and Mercians. The towns of the North East Midlands grew especially during the tenth century. Sometimes the dating of new growth appears to link closely with Viking settlement of the area, as at Lincoln and probably Stamford. Elsewhere, as at Northampton, development was slower and is hard to associate with Viking impact. York also experienced growth following its Viking takeover, though the town had been an important centre before. And development pre-dating the late ninth century occurred in southern towns like Winchester and Canterbury. The archaeological picture thus emphasizes the tenth and eleventh centuries in town development but provides no simple dating which would allow us to see Viking settlement or even the end of Viking raiding as sole or major motors to that growth. Indeed the patterns of local trade established for e.g.

Stamford pottery suggest a growth pattern linked to local and regional factors rather than to the long-distance trade affected by Viking raiding.[30]

The coinage tells a substantially similar story. The use of and minting of coin was well established by the mid ninth century, and the coinage of kings like Burgred of Mercia should already be estimated at 50 million or more pennies. There may have been temporary problems at the end of the ninth century, but not a permanent or significant setback. Edward the Elder's coinage is estimated at 20-30 million pennies struck at some twenty-odd mints. 36 million pence was paid as Danegeld alone in Æthelred II's reign.[31] Minting was decentralized in tenth- and eleventh-century England, and as the tenth century progressed the number of mints increased to more than forty. A few large mints always predominated. The bulk of the English coinage was always struck at Winchester, London and York. In the tenth century Chester joined them, eclipsed by Lincoln only during its second half. Taken together with the evidence on towns, a picture of a burgeoning exchange economy emerges.

During the tenth century Chester rivalled even London as a mint and its coins predominate in North West England and the Irish Sea area. Chester's dominance raises questions about what can be deduced from the coinage about the economy. Its large output may be related to tribute paid by the Welsh though the scale makes this unlikely as the major explanation. Chester was a point of entry into England of silver from a large area of north-west Britain. During the tenth century English kings effectively prevented the circulation of non-English coins within England. The most active mints were thus those which handled the most foreign silver, not simply those which had the most active local markets. Chester's situation as a town on many frontiers in the early tenth century is one key to its huge coinage. York and to a lesser extent Lincoln filled the same roles in relation to north-eastern England and the North Sea.

Chester also stood on what appears to have been the axis of early tenth-century trade, which was North West/South East between the Channel and the Irish Sea, rather than East and North East towards the Baltic and the Channel. This axis is deduced largely from the coinage and may be questioned by further research. If correct it suggests that the shift to a primarily eastern overseas trading pattern may be late in the tenth century, explaining the greater importance of the north-east mints and especially Lincoln by this date. But the rising importance of the north-eastern mints may have other causes. From the late tenth century onwards payments of tribute and later mercenary payments to Danes and other Scandinavians distorted the movement of coins towards the Baltic. It may also have distorted the production of coin within England itself to

30. The literature on tenth and eleventh-century towns is enormous. See e.g. M. Biddle, 'Towns', in *The Archaeology of Anglo-Saxon England*, ed. D. M. Wilson (1976), pp. 99–150; ed. R. Hall, *Viking Age York and the North*, CBA Research Report, no. 27 (1978) and his *The Viking Dig* (1984); P. A. Stafford, *The East Midlands in the Early Middle Ages* (Leicester, 1985); C. Mahany and D. Roffe, 'Stamford, the development of an Anglo-Scandinavian borough', ANS, 5 (1983), pp. 197–219; *Archaeology of Lincoln, Report* no. IX.I, CBA (1981); N Brooks, *The Early History of the Church of Canterbury* (Leicester, 1984)

31. D. M. Metcalf, 'The monetary history of England in the tenth century, viewed in the perspective of the eleventh century', *Anglo-Saxon Monetary History*, ed. M. A. S. Blackburn (Leicester, 1986), at pp. 137 and 141, and his 'Continuity and change in English monetary history, 973–1086', pt. 1, BNJ, 50 (1980), at p. 26 and pt 2, BNJ, 51 (1981), *passim*

meet these heavy payments. In the final picture given by the coins the relationship of political and economic factors is not easy to disentangle.

The association of *burh*-building and later town growth is only one of many indications of royal interest and involvement. The laws of the tenth century, from Athelstan onwards, attempted to confine trading to towns. This may not have been successful. Rates of coin loss uncovered by archaeological excavation at agrarian estate centres and in towns are too similar to point to towns as exclusive trading centres.[32] Royal motives were complex. Kings wished to make defensive centres viable by attracting trade and population to them, but they also desired easy supervision of the payment of tolls and may even have made arrangements and agreements with groups of townspeople or traders. By the eleventh century such groups had sufficient organization in the form of gilds or similar to negotiate the privileges which appear in Domesday.[33] Wulfstan's strange statement that well-established merchants could become thegns in the tenth century may well refer to privileged agreements made between kings and traders.[34] By 1066 all large towns and most small ones were in the king's hands. He had benefited directly from urban growth.

The king's hand is even clearer in the coinage. In the later ninth century minting mirrored the political structure of England. Each kingdom had a major mint, York for Northumbria, perhaps Ipswich for East Anglia, Canterbury for Kent, London for Mercia, Winchester for Wessex. The coinages were kingdom-wide rather than England-wide. Athelstan, as the first king of all England, was also the first to attempt a uniform coinage, though his experiments were not successful in North East Mercia. Royal control, economic need and local feeling all played their part. Thus the weight of Athelstan's coinage was uniform, but its styles retained strong regional diversity. Athelstan was king of all England but most effective in Wessex and central/southern Mercia. The proliferation of mints occurred chiefly in these areas, whilst East Anglia and York both retained the older pattern of 'kingdom' mints. The styles of his coinage and its minting pattern follow regional particularism as expressed in ealdormanries and suggest a need to woo East Anglia and York through the grant of a minting monopoly. The uniform weight, on the other hand, points to a coincidence of royal aim and traders' needs. Edgar, whose name has become synonymous with tenth-century reform of the coinage, built on Athelstan's foundations. Edgar successfully enforced what Athelstan had tried: a uniform, kingdom-wide penny bearing the king's head and title and the name of the mint and the moneyer who struck it. His aspiration and success are measures of the greater unity of the kingdom and development of its rule, though the return to regional die cutting under Æthelred and Cnut indicate the continuing limitations on royal power.

With the king so deeply involved in town and coinage, can the development of either be taken as a simple sign of economic growth? The siting of mints, the cutting of dies centrally or locally were as often questions of patronage and

32. D. Hinton, 'Coins and commercial centres in Anglo-Saxon England', in *Anglo-Saxon Monetary History*, ed. Blackburn, p. 24
33. S. Reynolds, 'Towns in Domesday Book', *Domesday Studies*, ed. Holt at pp. 306–9
34. EHD I, no. 51, p. 469

politics as of economic need.[35] Taxation in general stimulated the cash economy. The specific introduction of a regular tax to pay mercenaries in 1012 coincided with the lowering of the weight of the coinage, which did not rise again until the end of that tax *c.*1050. Mints were opened for royal as much as for trading needs, to facilitate the payment of taxes as well as trade, and some resulting mints were so small that it is questionable whether their moneyers could have covered the costs of the purchase of their dies.

But the king cannot be brought in as a *deus ex machina* to initiate economic growth. His control of the coinage was made possible and profitable by the rapid development of the use of coin. The common interests of king and traders enabled the changes of the tenth century. Not only did the number of mints increase steadily, the coin they produced circulated vigorously especially within southern and central England. Some small mints may have been doubtfully necessary in strict economic terms, but the great bulk of the English coinage was struck at a handful of large centres whose economic function is beyond doubt.

Rapid circulation of coin was a sign of trade and exchange reaching even into rural areas. When a young sheep could be valued at two pence the high-value silver penny could not have been the small change in a peasant's pocket. But a hierarchy of exchanges and markets was drawing the use of cash into the agrarian economy. In the mid eleventh century an English chronicler complained for the first time of price rises: the sester of wheat rose in 1040 to fifty five pence and higher.[36] That chronicler's religious community was presumably buying and selling. A land market had developed. As early as the reign of Edward the Elder land was bought from the Danes for ten pounds of gold and silver.[37] The Book of Ely is full of sales as well as gifts of land, regularly listing the price per acre. Its author was so accustomed to thinking in monetary terms that he complained of paying '60 shillings for 6½ *predia* [?dwellings] which no-one who knew anything would value at more than twenty shillings'.[38] Many place names of the tenth and eleventh century denote possession — x's *ton* or *by*. They indicate the emergence of a group of small-scale lords owning what had once been elements of large land units. Purchase and the operation of the land market had been one way these units had been dismantled.

Comparison of two Domesday shires, Lincolnshire and Somerset, demonstrates how far towns had genuine functions in the local economy yet how much might still be owed to royal stimulus. Both shires had a hierarchy of towns and markets, a sign of the spreading tentacles of an exchange economy.[39] In Lincolnshire Lincoln and Stamford were urban centres, Torksey almost certainly another. All three had mints, though that at Torksey worked only intermittently. Louth had a market and occasionally coins were minted there, whilst markets also existed at Barton-on-Humber, Bolingbroke, Partney,

35. P. A. Stafford, 'Historical implications of the regional production of dies under Æthelred II', BNJ, 48 (1987), pp. 35–51; M. Blackburn and S. Lyon, 'Regional die-production in Cnut's Quatrefoil issue', *Anglo-Saxon Monetary History*, ed. M. Blackburn, (Leicester, 1986) pp. 223–72; and A. Freeman, *The Moneyer and the Mint in the Reign of Edward the Confessor, 1042–66* (Oxford, 1985)
36. ASC MS E 1040
37. EHD I, no. 103, pp. 546–7
38. LE cap. 11a, p. 91
39. See R. Hodges, *Primitive and Peasant Markets* (Oxford, 1988)

Spalding, Threakingham, Thealby, Darby and Burton-on-Stather. A hierarchy of economic need was served from local markets, from small regular markets to those large enough to sometimes justify the occasional minting of coin to truly urban centres of regular trade, permanent settlement and industrial production demanding a permanent mint. In Somerset the picture is instructively blurred. Markets existed at Crewkerne, Frome, Ilchester, Ilminster, Milborne Port, Milverton and Taunton. All but Ilminster and Milverton were places where moneyers minted, and Bruton, Watchet, Axbridge, Petherton, Cadbury and Bath were also minting sites. Ilchester, Milborne, Taunton, Bath, Bruton, Axbridge and Langport had inhabitants whom Domesday deemed burgesses. The need for markets and their penetration into the rural economy is as clear as in Lincolnshire, but the hierarchy is less obvious, with many more and smaller places having burgesses and mints. The differences may be explained in many ways, not least the position of Lincolnshire's large towns on international as well as local trade routes. But one key is the role of the king in Somerset and his remoteness from Lincolnshire. No fewer than ten of these Somerset sites were in royal hands, often the centres of large royal manors. Another two were old ecclesiastical centres. The privileges and burdens of minting or of having burgess status had been spread by proximity to the king. Peasant dues required by the king in cash may have spread the need for money more widely. The impact of the king was felt in Lincolnshire. He was the holder of both Lincoln and Stamford. Here he had profited from economic growth. In Somerset his role had also been to influence it.

If lords and kings played so large a role in the economy, unification and conquest in the tenth and eleventh centuries should be reflected there. 1016 resulted in heavier taxation, 1066 in taxation, devastation and extensive exemptions. Destruction and devastation is the tale in many Domesday towns, though declining prosperity is less clear. William continued a coinage system which had proved profitable to his predecessors, and in towns like Winchester it long continued to be administered by Englishmen.[40] Here the moneyers were an urban elite who survived 1066 relatively unscathed and carried their English names and family pride on into the early twelfth century.

The wider economic impact of transfers of land cannot be assessed until arguments about the disruptiveness of these transfers are resolved (see chapter on *1066 and After*). The current picture is a patchwork: total disruption and falling land values in some places; immediate falls after 1066 followed by rapid recovery in others; elsewhere a pattern complicated by the nature of local estates and the survival of Old English estate managers or tenants.[41] Even this last question is not simple. Continuity of management might inhibit disruption, but English tenants could also prove vulnerable in competition with Normans, finding themselves forced to pay higher rents. The arrival of foreign landlords with needs to meet in Normandy as well as England may have accelerated pressures for cash renders. But the needs of English landlords had not been simple and localized and pressure in this direction was already strong.

40. M. Biddle, 'Early Norman Winchester', *Domesday Studies*, ed. Holt, pp. 311–31
41. See e.g. R. Fleming, 'Domesday Book and the tenurial revolution', ANS, 9 (1987), pp. 87–102, and J. D. Hamshere, 'Domesday Book: estate structures in the West Midlands', in *Domesday Studies*, ed. Holt, pp. 155–82

The taxation of moneyers rose sharply after 1066, an annual tax of between £200 and £250 rising to £750 to £1,000 under William.[42] By 1086 the overall picture is of a system milked to its limits, of excessive taxation raised further. Land assessments in 1066 were already sophisticated calculations of all resources, not merely measures of arable.[43] In 1086 William was considering a further reassessment,[44] partly to look again at the extensive taxation exemptions he himself had granted to his followers. Exemption and preferential treatment had been practiced pre-1066, but greatly extended afterwards.[45] In the towns many Norman immigrants were avoiding taxation.[46] A sophisticated and oppressive taxation system was being operated unequally. The combined demands of rents and taxes would probably have brought crisis by the late eleventh century without 1066. The results of 1066 shifted the taxation burden even more towards the productive small lords and peasants. If the demand for rent and tax had helped stimulate the tenth-century economy, by the end of the eleventh they may have been stifling it.

Unification is a broader question involving a century or more of change within which many other factors came into play. Unification was itself part conquest, hence the particularities of the coinage of York and East Anglia under Athelstan. It underpinned the prestige of a monarchy which was able to develop systems of taxation. It produced a great nobility with extended needs and extended estates from which to meet them. Economic and political boundaries coincided. York was the most northerly mint and town, Yorkshire the limit of administration and of shire-reeves and the Domesday enquiry, the Tees and Pennines effectively bounded both the cash economy and England. Were the political boundaries set by the economic division of Upland and Lowland Britain? England was far from being either an economic or political unity or community. Yet market and political activity were already sufficiently intrusive to ensure that neither was it a kingdom of isolated, self-sufficient peasant groups.

42.   D. M. Metcalf, 'The taxation of moneyers under Edward the Confessor and in 1086' in *ibid.*,
      pp. 279–93
43.   J. McDonald and D. Snooks, *Domesday Economy: A New Approach to Anglo-Norman History*
44.   S. Harvey, 'Taxation and the ploughland in Domesday Book', in *Domesday Book, a Reassessment*,
      ed. P. H. Sawyer (1985), pp. 86–103
45.   S. Harvey, 'Taxation and the economy', in *Domesday Studies*, ed. Holt, pp. 249–64
46.   S. Reynolds, 'Towns in Domesday Book', in *ibid.*, at pp. 308–9

Bibliographical Note

The following suggestions are intended merely to highlight general surveys and to draw attention to some recent work on sources. They are a supplement to, not a substitute for, the further reading provided throughout in footnotes.

A. Gransden, *Historical Writing in England, c. 500–1307* (1974) is the essential starting point for details of chronicles and their authors. Since she wrote the following important work on individual authors has appeared: M. Chibnall, *The Ecclesiastical History of Orderic Vitalis* (Oxford, 1969–80); R. Thomson, *William of Malmesbury* (Woodbridge, 1987); R. H. C. Davies, 'William of Poitiers and his *History of William the Conqueror*', *The Writing of History in the Middle Ages*, eds. R. H. C. Davis and J. M. Wallace Hadrill (Oxford, 1981), pp. 71–100, E. van Houtts, 'The *Gesta Normannorum Ducum* a history without an end', ANS 3, pp. 106–18 and 215–20 [on William of Jumièges] and her *Gesta Normannorum Ducum* (Groningen, 1983). The new edition of the Anglo-Saxon Chronicles under the general editorship of S. Keynes and M. Lapidge will eventually help elucidate the many problems which still surround this source. In the meantime the introductions to the Chronicle in the *English Historical Documents* vols. I and II remain essential. The importance of dating and placing individual sections of the Chronicle is brought out by S. Keynes, 'The declining reputation of King Æthelred the Unready', *Ethelred the Unready*, ed. D. Hill, B. A. R. British series, 59 (Oxford, 1978), pp. 227–53. The best guide to recent work on the charters is N. Brooks, 'Anglo-Saxon charters: the work of the last twenty years', ASE 3 (1974), pp. 211–31. For major new thinking on the laws see P. Wormald, '*Lex Scripta* and *verbum regis*: legislation and Germanic kingship from Euric to Cnut', *Early Medieval Kingship*, eds, P. H. Sawyer and I. N. Wood (Leeds, 1977), pp. 105–38.

Among recent general surveys of aspects of the period the following should be noted. P. A. Stafford, *The East Midlands in the Early Middle Ages* (Leicester, 1985) is a regional survey with particular discussion of the Viking settlements and impact. The government of tenth-and eleventh-century England is discussed in H. Loyn, *The Governance of Anglo-Saxon England, 500–1087* (1984) and W. L. Warren, *The Governance of Norman and Angevin England* (1987), and in essays by J. Campbell collected in his *Essays in Anglo-Saxon History* (1986). Important new thinking on Domesday and the England it describes is brought together in two essential collections of essays, *Domesday Book, a Reassessment*, ed. P. H. Sawyer (1985) and *Domesday Studies*, ed, J. C. Holt (Woodbridge, 1987). Both volumes are important not only for what they suggest about the ruling of England, but for religious and economic history and the impact of the Norman Conquest. No detailed general survey of the economy and coinage exists, but see Stafford, *The East Midlands* (above) and the articles gathered in *The Archaeology of Anglo-Saxon England*, ed. D. Wilson (Cambridge, 1976). The new volume of the *Cambridge Agrarian History* appeared too late to be used for this book, but is of central importance. M. Chibnall, *Anglo-Norman England 1066–1166* (Oxford, 1986) is the best modern survey of the century after the Norman Conquest. J. Le Patourel, *The Norman Empire* (Oxford, 1976) is a useful comparison with my argument since it presents the Norman Conquest from a Norman/French perspective. On the church the monastic emphasis of *Tenth-Century Studies*, ed. D. Parsons (Chichester, 1975) requires supplementing with the excellent articles on minsters and parishes by John Blair in the two Domesday volumes cited above. N. Brooks, *The Early History of the Church of Canterbury* (Leicester, 1984) is a magisterial account which should be read not only for general religious and intellectual history, but for the political relations between kings and archbishops.

Two studies of the reign of Æthelred have not only transformed views of this reign, but offer wide insight into late Saxon politics: *Ethelred the Unready*, a collection of essays ed. D. Hill (Oxford, 1978) and S. Keynes, *The Diplomas of King Æthelred, 'the Unready'* (Cambridge, 1980). That insight has also been deepened by two important articles by A. Williams, 'Princeps Merciorum gentis: the family, career and connections of Ælfhere, ealdorman of Mercia' in ASE 10 (1981), pp. 143–72 and 'Cockles among the Wheat, Danes and English in the west Midlands in the first half of the eleventh century', *Midland History*, 11 (1986), pp. 1–22.

Index

lordship 152; ties of 132–5, 154; role in law 140–1, 171, 209; and family 146, 154, 159–60, 162, 167, 170–1, 178–9, 208; and marriage 165–6 [*see also* loyalty, nobility]

Lotharingians 89

Lothian 56, 116, 122, 123, 127

Louis d'Outremer, k of W Frankia, nephew of k Athelstan and Edmund 36, 115

loyalty 70, 132, 154, 157; as ideal 63, 68, 75, 80, 82, 93; problems of 61–2, 68, 80, 82; churchmen and 14, 98, 104, 155

Lyfing, bp of Crediton and Cornwall 1027–46, bp of Worcester 1038–40, 1041–6 80, 86

Macbeth, mormær of Moray k of Scots 1040–57 95, 122, 124

Madselin, w of Ulf 178

Magnus of Limerick 121

Magnus, k of Norway 86

Malcolm I k of Scots 943–54 121–2

Malcolm II k of Scots 1005–34 123–4

Malcolm III s of Duncan, k of Scots 1058–93, married Margaret 95, 122, 124, 125, 127

Maldon, battle of 991 38

Malmesbury 192

Man, isle of 63, 116, 121

manumissions 210

Marches 137; organization of by Æthelred II 60–1, 112; organization of by Edward the Confessor 88–9, 91, 110, 120; organization of by William I 95, 104, 110, 112; Welsh 84, 88, 91, 95, 120

Maredudd k of Dyfed and Gwynedd 986/7–99 120–1

Margaret gt granddtr of Æthelred II si of Edgar the Ætheling, married Malcolm III k of Scots *c*.1069 85, 124

maritagium 166 [*see also* dowry]

markets 133, 209–10, 214–15 [*see also* towns]

marriage 162, 163, *165–73*; definition of 41–2, 76, 165, 167, 171–2; arrangement of 165–7, 171; property and 165–7, 171, 174–6; making of 167; consent in making of 146, 167, 171–2; feast 81; feelings in 165, 168–70; peasant 166; of priests 166–7; and church reform 57, 143, 167–18, 171–2, 185–6; as son's defiance 68; royal 40–1, 46–7, 51–3, 57, 58, 64, 67, 72, 76–7, 87, 117, 172; as alliance, between king and nobles 38, 52–3, 55, 58, 87, 154–5, among rulers 25–6, 28, 35–7, 64, 72, 76, 114–17, 126; [*see also* lordship, dower, dowry, divorce, incest]

Mathilda, w of William I 173, 177

Mathilda, w of Henry I gt gt granddtr of Æthelred II 20

Mathilda empress, dtr of Henry I 173

Mendham 190

mercenaries 63, 65, 77, 111–12, 117, 142, 143, 147, 212, 214

merchants 55, 135, 142, 213

merchet 166

Mercia 7, 8, 115, 142, 157, 183, 213; local feeling in 47–50, 183; relations with Wessex 24–6, 28, 32, 34–6, 41, 55, 115, compared with Strathclyde and Scots 121–2; possible underkingship of 41, 43, 48, 122; ealdormen of and Wales 120–1; in 1016 71; in 1035 77; in 1065 96–9

Mercian Register 7, 8, 26, 32

Milborne Port 215

military equipment 65, 111–12, 139, 141–2; and social status/definition 152, 209

military service 111–12, 135, 139, 141–2, 149, 152, 209

Milverton 215

minsters 73, 182, 183–4, 192, 194–5; patronage of 184, 189–91

mints 34, 78–9, 135, 141–2, 212–15 [*see also* moneyers]

Môn/Anglesey 121

monasteries 4, 10, 37, 52–5, 180–1, 184, *187–92*; land acquisitions of 131–3; attacks on after 975 4, 9, 11, 13, 16, 46, 57–8, 59, 63, 189

moneyers 141–2, 214; taxation of 142, 146, 216

monks 165, 184; as bishops 182, 187, 193–4

Morcar, NE Midlands noble fl early eleventh century 61–2, 66–8

Morcar, s of earl Ælfgar, b of earl Edwin, earl of Northumbria 1065–71 96–8, 104, 110, 168, 176, 178

Morgan Hen 'the old', k of Glywysing 119

morning gift 166, 171, 175–6

Muchelney 192

murder 89; political 61–2, 72–3, 80, 81, 96–8, 123–4; of Alfred 79, 80

names: and status 153–4; and social change 156; and family sense 168

neighbours, relations among 24, 25–6, 28–9, 32, 33–7, 56, 63–4, 71, 82, 87–8, 89, 95, 96–8, 100, 105, *114–28*; problems of interpreting 95, 116, 119, 121, 123, *125–7*; variety of 114, 117–18, 126–7 [*see also* alliances]

nepotism 168–9, 170, 185, 189, 191

nobility; nature of 111–12, 131–2; values of viii, 5, 75, 111–12, 132, 134–5, 154–5 [*see also* loyalty]; changes in structure of 74,